THE CIVIL WAR AND THE AMERICAN SYSTEM

THE CIVIL WAR
AND THE
AMERICAN SYSTEM

*America's Battle with Britain,
1860-1876*

by W. Allen Salisbury

1992

Cover: Detail of an 1862 Civil War poster (color lithograph); The Bettman Archive. The Assabet Manufacturing Company, Maynard, Massachusetts (color lithograph); The Library of Congress.

Back cover photograph: EIRNS

Cover design: Alan Yue

Compositor: World Composition Services

Printer: PMR Printing Company

For more information, contact the publisher:
  Executive Intelligence Review
  P.O. Box 17390
  Washington, D.C. 20041-0390

The body of this book has been reprinted by permission of University Editions, Campaigner Publications.

Library of Congress Cataloging in Publication Data: 92–75811
ISBN: 0-943235-06-5
EIB 92-005

To Wilbert Salisbury, Allen's father,
Estelle Young Salisbury, Allen's mother, and
Lucille Sharps Salisbury, Allen's dear stepmother.
They gave birth to Allen, raised him, and nurtured
his fighting and generous spirit.

CONTENTS

Preface

It is a tribute to my dear husband, who died on September 14, 1992, at the age of 43, that his book is more relevant now than when it was written. The final battles are being fought to save the United States, and to rededicate our nation as a force for good in our suffering world. Because of Allen's work, we know not only the face and methods of the enemy, not only the policies which created this nation as a great industrial power, but also the heroes who elaborated and fought for these policies, heroes like Henry Carey, who had otherwise been written out of our histories and our minds. Allen thwarted one of the great historical hoaxes of the enemy: He made a mockery of their desperate machinations to rob us of part of our heritage by hiding the truth of the history of the Civil War. And he had a great time doing it.

Allen, like Abraham Lincoln, and like Lyndon LaRouche, was a leader who rose from the level of "the common man," and created in himself the capacity to take responsibility for the world as a whole. Some might say he was born and raised in black rural poverty while segregation still reigned. Allen himself said that, while as a child he might not have had shoes with soles for the long walk to school, his family saw to it that there was always plenty of food and love, and Allen seemed to think this, and his books, were the components of a rich life. The walk to school always got made, and Allen used to chuckle as he walked past the much closer "white school" in his sometimes almost-bare feet. He took his "revenge" by making himself the chess champion of the county in his spare time.

While Allen's formal education stopped at high school, he taught himself to be one of the most poetic of writers. For Allen, the obvious was never worth stating. Like his hero Edgar Allan Poe, he wielded the method of metaphor and humor to address the universal in his reader, whatever the topic. As Poe wrote, Allen's "harshest idea will to melody run."

So, if we follow the example of Allen's courageous spirit, if we sing, laugh, and compose while we fight, we will not fail in our great tasks.

Patricia Salisbury
September 20, 1992

Remembering Allen Salisbury

A Fighter for the Truth

W. Allen Salisbury, a leader of the International Caucus of Labor Committees (ICLC) and the LaRouche movement for 20 years, died of colon cancer on September 14, 1992. Although only 43 years old at his passing, Salisbury had made lasting contributions to reviving the crucial ideas which are needed to take mankind out of the current Dark Age, and into a new renaissance of human civilization.

Salisbury's most recent article was published in *Executive Intelligence Review* magazine in April 1990, under the title "If the South Had Won, We'd All Be Slaves." That article served as an introduction to a reprint of Abraham Lincoln's favorite stump speech, entitled "On Discoveries and Inventions," which Salisbury had unearthed during his ground-breaking work during the late 1970s on the real story of the U.S. Civil War.

Salisbury's *The American System and the Civil War—America's Battle with Britain, 1860-76* was first published in 1978. Undertaken as a polemical attack against the fraud of Alex Haley's *Roots,* as well as a scholarly treatment of the American System economic policies of the political current which produced Abraham Lincoln, the book launched a devastating attack on free trade and British liberalism. It included extensive quotes from virtually unknown American economists of the 19th century, most prominently Lincoln's economist Henry Carey, which are essential to understanding the real nature of today's battle between oligarchism and republicanism.

Salisbury's work on the 19th-century American System economists
provided a solid foundation for the vast amount of historical work on
economics which the Labor Committees, and publications like *EIR,*
have produced in the subsequent 15 years. It became an integral and
vital part of LaRouche's own personal campaign for reviving American
System economic policy, not only within the United States, but in the
rest of the world.

Using Television to Educate

To get a vivid understanding of the quality of Salisbury's contribution to the LaRouche movement, the reader can reflect on his major
work in the 1980s—the series of half-hour television advertisements put
out by the LaRouche presidential campaigns. Working intimately with
LaRouche himself, Salisbury was the producer of the shows which both
educated and shook up the electorate.

To these "commercials," Salisbury brought a deep sense of irony
and humor, and the ability to give the viewer a vivid, unforgettable set
of images to convey the current world situation. The Soviet communist
nomenklatura will likely never forgive him for his 1984 show on their
drive for nuclear superiority; nor will Soviet agent-of-influence Walter
Mondale. Henry Kissinger, the chief target of LaRouche's 1984 presidential campaign broadcasts, will likely remember Salisbury unkindly
as well, for the treatment the shows gave to him.

The television show which Salisbury, and LaRouche, were most
happy with, however, was produced in the spring of 1988. It was entitled
"The Woman on Mars," and it addressed the issue of providing a mission
for the people of the United States, the mission of colonizing space,
especially the planet Mars. The fact that this show was truly a work of
art, immediately reflected itself in an outpouring of support from young
people who had watched it, young people who had been moved precisely
in the way which Salisbury and LaRouche had known they would be.

Salisbury was very happy after this television show, and he went
on to produce a couple more that fall, including the historic October
1988 show in which LaRouche projected the collapse of the Soviet
Union through its economic collapse, and called for the reunification of
the Germanys in conjunction with a western policy of "food for peace."
By the time the 1992 series of shows was produced, however, Salisbury
was too sick to lead the effort. He learned in April 1991 that he had

been stricken by cancer, and plunged immediately into an effort to conquer it.

Uplifting People Through Laughter . . .

Before describing Allen Salisbury's fight for life, it is appropriate to give some sense of where this extraordinary person came from. He was born in Lothian, Maryland. His family testifies to his early development of an infectious laugh, which he retained to the end of his life. They also testify to the fact that he was a fighter, who refused to tolerate degradation of himself, or others.

Salisbury was the first black person to become senior class president in his high school. He went on to become politically active, both in the civil rights and anti-war movements. At the same time, he worked in the advertising business, starting in late 1967.

As a creative writer for the Young & Rubicam firm, Salisbury was responsible for many popular commercials, including Eastern Airline's "The Wings of Man" theme.

In the early 1970s, Salisbury began to work with the LaRouche movement in New York City, and eventually took up major responsibility for the work among ghetto youths, which was organized under the rubric of the Revolutionary Youth Movement (RYM). While this work required considerable capability at self-defense—a skill which Salisbury had acquired to a notable extent—the most important qualification was intellectual guts. Salisbury followed LaRouche's advice: Use your mind the way a boxer uses his fists.

Salisbury's approach to the ghetto youths the LaRouche movement was trying to organize in the early 1970s was described by him in a deposition he gave in 1985, pursuant to a suit taken by LaRouche and several associates against FBI harassment of their work. One part of the deposition went as follows:

Q: What was the purpose of RYM?
Salisbury: Well, the purpose of it was to try and prevent these kids from killing—you know, shooting each other, killing each other, and to try to teach them. That was the purpose of the movement.
Q: How did you try to teach them?
A: What I would do is I would give them classes on economics. That's what I would do. I would give them classes on economics, philosophy, and it worked to an astonishing degree—well, a lot of instances. I would

go after the dope thing, which is horrendous, absolutely horrendous in the ghettoes, and so forth, and that's what I would do.

Q: How did you think that classes in economics were going to stop gang warfare?

A: That circumstance that they grew up in was much different than the circumstances I grew up in. When a kid grows up—kids five, four years old—every kid can think, regardless of what his circumstances are, and somewhere along the line the guy doesn't see any hope. He forgets how to think. He wants to get involved in turf, and everything else. By reminding an individual that he has the ability to think, to learn, and that that's truly who he is, sometimes can have an enormous impact on a person.

Salisbury became a member of the ICLC executive in the mid-1970s. Later he was a president of the National Anti-Drug Coalition.

. . . And Poetry

Salisbury's commitment to arousing that ability to think, in people who otherwise seemed determined not to do so, was also reflected in his other major intellectual contribution—the resurrection of the work of Edgar Allan Poe. Poe, Salisbury discovered, was not just a writer of strange stories and beautiful poems, as many American children know, much less a drug addict, but he was also an epistemological warrior for the American System of republican thinking and government against the British.

Poe's anti-Aristotelian method of thinking was the focus of Salisbury's work on the 19th-century poet. In his 1981 article on Poe, Salisbury brought out the poet's hilarious attacks on anti-human epistemology, the Baconian inductive method of "creeping," and the Aristotelian deductive method of "crawling." Salisbury was also one of the few individuals whom LaRouche collaborated with in attempting to revive the ability to recite poetry.

The Fight Against Cancer

Allen Salisbury's last major battle was his battle to conquer his cancer. In concert with his wife of 10 years, Pat, he determined to make every effort to defeat the disease. Indeed, his will to live defied all professional predictions, which had given him only three months to live.

The loving fight which the two made inspired everyone around them, from friends and colleagues, to the medical professionals who have been increasingly brainwashed into submitting to the culture of death. Appropriately, to his life and his death, his last words were: "Keep fighting."

The Civil War and the American System

America's Battle With Britain, 1860-1876

by Allen Salisbury

It would be slightly simplified, but essentially correct to say that there never was such a thing as a Civil War in the United States. The War Between the States that ravaged this country between 1861 and 1865 was the second military phase of the political battle which raged between Britain and the United States from the time a formal ceasefire was concluded at Yorktown in 1781.

While it is widely acknowledged that the British oligarchy supported the Confederacy until its defeat appeared inevitable, modern historians have covered over the more fundamental relationship between the slavocracy and Great Britain. Britain, in its desire to replace the American System of industrial progress with the British System of Malthusian poverty and looting, *created* the Confederacy. Like the Tories during the Revolutionary War, the Confederates were either the conscious or duped agents of the British monarchy, sworn to destroy the American nation.

During the Revolutionary War period, the battle lines were clear: industrialization and expansion, or agrarianism and looting; a national government committed to the principles of technological progress, or subservience to the British crown. Except for the period of open hostilities during the War of 1812, however, British subversion in the period after the Revolutionary War usually cloaked itself in superpatriotic garb. It requires close inspection to rip the American nationalist costume off the likes of Andrew Jackson and

1

Albert Gallatin but the invariant activity of these exemplary Tories, among others, was to turn over the financial reins of the nation to the British Empire.

It was British financial intervention, exercised through such agents, that subverted the implementation of a national development program as it had been put forward under George Washington and Alexander Hamilton. The resulting re-creation of the slave, cotton-growing South, then in alliance with certain New York and New England banking houses, served as an economic, political, and eventually military base for Britain's war against America.

To defeat this gameplan required the remobilization of the nation's workers, industrialists, and technology-proud farmers around the program that founded America. Henry Clay, John Quincy Adams, and Mathew Carey laid the groundwork, but the specific targeting of the treasonous British System, and the organization of the political party that could rout it were left to economist Henry Carey and the Republican Party of Abraham Lincoln.

The Republican Party of Lincoln was responsible for building the labor-industry alliance which won the war. That party's program has a surprisingly familiar ring to those fighting against the stagnation of the American and world economy under the British System today. Its key features were credits for rapid industrialization and realization of new technologies, debt moratoria on certain holdings that were crippling production, and measures to politically sever the U.S. credit generating mechanisms from British control.

It was not only the Democratic Party of Van Buren and Buchanan that Lincoln and his followers had to destroy. Their success depended on a constant battle against insidious agents *inside* the Republican Party as well — in some cases, agents who professed their loyalty to the Republican platform of industrial growth and protectionism, only to win their way into policymaking positions where they could sabotage Republican policies. The problem is similar to that experienced by Americans today: how to reorient politics around the basic scientific principles of economic growth and thus weed out the slogan-mongers *before* the damage is done.

The party of Lincoln succeeded in launching the United States of America as the greatest industrial power on earth — but the British were not brought to the ground. Through assassinations, divide-and-conquer tactics, and, most importantly, the deceptive offer of an "Anglo-American Imperial Alliance," the British oligarchs reestablished an ever-tightening stranglehold over the U.S. economy and political system. Americans' perception of their national interest was again viciously distorted and the war against the British System of austerity, deindustrialization, and mutually destructive class warfare conveniently forgotten. In this, American historians have played not the least significant role.

The Whig policies of Henry Carey and the Lincoln Administration live on in the largely un-self-conscious activities of millions of American workers, farmers, and industrialists today. Now, before the British succeed in manipulating the United States into economic or thermonuclear death, these policies must become a weapon for the reestablishment of the American System worldwide.

Reintroducing Henry Charles Carey, Whig Economist

Henry C. Carey, largely written out of or deliberately deemphasized in today's "revisionist" history books, is to be credited, perhaps more than any other single individual, with pursuing the policies which kept alive the Founding Fathers' program for industrial-capitalist republicanism known as the *American System*. From the late 1840s until his death in 1879, Carey organized for Hamilton and Franklin's dirigist system of political economy among the nation's political leaders, industrialists, bankers, farmers, and skilled workers. Carey's leadership in this effort, especially as exercised through Lincoln's Treasury Department, enabled much of the nineteenth century technological development of this nation to take place.

In the process, Carey and his cothinkers prevented a British attempt to divide and conquer the United States.

A reading of his major works establishes that Carey, like the Founding Fathers, saw his own republican capitalist outlook as the continuation of the humanist struggles of the Hofenstaufen Emperor Frederick II, of the England of John Milton, and of the France of Jean-Baptiste Colbert.

Even competent Civil War historians (e.g., Robert P. Sharkey,

Money, Class, and Party, 1959) conceptually block in their treatment of both Carey and the Civil War period. First, they refuse to recognize the line of development that links the outlook of the Founding Fathers with that of the Whigs — Henry Clay, Henry Carey, and Abraham Lincoln — and leads to the founding of the Republican Party. Second, they refuse to treat the Andrew Jackson Administration as the treasonous outfit it was, especially with regard to Jackson's violation of the intent of the U.S. Constitution when he dismantled Nicholas Biddle's National Bank in 1833.

What is clear from a reading of Hamilton's *Report on a National Bank,*[1] which he delivered to the Congress in December of 1790, is that the Founding Fathers' primary concern was to wed the new nation more closely to the production and promotion of useful manufactures, to the achievement of high rates of industrial growth and technological development, and to the discouragement of usurious banking practices, particularly those practiced by England. The Founding Fathers, following a dirigist policy of centralized national planning, intended the National Bank to so order the investment policies of the nation as to ensure that the production of real value (manufactures, internal improvements, inventions, and so forth) consistently outpaced mere interest on money or monetarist debt.

The Founding Fathers were guided by a labor theory of value, a theory commonly attributed to Karl Marx, but developed years earlier by Alexander Hamilton, particularly in his 1791 *Report on the Subject of Manufactures* to the Congress.[2]

What is the labor theory of value?

From the time that man emerged from the baboon-like existence of the Pleistocene epoch, his activity has been characterized by willful innovations in the modes of producing his means of existence — innovations which have, at the same time, increased his population and the amount of energy available to and consumed by society.

Advances in human society are not the outcome of some

---

1 Spannaus, Nancy B. and Christopher White, *The Political Economy of the American Revolution,* pp. 339-375.

2 Ibid., pp. 375-442.

biological or genetic variation (in the same way that some people glorify the continued adaptability of the ordinary house-roach to changing environmental circumstances). All great advances of humanity have been due to the intervention of humanists who have understood, along with Plato and his Neoplatonic successors, that man has the creative qualities to deliberately master the laws of nature and effect his own evolution. [3]

For such Neoplatonic humanists, the material basis for solving all the problems of human existence must be located in technological and cultural *progress*. There must be an increasing number of human beings available and trained to work on those problems, and each individual's power over nature (his or her "productivity" as defined by assimilation of new, more efficient scientific-technological discoveries) must be increasing. And this progress must be unceasing. Every time a technological advance brings human society to a new mode of production, that mode defines certain aspects of man-altered nature as relatively finite. This does not imply that there are any natural limits to progress. Rather, what appear to be finite limits in one productive mode compel man to make the breakthroughs which will bring him to the next, more advanced mode, thus redefining the domain of natural resources in a qualitative way.

The need and capacity of man to create and assimilate such new discoveries in his day-to-day practice is what the humanist Alexander Hamilton meant by "the productive powers of labor." It is what the Whig economist and humanist Henry C. Carey, in further developing Hamilton's work, meant by the "quality of labor." It is what the great American literary figure and defender of Neoplatonic epistemology, Edgar Allan Poe, termed the "quality of genius." It is what Karl Marx termed "labor power." And it is most emphatically what President Abraham Lincoln meant when he described himself as a follower of the "doctrine of necessity."

---

3 LaRouche, Lyndon H., "The Secrets Known Only to the Inner Elites," *The Campaigner*, Vol. 11, No. 3-4.

4 Carey was correct in his criticisms of both Sir Thomas More and the French mathamatician and philosopher Condorcet for assuming that there could ever be an equilibrium or a "point of rest" for technological progress.

This quality of labor was first treated in detail by Alexander Hamilton in his *Report on the Subject of Manufactures* as being the sole source of value or wealth creation in a capitalist economy. Both Hamilton's *Report on the Subject of Manufactures* and his *Report on a National Bank* were key to the elaboration of an official U.S. government policy that was in opposition to the British colonial policy of primitive accumulation and enforced cultural backwardness.[5]

Thus, the cornerstone of the humanist economic policy of the Founding Fathers — the policy which became known as the American System during the nineteenth century — was state direction of the nation's monetary and credit apparatus through a National Bank. The bank would ensure that the nation's currency and lending institutions acted as an aid to the productive process by issuing credit for industrialization, the fostering of scientific research, and the prevention of usury or at least the subordination of usurious practices to the process of production. Another included feature was government-financed internal improvements, which had the effect of ordering the investments of private individuals and companies into new manufactures, technological innovations in agriculture, and other, socially useful investments. A third policy associated with the American System was protective tariffs to prevent the British from wholesale dumping of their goods — as well as their debts — on the country in an effort to "strangle" American manufactures "in the cradle," as the British "liberal" David Hume put it.[6]

In other words, the aim of the Founding Fathers was to effectively safeguard the nation that had just emerged from a successful revolution against British raw materials looting practices which would have meant the effective recolonization of the United States. At the same time, the Founding Fathers sought to foster the development of the United States until the nation became powerful enough to free the rest of the world from the British System.

---

5 For a heuristic model of the British System versus the American System, see White, Christopher, "The Economy is Labor's Business," *The Campaigner Special Report*, No. 10, p. 5.

6 Carey, Henry C., *Miscellaneous Works of Henry C. Carey*, p. 36.

From this point of reference, Andrew Jackson's decision to withdraw government deposits from the National Bank was unquestionably an act of treason. The decision left the U.S. at the mercy of the credit policies of the Rothschild and Baring banking houses, and made the Baring-dominated Associated Banks of New York and New England (the major financiers of Southern cotton exports) the most powerful group of bankers in the nation.

More importantly, Jackson's actions gave direct support to the theory of "free trade" — an ideology synthetically created by British Royal Society agents like Parson Malthus, Adam Smith, David Ricardo, and John Stuart Mill for the express purpose of *subverting* America's commitment to dirigism.[7] This is the same subversive free trade ideology of "Cotton Is King" (see below), the outlook for which the South made its insurrection and against which Lincoln and his Whig allies fought.

Historians of the Sharkey school nobly, but incorrectly conclude that the Civil War was primarily a contest between finance and industrial capital, with Henry Carey as the latter's chief spokesman. Rather, Lincoln and Carey must be seen as continuing the struggle for industrial development begun by the Founding Fathers against the fundamentally *anticapitalist* policies of the monetarists of Great Britain and their agents in this country.

This view has immediate implications for today: it leads to the conclusion that the current financial policy of the United States, which was and is formulated largely by the British-based investment houses and their affiliated think tanks like the Brookings Institution, are, in fact, alien to the principles on which the United States was founded. Adherents to this British policy are today exerting a control over the nation's institutions and policies that is treasonous.

Carey's Roots

Henry Carey's background is rooted in republican humanist traditions. His father, Mathew Carey, was an Irish republican revolutionary strongly influenced by circles who were, in turn, in-

---

7 White, Carol and Christopher White, "The Royal Society: British Queens of Science," *New Solidarity*, Vol. 8, No. 63.

fluenced by Jonathan Swift. Mathew Carey's early Irish nationalism is humanist in the same sense as Franklin or Hamilton's American nationalism.

Mathew Carey was kicked out of Ireland for "defaming the British" when he resurrected Swift's *Modest Proposal for the Universal Use of Irish Manufactures.* He then made his way to France where he worked with Benjamin Franklin and the French General Lafayette.[8] From France, Carey began printing and distributing Franklin's *Notes from America* to leading humanist circles throughout Europe to keep them informed of the progress of the American Revolution. He later returned to Ireland to start a republican newspaper with the funds advanced for the purpose by Franklin and Lafayette.

Franklin, Lafayette, and Carey, too, were conspirators in a joint America-"League of Armed Neutrality" war against Britain of which the successful American Revolution was a part. The league of European continental powers stretching from Spain and France in the west to Russia in the east provided the decisive strategic element of humanist-organized monarchies to enable that battle against Britain to succeed. The plans did not end there; the league intended an invasion of Britain itself to bring an end to more than a century of British-based monetarist financial rule over Europe. To this end, Lafayette sought and received from the young Mathew Carey a detailed assessment of the possibility of establishing a republican state in Ireland. Ireland, at the time, was a probable launch point for an invasion force against Britain to be headed by Lafayette.

The plan became unworkable with the outbreak of the so-called French Revolution[9] which also nearly prevented the consolidation of

---

8 Jonathan Swift was a regular contributor to the young Franklin's network of American newspapers. See Pepper, Marcia Merry, "Franklin's Poor Richard's Almanacs" (unpublished, New York: Campaigner Publications, Inc., July 1977).

9 The French Revolution could be more accurately described as a destabilization by the British of France which significantly weakened the republican forces there until Lazare Carnot's reforms of the army and the emergence of the École Polytechnique in the late 1790s. See Frommer, Linda, "How Pitt's Jacobinism Wrecked the French Revolution," *New Solidarity,* Vol. 8, Nos. 28 and 29.

the gains of the American Revolution in the form of the present Constitution.

Upon his arrival in the U.S., Carey quickly became an ardent supporter of Alexander Hamilton; he continued his collaboration with Franklin until the latter's death. Contemporary opinion placed Carey second only to Hamilton as the nation's leading protagonist for the "American System." His work with Franklin encouraged him to found the nation's first book publishing company following their successful U.S. publication of Condorcet's *Historical Sketch for the Progress of the Human Mind.*

Mathew Carey adopted the humanist organizing method of Franklin. As Franklin reports in his *Autobiography,* the Junto, a secret organization, agitated for continual improvements, the first fire company, and the first network of printing establishments in the nation. It was this model that was followed by Carey and the Philadelphia Association for the Promotion of National Industry to effect such improvements as the construction of the first railroad in Pennsylvania. For this reason, Edgar Allan Poe once said of his publisher Mathew Carey that he reminded one of Ben Franklin.

Around Mathew Carey's Philadelphia circle developed the second generation of American political economists. The American humanist was not disposed to adopting a professorial chair of economics. They plunged into the study of political economy out of necessity as a deluge of classical British economics and economists threatened to stop development of the U.S. along the lines first elaborated by Franklin and adopted by the first U.S. Congress when it decided in favor of the celebrated reports of Alexcander Hamilton.

After the assassination of Hamilton by Aaron Burr in 1804,[10] major responsibility for keeping alive the American System program fell to this group of secondary leaders, which included as its chief spokesmen the Whig leaders John Q. Adams, Henry Clay, and John Calhoun (early in his career) and the members of Mathew Carey's Philadelphia circle, most notably such forgotten figures as

---

10 Hamilton at the time was in the process of writing for and publishing in the *New York Post* an eight-part attack on President Jefferson's Treasury Secretary Albert Gallatin.

Baltimore's Daniel Raymond, Hezikiah Niles, and the brilliant German leader Friedrich List.

As Mathew Carey documents his own contributions in his *Autobiography*, he vigorously pursued the policies put forward in Hamilton's report. In fact, he was a director for two terms of the Pennsylvania subdivision of the National Bank. Among other contributions was his defense of Joseph Priestley, the English chemist who collaborated closely with Franklin.

Priestley was forcibly exiled from England and had come under attack from William Cobbett. Cobbett was the chief U.S. publicist for the antihumanist circles around Jeremy Bentham and Parson Malthus in England. Cobbett's primary role was to conduct what today would be known as a Watergating operation against leading U.S. Hamiltonians. The ensuing newspaper war between Carey and Cobbett eventually led to the dissolution of Cobbett's Pennsylvania newspaper, the *Peter Porcupine Gazette*, and his departure to England.

It was only with the defeat of the "League of Armed Neutrality," sealed by the 1815 Treaty of Vienna, that Britain was again freed to continue open hostilities against the United States. In the eighteenth century, France was Europe's leading industrial power and the leading national power in the league. Objectively, Britain could not defeat France in a war, so Britain manipulated France to defeat itself. Using Swiss and French agents under London's direction, Britain wrecked French credit, mobilized the "sansculottes" slum population of Paris, and then set in motion the Jacobin Terror to abort any French humanist attempt at reproducing the American Revolution in Europe. By 1814, continental Europe was reduced to war ruin and the young American nation had fought another war against Britain — the War of 1812. The unfavorable aftermath of that war and continued trade war by the British against American commerce and industry was creating havoc within the United States.

The treaty that concluded the War of 1812 had given the New York merchants junior-partner status in the East India Company. Britain sought to "legalize" its trade war with the United States by having the U.S. drop its dirigist policy in favor of "free trade."

Albert Gallatin, the Secretary of the Treasury under both

President Madison and President Jefferson, was Britain's "agent-in-place" for this subversion attempt. The Treasury's London office under Gallatin was used as a training center for agents to influence U.S. economic policy toward free trade. There, Gallatin's staff met with both Jeremy Bentham and David Ricardo who instructed them not to have Hamilton's dirigist system taught in the schools and colleges of the United States. Bentham even offered to Gallatin his services to rewrite the U.S. Constitution — an offer Gallatin relayed to Jefferson, Madison, and the U.S. Congress.

It was Gallatin who sought to manipulate President Jefferson over the question of the Louisiana Purchase. Jefferson was properly concerned that the United States should expand its territory across the Mississippi River to the Rocky Mountains — from the Gulf of Mexico to Canada — to prevent occupation by hostile governments allied with the British. The actual policy debate over the Louisiana Purchase, however, occurred over whether the territories were to be developed *before* they were admitted as states in the union. Gallatin pushed a program of "free" plots of land, while the leading Federalists and Whigs insisted that the lands should be settled by men with enough capital to invest in manufactures and agricultural improvements. With the experience of the French Revolution fresh in mind, they had no intention of creating a state run by beggars and speculators.

As part of Britain's subversion, Adam Smith's *The Wealth of Nations* was taken off the dusty bookshelves and made popular throughout the country. *The Wealth of Nations* first appeared in this country during the first year of the Revolutionary War. During the period after 1815, it was revived especially by the shipping interests of New England and New York, and by the slave states of the deep South.

It was also during this period that Mathew Carey and other supporters of Hamilton sought out and wrote their own textbooks on political economy to refute the works of Smith and, later, Malthus and Ricardo.

With the publication of his *Olive Branch*, Mathew Carey opened a campaign throughout the country for a continued national commitment to Hamilton's economic policy. He immediately took up the study of political economy which, as he states in his

Autobiography, he had not paid any attention to before reading *The Wealth of Nations*. His first work took on Adam Smith's proposals to return the United States back to a colonial relationship with Great Britain. In this respect, *The Wealth of Nations* was British political intelligence propaganda. Of course, Smith paid due respect to the home market and its industries, but, as Carey states correctly, the whole proposal was a sham which he and Henry Clay's close associates Daniel Raymond and Friedrich List proceeded to expose.

To Mathew Carey, the foundation of Smith's proposal to establish "freedom of trade" was accompanied with "assurances" that the wiped-out American manufacturers and mechanics could find employment in "collateral manufactures," especially agriculture.

> "These positions, absurd, futile, and untenable as they are, form the basis of the *Wealth of Nations*. To a person wholly unbiased by prejudice, it must be a matter of astonishment how a work, resting on such sandy and miserable foundation, could have obtained, and still more, have so long preserved, its celebrity. The monstrous absurdity of these doctrines and the facility with which they might be refuted, induced me to enter the lists against this Goliath with the sling and stone of truth."[11]

Mathew Carey, Henry Clay, and others revived Hamilton's Society for the Promotion of Useful Manufactures. The new Philadelphia Association for the Promotion of National Industry included manufacturers, as well as agriculturists, scientists, and skilled mechanics. As part of their work, Mathew Carey republished several times Hamilton's *Report on the Subject of Manufactures*. In his prefaces to those editions, Carey correctly noted that Hamilton had already refuted all that Smith had to say and, in fact, Hamilton's report subsumed the work of the great seventeenth century French Finance Minister Colbert.

The impact of the association in at least sustaining Hamilton's system as the policy intention of the nation is evident in this letter from President Madison to Mathew Carey.

> "I have read the pamphlet on our commercial policy, which is

11 Carey, Mathew, *Autobiographical Sketches in a Series of Letters Addressed to a Friend*, p. 49.

another proof of your disinterested zeal on an important subject. You have placed in a strong light the evils necessarily resulting from the excess of our importations over our exports and the necessity for restoring an equilibrium. I have read your essays as well as the report of Hamilton...and I must confess that I see no possibility of resisting the facts, principles and arguments they contain. What adds to their weight too with me is that, as you remark, we cannot be worsted by the experiment, as far as economical expediency goes..."[12]

The remarks by the Senator from Pennsylvania, Andrew Stewart, during the 1827 debates on tariff legislation also evidences the impact of the association.

"The gentleman from New York has called this a 'New England Bill,' and, from principles of patriotism, he says he is opposed to it. 'It is immaterial,' he says, 'to us, whether we get our cloth from Manchester or Boston.' This may suit the patriotism of the representative of a city where it is said that three-fourths of the woolen business is in the hands of British merchants, and British manufacturers; but Mr. S. took his principles from another school. For he had been told in the course of the debate by a gentleman from South Carolina that there are two schools of political economy — one headed by Adam Smith, and the other by Mathew Carey — a British and an American school, and we are warned by that gentleman against giving up the sound doctrines of Smith, for what he is pleased to call the 'Statistical Nonsense of Mathew Carey.' Now Sir, although the views of Adam Smith and other British writers may suit the purposes of the gentlemen from New York and South Carolina, yet they must give me leave to say that I would not give one page of the 'Statistical Nonsense of Mathew Carey' on this subject for all the theories of Adam Smith, and their long and learned speeches into the bargain...."[13]

One of the more important figures engaged in the fight for the American System was the German republican Friedrich List. List was brought to America and introduced to the Pennsylvania circle by Lafayette in 1824. List was already familiar with the works of Daniel Raymond, Henry Clay, Alexander Hamilton, Mathew Carey, and others principally through Carey's earlier extensive colla-

---

12 Ibid., p. 7.

13 Stewart, Andrew. *The American System Speeches on the Tariff Question and on Internal Improvements*, (New York: Garland Publishing, Inc., 1974) pp. 146-147.

boration with the German educator Christopher Daniel Eberling. To combat propaganda from Britain that was defaming America as a land of savages, Eberling requested and got a steady stream of reports on the latest developments in internal improvements, books, and samples of every leading newspaper in the young nation. What Eberling faced was an international campaign on the part of Great Britain to prevent the model American republic from being exported.

Professor List himself played a leading role in exporting significant portions of the American System when he established the *Zoll-Verein* or German customs union upon his return to Germany in 1832. What List accomplished in part was the elimination of the customs duties between the various Germanic states. In its place, a national German customs policy was enacted, following the example of the United States. As Henry Carey later noted in his review of List's book, *The National System of Political Economy*, it was this accomplishment that enabled Germany to become a nation.

List, like Mathew Carey and Daniel Raymond, had nothing but contempt for Adam Smith. List even postulated that Adam Smith, while on his death bed, had all his personal papers burned so that the world would never know his evil.

List's book *The National System of Political Economy*, was written following his return to Germany, but was begun while List was in the United States working with the Philadelphia Association between 1825 and 1832. He was commissioned by Mathew Carey and Charles Ingersoll, the association's treasurer, to write a series of open letters attacking Adam Smith and free trade, and explicating the principles of the American System of political economy.

List did write a series of twelve open letters in which he proposed, among other things, that the U.S. save the Latin American countries from having to repeat the U.S. experience of carving a nation out of wilderness by exporting U.S. technological know-how to Latin America.

List's proposals on that account became a permanent feature of Whig foreign policy. His book was to be used by the association to counter what had become the hegemonic works of the British economists in the nation's colleges.

The programs enunciated by List and others remained the

A contemporary cartoonist's view of Andrew "Jack ass" Jackson's destruction of the national banking system to the cheers of the newspaper hounds tied to Administration policies. While the Globe wallows in a dung heap of lies, Vice President Van Buren, the sly fox, stalks the U.S. Bank. The rooster is Major Jack Downing, a political sage invented by a commentator of the age.

policy commitment of the nation until Andrew Jackson entered the White House in 1829. The factions led by Henry Clay then formed the Whig Party in opposition to Jackson. The vigorous fight in behalf of the American System, led by Clay in the Congress, prevented Jackson from doing much damage until he was reelected for a second term. After Jackson vetoed the charter of and withdrew federal money from the National Bank, the southern cotton planters forced Clay behind the Compromise Tariff of 1833. They threatened secession if U.S. tariffs against Great Britain were not ended. In fact, it was Great Britain's Prime Minister Lord Palmerston's policy in the early 1830s to get the United States to adopt the free trade policy in order to prevent the expense of another costly war.

The measures taken by Jackson, who was still publicly expressing his support for the American System, led to the depression of 1837. The bank's destruction handed large sections of the South to the nullifiers (or secessionists) because otherwise enlightened southerners were unable to obtain the needed credits to diversify out of cotton, tobacco, and other raw materials into industry. The institution of slavery, which had begun to die out, spread as the British were given a free hand to demand southern debt service payments to New York banks and eventually to the bottomless coffers to the Rothschild and Baring banking houses.

Martin Van Buren's election to the presidency and Rothschild agent August Belmont's later election to the leadership of the Democratic Party solidified the Rothschilds' control over the U.S. Democratic Party.

The abolitionist movement, which began attaching itself to the Whig Party, was also coming under Great Britain's direction. Consider the fact that Harriet Beecher Stowe's patron, Arthur Tappan, and William Lloyd Garrison were both on the Board of Directors of Albert Gallatin's Baring-connected bank. These abolitionists lobbied for the North's secession from the Union. So, it is by no means accidental that both the southern "slavocracy" and the northern abolitionist movement were British free traders in economic as well as social philosophy.

The actions of both were coordinated from the top by the London-based Cobden Clubs. This organization had on its Board of Directors the leading members of the House of Rothschild, and

Thomas Baring. John Stuart Mill, son of the detestable John Mill, was their chief political economist.

U.S. membership included such so-called liberals as the Boston cotton merchant, Edward Atkinson, the leading abolitionist, William Lloyd Garrison, as well as the top theorists for the southern slavocracy.

It was primarily the abolitionists together with the William Seward-Thurlow Weed New York faction of the Whig Party that prevented Clay or any other Whig leader of his calibre from winning the presidency. They forced compromise after compromise on the issue of the extension of slavery, all in the name of "states rights."

The Founding Fathers of this country had fully intended the slave trade and slavery to be stopped at the earliest possible date. The first draft of the Declaration of Independence, written by Thomas Jefferson with the aid of Benjamin Franklin, reads in part:

> "...He (the king — A.S.) has waged cruel war against human nature itself, violating its most sacred right of life and liberty, in the persons of a distant people, who never offended him, captivating and carrying them into slavery in another hemisphere, or to incur a miserable death in their transportation thither. This piratical warfare, the opprobrium of infidel powers, is the warfare of the Christian king of Great Britain. Determined to keep open a market where Men should be bought and sold, he has prostituted his negative for suppressing every legislative attempt to prohibit or to restrain this execrable commerce. And that this assemblage of horrors might want no fact of distinguished dye, he is now exciting those very people to rise in arms against us, and to purchase that liberty of which he has deprived them by murdering the people upon whom he also obtruded them — thus paying off former crimes committed against the liberties of one people with crimes which he urges them to commit against the lives of another...."[14]

This draft of the Declaration of Independence was not adopted out of deference to South Carolina and Georgia in order to gain their support in the prosecution of the Revolutionary War and the later signing of the U.S. Constitution. However, it was understood that both the slave trade and slavery would be halted as soon as practicable.

---

14 Colton, Calvin, *Junius Tracts*, No. V, p. 11.

Henry C. Carey and Karl Marx
vs. The Manchester School

In an essay published in the early 1960s, Arthur Schlesinger, like other British-tinged historians, recognized the significance of Karl Marx's assessment of Henry Carey as the "most important of the American economists."[15]

After making that statement and dutifully identifying Carey's humanist commitment as the reason for Marx's positive assessment, Schlesinger asserts that "after all, Carey was much closer to the classical economists (Mill and Ricardo — A.S.) than he was to Marx."[16]

The fact that Schlesinger could get away with publishing such nonsense and receive a Pulitzer Prize for his glorification of Andrew Jackson's Administration without a cry of moral indignation from the American population suffices as evidence of the utter ignorance in which most Americans have been kept regarding their own history.

In actual political practice, it was Henry Carey who sought to demonstrate to Marx the differences between the American System and the British System of the classical economists for whom they both shared a mutual hatred.

Such falsified historiography on the part of Schlesinger represents the on-going British-centered intelligence warfare against both the Soviet Union and the United States.

The populations of the United States and the Soviet Union share a common commitment to industrial and technological-progress. The Soviet Union's popularion associates such a commitment with the name of Karl Marx and its realization in the government's five-year plans. In the United States, Henry Carey and other supporters of the American System left this country a legacy which the average citizen associates with the "idea of progress."

On that account and especially after Lenin's successful 1917 revolution, British intelligence networks within both the U.S. and Soviet Union found it necessary to exploit both real and imagined

15 Schlesinger, Arthur M., Jr. and Morton White, eds., *Paths of American Thought*, (Boston: Houghton Mifflin Company, 1963) p. 117.

16 Ibid., p. 117.

differences in order to prevent the leadership of the two countries from making their shared humanist commitment the basis for international policy agreements and ventures — typified by the military collaboration between the U.S. and USSR during World War II and by current efforts at scientific collaboration.[17]

It is by no means accidental that Arthur Schlesinger, as a member of President Kennedy's National Security Council, was in part responsible for enhancing the credibility of British agents inside the Soviet Union associated with Georgii Arbatov and his USA-Canada Institute.[18] That Soviet institute controls the archives of Karl Marx and, in early 1977, reprinted in its *USA* magazine an error by Karl Marx regarding the Whig economist Henry Carey as evidence that Marx regarded Carey as a "bourgeois vulgar economist." That same epithet is repeated in most Moscow editions of the works of Karl Marx.

In truth, the term "vulgar" was used by Marx to characterize John Stuart Mill, the hated enemy of both Marx and Carey. Mill, a contemporary of Marx and Carey, was the chief economist of the Cobden Clubs, and thus published and organized in behalf of the House of Rothschild and the Baring Brothers' banking interests.

What is it that Marx actually had to say about Carey?

"...That bourgeois society in the United States has not yet developed far enough to make the class struggle obvious and comprehensible is most strikingly proved by H.C. Carey, the only American economist of importance. He attacks Ricardo, the most classical representative of the bourgeoisie and the most stoical adversary of the proletariat, as a man whose works are an arsenal for anarchists, socialists, and all the enemies of bourgeois society. He accuses not only him, but Malthus, Mill, Say, Torrens, Wakefield, McCulloch, Senior, Wakeley, R. Jones, etc., in short the economic masterminds of Europe, of tearing society apart and paving the way for civil war by their proof that the economic basis of the different classes must give rise to a necessary and ever-growing antagonism between them."[19]

---

17 LaRouche, Lyndon H., Jr., *The Case of Walter Lippmann,* passim.

18 Zoakos, Criton, "Open the Arbatov File," *Executive Intelligence Review,* Vol. IV, Nos. 18 and 19; also LaRouche, Lyndon H., Jr., "The Failure of Communist Ideology," *The Campaigner Special Report,* No. 8.

19 Marx, Karl, "Letter to Engels, March 5, 1852," *Marx-Engels Selected Correspondence,* p. 57.

What is true is that Marx was almost totally ignorant of the humanist struggle of the eighteenth century which culminated in the American Revolution.[20] Thus, he was unable, often to the point of ridiculous stubbornness, to recognize the difference between the American System and the British System, and took the latter to be the model for modern industrial capitalism.

Carey, on the other hand, in his first attempt at political economy, his 1840 *Principles of Political Economy*, thoroughly debunked Ricardo's theory of rent by showing it to be both factually and historically absurd. Carey demonstrates how yesterday's values are depreciated by today's advances in technology by focusing on the effects of technological progress in an economy on the determination of value. For this, Friedrich Engels credits him with being the first to state that the value of a commodity is its necessary cost of social reproduction and *not* its accounting cost. Carey, also in this context, defined the combined quantity and quality (or productive power) of labor to be the sole determinant of economic value in a capitalist economy.

Carey's book dealt a blow to the political-economic theory that was at that time reigning hegemonic. But Carey had not yet come around to the superior wisdom of his father, Mathew, and Alexander Hamilton that tariff barriers were needed to prevent the destruction of U.S. industry by Great Britain. He also accepted what was "positive" in Adam Smith's *Wealth of Nations* and stubbornly refused to recognize that it was merely bait. The eighteenth century French economist Pierre Dupont de Nemours has even charged that "everything that is true in this respectable, but tedious work" is to be found in Turgot's *Reflections on the Formation and Distribution of Wealth;* "everything added by Smith is inaccurate."[21]

But with the depression of 1848, Carey was to take over from Henry Clay the leadership of those forces committed to the

---

20 LaRouche, Lyndon H., Jr., "The *Karl Marx* Karl Marx Did Not Know," *The Campaigner*, Vol. 10, pp. 11-30.

21 Dakin, Douglas, *Turgot and the Ancien Regime in France*, (New York: Octagon Books, Inc., 1965) p. 346. Turgot, Minister of State under French King Louis XVI, was an economist whose cited work predates Smith's.

protective policy. This leadership position forced Carey to hone his analysis of British monetarism.

In *The Past, The Present, and The Future* (1848), Carey begins to argue correctly that the entire British economic system was nothing more than an apology for a foreign policy of looting, bent on destroying the industrial capability of the rest of the world.

The *Harmony of Interest,* written in 1851, is a polemical restatement of his proposal for a labor-industry (or "producing classes") alliance against the free trade movement in the U.S.

In *Harmony of Interest,* Carey singles out the Ricardo-Malthus school of British economists for the particular attention of his readers. The Malthusian doctrine of overpopulation is false, says Carey, because industrialization and improvements in agriculture have historically enabled man to increase his population. The Ricardian doctrine of ground rent is equally absurd. Using examples of settlement patterns in Pennsylvania, Carey proves that man does not move from the "best" lands to poorer ones. Rather, there are no "best" lands until they become man-improved by the introduction of agricultural implements, fertilizer, and dredging techniques. As further evidence against the Ricardian doctrine, Carey discusses the work of his German friend and chemist Liebig in the application of fertilizer and crop rotation methods to farmland. In capitalist society, such improvements by man give value to land and justify rent; Ricardo's is the system of a common thief.

Carey then describes the British System:

"The impoverishing effects of the system were early obvious, and to the endeavor to account for the increasing difficulty of obtaining food where the whole action of the laws tended to increase the number of consumers of food, and to diminish the number of producers, was due the invention of the Malthusian theory of population, now half-a-century old. That was followed by the Ricardo doctrine of rent, which accounted for the scarcity of food by asserting, as a fact, that men always commenced the work of cultivation on rich soils, and that as population increased they were obliged to resort to poorer ones, yielding a constantly diminishing return to labor, and producing a constant necessity for separating from each other, if they would obtain a sufficiency of food. Upon this theory is based the whole English politico-economical system."

"We thus have here, first, a system that is unsound and un-natural, and second, a theory invented for the purpose of accounting

for the poverty and wretchedness which are its necessary results. . .
Overpopulation is the ready excuse for all the evils of a vicious system, and so will it continue to be until that system shall see its end, the time for which is rapidly approaching." [22]

On the Rothschilds' role in the British System, Carey remarks:

"Rothschild may be taken as the type of the whole system, and the following notice of him and of his modes of taxing those by whom he was surrounded, furnishes a picture of the speculators of every kind, in England, who live at the cost of the labourers of the world.

"The name of Nathan Meyer Rothschild was in the mouths of all city men as a prodigy of success. Cautiously, however, did the capitalist proceed, until he had made a fortune as great as his future reputation. He revived all the arts of an older period. He employed brokers to depress or raise the market for his benefit, and is said in one day to have purchased to the extent of four millions. The name of Rothschild as a contractor for an English loan made its first public appearance in 1819....The Old and the New World alike bore witness to his skill....Minor capitalists, like parasitical plants, clung to him, and were always ready to advance their money in speculations at his bidding. He became the high-priest of the temple of Janus, and the coupons raised by the capitalist for a despotic state were more than a match for the cannon of the revolutionist." [23]

The Slave Trade, Foreign and Domestic, written in 1853, identifies Harriet Beecher Stowe's *Uncle Tom's Cabin* as an important element in a British attempt to balkanize the United States. In it, there are many of Karl Marx's contributions to the *New York Tribune,* including one which exposes the hypocrisy of the British liberal's antislavery movement by showing Stowe's connection to the landed aristocracy of Great Britain, most particularly Lady Sunderland who was financing Stowe and who had just kicked all the peasants off her land to make room for a game preserve. Marx's appellation, "The Lady Sunderland Self-Glorification Society," became "canonized" among Whig circles in the U.S.

Carey's discussion of chattel slavery deals with the effects of

---

22 Carey, Henry C., *Harmony of Interest* in *Miscellaneous Works of Henry C. Carey,* pp. 63-64.
23 Ibid., p. 75. The temple of Janus, referred to by Carey, was always closed during peacetime.

British policy worldwide. Entire populations were enslaved, restricted to engaging in primitive agriculture and mineral extraction, and denied participation in technological progress. Carey treats India and how the British East India Company systematically supplanted the positive influence of Mohammedan culture with the introduction of the vicious ideology of Hinduism.

In a letter to Friedrich Engels, discussing *The Slave Trade,* Marx shows his stubbornness on the issue of the American System versus the British System.

"Carey, the American national economist, has published a new book, *Slavery At Home and Abroad.* Under "slavery" are here included all forms of servitude, wage slavery, etc. He has sent me his book and has quoted me repeatedly (from the *Trib*). I told you before that in this man's previously published works the harmony of the economic foundations of the bourgeois system was described and all the mischief was attributed to superfluous interference by the state. The state was his bogey....The root of all evil is the centralizing effect of big industry. But this centralizing effect is England's fault because she turns herself into the workshop of the world and forces all other countries back into the rudest agriculture, divorced from manufacture. For the crimes of England the Ricardo-Malthus theory and especially Ricardo's theory of ground rent are in their turn responsible. The necessary consequences alike of Ricardo's theory and of industrial centralization would be Communism. And in order to avoid all this, to oppose centralization by localization and a combination of factories and agriculture all over the country, the final recommendation of our ultra-free trader is — protective tariffs. In order to escape the effects of bourgeois industry, for which he makes England responsible, he resorts like a true Yankee to hastening this development in America itself by artificial means.

"...The only thing of positive interest in his book is the comparison between the former English Negro slavery in Jamaica and the Negro slavery in the United States. He shows that the main body of Negroes in Jamaica, etc., always consisted of newly imported barbarians, as under English treatment the Negroes were not only unable to maintain their population, but lost two thirds of the number annually imported; the present generation of Negroes in America, on the other hand, is a native product more or less Yankee-ised, English-speaking etc., and therefore fit for emancipation.

"Your article on Switzerland was of course a direct smack at the leader in the *Tribune* and their Carey. I have continued this hidden warfare in a first article on India in which the destruction of the native industry by England is described as revolutionary. This will be very shocking to them. For the rest, the whole rule of Britain in India was swinish, and is to this day."[24]

Marx repeats this error throughout *Das Capital* and in the following quote from *Grundrisse:*

"...It is not surprising that the production relationships in which this immense new world has developed so surprisingly, quickly and fortunately are considered by Carey as the normal, eternal conditions of social production and distribution, contrary to what has taken place in Europe, especially in England — which for Carey is the real Europe where the production relationships have been hindered and disturbed by the inherited obstacles of the feudal period. What more natural from his point of view, than that these relationships should have been caricatured and falsified by the English economists, who have confused the fortuitous distortions of these relationships with their inherent character."[25]

To this view, Marx objects that, according to Carey,

"It is a law of nature, for example, that wages should increase with the productivity of labor. So if reality does not correspond with this law, whether in India or in England, we have to make an abstraction of the influence of the state . . . taxes, monopolies, etc. Naturally, Carey does not inquire to what extent these state influences — public debt, taxes, etc. — themselves grow out of bourgeois conditions; thus, in England, for example, they are not at all the result of feudalism, but rather of its dissolution and defeats.

"Carey's criticism of the English theory of landed property wages, population, class contradictions, etc. resolves itself into one thing only — American conditions against English conditions. Bourgeois society does not exist in the pure state in England; it does not there conform to its nature and definition. So why should the ideas of English economists on bourgeois society be the true and untroubled expression of a reality they have never known."[26]

Marx's errors regarding the American Revolution duly noted, Marx as well as his close associates counted among the most potent allies of the nation during the Civil War, which was recognized by

---

24 Marx, Karl, "Letter to Engels, June 14, 1853," *Selected Correspondence,* pp. 68-69.
25 Marx, Karl, *Grundrisse,* p. 48.
26 Ibid., p. 49.

President Lincoln in his distinction between the British abolition societies and Marx's International Workingman's Association. [27]

Marx wrote for the *New York Tribune* during that period when, for all intents and purposes, Carey was the financial editor of the paper. Carey's personal friend and collaborator at the *Tribune*, Charles Dana, had added Marx to the *Tribune* staff and requested that Marx begin to write articles on English domestic and foreign policy. Marx's tenure stretched from the early 1850s through 1860. During that decade, Carey had more or less determined that the survival of the American System largely rested with himself and what became known as his Philadelphia Vespers circle — the center of Whig humanism in the United States.

Although Marx, in his theoretical work, rejected Carey's *Harmony of Interest*, which, in essence, was Carey's proposal for the cooperation of the industrialists, laborers, and farmers under an American System, in point of fact, Marx's actual political practice defended the American System forces against the British free traders and the social reformers and assorted liberals associated with them. Hence, the hatred bestowed on both Marx and Carey by the British liberals which continues to this day. Charles Dana even penned a letter defending Karl Marx from the slanders of British agent Herr Vogt. The letter was published in the first edition of Marx's work *Herr Vogt*.

The Carey-Lincoln Tradition
and the Fight for the Republican Party

The dissolution of the Whig Party following the death of Henry Clay in 1852 and the passage of the Kansas-Nebraska Act in 1854, which effectively repealed the Missouri Compromise of 1820 prohibiting slavery in the Louisiana Territory north of Arkansas, sparked what can only be described as a mass strike movement which gave birth to the Republican Party. The first national campaign of the Republican Party in 1856 gave them a majority in the U.S. House of Representatives despite the electoral defeat of their presidential candidate John C. Frémont.

---

27 Abraham Lincoln's letter to the workingmen of Manchester, England is included in the selection of extracts which follows, pp. 245-246.

The difficult task which the Whigs, Lincoln and Carey, faced was to establish the hegemony of Whig policy in the new party. Frémont was the candidate of a coalition led by New York's William Seward and the Jacksonian-turned-free-soiler and abolitionist William Cullen Bryant: the British free trade wing of the party. Lincoln was a supporter of Henry Clay and the American System all his political life. Contrary to the populist garbage peddled by the poet Carl Sandburg, Lincoln was the heir of earlier republicans who fought the political battles for the most rapid introduction of internal improvements to civilize the Midwest and West of the United States and against the Jacksonian notion of "rugged individualism." Lincoln detested the proletarianism (in the Roman, not Marxian, sense of the word) in his own Vice-President Andrew Johnson.

The state of American politics at the time made Whig control of the Republican Party a matter of urgency. The Democratic Party was led by Rothschild agent August Belmont, and the South, beginning with the Administration of President Buchanan — a documented embezzler — was preparing for a secession war through appropriation of the nation's military arsenals.

In 1855, the southern planters had prepared their secessionist raison d'etre in a work that was widely distributed throughout the South, titled *Cotton is King.*[28] Representative William D. Kelley (R-Pa.) concluded the following discussion of the South's free trade policy with a quote from that book.

"...The opposition to the protective tariff by the South arose from two causes; the first openly avowed at the time, and the second clearly deducible from the policy it pursued; the one to secure the foreign market for its cotton, the other to obtain a bountiful supply of provisions at cheap rates.

"...But they could not monopolize the market unless they could obtain a cheap supply of food and clothing for their Negroes, and raise their cotton at such reduced prices as to undersell their rivals. A manufacturing population with its mechanical coadjutors in the

---

28 The full title of this pamphlet, which was later published by Prichard, Abbott and Loomis of Augusta, Georgia in 1860, is: *Cotton is King, and Pro-Slavery Arguments, comprising the Writings of Hammond, Harper, Christie, Stringfellow, Hodge, Bledsoe, and Cartwright on this Important subject, by E.N. Elliot, LL.D., President of Planters' College, Mississippi with an Essay on Slavery in the Light of International Law, by the Editor.*

midst of the provision growers, on a scale such as the protective policy contemplated it, was conceived would create a permanent market for their products and enhance the price; whereas if this manufacturing could be prevented, and a system of free trade be adopted, the South would constitute the principal provision market of the country, and the fertile lands of the North supply the cheap food demanded for its slaves.... By the protective policy, the planters expected to have the cost of both provisions and clothing increased, and their ability to monopolize the foreign markets diminished in a corresponding degree. If they could establish free trade, it would insure the American markets to foreign manufacturers, secure the foreign markets of their leading staples, repress home manufactures, force a large number of northern men into agriculture, multiply the growth and diminish the price of provisions feed and clothe their slaves at lower rates, produce their cotton for a third or fourth of former prices, rival all other countries in its cultivation, monopolize the trade in the article throughout all of Europe, and build up a commerce that would make us the ruler of the seas.

"...As the protective system coupled with the contemplated internal improvements, if successfully accomplished, would inevitably tend to enhance the price of agricultural products, while the free trade, anti-internal improvements policy would as certainly reduce their value, the two systems were long considered so antagonistic that the success of one must mean the death knell of the other. Indeed, so fully was Ohio impressed with the necessity of promoting manufactures that all capital thus employed was for many years entirely exempt from taxation....

" 'We must prevent the increase of manufactures, force the surplus labor into agriculture, promote the cultivation of our unimproved western lands until provisions are so multiplied and reduced in price that the slave can be fed so cheaply as to enable us to grow our sugar at three cents a pound. Then without protective duties, we can rival Cuba in the production of that staple and drive her from our markets....' "[29]

Southern policy was the very antithesis of the technologically vectored growth demanded by the American System. Both Lincoln and Henry Carey were right when they insisted that slavery not only oppressed and degraded the slave, but degraded the productive and mental power of all American labor. It was precisely on this point

29 Kelley, William D., "Protection to American Labor," *Speeches, Addresses and Letters,* pp. 16-18, 21.

that Lincoln distinguished himself as a presidential candidate in his 1858 senatorial contest with Stephen Douglas, the intellectual author of the Kansas-Nebraska Act and the Dred Scott decision. The latter allowed the southern slave owner to cross state lines, if necessary, to reclaim his property — the slave.

It was also on this question of labor power that Karl Marx's closest American collaborator, Joseph Weydemeyer, was drawn closer to support of Whig industrialists. Weydemeyer's polemic from 1853 on was aimed at refuting the "over-population" theories of Malthus. In 1853, Weydemeyer published a series of pamphlets, *Sketches of National Economy,* to recruit the German émigré population, particularly in the U.S. West, away from the "spread the poverty" notions of the German émigré agent Weitling.[30]

Following the passage of the Homestead Act in 1854, Weydemeyer again intervened to prevent the newly opened lands from becoming the domain of agriculture only, as the southern free traders wanted. In early 1855, the Central Committee of the American Workers League published a series of pamphlets by Weydemeyer which called for, in part:

> "Introduction of large-scale agriculture on those vast areas known as state lands, not in the interests of big capital, but in the interest of workers who constitute the great mass of the nation. Hence, inviolability and indivisibility of state property, development of these lands by workers' associations under the control and with the help of the states. Connecting industrial enterprises with agriculture and administering them in the same way, so that the saving of human labor by the introduction of machines is not at the expense of the workers, and so that a healthy life and healthy home no longer seem incompatible with large-scale business undertakings."[31]

Henry Carey, too, was insistent that the Republican Party adopt the American System as its policy. He perceived that unless the new party did so, the nation would be hopelessly divided into competing sections — all ruled by the British ideology of free trade. From 1856 until the presidential contest of 1860, Carey's

---

30 Oberman, Karl, *Joseph Weydemeyer, Pioneer of American Socialism,* (New York: International Publishers, 1947) pp. 69-78.

31 Ibid., pp. 83-84.

Vespers circle organized industrial associations in the Midwest, West, and especially, the border states to agitate for the American System.

Much of this agitation was initiated by the Home Protective Union of Pennsylvania of which Carey was president.

Carey and his circle were determined that William Seward would not get the presidential nomination of the Republican Party.[32]

Of primary importance in the fight which preceded the adoption of a national development platform at the 1860 Republican Party convention were the open letters from Henry Carey to the "free trade" wing of the Republican Party and its leader, William Cullen Bryant.[33]

The policy discussions that were generated around these open letters, which were printed in the nation's protectionist press, reoriented the Republican's campaign focus for the upcoming presidential race. As late as 1856, nearly everyone, including some leading Whigs, were content to wage the campaign just on the issue of slavery and its prohibition or extension. Carey said as much in a letter to Ohio Whig leader Judge McLean in June 1858:

"... We have had a great meeting here, having for it's object the reinauguration of protection as a part of the political platform. The ultra-Republicans do not like it, and yet they will be forced to stand by it — Pennsylvania, New Jersey, Delaware, and Maryland being fully determined as I think to have nothing to do with any party that has yet to determine between free trade and protection...."[34]

At the same time, Carey continued to warn against the "radical" abolitionists around Harriet Beecher Stowe. In 1859, following the John Brown raid on the arsenal at Harper's Ferry,

---

32 See E. Pershine Smith's letters to Henry Carey during 1859-1860 in Henry C. Carey Papers. A friend of Carey's, Smith also held an office in Seward's New York machine and was peeved by Carey's efforts to prevent Seward's nomination.

33 See Carey's open letters to William Cullen Bryant included in the selection of extracts which follows, pp. 121-140.

34 Henry C. Carey Papers. Also quoted in Smith, George Winston, *Henry C. Carey and the American Sectional Conflict*, p. 73.

West Virginia, which was financed and planned in large part by agents of the British East India Company, [35] Carey wrote:

> "...A year ago, we had the Kansas murders on our side. Now, our opponents have the Harper's Ferry riots on theirs, and if we do not act with great caution, we shall fail to win the race.... It is my final belief that Messrs. Beecher, Phillips, and others, are in this quarter, the most efficient allies of the proslavery power. Reflect upon this and then try and persuade your editors to pursue such a course of action as will permit that we may reelect a good mayor... and that we may give the Republican candidates in the autumn a handsome majority...." [36]

Carey, particularly in his open letters to Bryant, warned the nation that the British were behind the attempts to wreck the Union.

> "...In common with Franklin and Adams, Hancock and Hamilton, those men clearly saw that it was to the industrial element we were to look for that cement by which our people and our States were to be held together. Forgetting all the lessons they had taught, we have now so long been following in the direction indicated by our British Free Trade friends — by those who now see, as was seen before the Revolution, in the dispersion of our people the means of maintaining colonial vassalage — that already are they congratulating themselves upon the approaching dissolution of the Union, and the entire reestablishment of Britsh influence over this northern portion of the continent. For proof of this, permit me to refer you to the following extracts from the *Morning Post,* now the recognized organ of the Palmerstonian government:

> " 'If the Northern States should separate from the Southern on the question of slavery — one which now so fiercely agitates the public mind in America — that portion of the Grand Trunk Railway which traverses Maine, might at any day be closed against England, unless indeed the people of that State, with an eye to commercial profit, should offer to annex themselves to Canada. On military as well as commercial grounds it is obviously necessary that British North America should possess on the Atlantic a port open at all times of the year — a port which, whilst the terminus of that railway communication which is destined to do so much for the development and consolidation of the wealth and prosperity of British North

---

35 Sawicky, A.M., "Why the British Built Uncle Tom's Cabin" (unpublished, New York: Campaigner Publications, Inc., 1978).

36 Smith, *American Sectional Conflict,* p. 73.

America, will make England equally in peace and war independent of the United States. We trust that the question of confederation will be speedily forced upon the attention of Her Majesty's ministers.

" 'The present time is the most propitious for its discussion.... If slavery is to be the nemesis of Republican America — if separation is to take place — the confederated States of British North America, then a strong and compact nation, would virtually hold the balance of power on the continent, and lead to the restoration of that influence which, more than eighty years ago, England was supposed to have lost. This object, with the uncertain future of Republican institutions in the United States before us, is a subject worthy of the early and earnest consideration of the Parliament and people of the mother country.'

"Shall these anticipations be realized? That they must be so, unless our commercial policy shall be changed, is as certain as that the light of day will follow the darkness of night. Look where we may, discord, decay, and slavery march hand-in-hand with the British free trade system — harmony and freedom, wealth and strength, on the contrary, growing in all those countries by which that system is resisted. Such having been, and being now the case, are you not, my dear sir, in your steady advocacy of the Carolinian policy among ourselves, doing all that lies in your power toward undoing the work that was done by the men of '76?

"Repeating once again my offer to place your answers to this and other questions within the reach of a million and a half protectionist readers, I remain Yours, very respectfully, Henry C. Carey." [37]

Needless to say, Bryant could not effectively answer at the time. When the Republican Party convened for the Chicago Convention of 1860, they committed themselves to a program of internal improvements and to building a continental railway. They adopted this resolution penned by Henry Carey.

"... That while providing revenue for the support of the general government by duties upon imports, sound policy requires such an adjustment of these imports as will encourage the development of the industrial interest of the whole country; and we commend that policy of national exchanges which secures to working-men liberal wages, to agriculture remunerative prices, to mechanics and manufacturers

---

37 Carey, Henry C., "The Financial Crisis, Their Causes and Effects," in *Miscellaneous Works,* pp. 21-24.

adequate reward for their skill, labour, and enterprise, and to the nation commercial prosperity and independence."[38]

After the Chicago convention, Carey wrote to a friend:

"Happily the Republican, or antislavery, party has recently re-adopted Protection as one of the essential parts of its platform, and has nominated as its candidate for the presidency a man who has been all his life a protectionist. He will be elected, and we shall then have a total change in the policy of the country, as you shall see."[39]

The Fight for the American System

When Abraham Lincoln entered office in March of 1861, the Civil War was weeks away. Four southern states had seceded from the Union immediately after the announcement of Lincoln's victory in the October 1860 election; the rest were to follow in rapid succession. The immediate cause of the Civil War was the firing on Fort Sumter, a federal fort in South Carolina, by the Confederate insurrectionists. But what drove the North and the South to war was the British conspiracy to overthrow the American System in favor of free trade policies.[40]

The new Lincoln Administration found the United States Treasury virtually bankrupt. The actions taken by Andrew Jackson against the National Bank had set the standard for federal nonintervention into the currency and banking affairs of the nation, which was followed by subsequent presidents in deference to states rights. Jackson's dismantling of "Biddle's Bank" was followed by the 1846 passage of the Independent Treasury Act by the "free trade" Democrats. The act prevented the U.S. government from regulating the affairs of the banks and stipulated that the government should be treated like any other depositor.

Thus, in 1861, Abraham Lincoln and his Administration were faced with waging a dual war: one against the monetarist bankers of particularly New York and New England, the other against their surrogate, the Confederate Army.

---

38 The Republican Party Platform of 1860, Point 12.

39 Smith, *American Sectional Conflict*, p. 85.

40 See Goldstein, Paul "The Rothschilds' International Plot to Kill Lincoln," *New Solidarity*, Vol. 7, No 67.

It was Great Britain's intent to gain full financial control over not only the southern Confederacy, but the North. Anyone familiar with the history of British financial manipulation of foreign wars knows that the ABCs of counterinsurgency entail such control of the purse strings of all warring parties as to predetermine the outcome of the battle or the war itself.[41]

Congress was out of session following Lincoln's inauguration, so Secretary of the Treasury Solomon Chase turned to the Associated Banks, headed by James Gallatin, the son of Albert Gallatin, for an immediate loan to the Treasury of $150 million in specie (gold coin). Chase arranged to have the banks buy government bonds in three sets of $50 million each in intervals of six days. The specie returned to the banks after it was paid out by the Treasury Department as salaries, materials purchases, and so forth. The Associated Banks also had the right of marketing several million dollars worth of government refinancing bonds, known as 7:30 bonds.

The Associated Banks intended to sell the U.S. debt overseas to the Rothschild and Baring banking houses. In fact, the Barings wrote continually to Chase saying they would be glad to take a part of the securities the Associated Banks had assumed.

U.S. historians widely hold and propagate the belief that the reason behind the Associated Banks' abrogation of their agreement with Treasury Secretary Chase and suspension of specie payments to the government on December 28, 1861 was the Trent Affair. Two Confederates, Mason and Slidell, who were carrying diplomatic and financial papers, were enroute to London aboard the British vessel *Trent*. The ship was stopped by an American vessel and the Confederates were removed.

The November 1 Trent Affair indeed provoked a "diplomatic scandal." But, there had been other, more important developments in early December which forced the hand of the British and their Associated Banks' agents...the American System was adopted as government policy.

While Chase was negotiating for loans, Carey and his Vespers circle were engaged in furious letter-writing, negotiating, and lobby-

---

41 LaRouche, Lyndon, H., Jr., "The Secrets Known Only to the Inner Elites," *The Campaigner*, Vol. 11, Nos. 3 and 4.

ing efforts with senators, congressmen, and even the President to have the policies of Alexander Hamilton adopted.

In the fall of 1861, Carey received the following letter from Senator Morrill, the author of the protective Morrill Tariff:

> "I have had a full and fair conference with Secretary Chase. His philosophy is free trade and *ad valorems,* but he confessed that in his present agony for money the latter failed. He suggested something like the Tariff of 1846. I told him it could not get 20 votes of the Republican Party in the House. At last he came into the same channel and agreed with me that all we could do with the Tariff was to increase it upon several or even many things.... The Secretary prefers a new bill, but almost identical with the one passed. I have aided in preparing it and have found him willing to yield in all save three or four points. On the whole, he is willing to throw his theories to the dogs. All this, of course, you must regard as confidential and if you find a little not quite satisfactory you may thank your stars and possibly your humble servant that it was not worse. I think Chase, considering his antecedents, should receive generous treatment by all our friends. He is doing the best he can practically." [42]

Secretary Chase's report to Congress in December 1861 proposed the passage of a Hamiltonian policy, a proposal seconded by Lincoln in his address to Congress on December 3, 1861. [43] The Hamiltonian policy proposed by Carey and others included the Morrill protective tariff, the issuance of a currency that was internal to the United States and backed by the U.S. government's commitment to a policy of rapid industrial expansion, the sale of United States bonds (popularly known as the 5:20 bonds), the establishment of a national banking system regulated by the federal government, and a peace-winning program to industrialize the South. The national banks were intended to serve as investors in the future wealth of the United States through the purchase of 5:20 bonds and the issuance of long-term, low-interest loans to manufacturers, and by acting as a medium for the circulation of currency. (Carey had proposed such a banking system to Henry Clay years earlier; the system would have been under the jurisdiction of the United States Bank.)

---

42 Henry C. Carey Papers.

43 Lincoln's Annual Address to the U.S. Congress, December 3, 1861, is included in the selection of extracts which follows, pp. 224-242.

In the fall preceding Lincoln's December address, Carey sent the President the following letters with a copy of his pamphlet urging the construction of a North-South Railroad to facilitate future attempts at industrializing the South:

> "If Henry Clay's tariff views would have been carried out sooner there would have been no secession because the southern mineral region would long since have obtained control of the planting area. Some means must be found to enable these people of the hill country to profit of our present tariff...."

Later Carey wrote:

> "How much more firm and stable might the antebellum union have been, had there developed then a policy which would have filled the hill country of the South with free white men engaged in mining coal and ore, making iron and cloth, and building school houses and churches, and establishing little libraries...." [44]

Carey repeated the same message to Chase and Secretary of State Seward, particularly to encourage immigration to the U.S. The South, Carey argued, would need skilled mechanics and other tradesmen if reconstruction were to be a success.

On December 3, 1861, Lincoln laid out the American System as the guiding principle of his Administration, a course he was to follow up to and including the day of his assassination. He urged Congress to consider the proposal by Carey to begin the construction of a railroad system into North Carolina, Kentucky, and Tennessee for the purpose of enabling the development of the mining and ore and other industrial interests in these southern states. Such transportation facilities were the obvious first step toward industrializing the South, a fact left out of the texts of modern day U.S. historians to create the myth that Lincoln's reconstruction policy was to readmit the South as it was. I quote here from the relevant sections of the December 3 address.

> "I deem it of importance that the loyal regions of east Tennessee and western North Carolina should be connected with Kentucky and other faithful parts of the Union, by railroad. I therefore recommend, as a military measure, that Congress provide for the construction of such road as speedily as possible. Kentucky, no doubt, will

---

44 Henry C. Carey Papers.

cooperate and, through her legislation, make the most judicious selection of a line. The northern terminus must connect with some existing railroad; and whether the route shall be from Lexington, or Nicholasville, to the Cumberland Gap; or from Lebanon to the Tennessee line, in the direction of Knoxville; or on some still different line, can easily be determined. Kentucky and the general government cooperating, the work can be completed in a very short time; and when done, it will be not only of vast present usefulness, but also a valuable permanent improvement, worth its cost in all the future...."[45]

Regarding financial policy:

"The operations of the Treasury during the period which has elapsed since your adjournment have been conducted with signal success. The patriotism of the people has placed at the disposal of the government the large means demanded by the public exigencies. *Much of the national loan has been taken by citizens of the industrial classes, whose confidence in their country's faith and zeal for their country's deliverance from present peril, have induced them to contribute to the support of the government the whole of their limited acquisitions. This fact imposes peculiar obligations to economy in disbursement and energy in action."* [46]

Lincoln concluded the address by clearly stating labor's priority over capital:

"It is not needed, nor fitting here, that a general argument should be made in favor of popular institutions; but there is one point, with its connections, not so hackneyed as most others, to which I ask a brief attention. *It is the effort to place capital on an equal footing with, if not above labor, in the structure of government. It is assumed that labor is available only in connection with capital; that nobody labors unless somebody else, owning capital, somehow by use of it, induces him to labor.... (However,) labor is prior to, and independent of capital. Capital is only the fruit of labor and could never have existed if labor had not first existed. Labor is superior of capital, and deserves much the higher consideration."* [47]

The present author expects the British-tinged writer of U.S.

---

45 Lincoln, Abraham, *The Collected Works of Abraham Lincoln,* Vol. 5, p. 37. The full text of Lincoln's speech is included in the selection of extracts which follows, pp. 224-242.

46 Ibid., p. 39 (emphasis added).

47 Ibid., pp. 51-52 (emphasis added).

history to indignantly protest this interpretation of Lincoln's annual address. The following brief quote from one of Lincoln's favorite "stump" speeches should firmly establish Lincoln as a self-conscious Whig humanist:

> "... Man is not the only animal who labors; but he is the only one who improves his workmanship. This improvement he effects by Discoveries and Inventions...."[48]

The policies which Lincoln would follow during his Administration could only conform to his own personal identity and commitment to the "idea of progress."

When Gallatin and the Associated Banks got wind of the new policy — even before Lincoln and his Treasury Secretary addressed the Congress — they instantly and incessantly wrote to Secretary Chase urging him to adopt instead a stringent taxing policy.

On December 28, 1861, the Associated Banks suspended specie payments to the government. Fearing that all was lost, James Gallatin arranged a meeting with Treasury Secretary Chase and the group of congressmen who would be responsible for steering the "Hamiltonian" legislation through the U.S. Congress.

On January 9, Gallatin outlined his proposal; the Associated Banks proposed that Chase adopt a policy of immediate and direct taxation, allow them to sell an unlimited number of government six percent (or 7:30) bonds below par on the London market, suspend the "sub treasury law" by which the government gained regulatory control over the banks, and halt the issuance of government legal tender.

This plan was dismissed by Congress; Congressman Samuel Hooper (R-Ma.) commented that he would adopt no plan which called for "government shinning (begging) before Wall Street."

British reaction was furious over the failure to get this proposal through. On February 22 *The Economist* of London ran this editorial:

---

48 This speech by Lincoln has never been published in any collected works to the author's knowledge. A printed, but unpublished edition of the speech can be found at the University of Pennsylvania Library. It is also included in the selection of extracts which follows, pp. 217-222.

"...If Congress had adopted an efficient system of direct taxation at the outset of the struggle, the European credit of the government might have been preserved. At a price they would have got some money, but now they will not get a sixpence in Lombard Street or on the continent, no matter what interest they offer."

William Cullen Bryant, editor of the *New York Post* and free trade spokesman in the Republican Party, began, at the behest of Boston cotton merchant and financier John Murray Forbes, a series of editorials attacking Lincoln's financial policy and calling for direct taxation of industry to pay off the war debts. After congressional passage of the legislation, Bryant met with Lincoln and editorially implored him to veto the measure. Lincoln refused.

From Britain, August Belmont, then meeting with the Rothschild bankers, and Thurlow Weed dispatched a plethora of protesting messages to Lincoln and Secretary of State Seward. At a meeting arranged by the Rothschilds with Prime Minister Palmerston and Chancellor of the Exchequer William E. Gladstone, Belmont was questioned as to the state of the American nation's defenses and the popular attitude toward England. In one outburst, Palmerston had the gall to say: "We do not like slavery, but we want cotton and we dislike your Morrill tariff."[49]

Belmont wrote to Seward:

"...The English government and people could not accept the North's justification for fighting the confederacy as long as this war is not carried on for the abolition of slavery in the southern states. Perhaps English sentiment could use the tonic of a reduction in the objectionable Morrill tariff? Nothing else could contribute so effectively toward disproving widespread southern assertions that the war was merely a contest between free trade and protection."[50]

Palmerston certainly had his reasons for "disliking" the tariff — and the rest of American System policy being implemented. Such a policy on the part of the United States was once again bringing to the fore various international currents which had almost succeeded in destroying British domination at the time of the American Revolution.

Both Germany and Russia began adopting protective systems.

---

49 Katz, Irving, *August Belmont, A Political Biography,* pp. 102-103.
50 Ibid.

The case of Russia is particularly important because it illustrates the point that the protective policy of the U.S. was absolutely not to be equated with isolationism.

Leading U.S. protectionists stated time and again that their aim was to enable the United States to become strong enough to rid the world of the odious British System once and for all. Thus, during the early part of the Lincoln Administration, the U.S. exported to Russia both the blueprints and the technicians for construction of American iron-clad ships which provided the basis for the modernization of the Russian navy and the brute-force development of Russia's iron industry. It was Henry Carey who, by stating the *Tribune's* editorial policy, was responsible in 1856 for U.S. diplomatic support of Russia against England during the Crimean War.

Within England itself, Karl Marx took hold of the international ferment to give direction to the International Workingman's Association. In the words of Pennsylvania Congressman William Kelley, "the producing classes" in England were engaged in a struggle which would finally force that country to adopt some of the best aspects of the American System. Insight into the danger which the British faced is afforded by two letters written by Karl Marx to Friedrich Engels.

On March 6, 1862, Marx writes:

> "...Of (England's —A.S.) total exports, amounting to 125,115,133 pounds (1861), 42,260,970 pounds' worth to go to English 'possessions' and 'colonies.' If one adds to these England's further exports to Asia, Africa, and America, 23 to 24 percent at most then remain for export to the European states. If Russia goes forward in Asia at the double quick march of the last ten years, until she concentrates all her efforts on India, then it is all up with John Bull's world market, and this end is further hastened by the protectionist policy of the United States, which now, if only to revenge themselves on John Bull, will assuredly not give it up so soon. Moreover, John Bull discovers with horror that his principal colonies in North America and Australia become protectionist in precisely the same measure as John Bull becomes a free trader. The self-conceit, brutal stupidity with which John admires Pam's spirited policy in Asia and America, will cost him damned dear...." [51]

---

51 Marx, Karl and Friedrich Engels, *The Civil War in the United States,* pp. 236-237. "Pam" is British Prime Minister Palmerston.

Again, on May 27, Marx writes Engels on the response of Britain to American financial policy.

"... It is wonderfully fine how the *Times* (of London — A.S.) wails that... liberty must be lost in the event of the North tyrannizing the South. The *Economist* is also good. In its last number, it declares that the Yankees' financial prosperity — the non-depreciation of their paper money — is incomprehensible to it (although the matter is perfectly simple). It had hitherto consoled its readers from week to week with this depreciation. Although it now admits that it does not understand what is its business and has misled its readers concerning this, it is at present solacing them with dark doubts about the military operations of which it officially knows nothing. What extraordinarily facilitated the paper operations of the Yankees (the main point being the confidence placed in their paper money and therewith in their government) was without question the circumstance that in consequence of secession the West was almost denuded of paper money and therefore of a circulating medium generally. All the banks whose principal securities consisted of the bonds of slave states, were bankrupted.

"... Then partly in consequence of the Morrill tariff, partly in consequence of the war itself, which largely put an end to the import of luxuries, the Yankees had a balance of trade and therefore a rate of exchange favorable to themselves and against Europe the whole time. An unfavorable rate of exchange might have badly affected the patriotic confidence in their paper on the part of the philistines.

"For the rest — this comical concern of John Bull for the interest on the national debt that Uncle Sam will have to pay! As if it were not a mere bagatelle in comparison with Bull's national debt; moreover the United States are unquestionably richer today than were the Bulls with their debt of a billion in 1815."

Frantic over the American System financial policy adopted by the U.S. government, the British government shifted the emphasis of its policy away from the "hardline" of Palmerston, who had intended to go to war against the Union on the side of the South. The new approach was to be "softer" and guided by the liberals under John Stuart Mill and Chancellor of the Exchequer Gladstone, who was later to become Prime Minister. Mill, who was heard to exclaim "what are we to do without our New York banks," argued for such a shift: the South, after all, had defaulted on its debt payment and was unreliable.

---

52 Ibid., pp. 246-247.

Mill's circle of liberals, connected to both the British manufacturers and the Rothschild and Baring banks, controlled the Cobden Clubs — Britain's world-wide agitators for "free trade." The clubs' U.S. members could be found within the free-trade wing of the Republican Party and within the U.S. abolitionist movement. The leading figures in the United States were Edward Atkinson, the Massachusetts liberal and cotton merchant; William Cullen Bryant, the editor of the *Evening Post* and the leading transcendentalist literary figure; Charles Sumner; the abolitionist and Senator from Massachusetts William Lloyd Garrison; Harriet Beecher Stowe; Charles Francis Adams, the U.S. Ambassador to England; and a host of others. The Cobden Clubs, as the true descendants of Jeremy Bentham, were primarily responsible for disseminating and popularizing the Manchester school of economics, the school of Ricardo, Malthus, and Smith, as well as every degraded form of nominalist thought which passed for science, including the theories of Charles Darwin.

The network of free-trade radicals in the U.S. were largely tied to East Coast shipping and banking interests, and to New England textile manufacturers and export-import bankers. The merchants and bankers depended largely on England, the export of cotton and other unfinished raw materials, and the import of finished goods from Britain. They would, on economic matters, support the interests of Britain against the United States. Their party loyalties were largely to the Democratic Party, particularly after Andrew Jackson's election to the presidency.

This is the network which was employed in the operation to destabilize Lincoln's government, utilizing well-tested British counterinsurgency methods and underwritten by Britain. There was speculation in gold on Wall Street in order to depreciate the Greenback currency, and an effort was made to undermine the Union's war effort through an attack on the Commanding General of the Army McClellan and through a manipulation of the slavery issue.

The following letter, written by Henry Carey to Treasury Secretary Chase in January 1862, illustrates the problem.

> "... Last night at a large public meeting in this city one of the speakers asserted clearly and distinctly that General McClellan had been ordered by the President and the Secretary to take the South by the Peninsula — that he had protested it — that he had said however

that he was only a soldier and must obey orders — and that he would do so, although it would certainly involve the ruin of the army. That the reverse of all this was true was not for a moment doubted by many of the audience, but who among them was there, who could certainly expect that such was the fact? Not even a single person present. The real facts, as given to me by a friend almost at the moment of their occurrence I have always believed to be, that General McClellan urged the Peninsula route — that the Secretary opposed it — and that it was with no small difficulty he was induced to side with the former. If this is really so, why should not the world know about it? All believe the President honest, and all would be found ready to excuse any error of judgement that he might admit.

"Some explanation must certainly soon be given for if it be not we shall have war among ourselves — the McClellan and anti-McClellan factions as bitter as are now the patriots and the rebels. Let things go on as they are now going and there may arise a danger yet overlooked for — the appearance of McClellan and his army at the gates of Washington and not at those of Richmond. A more unscrupulous faction than that which is now advocating ruin does not exist even in Carolina, and the government, by its silence, is doing all in its power to give it strength. Let us go on for another month and you will, my dear sir, find it very difficult to negotiate the notes you are now authorized to issue. For every reason then, I pray you to let your friends know what are the real facts."[53]

What had been unleashed upon the American nation was "countergang" warfare in the midst of the war against the secessionists. The Commanding General of the Army, McClellan, was an ardent "states rights" Democrat who, by his own admission, was not politically motivated to wage war against the South and would have accepted peace at any price.

Having a target in McClellan, the radicals opened a campaign against the Administration on two fronts: demand for the removal of McClellan from office and agitation for an immediate proclamation ending slavery. It cannot be overly emphasized that the so-called radicals of the stripe of Charles Sumner, William Lloyd Garrison and William Cullen Bryant did not give a damn about ending slavery. It was merely a convenient issue around which to destabilize the Lincoln Administration. William Cullen Bryant's newspaper, *The Evening Post,* opened the campaign, early in 1862, shortly after Lincoln refused to veto the legal tender bill.

---

53 Henry C. Carey Papers.

The focus of the slavery issue was the Wade-Davis emancipation bill, passed by Congress, but vetoed by Lincoln — and for a very good reason. The measure would have placed a lien on southern cotton for the accounts of New England textile manufacturers and the Rothschild-connected bankers Belmont and Seligman as security for payment of southern debt contracted before the war.

Lincoln incurred the wrath of the free traders for his veto of the bill, not because he was unwilling to free the slave, but because he would not set up the South for postwar financial looting against the South's entire population, including the freedmen.

The Wade-Davis Bill had the added onerous feature of treating slaves as southern property which could be confiscated together with the bales of cotton.[54]

The newspapers of William Cullen Bryant and others harangued Lincoln for being proslavery; in their private correspondence, they were vexed. Cobden Club member Edward Atkinson received many such letters, including one from New England cotton merchant Forbes who wanted to "wring Lincoln's scrawny neck" for vetoing the legislation.

Free trade radicals infested Congress; they were even members of the congressional committee on the conduct of the war.[55] Their waving of the Wade-Davis banner forced Lincoln to bypass Congress. As Commander in Chief of the Union's armed forces, Lincoln issued his Emancipation Proclamation as a military decree. He also proposed a period of apprenticeship for the newly freed men to enable them to contribute to a postwar industrializing South.

Another "free trade" attack which Bryant led was against the Greenbacks and the government's investment policy which centered

---

54 For the benefit of those historians who may cite sections of the 1861 message to Congress where Lincoln moots a colonization program, suffice it to say that it was Henry Carey who argued against it. Once Lincoln realized that such colonization schemes implemented slavery in an unchained form, he quickly dropped the idea.

55 This group of dyed-in-the-wool free traders, both within and outside the Congress pushed General John Charles Frémont to campaign for the presidency in 1864, a campaign that would have led to a Democratic Party victory. The Frémont for President movement was led by German radical émigré and free trader Carl Schurze; Marx's American collaborator Weydemeyer did much to convince Frémont not to run.

Henry Clay

Henry Carey

Mathew Carey

The American Whigs

Abraham Lincoln

William D. Kelley

William Elder

August Belmont

William Cullen Bryant

Nathan Rothschild

The "Free Trade" Tories

John Stuart Mill

David Ames Wells

Harriet Beecher Stowe

on creating a national banking system. Government 5:20 bonds would be sold to those banks as a basis for issuing low-interest credits to industry and to facilitate the circulation of currency. Gallatin's Associated Banks refused to participate in the national banking system and gave the government no aid in its sale of the 5:20 bonds.

Philadelphia banker Jay Cooke had been employed by Treasury Secretary Chase to become the sole agent for the sale of 5:20 bonds. Several of Henry Carey's associates, principally Stephen Colwell and William Elder, both important Whig economists in their own right, and Samuel Wilkerson, prepared the propaganda Cooke utilized to sell the bonds. Elder and Colwell were later appointed by Lincoln to posts in the Treasury Department: Elder as the official Treasury statistician and Colwell as an economist.

The original bill, authorizing the sale of 5:20 bonds, contained no provision for paying the interest on the bonds in gold. Thus, if the bill as it was prepared by Thaddeus Stevens's House Ways and Means Committee had passed the House, it would have had the effect of severing the domestic economy of the United States from the British early in Lincoln's Administration. The British pound sterling, at the time, was the gold-backed world reserve currency. But before the bill was passed, August Belmont and James Gallatin worked out a compromise with Republican Congressman Spaulding of New York which allowed the bonds to be purchased with Greenbacks, but their interest was to be paid in specie.

The compromise was the first step in pegging the value of the U.S. Greenback to gold, and allowed Belmont and other New York merchants engaged in the export-import trade to speculate in gold through the Associated Banks and thus create fluctuations in the value of Greenbacks as measured by the British gold standard.

Congress was eventually forced to pass two bills in 1864: one coerced the Associated Banks to join the national banking system by forcing them to pay a ten percent tax on every transaction outside the system; and another, authored by Thaddeus Stevens at Lincoln's request, outlawed all sale of gold in the New York Gold Room.

In the meantime, the actions of the Associated Banks prompted the Whig mayor of New York, George Opdyke, an ardent opponent of John Stuart Mill, to seek Jay Cooke's assistance in founding a national bank in New York with twice the reserves of the Associated Banks. Opdyke had been instrumental in organizing, through a small faction in the New York City Chamber of Commerce, petitions to Treasury Secretary Chase and to Congress to make the Greenbacks legal tender. He was well informed and sought to keep the protectionist forces up to date on the work being done in England by Karl Marx and the IWMA, and constantly pointed to the fact that they were holding demonstrations all over England in support of the Union. As Marx writes in a letter to Engels on January 2, 1863:

> " The *Times* and Co. are utterly furious over the workers' meetings in Manchester, Sheffield, and London. It is very good that the eyes of the Yankees are opened in this way. For the rest, Opdyke has already said at a meeting in New York: 'We know that the English working class are with us, and that the governing classes of England are against us.' " [56]

Both Elder and Wilkerson's pamphlets and circulars, produced for the government loan office, were largely educational on the national banking system and informed the world of the development policy of the country. A report by William Elder, written in the latter part of 1863 and titled *The Debt and Resources of the United States*, puts forth the Whig perspective on abolition as well as the nation's development policy.

> ". . . The very best and healthiest of all the causes of this prosperity is that one which has given us our own work to do — the congressional legislation of 1861-1862 upon import duties aided by the high rate of foreign exchange. For more than a year, we have had the competing industry of Europe under a tolerable commercial blockade, and the policy which saves a Nation's work for its own hands has had a demonstration of its wonder working power among us, which will not be lost when gold falls to par and peace puts in practice the wisdom that war has taught.... Someone may turn upon us with impatience and ask whether we mean to prove that war is a blessing? No, alas! No. War, Pestilence, and Famine are a leash of evils, usually associated, but happily separated in our case, sparing us the most terrible, and so far modifying the fury of the leader of the train, and with this further mitigation, that for the time it has broken up a wretched system of commercial policy, greatly more destructive to the industrial interests of the nation than all the usual waste of war. It has muzzled the two blood-hounds that always hunt in couples,

---

56 Marx and Engels, *The Civil War in the United States*, p. 264.

slavery and free trade, slavery ever crying for free foreign trade, and free trade meaning nothing but slave men. Even a national debt may be lighter than a paralyzed industry, and may indirectly give the strength to bear its burden, by protecting labor itself from foreign invasion, and keeping it free to build up a Nation's wealth."[57]

This fifty-page pamphlet and others like it were translated into German, Spanish, French, and Russian, and were distributed throughout. The pamphlet included charts of U.S. growth since the adoption of the protective policy, and the projected development of U.S. resources once the war is ended. Most importantly, the pamphlet contrasted the U.S. national debt with the British national debt, and the U.S. development policy with British looting. In short, it was a "how-to-do-it" pamphlet for other nations to follow.

The Assassination of Lincoln:
British Coup Against the American System

It is the general conclusion among historiographers that Lincoln was somehow not involved in the financial policy pursued by Treasury Secretary Chase. On the day he was assassinated, Lincoln was in fact considering the problem of how to combat speculation by bringing the national currency (the Greenbacks) up to par value without contracting the supply. He told a gathering of Congressmen:

"Grant thinks we can reduce the cost of the army establishment at least half a million a day, which, with the reduction of expenditures of our navy, will soon bring down our national debt to something like decent proportions, and bring our national paper up to par, or nearly so, with gold."[58]

At Lincoln's request, Henry Carey wrote a series of open letters to the Speaker of the House of Representatives Schuyler Colfax that were titled, "How to Outdo England Without Fighting Her."[59]

---

57 Elder, Dr. William, *The Debt and Resources of the United States and the Effect of Secession upon the Trade and Industry of the Loyal States*, (Philadelphia: Ringwalt and Brown, 1863) pp. 23-24.

58 Bishop, James, *The Day Lincoln Was Shot* (New York: Harper, 1955) p. 191.

59 A selection from these open letters is included in the extracts which follow, pp. 140-154.

Carey argued against the heteronomy with which U.S. economic policy was carried out. Lincoln had been forced to put his signature on bills that he did not consider in the national interest, Carey pointed out. He called for the creation of a national economic policy planning body under the control of the executive branch. Lincoln did set up the Revenue Commission and appointed at its head David Ames Wells, a person everyone thought to be a Careyite.

British financial warfare against the United States followed the conclusion of the Civil War, and assassination was a strategic part of this renewed assault. Secretary of the Treasury McCulloch, Lincoln's third Treasury Secretary, actually initiated the attack on the American System with an open letter to Henry Carey which was published in the *Chicago Tribune* just three days before Lincoln's death. He advocated a reduction of the tariff, an immediate return to specie payments, and a contraction of the currency. The article was accompanied by the following excerpt from the *London Times:*

> "He (McCulloch — A.S.) is what few Americans are; a sound political economist. He has studied the philosophy and theory as well as the practice. To read his letters and Treatise anyone who did not know that he was an American might imagine that he was an Englishman or a Scotsman, who had never embraced the delusion so prevalent on this side of the Atlantic, that as the resources of America are not half developed it is competent to American statesmen to run riot in wild experiment and set at defiance the dearly bought experience of older communities. Mr. McCulloch is, as far as his published opinions testify, a worthy successor of Adam Smith, Mill, Ricardo and his quasi-namesake the late J.K. McCulloch."[60]

Lincoln chastised McCulloch for the article. Three days later the President was assassinated; a virtual coup d'etat within the executive branch of the government had been perpetrated by the British.

Contemporary revisionist history has promulgated the myth that Andrew Johnson, Lincoln's successor, angered the Congress because he committed himself to carrying out Lincoln's "lenient" policy toward the South. In fact, Johnson's Inaugural Address marked a total reversal of Lincoln's economic policy.

---

60 Hugh McCulloch Papers. The article was attached to a letter from J. Medill, the editor of the *Chicago Tribune.*

"... The present law of tariff is being rapidly understood. It is no longer a deception, but rather a well defined, and clearly recognized outrage. The agricultural labor of the land is driven to the counters of the most gigantic monopoly ever before sanctioned by law. From its exorbitant demands there is no escape. The European manufacturer is forbidden our ports of trade for fear he might sell his goods at cheaper rates and thus relieve the burdens of the consumers. We have declared by law that there is but one market into which our citizens shall go to make their purchases, and we have left it to the owners of the market to fix their own prices. The bare statement of such a principle foreshadows at once the consequences which flow from it. One class of citizens, and by far the largest and most useful is placed at the mercy, for the necessaries as well as luxuries of life, of the fostered, favored, and protected class to whose aid the whole power of the government is given.

". . . Free trade with all the markets of the world is the true theory of government." [61]

Almost the entire Johnson Cabinet were either outright British agents or corrupted by British ideology: the President, Secretary of War Stanton, Secretary of State Seward, and Secretary of the Treasury McCulloch. In a celebrated speech in Fort Wayne, Indiana in late 1865, McCulloch announced his intention of reversing the American System. His policy was to rapidly contract the national currency and return the nation immediately to specie payments and direct taxation of productive wealth (looting) to pay off the national debt.

Within the context of a policy which called for destroying the nation's industrial base to pay off foreign debts, any positive program for reconstruction of the South was impossible.

The Case of David Ames Wells: How British Counterinsurgency Worked

The Whig congressmen and senators around Henry Carey opened a counterattack in defense of Lincoln's program that is responsible for the growth of American industry and the scientific development which turned this nation into the most advanced technological nation in the world. The fight, in its conscious terms, was the American System versus the British System which was slowly being

---

61 "Inaugural Address of Andrew Johnson," *Congressional Globe*, 1866.

adopted as U.S. banking and credit policy. The fight lasted into the early part of the twentieth century. William McKinley summed up more than a hundred years of history when he wrote in 1896 that "there has existed a fight between two social systems." He made clear in his book, *The History of Tariff Legislation From Henry Clay To The Present*, that those two systems were the British and the American.

The traitor, the agent-in-place, who carried out the most devastating British operation against the Lincoln Administration — next to the assassination of the President — and the American System was David Ames Wells, the head of the Special Commission on the Revenue.

Wells was appointed to the position by Lincoln, after the President read one of Wells's pamphlets, *Our Burden and Our Strength*, (1864). He was ordered to review the nation's currency situation and to formulate proposals for implementation at the end of Civil War hostilities. It is important to note that Wells was appointed to the Treasury post at the behest of Henry Carey. Throughout the war, Wells professed himself to be a committed protectionist. His pamphlet, *Our Burden and Our Strength*, was, in fact, very similar to the pamphlet written earlier by Elder.

One of the first acts of Treasury Secretary McCulloch was to begin — again — selling the 7:30 bonds, first tried unsuccessfully by Chase. The 7:30s and the new 10:40s were sold by Jay Cooke, August Belmont, and investment banker Joseph Seligman. They represented further leverage for the British to begin "consolidation" of the U.S. debt.

In terms of policy, the principal difference to be understood between the 5:20 bonds, and the 7:30 and 10:40 bonds was that purchase of the former was an investment in the future growth of U.S. industry, in the development of natural resources, and in the mechanization of agriculture. The latter two bonds were a part of a debt payment policy which included contraction of the currency, heavy taxation, and the removal of the tariff barrier; in short, a loan to the government which would be paid by looting present and future production, and labor power.

McCulloch's proposed reversal of U.S. policy was seen as crucial by the Bank of England, and the Rothschild and Baring banking houses. Opposition to British looting policies at home and abroad was growing stronger with every success at restoring the American System in the U.S. At the end of 1865, the panic provoked by the bankruptcy of the Overend Gurney company threatened to bring down the Bank of England and with it substantial portions of the British Empire. McCulloch's "immediate return to specie payments" meant a bail-out of the Bank of England, a fact whose significance leading Whigs well understood. At the height of the "Overend Gurney" panic, McCulloch released some $30,000,000 in U.S. gold to England as part of the bail-out.

David Wells, however, was the most important British "agent-in-place" in this bail-out operation.

The day following congressional approval of his appointment as Special Revenue Commissioner on July 17, 1866, Wells wrote the following letter to Boston cotton merchant and Cobden Club member Atkinson:

> "As you know the tariff bill is laid on the shelf until next winter, and on the whole I am not sorry for it. I sent you a copy of the Senate bill, with the House amendments. . . . I have changed my mind respecting tariffs and protection very much since I came to Washington and am coming over to the ground which you occupy. . . ." [62]

Just a few weeks before, New York Congressman John Griswold, an iron manufacturer, and Henry Carey got the following communiqué from the United States Consul in Liverpool Thomas Dudley. The communiqué was read by Griswold from the floor of the House and printed in all the protectionist press.

> "They are making great efforts on this side to repeal our tariff and admit British goods free of duty. If effort and money can accomplish it, you may rest assured it will be done. The work is done through the agents of foreign houses in Boston and New York. Their plan is to agitate in the western States, and to form free-trade associations all over the country." [63]

The first series of reports by Stephen Colwell, also a member of

---

62 Ferleger, Herbert Ronald, *David A. Wells and the American Revenue System, 1865-1870,* p. 154.

63 Ibid., p. 300.

the Revenue Commission, was devoted to attacking British free trade and warning the United States Congress on what the British were up to.

Thinking that Wells was still a patriot, Colwell addressed the following note to him:

> "I took these reports to the Secretary only from the proof to let him know what was coming. I intended to submit them personally to my colleagues before reporting them to the Secretary....Our conversation was wholly as to the one upon high prices. I believe he agreed with the others, but the one on high prices evidently annoyed him. He thought it would operate unfavorably upon his plans and views in reference to Wall Street. I regard my views, though differing widely from his, as vital to the interests of the country, and to our revenue system, whatever shape it may take."[64]

Thus Colwell, along with industrialists and congressmen led by the Pennsylvania contingent of Senator Moorehead, Representative Thaddeus Stevens and Representative William Kelley, began an attempt to impose a congressional dictatorship of sorts over the nation's economic policy. Their goal was the passage of a higher general tariff law while McCulloch was stripped of his power to contract the currency.

One of Colwell's reports which was not suppressed by McCulloch and Wells[65] in his *Claims of Labor*. It warns against any attempt by the Secretary of the Treasury to adopt a system of economics modeled on the British System, since it would wholly exclude as a consideration the labor theory of value. It reads in part:

> "The interests of that immense majority of men who do not merely labor for their living, but whose industry and skill produce all that is called wealth....deserve to be studied directly and specially, and not merely as incidents of national wealth. No system of social economy can be trusted which suppresses or overlooks the duties which men owe to their fellow men; and no system of social duties can for a moment be compared with that which was propounded by Him who gave the commandment 'Love thy neighbor as thyself.'

---

64 Ibid., p. 94. The "plans Colwell refers to are the sales of 7:30 and 10:40 bonds.

65 One such suppressed report by Colwell, *The Relations of Foreign Trade to Domestic Industry and Internal Revenue,* is included in excerpted form in the extracts which follow, pp. 367-381.

"... The prevailing systems (The Manchester school — A.S.) ... take wealth for their subject and treating it under the special topics of production, distribution, and consumption, proceed to develop it mainly from a commercial point of view. The production of wealth is its appearance in the channels of commerce, that is supply; its distribution is commerce; its consumption, its movement to the consumers, that is demand.

"In fact, however, the producers and consumers are substantially the same. In a state of advanced civilization, the extreme division of labor makes it necessary to institute a system of exchange of products, which involves that complicated movement for the assortment of products which is called trade; an agency which is not designed to promote the interests of that class of men called merchants, but to promote the comfort and well-being of all classes of society, especially that largest class, of which those who labor for a living are the members. This is the class that furnishes the producers and the chief part of the consumers. The point of view, then, from which to regard social industry is not trade, but labor and social well-being. Trade is but one of the branches of this industry, a department which becomes more important as civilization advances, but can never be otherwise than subordinate to the interests of the great body of producers and consumers. Merchants form a necessary class, but their private interests prompt them to make the largest profits possible out of their agency. It is therefore assuming a false position to study the interests of those who produce by the light furnished by those who merely assort and distribute the commodities of industry."[66]

In late 1865, after Colwell learned of the British antitariff scheme, he successfully organized the wool growers of the West and the wool manufacturers of the East into one lobbying association which could act in concert with the nation's industrialists, centered around the Pennsylvania Iron and Steel Association. Their chief spokesman was John Williams, editor of *Iron Age* magazine; they were backed by the *New York Tribune* and the Washington-Philadelphia newspaper chain owned by an associate of Carey's, John Forney. Forney, who had been Secretary of the Senate, had drafted his Pennsylvania papers in support of Lincoln, silencing those who would "dump Lincoln" from the Republican slate in 1864.

---

66 Colwell, Stephen, *Claims of Labor,* Report of the U.S. Department of Treasury, Library of Congress, 1866.

Although the vigorous campaign led by Carey was only partially successful, both the House of Representatives and the Senate received memorializations from industrialists nationwide to legislate against McCulloch's contraction policy. The memorializations were the result of a series of open letters from Carey to McCulloch and Massachusetts free trader, Congressman Henry Wilson.

The nation, however, was still awaiting the reports of the Special Revenue Commission headed by David Wells.

By the time Carey published his letters to Wilson, British plans were well underway. Edward Atkinson wrote to Carey on November 11, 1867, offering his opinion of the open letters.

> ...I will frankly admit that I am rejoiced at its publication as it will achieve no New England men from any supposed or implied obligation to vote for protectionist measures next winter, as many of them did at the last session against their own conviction. We have had to bear the odium of what I call the Pennsylvania policy and we can join the Northwest and the new South in promoting a simple revenue system and speedy return to specie payments."[67]

Atkinson could afford to be cocksure; Wells had been in England all that summer on a "fact-finding mission" to give some depth to his upcoming revenue report. In his letters to McCulloch and Atkinson, Wells said that he was gathering information to refute Carey's *Harmony of Interest*. Thus, he met with Thomas Baring of the Baring Brothers investment house, John Stuart Mill, and various representatives of the Cobden Clubs — the most vociferous international proponents of free trade.

This was no mere fact-finding mission, but an effort to make the British System the policy of the American nation. On July 10, 1867, McCulloch instructed him:

> "I have been hearing from time to time favorable accounts of yourself and the work which you are doing in the way of obtaining valuable information in regard to the industry and the revenue system of England. I have no question that your visit will be of great service to this Department and to the country...."[68]

Two days later, he wrote:

---

67 Henry C. Carey Papers.
68 Ferleger, *David A. Wells,* p. 187.

"I am greatly pleased to learn that you have been so handsomely received by Mr. Gladstone, and am not a little gratified by the assurances which you give me that my administration of the Treasury is approved by intelligent men in England....Some of our high tariff men are very apprehensive that you will become too much in-doctrinated with free trade notions by a visit to England." [69]

Up to the time Wells left for England, he was still professing protection as his policy with the intent of delaying effective action during the difficult years of the Andrew Johnson Administration. Before his departure, he wrote to Carey:

"I hope to join your Vesper circle of worshipers on Sunday eve; but as I may not be able to leave I will make a provisional appointment for Monday eve. There seems to be a most persistent and determined effort on the part of some to brand me as with the ranks of the free traders; or to make the country believe that I am dangerous and disloyal to the best interest of American industry. Now I am determined not to be sent out of the ranks of my old friends and supporters....Invite a few of your intimates over, say McMichael, Lewis, Reeves, Blodgell, Baird, and Tucker, or whoever else you may think proper and let's talk this matter over. I will state how matters look from my ... views and hear what you all have to say; and see if we can agree." [70]

When Wells returned from England to the U.S. in 1867, he was still publicly insisting that he was a protectionist; in his private letters to James Garfield, Edward Atkinson, and Thomas Baring, he confessed that he was a British free trader.

In the fall congressional session of 1867, the industrialist faction led by Carey succeeded in stripping McCulloch of his power to contract the currency. Legislation was framed to perfect the tariff system that had been set up during the war and an interconvertible bond measure was introduced allowing the 5:20 bonds to be redeemed in Greenbacks and setting at 3.65 percent the interest rate on the government-funded debt which was the credit-generating base of the national banking system.

On November 7, 1867, Edward Atkinson wrote McCulloch to warn him of the Whig proposal for controlling the national banks.

---

69 Ibid., pp. 187-188.

70 Ibid., pp. 181-182.

"...The only point of danger is the plausible scheme of substituting legal tenders for banknotes. If you allow me to say what I
intended before I learned from Wells that it would probably coincide
with your views. I think you will be supported in a bold and determined stand for specie payment at the earliest moment and at any
cost....That the banks must be used as the agents to promote the end
in view and not destroyed and that the government cannot assume
the function of a bank by issuing a convertible currency."[71]

Throughout the summer before, *Iron Age*, the unquestioned
spokesman for U.S. iron interests, the developing agribusiness in
the Midwest, and the tool and dye industry, wrote editorial after
editorial urging the formation of industry and labor alliances, and
issued sharp attacks against British System economists.

At issue was the fact that while there had been a substantial
rate of growth of U.S. industry under the Lincoln Administration,
under McCulloch the production of wealth in the nation was being
sharply curtailed. As Carey put it, "Lincoln had 'wed' the nation's
treasury to the producers of wealth"; the hallmark of Lincoln's
economic program was the protective Morrill Tariff. Under Mc-
Culloch, the supply of currency was being steadily contracted, the
national debt was being sold to the Rothschild and Baring banks by
way of New York, and heavy taxation of industry was promised.

The nation's manufacturers found it nearly impossible to get
loans for investment in plant and machinery. What money the iron
industry did get was used to convert almost entirely to the Bessemer
process that allowed for the production of steel.

Carey's open letters attacking McCulloch and the British free
traders were distributed by these industrialists all over the country
and were reprinted in three-fifths of the nation's newspapers, according to contemporaries.

Reflecting the pressure coming from the nation's manufacturers, Senator John Sherman took the Senate floor on January 9,
1868, to comment on congressional suspension of McCulloch's
currency contraction powers.

"It will satisfy the public mind that no further contraction will be
made when industry is in a measure paralyzed. We have the com-

---

71 Hugh McCulloch Papers.

plaint from all parts of the country, from all branches of industry from every state in the union that industry for some reason is paralyzed and that trade and enterprise are not so well rewarded as they were. Many perhaps erroneously attribute all this to the contraction of the currency — a contraction which I believe is unexemplified in the history of any nation. One hundred and forty-million dollars have been withdrawn…in less than two years. It may be wise, it may be beneficial, but still so rapid as to excite a stingency that is causing complaint, and I think the people ought to be relieved from that.

"This will strongly impress upon Congress the imperative duty of acting wisely upon financial measures for the responsibility will then rest squarely upon Congress and will not be shared with them by the Secretary of the Treasury.

"It will encourage businessmen to continue old and embark in new enterprises when they are assured that no change will be made in the measure of value without the open and deliberate consent of their representatives." [72]

The London *Daily News* of January 28, 1868, displayed its chagrin to the world.

"In all questions relating to the tariff and taxation, both houses were largely influenced by the lobby which represented various interests looking for special protection, and which invariably succeeded in shutting out students and economists. These gentry have, in fact, had full swing for the last five years, and perhaps they succeeded in imposing on the country a system of taxation (tariffs) which perhaps has every fault which any system of taxation ever had, with some which no system has ever had and against which no economist ever thought of warning the world."

In late December 1868, Carey wrote to McCulloch, signing his letter "Alexander Hamilton."

"…In the first place I do not agree with you in your sweeping denunciation of our legal tender circulation, except so far as it is subject to terrible abuse such as has been experienced in the currency of every age. In this country we have never had a paper money simply and truly, only nominally based on a specie platform…The U.S. Bank did not give us specie, its notes were current almost on the same fundamental hypothesis, which has given useful circulation to the Legal Tender issues.

---

72 *The Congressional Globe*, January 9, 1868.

"...It was not as a mere war incident that Legal Tenders were put into circulation, that necessitous ingredient would not have given them currency, it was the intellectual acknowledgement that the power and right to issue Legal Tender notes was nothing more than the plain and enlightened exercise of a high sovereign prerogative, never to be doubted although always to be deployed with the most severe and scrupulous discretion — as a sacred trust...To revert to the Legal Tenders, permit me to ask a single sober question. What should we do, if Europe were to become involved in a general warfare, with any other currency than that which we now have? In less than three months we should be disgraced with the charge of bankruptcy for the non-payment of specie."[73]

The Pendleton Plan

It soon became clear to the British that merely an "agents-in-place" operation would not suffice to break the Whig's grip on the Republican Party. What was needed was something more, an arousal of popular opinion to give their agents in Congress more maneuvering room and to force the national banks to support the various debt refunding schemes. As Atkinson expressed the matter to Wells, "Jay Cooke was hurting the cause because he was willing to compromise too much" with the Whigs on the refunding issue. [74]

The national banks were established to utilize the 5:20 bonds (the government-funded debt) as a basis for issuing credit. The enacting legislation allowed for only the interest on the 5:20 bonds to be payable in gold coin; the bonds themselves could be purchased with Greenbacks. The 5:20 bonds under Lincoln's Administration represented the basis for issuing long-term, low-interest loans to industry. Thus, if the Rothschild-Baring refunding measures were to be enacted, the grouping of bankers essentially identified as the Jay Cooke wing of the Republican Party had to be shaken loose from Whig control. The Democratic Party was mobilized.

George Pendleton was an Ohio "Copperhead" Democrat and Jacksonian congressman. During the Civil War, while the American System measures were being debated, he professed that "God had ordained gold to be money." Later, in the Ohio elections of 1867,

---

73 Hugh McCulloch Papers.

74 Ibid.

Pendleton led the Democratic Party on a campaign to tap the old Jacksonian populism that was deep seated in the Midwest, especially among the backward butternut farmers. Pendleton campaigned on a a platform that called for only the 5:20 bonds to be paid off in Greenbacks and outright repudiation of interest on the bonds. He raised the old Jacksonian cry about getting rid of the national banks and the funded debt.

Henry Clay Dean, another old Jacksonian and "Copperhead," inundated the midwestern press with articles attacking Alexander Hamilton, Nicholas Biddle, and the funded debt. He, too, wanted to bring back the days of Jacksonian pluralism.

The platform adopted at the Democratic Party convention for the 1868 presidential election was the Pendleton plan *in toto*. August Belmont made sure that the Democratic presidential candidate, Horatio Seymore, was a "hard money" man.

This populist agitation forced a change in the Republican Party which gave the upper hand to the "liberals." The campaign platform of Republican candidate Ulysses S. Grant called for an early return to specie payments and the payment of all government obligations in gold. The demagogic propaganda attempted to brand the Carey faction as "repudiationist," no different than the Democrats.

Sufficient pressure had thus been built up to push Jay Cooke behind a refunding measure which would allow the British banking group to purchase the entire U.S. debt. The scheme followed by Senators Sherman and Sumner called for a new bond issue to be sold primarily in Europe; the principal and interest would be gold-backed. The special feature of this funding scheme was that it would allow the network of national banks to trade in their 5:20 bonds for the new issue, which would both increase the national indebtedness and, at the same time, destroy the productive capacity of the nation.

Pennsylvania Congressman William D. Kelley wrote to Carey describing the situation in Congress.

"...I have no idea that the funding bill will get through in any shape. For myself I will not vote for a bill that proposes to pay our bonds abroad and in foreign currency or to extend our debt without option on the part of the government over a period of 40 years." [75]

---

75 Henry C. Carey Papers.

Senator Charles Sumner, writing to Carey, answered the Whig protest.

> "I am sorry that the bill I have introduced seems to you likely to prove ruinous. I cannot think that you are right. And though I have had long conversations with many opposed to my place and have received many letters from many more . . . what Congress will do remains to be seen — it certainly should not adjourn without adopting some measure to bring about the desired result but the opposition to all measures to maintain the National honesty is very strong, and may prevail."[76]

Even John Stuart Mill, although sensing a British victory, wrote a long article for Edwin L. Godkin's *Nation* saying how unfortunate it was that the Democratic Party was advocating such financial heresy.

The Whig leader of the House of Representatives, Thaddeus Stevens, had few alternatives but to attempt to run a "congressional dictatorship" in the absence of an effective executive like Abraham Lincoln. He was determined to industrialize the South, breaking up and confiscating the large southern plantations as a step in industrialization. He opposed the refunding measure.

It was Stevens who, to the annoyance of abolitionist Harriet Beecher Stowe, insisted on granting suffrage to the freedmen as a means of creating an alliance of the freedmen with enlightened southern Whigs and assuring the ascendancy of the Republican Party in the South.

He did not lead the impeachment move against President Andrew Johnson as most historians suggest. He did, however, sponsor the bill upon which the impeachment case rested. Johnson had been replacing Whig officeholders with southern Confederates of the worst sort. Stevens pushed through Congress a bill requiring congressional approval of presidential hiring or firing of Cabinet members.

A letter from Cobden Club member Edward Atkinson to Treasury Secretary McCulloch attests to Stevens's character — and also what the agents themselves were up to.

> "...I am endeavoring, in connection with some others known as

---

76 Ibid.

extreme radicals, to give such direction to the reorganization of the South as shall prevent the creation of an exclusive Black men's party and also to kill the scheme of confiscation. I also hope we may be able to secure the election of a Southern delegation who shall not be under *Thad Stevens's* lead on tariff and currency questions, but of this I am not hopeful. The new men from the South will be likely to be the very men who will follow Stevens even to prohibition of imports. They will be misled by the desire to establish manufactures and to diversify employment.

"...I am led to make certain suggestions to you by the rumors of a diversity of opinion between you and the President. You must now feel assured that the President's policy is dead; even any merit which his views may have had will not be recognized...your fame and reputation will rest on your successful administration of the Treasury. A large section of the Republicans desires to see financial and all revenue questions separated from party questions. If you have reason to do so and can separate yourself from A.J. (Andrew Johnson — A.S.) and let it be known that while you do not fully approve the action of the Congress you will submit to its decision and desire to work in harmony, you will be able to secure such support for your plans for administering the Treasury as will insure success....Only give the Republicans who hold sound views on financial questions a chance to support you as the Secretary of the United States Treasury and not as a member of the present cabinet and you can almost dictate future policy....I don't expect an answer to this."[77]

The refunding bill failed in Congress.

After the election of Grant to the presidency, Special Commissioner on the Revenue David Wells was ready with his report, on which the nation was depending for a more thorough inauguration of the American System. It was released on January 5, 1869. Although cloaked in protective phraseology, the report directly attacked the American System as inequitable. British newspapers, especially the *Times*, would later say that Wells "felt his countrymen would be more willing to adopt free trade could it only be called by some other name."

The report attacked "special interests groups" and called for contraction of the currency and an end to the tariff on iron because it hurt the producers of penknives in New England. The problem of

77 Hugh McCulloch Papers.

unemployment in the country was due to overproduction as a result of advances in technology, the report alleged.

Two letters written by Wells in 1867, before his trip to England, provide irrefutable evidence of his British agentry. At a meeting held by the Iron and Steel Association on January 16, Wells protests,

> "I desire here and now, unequivocally and unreservedly, to declare that, in the British sense of the word, there is no free trade about me...and it has been my fortune to sit at the feet of that great teacher of political economy Henry C. Carey, and learn from him the great principles on which these doctrines are founded — the complete and universal harmony between all the producing interests of the country."[78]

But just two weeks later, Wells wrote in a letter to the leading Social Darwinist and exponent of the British System in the U.S., Arthur Laymen Perry:

> "I have been intending to write you for some time past and tell you confidentially of the change which my recent intimate connection with the tariff legislation has produced in my opinions, in respect to Free Trade and protection...and am about prepared to place myself on the ground occupied by you and Walker. The time has not come however for me to distinctly avow my sentiments. I am accumulating a store of facts, which private individuals could not obtain, and which when made public will I think go very far toward settling our future commercial policy. To provoke opposition now, would probably close the door to some important investigations; so for the present I must work on silently. In the present discussion of the tariff in Congress, New England — and especially Massachusetts — went almost always for the most extreme propositions. There was a lack of moral courage on the part of Dawes and Boutwell ... which prevented them from acting or speaking according to their convictions. The members of Congress from New England are, for the most part, inclined to liberal views — Boutwell is an old free trader — but they are afraid of their constituents, and think that public opinion will not sustain them in anything contrary to the requirements of the Carey school. Dawes might be punched a little for his course....I urged him to come out boldly, and declare that while Massachusetts would be just and generous, yet she would not agree to endorse everything labeled protection to American industry. He however...made a speech in which he took the strongest ground for protection. I have written hurriedly...and perhaps not clearly;

but I think you will get my views in the main. Are there any documents which you wish sent you. If so let me know." [79]

Wells wrote to Perry again on March 11, corroborating all that the Whig consul in Liverpool Dudley had warned about British plans to finance free trade clubs and promote western agitation.

"I have arranged with Atkinson, Raymond of the *New York Times*, Nordhoff of the *Post*, and several writers and editors of the West that during the next six months there shall be an earnest discussion of the subject (free trade — A.S.) kept up through the papers; and a more vigorous attempt than ever made to change public sentiment, and my main object in writing you is to ask that you will commence at once and write every week an article for the *Springfield Republican* on the subject — short and pithy. Ridicule will I think be fully as effective as argument...." [80]

Before the spring 1867 session of Congress adjourned, Senator Sherman pushed through the Senate the Wool and Woolens Act which had been passed sometime before by the House. The measure as passed by the Senate afforded high duties for the wool and wool growing industry. Wells urged President Johnson not to veto the measure because its passage opened possibilities of winning the wool growers away from supporting the protection demands of the iron industry — the old divide-and-conquer routine.

Wells had prepared the nation's free trade press for the release of his revenue report. They were ready to print and distribute thousands of copies all over the country with the aim of provoking the labor movement to oppose the "special interests of the industrialist."

Congressman Kelley wrote to Henry Carey on January 9, 1869:

"I meant to find time to ask you what you think of Wells by this time. I regard his report supplemented by Walker's letters as the most insidious Free Trade document that has ever been published in this country. I have all along assured you that his protectionism was affected and that he meant to cause harm. I think even Greeley sees that now though his faith in him was so great he endorsed the report unconditionally before he had read a word of it...." [81]

---

79 Ibid., p. 178.

80 Ibid., p. 181.

81 Henry C. Carey Papers. Amasa Walker was a leading U.S. Malthusian.

In his report, Wells aimed straight at the humanists in the U.S. in general and Henry Carey in particular.

"No nation acted on grounds of liberality or humanitarianism in framing financial legislation. Enlightened selfishness was a satisfactory basis for policy. Though other countries sought to protect industry, the method employed especially in England differed greatly from what was called protection in the United States. The British aim is to remove burdens to cheapen cost, and reduce prices. Our method on the contrary is to levy a tax, thereby increasing cost and reducing consumption. The one method to be called a bounty to the consumer, the other a bounty to the producer; one the method of abundance, the other of scarcity or privation...."[82]

The Wells plan to subjugate the U.S. economy to the British Baring and Rothschild banking houses was trumpeted in all the free trade press in the country, including August Belmont's *Democratic World*. At the urging of Belmont, Wells wrote to Manton Marble, the editor of the *World*, during the Grant-Seymore race. Wells was then writing tracts for the Grant campaign and so was being attacked in the *World*. Wells's letter concluded by saying:

"Besides I shall want your aid and that of the *World* next winter, when I expect the Republicans will be about ready to hang me."[83]

The Wells report rallied what was later known as the liberal Repubicans; James Garfield, William Cullen Bryant, the Free Trade Leagues, and the Social Science Associations all began applying pressure on President Grant to name Wells as the new Secretary of the Treasury. In private, Grant's two New York merchant friends Stewart and Seligman put the pressure on too.

This latest and most dangerous coup attempt did not go unanswered by the Carey Whigs, the nation's industrialists, and the labor movement. Carey answered Wells in twelve public letters printed in the *New York Tribune*, *Iron Age*, and the rest of the nation's protectionist press.[84]

---

82 Ferleger, *David A. Wells*, p. 255.

83 Ibid., p. 231.

84 Henry Carey's open letters to Wells are included in the selection of extracts which follows, pp. 186-205.

"...To whom, however, are to be attributed the oft-repeated misstatements by which the committee had been deceived? No name is given, but you of course refer to me, the statements thus controverted having been first published over my own signature, so early as 1851, and since then many times republished; and the committee having been misled, if misled at all, by no other than myself. To me, therefore, it is that you have thus thrown down the glove, and I now take it up prepared on the one hand to prove the accuracy of the views you have thus called in question; or, on the other, to admit of having through a long series of years misled my fellow citizens. Admit that such proof be furnished — that the "mere assertions" be now proved to be real "historical truths" fitted for even your own acceptance, where I beg to ask, will you yourself then stand? Should it chance to be proved that it is not I that am required to impale myself on the horns of a dilemma which leaves but a choice between the admission of gross carelessness on the one hand, or grosser dishonesty on the other, does it not follow necessarily that you must be compelled to take the place you had prepared for me, and thus furnish yourself the proof required for establishing the fact that you are wholly disqualified for the office of public teacher?"[85]

To the Swedish and German press, Carey declared that Wells had been bought by British gold. In their press, William Sylvis and the National Labor Union attacked Wells as a British agent. Sylvis was particularly upset about the attempt to degrade U.S. labor to the state of labor in Great Britain.

William Sylvis was the leader of the National Labor Union which was fraternally connected to Karl Marx's IWMA. In 1866, Sylvis brought his Pennsylvania Iron Molders Union out in favor of protection. In 1867, he began printing editorial attacks on British economists in the *Chicago Workingmans Advocate*:

"The whole system of political economy from beginning to end is an apology for tyranny and the whole tribe of political economists are humbugs...and at their head stands the prince of humbugs, John Stuart Mill.

"The manufacturer, the farmer, the businessman of any kind needing money, must pay from 10 to 30 percent for the use of it. In many cases the profits of his business are less than the rates of interest demanded. To borrow would be ruinous, therefore his business must languish or, what is very frequently the case, a

---

85 Carey, Henry C., *Review of the Report of the Hon. D.A. Wells*, (Philadelphia: Collins, Printer and Jayne Street, 1869), p. 4.

reduction in wages is made. This reduction does not always go into the pocket of the employer, but into that of the money lender. Thus do employer and employee suffer from this system of legal robbery called interest on money."[86]

There were many differences between the NLU and the Carey Whigs, but they agreed on one basic point: as long as the Whigs were leading a strong fight against British credit policies, they had an ally in the labor movement.

Wells did not go unrewarded for his efforts; he was elected president of the Cobden Clubs in the U.S. The Whigs in Congress first planned to remove him from office by discontinuing his salary, but finally decided to simply let the office expire. The four years of damage done by Wells and McCulloch gave the British room to maneuver, and the nation was still without an official economic policy.

McCulloch's contraction policy toward money supply had made any attempt at southern industrial reconstruction virtually impossible. Because of the refunding schemes, the national banks had become a major rallying point for Jacksonian populism across the country which demanded an end to the funded debt.

The political-economic geometry which subsumed the debates of free trade versus protection gave the Whigs some leverage on the question of tariff legislation. Their victory in the tariff battle afforded a modest rate of economic growth and an occasional increase in the supply of money in the face of British determination to control the U.S. economy.

Wells did not get the Treasury post under Grant; Whig propaganda prevented the New York banker Seligman from accepting the post when it was offered; and Congress further opposed Grant's appointment of New York merchant A.T. Stewart. A compromise finally gave the post to George S. Boutwell.

The "liberals" William Cullen Bryant, David Wells, Amasa Walker, and Charles Graham Sumner, began to "Watergate" (using twentieth century terminology) the Whig influences within the Grant Administration. The 1869 Black Friday scandal of Jay

---

86 Sylvia, James C., *The Life, Speeches, Labor, and Essays of William H. Sylvis,* p. 374.

Gould and Jim Fisk is probably the most notorious. The two drove the price of gold to the sky and then quickly sold their shares, collapsing the market. That gold-cornering operation was, in point of fact, run by the New York banker Seligman.

During congressional hearings — a whitewash by James Garfield — Seligman's role in the affair was downplayed: after all, he was only Gould's "broker." The affair tied in with efforts by the free traders for so-called currency and civil service reform.

In the flurry of investigations, Grant pushed through Congress the refunding scheme which McCulloch had failed to have legislated. Treasury Secretary Boutwell formed a consortium of Jay Cooke and the House of Rothschild in London, Seligman and Morton in New York, and the Baring Brothers to begin selling the U.S. debt to Great Britain. The new bond issue offered the national bankers the possibility of trading in their 5:20 bonds for the new 10:40 bonds, increasing drastically the amount of future debt the country would have to pay to the British.[87]

Carey, Kelley, and others repeatedly warned that such a policy would only lead to a new depression. They set their sights on the 1872 elections and a Whig Congress. Kelley, especially, was relying on the working class in England to begin forcing changes in the British System.

In 1871, he wrote to Carey:

"Mr. Dudley is right in his estimate of the influences British manufacturers will put forth in our next campaign. They can afford to spend several millions pound sterling to control our election. The question is vital with them. Should we elect a protectionist President and Congress in 1872, England will have to modify her revenue system and perhaps her fundamental institutions. Things in that country cannot continue as they are unless they can monopolize our markets....But how shall we make those whose interests it is to secure this election understand and perform their duties. Will you not impress the importance of such contributions to the South as I propose to Mr. Wharton and all the Gentlemen who gather under your hospitable roof?"[88]

---

87 For a contemporary discussion of these issues, see the selection by William D. Kelley, *The Causes and Authors of the Financial Depression,* included in the extracts which follow, pp. 323-342.

88 Henry C. Carey Papers.

Carey then wrote to John Forney, the former Secretary of the Senate.

"You are going to Washington on a business of a most agreeable kind. Let me try to add to it a little of the useful, presenting for your consideration and that of your friend a brief exhibit of what is going on around us, and of the consequences that may reasonably be anticipated from its continuance.

"The country is producing too much of all the good things of life, coal, iron, food, wool, cotton, cloth, houses, etc. Why is it so? Because our financial policy is destroying the demand for labor of body and of mind and, as a necessary consequence, the power of purchase. Look where we see diminishing power of consumption and with every further step in that direction we shall hear more and more of overproduction.

"For five years past the financial affairs of the country have been controlled by men in and out of the Cabinet, in and out of Congress who have been troubled with such an excess of knowledge that they could learn nothing whatsoever. For years they howled contraction. Finding that not the answer they now howl resumption not seeing that by thus destroying confidence they are daily making it more and more impossible that we should resume. Sangrado like, they have bled the patient until he can scarcely stand, and now deny him food until he shall prove his ability to walk. Free banking is, they say, a good thing and we shall be allowed to have it after resumption, yet are they daily diminishing that power of production to whose increase alone can we look for power to resume the use of the precious metals. This is a great country, but it is at this moment governed financially by as small a set of charlatans as anyone has yet produced. Some of them read books and imagine they are learning something, but, as the farmer said, the more cows his calf sucked the greater calf he grew.

"Their policy is now, as we are told, to be endorsed by our friend Blaine, who is to place one of them at the head of the Ways and Means, and another at that of the Currency Committee. Should this be done it will as I believe result in the ruin of the Party and of the speaker himself. Three years since all looked to the inauguration of Grant as to the reinauguration of that confidence without which there can be no activity of circulation, nor increase of strength. So far the reverse has been the case, the country having been becoming from day to day more paralyzed.

"The *Tribune* has this moment brought me Amasa Walker's letter advocating the establishment of a great monopoly bank in New York. (Seligman was planning to open a house modeled after the London

House of Rothschild — A.S.) He should and I presume is well paid for writing all the nonsense of which he has made himself the father. Such men can afford to spend their winters in Washington, but those who have no private axes to grind cannot.

"The policy of the next 20 years will probably be decided in the first week of March and by the speaker's fiat. Can you not see and talk with him on the subject? What shall then be done will probably be determined by the question as to whether England or America shall rule the world."[89]

For his role in pushing the refunding and related measures through the U.S. Congress, Jay Cooke won an agreement with the Rothschilds to help fund his Northern Pacific Railroad project. Former Secretary of the Treasury McCulloch was dispatched to England to set up Cooke's banking house there.

Regardless of his connections, Cooke was an entrepreneur at heart. He poured capital into the development of the roads, the iron industry, and the rails, hoping that McCulloch and the Rothschild and Baring bankers would be able to dispose of their share of the bonds that were floated for the project at a later date.

When the books were opened for the sale of the bonds, neither the Rothschilds nor the Barings sold their bonds. Overextended, the House of Cooke collapsed in 1873, setting the stage for the collapse of 1876.

The Heritage of the Civil War

The Whig fight continued into the twentieth century. The concessions they won made this nation the greatest industrial power on earth.

As early as 1871, the Pennsylvania Congressmen Kelley and Moorehead began lobbying for congressional funding of the 1876 celebration of the U.S. Centennial. They saw the Centennial fair as a means to develop the nation's resources and to bring into practical use its inventions in spite of growing British control of the finances. The measures were opposed by the liberal senators and congressmen from New York and New England.

The 1871 Congress refused to fund the fair, but, as former

---

89 Ibid.

The Corliss Centennial Steam Engine, built for the 1876 Centennial Celebration in Philadelphia, was the largest steam engine in the world. George Corliss built the engine to drive all the machinery in Machinery Hall and it is a testament to America's commitment to technological progress.

California Governor Ronald Reagan is fond of telling the story today, the 1876 Centennial Celebration gave the nation the electric lightbulb, the elevator, and numerous other inventions, and mechanical and industrial improvements. These advances in technology were the net result of the American System battles the Whigs waged in Congress.

The free trade papers of William Cullen Bryant and others were cynical of the Centennial fair, printing poems like the following by the transcendentalist James Russell Lowell:

Columbia puzzled what she should display
Of True home-make on her Centennial
Asked Brother Jonathan; he scratched his head,
Whittled a while reflectively, and said,
"Your own invention, and own making too?
Why, any child could tell ye what to do;
How all men's loss is everybody's gain;
Show your new patent to increase your rents
By paying quarters for collecting cents;
Show your short cut to cure financial ills
By making paper-collars current bills;
Show your new bleaching-process, cheap and brief,
To wit; a jury chosen by the thief;
Show your State Legislatures; show your Rings;
And challenge Europe to produce such things,
As high officials sitting half in sight
To share the plunder and to fix things right;
If that don't fetch her, why you only need
To show your latest style in martyrs-Tweed;
She'll find it hard to hide her spiteful tears
At such advance in one poor hundred years."

The 1876 Centennial Celebration and the new technologies displayed proves a lie the much touted analysis of the historiographers — and economists like Milton Friedman in his *Capitalism and Freedom* — that the nation became the industrial powerhouse of the world not because the Whigs fought for a policy of protection and credit for industry, but because the British ideology of *laissez-faire* emerged victorious. The celebration clearly unnerved the Rothschilds who, during the height of the fair's activities — and the depression of that year — made a point of sending to President Hayes's Secretary of the Treasury, John Sherman, a little note explaining that they would not buy government bonds on the basis of "speculative activities" as they had lost money before on such enterprises.

America's battle against Britain during the Civil War period left the nation a heritage, a commitment to fully develop and utilize the industrial potential of the U.S. Yet, to the extent that British monetarist control over the credit mechanisms of the country were allowed to remain intact, the war was not won. If the American System is not now restored, adherence to British economic policy threatens to plunge the nation and the world into thermonuclear disaster.

Henry C. Carey
(1783 - 1879)

The Harmony of Interest

The Slave Trade, Foreign and Domestic

Money

Financial Crises: Their Causes and Effects

How to Outdo England

Open Letters to Hugh McCulloch

Open Letters to Henry Wilson

Protection and Revenue, Public and Private

Shall We Have Peace?

The Harmony of Interest

Henry Carey first published this pamphlet in 1851 after compiling the series of articles he had written for the Plough, Loom and Anvil, *a newspaper published by his associate William Skinner and intended largely for circulation in the South and West. The selection which follows is from the last article of the series and served as a rallying cry for the restoration of the American System.*

...Two systems are before the world; the one looks to increasing the proportion of persons and of capital engaged in trade and transportation, and therefore to diminishing the proportion engaged in producing commodities with which to trade, with *necessarily* diminished return to the labour of all; while the other looks to increasing the proportion engaged in the work of production, and diminishing that engaged in trade and transportation, with increased return to all, giving to the labourer good wages, and to the owner of capital goods profits. One looks to increasing the quantity of raw materials to be exported, and diminishing the inducements to the import of men, thus impoverishing both farmer and planter by throwing on them the burden of freight; while the other looks to increasing the import of men, and diminishing the export of raw materials, thereby enriching both planter and farmer by relieving them from the payment of freight. One looks to giving the *products* of millions of acres of land and of the labour of millions of men for the *services* of hundreds of thousands of distant men; the other to bringing the distant men to consume on the land the products of the land, exchanging day's labour for day's labour. One looks to compelling the farmers and planters of the Union to continue their contributions for the support of the fleets and the armies, the paupers, the nobles, and the sovereigns of Europe; the other to enabling ourselves to apply the same means to the moral and intellectual improvement of the sovereigns of America.† One looks to the con-

---

† Russia is now raising by loan five millions of pounds sterling to pay the expenses of the war in Hungary. The farmers and planters of the Union are the chief contributors to this loan.

75

tinuance of that *bastard* freedom of trade which denies the principle
of protection, yet doles it out as revenue duties; the other to extending the area of *legitimate* free trade by the establishment of perfect
protection, followed by the annexation of individuals and communities, and ultimately by the abolition of custom-houses. One
looks to exporting men to occupy desert tracts, the sovereignty of
which is obtained by aid of diplomacy or war; importing men by
millions for their occupation. One looks to the *centralization* of
wealth and power in a great commercial city that shall rival the great
cities of modern times, which have been and are being supported by
aid of contributions which have exhausted every nation subjected to
them; the other to *concentration*, by aid of which a market shall be
made upon the land for the products of the land, and the farmer and
planter be enriched. One looks to increasing the necessity for commerce; the other to increasing the power to maintain it. One looks to
underworking the Hindoo, and sinking the rest of the world to his
level; the other to raising the standard of man throughout the world
to our level. One looks to pauperism, ignorance, depopulation, and
barbarism; the other to increasing wealth, comfort, intelligence,
combination of action, and civilization. One looks toward universal
war; the other toward universal peace. One is the English system;
the other we may be proud to call the American system, for it is the
only one ever devised the tendency of which was that of *elevating*
while *equalizing* the condition of man throughout the world.

Such is the true *mission* of the people of these United States. To
them has been granted a privilege never before granted to man, that
of the exercise of the right of perfect self-government; but, as rights
and duties are inseparable, with the grant of the former came the
obligation to perform the latter. Happily their performance is
pleasant and profitable, and involves no sacrifice. To raise the value
of labour throughout the world, we need only to raise the value of
our own. To raise the value of land throughout the world, it is
needed only that we adopt measures that shall raise the value of our
own. To diffuse intelligence and to promote the cause of morality
throughout the world, we are required only to pursue the course that
shall diffuse education throughout our own land, and shall enable
every man more readily to acquire property, and with it respect for
the rights of property. To improve the political condition of man

throughout the world, it is needed that we ourselves should remain at peace, avoid taxation for the maintenance of fleets and armies, and become rich and prosperous. To raise the condition of woman throughout the world, it is required of us only that we pursue that course that enables men to remain at home and marry, that they may surround themselves with happy children and grandchildren. To substitute true Christianity for the detestable system known as the Malthusian, it is needed that we prove to the world that it is population that makes the food come from the rich soils, and that food tends to increase more rapidly than population, thus vindicating the policy of God to man. Doing these things, the addition to our population by immigration will speedily rise to millions, and with each and every year the desire for that perfect freedom of trade which results from incorporation within the Union, will be seen to spread and to increase in its intensity, leading gradually to the establishment of an empire the most extensive and magnificent the world has yet seen, based upon principles of maintaining peace itself, and strong enough to insist upon the maintenance of peace by others, yet carried on without the aid of fleets, or armies, or taxes, the sales of public lands alone sufficing to pay the expenses of government.

To establish such an empire — to prove that among the people of the world, whether agriculturists, manufacturers, or merchants, there is perfect harmony of interests, and that the happiness of individuals, as well as the grandeur of nations, is to be promoted by perfect obedience to that greatest of all commands, "Do unto others as ye would that others should do unto you," — is the object and will be the result of that mission. Whether that result shall be speedily attained, or whether it shall be postponed to a distant period, will depend greatly upon the men who are charged with the performance of the duties of government. If their movements be governed by that enlightened self-interest which induces man to seek his happiness in the promotion of that of his fellow-man, it will come soon. If, on the contrary, they be governed by that ignorant selfishness which leads to the belief that individuals, party, or national interests are to be promoted by measures tending to the deterioration of the condition of others, it will be late.

The Slave Trade
Foreign and Domestic

Henry Carey authored this book in 1853 largely as a polemic against Harriet Beecher Stowe's Uncle Tom's Cabin. *Stowe's primary literary achievement before the publication of this book was as a writer of Pell Romance novels.* Uncle Tom's Cabin *was the first popular attempt to justify British cultural relativism or enforced cultural backwardness. Hence, it was hardly distinguishable from the "racial superiority" tracts written by the slavocracy and, from its first appearance, was taken to be a defense of slavery.*

Carey's work, of which Chapter XV is excerpted here, demonstrated that the cause for the continuation of chattel slavery in the United States could be found in the nation's adherence, since the presidency of Andrew Jackson, to the British system of cheapening and degrading labor. That hideous system of chattel slavery, Carey insists, is just one particular form of the slavery which Great Britain had enforced on the world.

The Slave Trade Foreign and Domestic *served its purpose of winning the best of the abolitionist movement away from the British-controlled leadership of William Lloyd Garrison and Harriet Beecher Stowe, and to a program of national industrial development.*

Chapter XV
How Can Slavery Be Extinguished?

How can slavery be extinguished, and man be made free? This question, as regarded England, was answered some years since by a distinguished anti-corn-law orator, when he said that for a long time past, in that country, two men had been seeking one master, whereas the time was then at hand when two masters would be seeking one man. Now, we all know that when two men desire to purchase a commodity, it rises in value, and its owner finds himself more free to determine for himself what to do with it than he could do if there were only one person desiring to have it, and infinitely more free than he could be if there were two sellers to one buyer. To make men free there must be competition for the purchase of their services, and the more the competition the greater must be their value, and that of the men who have them to sell.

It has already been shown that in purely agricultural communities there can be very little competition for the purchase of labour; and that such is the fact the reader can readily satisfy himself by reflecting on the history of the past, or examining the condition of man as he at present exists among the various nations of the earth. History shows that labour has become valuable, and that man has become free, precisely as the artisan has been enabled to take his place by the side of the ploughman — precisely as labour has become diversified — precisely as small towns have arisen in which the producer of food and wool could readily exchange for cloth and iron — precisely as manure could more readily be obtained to aid in maintaining the productiveness of the soil — and precisely, therefore, as men have acquired the power of associating with their fellow-men. With the growth of that power they have everywhere been seen to obtain increased returns from land, increased reward of labour, and increased power to accumulate the means of making roads, establishing schools, and doing all other things tending to the improvement of their modes of action and their habits of thought; and thus it is that freedom of thought, speech, action, and trade have always grown with the growth of the value of labour and land.

It is desired to abolish the *trade* in slaves. No such trade could exist were men everywhere free; but as they are not so, it has in many countries been deemed necessary to prohibit the sale of men from off the land, as preliminary to the establishment of freedom. Nothing of this kind, however, can now be looked for, because there exists no power to coerce the owners of slaves to adopt any such measures; nor, if it did exist, would it be desirable that it should be exercised, as it would make the condition of both the slave and his master worse than it is even now. Neither is it necessary, because there exists "a higher law" — a great law of the Creator — that will effectually extinguish the trade whenever it shall be permitted to come into activity.

Why is it that men in Africa sell their fellow-men to be transported to Cuba or Brazil? For the same reason, obviously, that other men sell flour in Boston or Baltimore to go to Liverpool or Rio Janeiro — because it is cheaper in the former than in the latter cities. If, then, we desired to put a stop to the export, would not our object be effectually accomplished by the adoption of measures that would cause prices to be higher in Boston than in Liverpool, and higher in Baltimore than in Rio? That such would be the case must be admitted by all. If, then, we desired to stop the export of negroes from Africa, would not our object be effectually and permanently attained could we so raise the value of man in Africa that he would be worth as much, or more, there than in Cuba? Would not the export of Coolies cease if man could be rendered more valuable in India than in Jamaica or Guiana? Would not the destruction of cottages, the eviction of their inhabitants, and the waste of life throughout Ireland, at once be terminated, could man be made as valuable there as he is here? Would not the export of men, women, and children of Great Britain cease, if labour there could be brought to a level with that of Massachusetts, New York, and Pennsylvania? Assuredly it would; for men do not voluntarily leave home, kindred and friends. On the contrary, so great is the attachment to home, that it requires, in most cases, greatly superior attractions to induce them to emigrate. Adam Smith said that, of all commodities, man was the hardest to be removed — and daily observation shows that he was right.

To terminate the African slave trade, we need, then, only to raise the value of man *in Africa*. To terminate the forced export of men, women, and children from Ireland, we need only to raise the value of men *in Ireland*; and to put an end to our own domestic slave trade, nothing is needed except that we raise the value of man *in Virginia*. To bring the trade in slaves, of all colours and in all countries, at once and permanently to a close, we need to raise the value of man *at home*, let that home be where it may. How can this be done? By precisely the same course of action that terminated the export of slaves from England to Ireland. In the days of the Plantagenets, men were so much more valuable in the latter country than in the former one, that the market of Ireland was "glutted with English slaves;" but as, by degrees, the artisan took his place by the side of the English ploughman, the trade passed away, because towns arose and men became strong to defend their rights as they were more and more enabled to associate with each other. Since then, the artisan has disappeared from Ireland, and the towns have decayed, and men have become weak because they have lost the power to associate, and, therefore, it is that the market of England has been so glutted with Irish slaves that man has been declared to be "a drug, and population a nuisance."

Such precisely has been the course of things in Africa. For two centuries it had been deemed desirable to have from that country the same "inexhaustible supply of cheap labour" that Ireland has supplied to England; and, therefore, no effort was spared to prevent the negroes from making any improvement in their modes of cultivation. "It was," says Macpherson, "the European policy" to prevent the Africans from arriving at perfection in any of their pursuits, "from a fear of interfering with established branches of trade elsewhere." More properly, it was the English policy. "The truth is, said Mr. Pitt, in 1791,

> "There is no nation in Europe which has plunged so deeply into this guilt as Britain. *We* stopped the natural progress of civilization in Africa. *We* cut her off from the opportunity of improvement. *We* kept her down in a state of darkness, bondage, ignorance, and bloodshed. We have there subverted the whole order of nature; we have aggravated every natural barbarity, and furnished to every man motives for committing, under the name of trade, acts of perpetual hostility and perfidy against his neighbour. Thus had the perversion of British commerce carried misery instead of happiness to one whole quarter of the globe. False to the very principles of trade, unmindful of our duty, what almost irreparable mischief had we done to that continent! We had obtained as yet only so much knowledge of its productions as to show that there was a capacity for trade which we checked."

How was all this done? By preventing the poor Africans from obtaining machinery to enable them to prepare their sugar for market, or for producing cotton and indigo and combining them into cloth — precisely the same course of operation that was pursued in Jamaica with such extraordinary loss of life. Guns and gunpowder aided in providing cheap labour, and how they were supplied, even so recently as in 1807, will be seen on a perusal of the following passage, from an eminent English authority, almost of our own day:

> "A regular branch of trade here, at Birmingham, is the manufacture of guns for the African market. They are made for about a dollar and a half: the barrel is filled with water, and if the water does not come through, it is thought proof sufficient. Of course, they

burst when fired, and mangle the wretched negro, who has purchased them upon the credit of English faith, and received them,
most probably, as the price of human flesh! No secret is made of this
abominable trade, yet the government never interferes, and the persons concerned in it are not marked and shunned as infamous." —
Southey's "Espriella's Letters."

It is deemed now desirable to have cheap labour applied to the
collection of gold-dust and hides, palm-leaves and ivory, and the description of commodities at present exported to that country will be
seen by the following cargo-list of the brig Lily, which sailed from
Liverpool a few weeks since for the African coast, but blew up and
was destroyed in the neighborhood of the Isle of Man, to wit:

> 50 tons gunpowder,
> 20 puncheons rum,
> A quantity of firearms, and
> Some bale-goods.

Such are not the commodities required for raising the value of
man in Africa, and until it can be raised to a level with his value in
Cuba, the export of men will be continued from the African coast as
certainly as the export from Ireland will be continued so long as men
are cheaper there than elsewhere; and as certainly as the trade described in the following letter will be continued, so long as the
people of India shall be allowed to do nothing but raise sugar and
cotton for a distant market, and shall thus be compelled to forego all
the advantages so long enjoyed by them under the native governments, when the history of the cotton manufacture was the history of
almost every family in India:

"Havana, Feb. 11, 1853.

"On the morning of the 7th, arrived from Amoa, Singapore, and
Jamaica, the British ship Panama, Fisher, 522 tons, 131 days'
passage, with 261 Asiatics (Coolies) on board, to be introduced to the
labour of the island, *purchased* for a service of four years. The loss
on the passage was considerable percentage, being 90 thrown over-
board. The speculators in this material are Messrs. Viloldo, War-
drop and Co., who have permission of the government to cover five
thousand subjects. The cargo is yet held in quarantine.

"On the 8th inst., arrived from Amoa and St. Helena, the ship

Blenheim, Molison, 808 tons, 104 days' passage, bringing to the same consignees 412 Coolies. Died on the voyage, 38. Money will be realized by those who have the privilege of making the introduction, and English capital will find some play; but I doubt very much whether the purposes of English *philanthropy* will be realized, for, reasoning from the past, at the expiration of the four years, nearly all have been sacrificed, while the condition of African labour will be unmitigated. A short term and cupidity strain the lash over the poor Coolie, and he dies; is secreted if he lives, and advantage taken of his ignorance for extended time when once merged in plantation-service, where investigation can be avoided." — *Correspondence of the New York Journal of Commerce.*

This trade is sanctioned by the British government because it provides an outlet for Hindoo labour, *rendered surplus* by the destruction of the power of association throughout India, and yet the same government expends large sums annually in closing an outlet for African labour, *rendered surplus* by the rum and the gunpowder that are supplied to Africa!

To stop the export of men from that important portion of the earth, it is required that we should raise the value of man in Africa, and to do this, the African must be enabled to have machinery, to bring the artisan to his door, to build towns, to have schools, and to make roads. To give to the African these things, and to excite in his breast a desire for something better than rum, gunpowder, and murder, and thus to raise the standard of morals and the value of labour, has been the object of the founders of the Republic of Liberia, one of the most important and excellent undertakings of our day. Thus far, however, it has been looked upon very coldly by all the nations of Europe, and it is but recently that it has received from any of them the slightest recognition; and even now it is regarded solely as being likely to aid in providing *cheap labour*, to be employed in increasing the supplies of sugar and cotton, and thus cheapening those commodities in the market of the world, at the cost of the slaves of America and of India.

Nevertheless it has made considerable progress. Its numbers now amount to 150,000, a large proportion of whom are natives, upon whom the example of the colonists from this country has operated to produce a love of industry and a desire for many of the comforts of civilized life. By aid, generally, of persuasion, but oc-

casionally by that of force, it has put an end to the export of men
throughout a country having several hundred miles of coast. The
difficulty, however, is that wages are very low, and thus there is but
little inducement for the immigration of men from the interior, or
from this country. Much progress has thus been made, yet it is small
compared with what might be made could the republic offer greater
inducements to settlers from the interior, or from this country; that
is, could it raise the value of man, ridding itself, of *cheap labour*.
Where there is nothing but agriculture, the men must be idle for
very much of their time, and the women and children *must* be idle or
work in the field; and where people are forced to remain idle they remain poor and weak, and they can have neither towns, nor roads,
nor schools. Were it in the power of the republic to say to the people
for hundreds of miles around, that there was a demand for labour
every day in the year, and at good wages — that at one time cotton
was to be picked, and at another it was to be converted into cloth —
that in the summer the cane was to be cultivated, in the autumn the
sugar was to be gathered, and in the winter it was to be refined —
that at one time houses and mills were to be built, and at another
roads to be made — that in one quarter stone was to be quarried,
and in another timber to be felled — there would be hundreds of
thousands of Africans who would come to seek employment, and
each man that came would give strength to the republic while
diminishing the strength of the little tyrants of the interior, who
would soon find men becoming less abundant and more valuable,
and it would then become necessary to try to retain their subjects.
Every man that came would desire to have his wife and children
follow him, and it would soon come to be seen that population and
wealth were synonymous, as was once supposed to be the case in
Europe. By degrees, roads would be made into the interior, and
civilized black men would return to their old homes, carrying with
them habits of industry and intelligence, a knowledge of agriculture
and of the processes of the coarser manufactures, and with every
step in this direction labour would acquire new value, and men
would everywhere become more free.

To accomplish these things alone and unassisted might, however, require almost centuries, and to render assistance would be to
repudiate altogether the doctrine of cheap labour, cheap sugar, and

cheap cotton. Let us suppose that on his last visit to England, President Roberts should have invoked the aid of the English Premier in an address to the following effect, and then see what must have been the reply:

"My Lord:

"We have in our young republic a population of 150,000, scattered over a surface capable of supporting the whole population of England, and all engaged in producing the same commodities, — as a consequence of which we have, and can have, but little trade among ourselves. During a large portion of the year our men have little to do, and they waste much time, and our women and children are limited altogether to the labours of the field, to the great neglect of education. Widely scattered, we have much need of roads, but are too poor to make them, and therefore much produce perishes on the ground. We cannot cultivate bulky articles, because the cost of transportation would be greater than their product at market; and of those that we do cultivate nearly the whole must be sent to a distance, with steady diminution in the fertility of the soil. We need machinery and mechanics. With them we could convert our cotton and our indigo into cloth, and thus find employment for women and children. Mechanics would need houses, and carpenters and blacksmiths would find employment, and gradually towns would arise, and our people would be from day to day more enabled to make their exchanges at home, while acquiring increased power to make roads, and land would become valuable, while men would become from day to day more free. Immigration from the interior would be large, and from year to year we should be enabled to extend our relations with the distant tribes, giving value to their labour and disseminating knowledge, and thus should we, at no distant period, be enabled not only to put an end to the slave trade, but also to place millions of barbarians on the road to wealth and civilization. To accomplish these things, however, we need the aid and countenance of Great Britain."

The reply to this would necessarily have been:

"Mr. President:

"We are aware of the advantage of diversification of employments for to that were our own people indebted for their freedom. With the immigration of artisans came the growth of our towns, the value of our land, and the strength of the nation. We are aware, too, of the advantages of those natural agents which so much assist the powers of man; but it is contrary to British policy to aid in the establishment of manufactures of any description in any part of the world. On the contrary, we have spared no pains to annihilate those existing in India, and we are now maintaining numerous colonies, at vast expense, for the single purpose of 'stifling in their infancy the manufactures of other nations.' We need large supplies of cotton, and the more you send us, the cheaper it will be; whereas, if you make cloth, you will have no cotton to sell, no cloth to buy. We need cheap sugar, you will have none to send us to pay for axes or hammers. We need cheap hides, palm-leaves, and ivory, and if your people settle themselves in towns, they will have less time to employ themselves in the collection of those commodities. We need cheap labour, and the cheaper your cotton and your sugar the lower will be the price of your labour. Be content. Cultivate the earth, and send its products to our markets, and we will send you cloth and iron. You will, it is true, find it difficult to make roads, or to build schools, and your women will have to work in the sugar-plantations; but this will prevent the growth of population, and there will be less danger of your being compelled to resort to 'the inferior soils' that yield so much less in return to labour. The great danger now existing is that population may outrun food, and all our measures in Ireland, India, Turkey, and other countries are directed toward preventing the occurrence of so unhappy a state of things."

Let us next suppose that the people of Virginia should address the British nation, and in the following terms:

"We are surrounded by men who raise cotton wool, and we have in our own State land unoccupied that could furnish more sheep's wool than would be required for clothing half our nation. Within our limits there are water-powers now running to waste that could, if properly used, convert into cloth half the cotton raised in the Union. We have coal and iron ore in unlimited quantity, and are wasting almost as much labour as would be required for making all the cloth and iron we consume in a month. Nevertheless, we can make neither cloth nor iron. Many of our people have attempted it, but they have, almost without exception, been ruined. When you charge high prices for cloth, we build mills; but no sooner are they built than there comes a crisis at 'the mighty heart of commerce,' and cloths are poured into our markets so abundantly and sold so cheaply, that our people become bankrupt. When you charge high prices for iron, as you *now* do, we build furnaces; but no sooner are they ready than your periodical crisis comes, and then you sell iron so cheaply that the furnace-master is ruined. As a consequence of this, we are compelled to devote ourselves to raising tobacco and corn to go abroad, and our women and children are barbarized, while our lands are exhausted. You receive our tobacco, and you pay us about three pence for that which sells for six shillings, and we are thus kept poor. Our corn is too bulky to go abroad in its rude state, and to enable it to go to market we are obliged to manufacture it into negroes for Texas. We detest the domestic slave trade, and it is abhorrent to our feelings to sell a negro, but we have no remedy, nor can we have while, because of inability to have machinery, labour is so cheap. If we could make iron, or cloth, we should need houses, and towns, and carpenters, and blacksmiths, and then people from other States would flock to us, and our towns and cities would grow rapidly, and there would be a great demand for potatoes and tur-nips, cabbages and carrots, peas and beans, and then we could take from the land tons of green crops where now we obtain only bushels of wheat. Land would then become valuable, and great plantations would become divided into small farms, and with each step in this direction labour would become more productive, and the labourer would from day to day acquire the power to determine for whom he would work and how he should be paid — and thus, as has been the case in all other countries, our slaves would become free as we be-came rich.''

To this what would be the reply? Must it not be to the following effect:

''We need cheap food, and the more you can be limited to agri-culture, the greater will be the quantity of wheat pressing upon our market, and the more cheaply will our cheap labourers be fed. We need large revenue, and the more you can be forced to raise tobacco, the larger our consumption, and the larger our revenue. We need cheap cotton and cheap sugar, and the less the value of men, women, and children in Virginia, the larger will be the export of slaves to Texas, the greater will be the competition of the producers of cotton and sugar to sell their commodities in our markets, and the lower will be prices, while the greater will be the competition for the purchase of our cloth, iron, lead, and copper, and the higher will be prices. Our rule is to buy cheaply and sell dearly, and it is only the slave that submits dearly to buy and cheaply to sell. Our interest requires that we should be the great work-shop of the world, and that we may be so it is needful that we should use all the means in our power to prevent other nations from availing themselves of their vast deposits of ore and fuel; for if they made iron they would obtain machinery, and be enabled to call to their aid the vast powers that nature has everywhere provided for the service of man. We desire that there shall be no steam-engines, no bleaching apparatus, no furnaces, no rolling-mills, except our own; and our reason for this is, that we are quite satisfied that agriculture is the worst and least profitable pursuit of man, while manufactures are the best and most profitable. It is our wish, therefore, that you should continue to raise tobacco and corn, and manufacture the corn into negroes for Texas and Arkansas; and the more extensive the slave trade the better we shall be pleased, because we know that the more negroes you export the lower will be the price of cotton. Our people are becoming from day to day more satisfied that it is 'for their advantage' that the negro shall 'wear his chains in peace,' even although it may cause the separation of husbands and wives, parents and children, and although they know that, in default of other employment, women and children are obliged to employ their labour in the culture of rice among the swamps of Carolina, or in that of sugar among the richest and most unhealthy lands of Texas. This will have one advantage. It will lessen the danger of over-population."

Again, let us suppose the people of Ireland to come to their brethren across the Channel and say,

"Half a century since we were rapidly improving. We had large manufactures of various kinds, and our towns were thriving, and schools were increasing in number, making a large demand for books, with constantly increasing improvement in the demand for labour, and in its quality. Since then, however, a lamentable change has taken place. Our mills and furnaces have everywhere been closed, and our people have been compelled to depend entirely upon the land; the consequence of which is seen in the fact that they have

been required to pay such enormous rents that they themselves have
been unable to consume anything but potatoes, and have starved by
hundreds of thousands, because they could find no market for
labour that would enable them to purchase even of them enough to
support life. Labour has been so valueless that our houses have been
pulled down by hundreds of thousands, and we find ourselves now
compelled to separate from each other, husbands abandoning wives,
sons abandoning parents, and brothers abandoning sisters. We fear
that our whole nation will disappear from the earth; and the only
mode of preventing so sad an event is to be found in raising the value
of labour. We need to make a market at home for it and for the products of our land; but that we cannot have unless we have machinery. Aid us in this. Let us supply ourselves. Let us make cloth and
iron, and let us exchange those commodities among ourselves for the
labour that is now everywhere being wasted. We shall then have
schools, and our land will become valuable, while we shall become
free.''

The answer to this would necessarily be as follows:

''It is to the cheap labour that Ireland has supplied that we are
indebted for 'our great works,' and cheap labour is now more than
ever needed, because we have not only to underwork the Hindoo,
but also to underwork several of the principal nations of Europe and
America. That we may have cheap labour we must have cheap food.
Were we to permit you to become manufacturers you would make
a market at home for your labour and wages would rise, and you
would then be able to eat meat and wheaten bread, instead of potatoes, and the effect of this would be to raise the price of food; and
thus should we be disabled from competing with the people of
Germany, of Belgium, and of America, in the various markets of the
world. Further than this, were you to become manufacturers you
would consume a dozen pounds of cotton where now you consume
but one, and this would raise the price of cotton, as the demand for
Germany and Russia has now raised it, while your competition with
us might lower the price of cloth. We need to have cheap cotton
while selling dear cloth. We need to have cheap food while selling
dear iron. Our paramount rule of action is, 'Buy in the cheapest
market and sell in the dearest one' — and the less civilized those
with whom we have to deal the cheaper we can always buy and the

dearer we can sell. It is, therefore, to our interest that your women should labour in the field, and that your children should grow up uneducated and barbarous. Even, however, were we so disposed, you could not compete with us. Your labour is cheap, it is true, but after having, for half a century, been deprived of manufactures, you have little skill, and it would require many years for you to acquire it. Your foreign trade has disappeared with your manufactures, and the products of your looms would have no market but your own. When we invent a pattern we have the whole world for a market, and after having supplied the domestic demand, we can furnish of it for foreign markets so cheaply as to set at defiance all competition. Further than all this, we have, at very short intervals, periods of monetary crisis that are so severe as to sweep away many of our own manufacturers, and at those times goods are forced into all the markets of the world, to be sold at any price that can be obtained for them. Look only at the facts of the last few years. Six years since, railroad iron was worth £12 per ton. Three years since, it could be had for £4.10, or even less. Now it is at £10, and a year hence it may be either £12 or £4; and whether it shall be the one or the other is dependent altogether upon the movements of the great Bank which regulates all our affairs. Under such circumstances, how could your infant establishments hope to exist? Be content. The Celt has long been 'the hewer of wood and drawer of water for the Saxon,' and so he must continue. We should regret to see you all driven from your native soil, because it would deprive us of our supply of cheap labor; but we shall have in exchange the great fact that Ireland will become one vast grazing-farm, and will supply us with cheap provisions, and thus aid in keeping down the prices of all descriptions of food sent to our markets."

The Hindoo, in like manner, would be told that his aid was needed for keeping down the price of American and Egyptian cotton, and Brazilian and Cuban sugar, and that the price of both would rise were he permitted to obtain machinery that would enable him to mine coal and iron ore, by aid of which to obtain spindles and looms for the conversion of his cotton into cloth, and thus raise the value of his labour. The Brazilian would be told that it was the policy of England to have cheap sugar, and that the more he confined himself and his people — men, women, and children — to the culture of the cane, the lower would be the prices of the product of the slaves of Cuba and the Mauritius.

Seeing that the policy of England was thus directly opposed to every thing like association, or the growth of towns and other local places of exchange, and that it looked only to cheapening labour and enslaving the labourer, the questions would naturally arise: Can we not help ourselves? Is there no mode of escaping from this thraldom? Must our women always labour in the field? Must our children always be deprived of schools? Must we continue for ever to raise negroes for sale? Must the slave trade last for ever? Must the agricultural communities of the world be compelled for all time to compete against each other in one very limited market for the sale of all they have to sell, and the purchase of all they have to buy? Are there not some nations in which men are becoming more free, and might we not aid the cause of freedom by studying the course they have pursued and are pursuing? Let us, then, inquire into the policy of some of the various peoples of Continental Europe, and see if we cannot obtain an answer to these questions....

In considering what is the duty of this country, every man should reflect that whatever tends to increase the quantity of raw produce forced on the market of England, tends to the cheapening of labour and land everywhere, to the perpetuation of slavery, and to the extension of its domain — and that whatever tends to the withdrawal of such produce from that market tends to raising the value of land and labour everywhere, to the extinction of slavery, and to the elevation of man.

The system commonly called free trade tends to produce the former results; and where man is enslaved there can be no real freedom of trade. That one which looks to protection against this extraordinary system of taxation, tends to enable men to determine for themselves whether they will make their exchanges abroad or at home; and it is in this power of choice that consists the freedom of trade and of man. By adopting the "free trade," or British, system we place ourselves side by side with the men who have ruined Ireland and India, and are now poisoning and enslaving the Chinese people. By adopting the other, we place ourselves by the side of those whose measures tend not only to the improvement of their own subjects, but to the emancipation of the slave everywhere, whether in the British Islands, India, Italy, or America.

It will be said, however, that protection tends to destroy commerce, the civilizer of mankind. Directly the reverse, however, is the fact. It is the system now called free trade that tends to the destruction of commerce, as is shown wherever it obtains. Protection looks only to resisting a great scheme of foreign taxation that everywhere limits the power of man to combine his efforts with those of his neighbor man for the increase of his production, the improvement of his mind, and the enlargement of his desires for, and his power to procure, the commodities produced among the different nations of the world. The commerce of India does not grow, nor does that of Portugal, or of Turkey; but that of the protected countries does increase, as has been shown in the case of Spain, and can now be shown in that of Germany. In 1834, before the formation of the *Zoll-Verein*, Germany took from Great Britain, her own produce and manufactures, only £4,429,727
Whereas in 1852 she took £7,694,059

And as regards this country, in which protection has always to some extent existed, it is the best customer that England ever had, and our demands upon her grow most steadily and regularly under protection, because the greater our power to make coarse goods, the greater are those desires which lead to the purchase of fine ones, and the greater our ability to gratify them.

Whatever tends to increase the power of man to associate with his neighbor man, tends to promote the growth of commerce, and to produce that material, moral, and intellectual improvement which leads to freedom. To enable men to exercise that power is the object of protection. The men of this country, therefore, who desire that all men, black, white, and brown, shall at the earliest period enjoy perfect freedom of thought, speech, action, and trade, will find, on full consideration, that duty to themselves and to their fellow-men requires that they should advocate efficient protection, as the true and only mode of abolishing the domestic trade in slaves, whether black or white.

It will, perhaps, be said that even although the slave trade were abolished, slavery would still continue to exist, and that the great object of the anti-slavery movement would remain unaccomplished. One step, at all events, and a great one, would have been made. To render men *adscripti glebae*, thus attaching them to the soil, has been in many countries, as has so recently been the case in Russia, one of the movements toward emancipation; and if this could be here effected by simple force of attraction, and without the aid of law, it would be profitable to all, both masters and slaves; because whatever tends to attract population tends inevitably to increase the value of land, and thus to enrich its owner. There, however, it could not stop, as the reader will readily see. Cheap food enables the farmer of Virginia to raise cheap labour for the slave market. Raise the price of food, and the profit of that species of manufacture would diminish. Raise it still higher, and the profit would disappear; and then would the master of slaves find it necessary to devolve upon the parent the making of the *sacrifice* required for the raising of children, and thus enable him to bring into activity all the best feelings of the heart.

Cheap food and slavery go together; and if we desire to free ourselves from the last, we must commence by ridding ourselves of the first. Food is cheap in Virginia, because the market for it is distant, and most of its value there is swallowed up in the cost of transportation. Bring the consumer close to the door of the farmer, and it will be worth as much there as it now commands in the distant market. Make a demand everywhere around him for all the food that is raised, and its value will everywhere rise, for then we shall cease to press upon the limited market of England, which fixes the price of our crop, and is now borne down by the surplus products of Germany and Russia, Canada and ourselves; and the price will then be higher in the remote parts of Virginia than can now be obtained for it in the distant market of England. It will then become quite impossible for the farmer profitably to feed his corn to slaves.

With the rise in the price of food the land would quadruple in value, and that value would continue to increase as the artisan more and more took his place by the side of the producer of food and wool, and as towns increased in number and in size; and with each step in this direction the master would attach less importance to the ownership of slaves, while the slave would attach more importance to freedom. With both, the state of feeling would improve; and the

more the negro was improved the more his master would be disposed
to think of slavery, as was thought of old by Jefferson and Madison,
that it was an evil that required to be abated; and the more rapid the
growth of wealth, the greater the improvement in the value of land,
the more rapid would be the approach of freedom to all, the master
and the slave.

It will be said, however, that if food should so much increase in
value, as to render it desirable for Virginia to retain the whole
growth of her population, black and white, the necessary effect
would be a great rise in the price of cotton, and a great increase in
the wealth of the planters further South, who would be desirous to
have negroes, even at greatly increased prices. That the price of
cotton would rise is quite certain. Nothing keeps it down but the low
price of food, which forces out the negroes of the Northern States,
and thus maintains the domestic slave trade; and there is no reason
to doubt that not only would there be a large increase in its price,
but that the power to pay for it would increase with equal rapidity.
More negro labour would then certainly be needed, and then would
exist precisely the state of things that leads inevitably to freedom.
When two masters seek one labourer, the latter becomes free; but
when two labourers seek one master, the former become enslaved.
The increased value of negro labour would render it necesssary for
the owners of negroes to endeavor to stimulate the labourer to
exertion, and this could be done only by the payment of wages for
over-work, as is even now done to a great extent. At present, the
labour of the slave is in a high degree unproductive, as will be seen
by the following passage from a letter to the New York *Daily Times*,
giving the result of information derived from a gentleman of
Petersburgh, Virginia, said to be "remarkable for accuracy and
preciseness of his information:"—

"He tells me," says the writer, "he once very carefully observed
how much labour was expended in securing a crop of very thin
wheat, and found that it took four negroes one day to cradle, rake,
and bind one acre. (That is, this was the rate at which the field was
harvested.) In the wheat-growing districts of Western New York,
four men would be expected to do five acres of a similar crop.

"Mr. Griscom further states, as his opinion, that four negroes do
not, in the ordinary agricultural operations of this State, accomplish

as much as one labourer in New Jersey. Upon my expressing my astonishment, he repeated it as his deliberately formed opinion.

"I have since again called on Mr. Griscom, and obtained permission to give his name in the above statement. He also wishes me to add, that the ordinary waste in harvesting, by the carelessness of the negroes, above that which occurs in the hands of Northern labourers, is large enough to equal what a Northern farmer would consider a satisfactory profit on the crop."

To bring into activity all this vast amount of labour now wasted, it is needed to raise the *cost of man*, by raising the price of food; and that is to be done by bringing the farmer's market to his door, and thus giving value to labour and land. Let the people of Maryland and Virginia, Carolina, Kentucky, and Tennessee be enabled to bring into activity their vast treasures of coal and iron ore, and to render useful their immense water-powers — free the masters from their present dependence on distant markets, in which they *must* sell all they produce, and *must* buy all they consume — and the negro slave becomes free, by virtue of the same great law that in past times has freed the serf of England, and is now freeing the serf of Russia. In all countries of the world man has become free as land has acquired value, and as its owners have been enriched; and in all man has become enslaved as land has lost its value, and its owners have been impoverished....

Money

This speech was delivered by Henry Carey to the New York Philosophical Society in 1857. In part, Carey demonstrated the effects of the London Rothschild and Baring families' control of the world's currency supplies. The speech, excerpted here, formed a part of Carey's polemical attack against the "Free Traders" in the young Republican Party.

1. The single commodity that is of universal request is money. Go where we may, we meet persons seeking commodities required for the satisfaction of their wants, yet widely differing in their demands. One needs food; a second, clothing; a third, books, newspapers, horses, or ships. Many desire food, yet while one would have fish, another rejects the fish and seeks for meat. Offer clothing

to him who sought for ships, and he would prove to have been supplied. Place before the seeker after silks, the finest lot of cattle, and he will not purchase. The woman of fashion rejects the pantaloons; while the porter regards her slipper as wholly worthless. Of all these people, nevertheless, there would not be found even a single one unwilling to give labor, attention, skill, houses, bonds, lands, horses, or whatever else might be within his reach in exchange for money — provided, only, that the quantity offered were deemed sufficient.

So has it been in every age, and so is it everywhere. Laplander and Patagonian, almost the antipodes of each other, are alike in their thirst after the precious metals. Midianite merchants paid for Joseph with so many pieces of silver. The gold of Macedon bought the services of Demosthenes; and it was thirty pieces of silver that paid for the treason of Judas. African gold enabled Hannibal to cross the Alps; as that of Spanish America has enabled France to subjugate so large a portion of Northern Africa. Sovereigns in the East heap up gold as provision against future accidents; and finance ministers in the West, rejoice when their accounts enable them to exhibit a full supply of the precious metals. When it is otherwise the highest dignitaries are seen paying obsequious court to the Rothschild and the Baring, controllers of the supply of money. So, too, when railroads are to be made, or steamers to be built. Farmers and contractors, landowners, and stockholders, then go, cap in hand, to the Croesuses of Paris and London, anxious to obtain a hearing, and desiring to propitiate the man of power by making whatsoever sacrifice may seem to be required.

2. Were a hundred ships to arrive in your port tomorrow, a single one of which was freighted with gold, she alone would find a place in the editorial columns of your journals — leaving wholly out of view the remaining ninety-nine, freighted with silks and teas, cloth and sugar. The news, too, would find a similar place in almost all the journals of the Union, and for the reason that all their readers, the "bears" excepted, so much rejoice when money comes in, and so much regret when it goes out. Of all the materials of which the earth is composed, there are none so universally acceptable as gold and silver — none in whose movements so large a portion of every community feels an interest.

Why is this the case? Because of their having distinctive qualities that bring them into direct connection with the distinctive qualities of man — facilitating the growth of association, and promoting the development of individuality. They are the *indispensable* instruments of society, or commerce.

That they *are* so would seem to be admitted by those journalists when giving to their movements so much publicity; and yet, on turning to another column, you would probably find it there asserted that all this anxiety in regard to money was evidence of ignorance — the condition of man being improved by parting with gold that he can neither eat, drink, nor wear, in exchange for sugar that he *can* eat, and cloth that he *can* wear. Such may be the case, says one reader, but, for my part, I prefer to see money come in, because when it does so, I can borrow at six percent; whereas, when it is going out, I have to pay ten, twelve, or twenty. This is doubtless true, says another, but I prefer to see money arrive — being then able to sell my hats and shoes, and to pay the people who make them. It may be evidence of ignorance, says a third, but I always rejoice when money flows inwards, for then I can always sell my labor; whereas, when it flows outwards, I am unemployed, and my wife and children suffer for want of food and clothing. Men's natural instincts look, thus, in one direction, while mock science points in another. The first *should* be right, because they are given of God. The last *may* be wrong — being one among the weak inventions of man. Which is right, we may now inquire.

3. The power of man over matter is limited to effecting changes of place and of form. For the one he needs wagons, horses, ships, and railroads; for the other, spades, plows, mills, furnaces, and steam-engines. Among men, changes of ownership are to be effected, and for that purpose they need some general medium of circulation.

The machinery of exchange in use is, therefore, of three kinds — that required for producing changes of place, that applied to effecting changes of form, and that used for effecting changes of ownership; and were we now to examine the course of proceeding with regard to them, we should find it to be the same in all — thus obtaining proof of the universality of the natural laws to whose government man is subject. For the present, however, we must limit ourselves to an examination of the phenomena of the machinery of circulation.

In the early periods of society, man has little to exchange, and there are few exchanges — those which are made being by direct barter — skins being given for knives, clothing, meat, or fish. With the progress of population and wealth, however, all communities have endeavored to facilitate the transfer of property, by the adoption of some common standard with which to compare the value of the commodities to be exchanged — cattle having thus been used among the early Greeks — while slaves and cattle, or "living money," as it was then denominated, were commonly in use among the Anglo-Saxons — wampum among our aborigines — codfish among the people of New England — and tobacco among those of Virginia. With further progress, we find them adopting successively iron, copper, and bronze, preparatory to obtaining silver and gold, to be used as the machinery for effecting exchanges from hand to hand.

For such a purpose, the recommendations of those metals are very great. Being scantily diffused throughout the earth, and requiring, therefore, much labor for their collection, they represent a large amount of value — while being themselves of little bulk, and therefore capable of being readily and securely stored, or transported from place to place. Not being liable to rust or damage, they may be preserved uninjured for any length of time, and their quantity is, therefore, much less liable to variation than is that of wheat or corn, the supply of which is so largely dependent upon the contingencies of the weather. Capable of the most minute subdivision, they can be used for the performance of the smallest as well as the largest exchanges; and we all know well how large an amount of commerce is effected by means of coins of one and of three cents that would have to remain unaffected; were there none in use of less value than those of five, six, and ten cents.

To facilitate their use, the various communities of the world are accustomed to have them cut into small pieces and weighed, after which they are so stamped as to enable every one to discern at once how much gold or silver is offered in exchange for the commodity he has to sell; but the value of the piece is in only a very slight degree due to this process of coinage.† In the early periods of society, all the metals passed in lumps, requiring, of course, to be weighed; and such is now the case with much of the gold that passes between America and Europe. Gold dust has also to be weighed, and allowance has to be made for the impurities with which the gold itself is connected; but with this exception, it is of almost precisely the same value with gold passed from the mint and stamped with an eagle, a head of Victoria, or of Nicholas.

4. A proper supply of those metals having been obtained, and this having been divided, weighed, and marked, the farmer, the miller, the clothier, and all other members of society are now enabled to effect exchanges, even to the extent of purchasing for a single cent their share of the labors of thousands, and tens of thousands of men employed in making railroads, engines, and cars, and transporting upon them annually hundreds of millions of letters; or, for another cent, their share of the labor of the hundreds, if not thousands, of men who have contributed to the production of a penny newspaper. The mass of small coin is thus a *saving fund* for labor, because it facilitates association and combination — giving utility to billions of millions of minutes that would be wasted, did not a demand exist for them at the moment the power to labor had been produced. Labor being the first price given for everything we value, and being the commodity that all can offer in exchange, the progress of communities in wealth and influence is in the direct ratio of the presence or absence of an *instant* demand for the forces, physical and mental, of each and every man in the community — resulting from the existence of a power on the part of each and every other man to offer something valuable in exchange for it. It is the only commodity that perishes at the instant of production, and that, if not then put to use, is lost forever.

We are all momently producing labor-power, and daily taking in the fuel by whose consumption it is produced; and that fuel is

† The heap of paper in the mill becomes slightly more valuable when it is counted off and tied up in reams, and the heap of cloth is in like manner increased in value when it is measured and tied up in pieces, for the reason that both can be more readily exchanged. Precisely similar to this is the increase of value resulting from the process of coinage.

wasted unless its product be on the instant usefully employed. The most delicate fruits or flowers may be kept for hours or days; but the force resulting from the consumption of food cannot be kept, even for a second. That the instant power of profitable consumption may be coincident with the instant production of this universal commodity, there must be incessant combination, followed by an incessant division and subdivision, and that in turn followed by an incessant recomposition. This is seen in the case above referred to, where miners, furnace-men, machine-makers, rag-gatherers, carters, bleachers, paper-makers, railroad and canal men, type-makers, compositors, pressmen, authors, editors, publishers, newsboys, and hosts of others, combine their efforts for the production in market of a heap of newspapers that has, at the instant of production, to be divided off into portions suited to the wants of hundreds of thousands of consumers. Each of these latter pays a single cent — then perhaps subdividing it among half a dozen others, so that the cost is perhaps no more than a cent per week; and yet each obtains his share of the labors of all of the persons by whom it had been produced.

Of all the phenomena of society, this process of division, subdivision, composition, and recomposition is the most remarkable; and yet — being a thing of such common occurrence — it scarcely attracts the slightest notice. Were the newspaper above referred to partitioned off into squares, each representing its portion of the labor of one of the persons who had contributed to the work, it would be found to be resolved into six, eight, or perhaps even ten thousand pieces of various sizes, small and great — the former representing the men who had mined and smelted the ores of which the types and presses had been composed, and the latter the men and boys by whom the distribution has been made. Numerous as are these little scraps of human effort, they are, nevertheless, all combined in every sheet, and every member of the community may — for the trivial sum of fifty cents per annum — enjoy the advantage of the information therein contained; and as fully as he could do, had it been collected for himself alone.

Improvements in the mode of transportation are advantageous to man, but the service they render, when compared with the cost, is very small. A ship worth forty or fifty thousand dollars cannot effect exchanges between men at opposite sides of the Atlantic to an extent exceeding five or six thousand tons per annum; whereas, a furnace of similar cost will effect the transmutation of thirty thousand tons' weight of coal, ore, limestone, food, and clothing, into iron. Compared with either of these, however, the commerce effected by the help of fifty thousand dollars' worth of little white pieces representing labor to the extent of three or five cents — labor which by their help is gathered up into a heap, and then divided and subdivided day after day throughout the year — and it will be found that the service rendered to society, in economizing force, by each dollar's worth of money, is greater than is rendered by hundreds, if not thousands, employed in manufactures, or tens of thousands in ships or railroads; and yet there are able writers who tell us that money is so much "dead capital" — being "an important portion of the capital of a country that produces nothing for the country."

"Money, as money," says an eminent economist, "satisfies no want, answers no purpose....The difference between a country with money, and a country altogether without it, would," as he thinks, "be only one of convenience, like grinding by water instead of by hand." A ship, as a ship — a road, as a road — a cotton-mill, as a cotton-mill — in like manner, however, "satisfies no want, answers no purpose." They can be neither eaten, drunk, nor worn. All, however, are instruments for facilitating the work of association, and the growth of man in wealth and power is in the direct ratio of the facility of combination with his fellow-men. To what extent they do so, when compared with money, we may now inquire. To that end, let us suppose that by some sudden convulsion of nature all the ships of the world were at once annihilated, and remark the effect produced. The ship-owners would loose heavily; the sailors and the porters would have less employment; and the price of wheat would temporarily fall; while that of cloth would, for the moment rise. At the close of a single year, by far the larger portion of the operations of society would be found moving precisely as they had done before — commerce at home having taken the place of that abroad. Cotton and tropical fruits would be less easily obtained in Northern climes, and ice might be more scarce in Southern ones; but, in regard to the chief exchanges of a society like our own, there would be no suspension, even for a single instant. So far, indeed, would it be to the contrary, that in many countries commerce would be far more active than it had been before — the loss of ships producing a demand for the opening of mines, for the construction of furnaces and engines, and for the building of mills, that would make a market for labor, mental and physical, such as had never before been known.

Let us next suppose that the ships had been spared, and that all the gold and silver, coined and not coined, mined and not mined, were annihilated, and study the effect that would be produced. The reader of newspapers — finding himself unable to pay for them in beef or butter, cloth or iron — would be compelled to dispense with his usual supply of intelligence, and the journal would be no longer printed. Omnibuses would cease to run for want of sixpences; and places of amusement would be closed, for want of shillings. Commerce among men would be at an end, except so far as it might be found possible to effect direct exchanges, food being given for labor, or wool for cloth. Such exchanges could, however, be few in number, and men, women, and children would perish by millions, because of inability to obtain food and clothing in exchange for service. Cities whose population now counts by hundreds of thousands would, before the close of a single year, exhibit hundreds of blocks of unoccupied buildings, and the grass would grow in their streets. A substitute might, it is true, be found — men returning to the usages of those primitive times when wheat or iron, tobacco or copper, constituted the medium of exchange; but under such circumstances, society, as at present constituted, could have no existence. A pound of iron would be required to pay for a *Tribune* or a *Herald*, and hundreds of tons of any of the commodities above referred to, would be needed for the purchase of the weekly emission of either. Tons of them would be needed to pay for the food consumed in a single eating-house, or the amusement furnished in a single theatre; and how the wheat, the iron, the corn, or the copper could be fairly divided among the people, who had contributed to the production of the journal, the food, or the amusement, would be a problem entirely incapable of solution.

The precious metals are to the social body what atmospheric air is to the physical one. Both supply the machinery of circulation, and the resolution of the physical body into its elements when deprived of the one is not more certain than is that of the social body when deprived of the other. In both these bodies the amount of force is dependent upon the rapidity of circulation. That it may be rapid, there must be a full supply of the machinery by means of which it is to be effected; and yet there are distinguished writers who mourn over the cost of maintaining the currency, as if it were altogether lost, while expiating on the advantages of canals and railroads — not perceiving, apparently, that the money that can be carried in a bag, and that scarcely loses in weight with a service of half a dozen years, effects more exchanges than could be effected by a fleet of ships, many of which would be rotting on the shores on which they had been stranded, at the close of such a period of service, while the remainder would already have lost half of their original value.†

Of all the labor-saving machinery in use, there is none that so much economizes human power, and so much facilitates combination, as that known by the name of money. Wealth, or the power of man to command the services of nature grows with every increase in the facility of combination — this latter growing with the growth of the ability to command the aid of the precious metals. Wealth, then, should increase most rapidly where that ability is most complete.

5. The power of a commodity to command money in exchange is called its *price*. Prices fluctuate with changes of time and place — wheat being sometimes low, and at others high — and cotton commanding in one country thrice the quantity of silver that would be given for it in another. In one place, much money is required to be given for a little cloth; whereas, in another, much cloth may be obtained for little money. What are the causes of all these differences, and what the circumstances which tend to affect prices generally, we may now inquire.

A thousands tons of rags at the Rocky Mountains would not exchange for a piece of silver of the smallest conceivable size; whereas, a quire of paper would command a piece so large that it

---

† A three-cent piece, changing hands ten times in a day, effects exchanges in a year to the extent of $100; or, if we take both sides of the exchanges, to that of $200. Two thousand such pieces — costing $60 — engaged in circulating bread at home, are capable of maintaining a greater amount of commerce than can be maintained by a ship that has cost $30,000, engaged in effecting exchanges between the producers of cloth in Manchester and tea in China.

would weigh an ounce. Passing thence eastward, and arriving in the plains of Kansas, their relative values, measured in silver, would be found so much to have changed, that the price of the rags would pay for many reams of the paper. Coming to St. Louis, a further change would be experienced — rags having again risen and paper having again fallen. Such, too, would prove to be the case at every stage of the progress eastward — the raw material steadily gaining, and the finished commodity losing, in price, until, at length, in the heart of Massachusetts, three pounds of rags would be found to command more silver than would be needed for the purchase of a pound of paper. The changes of relation thus observed are exhibited in the following diagram:—

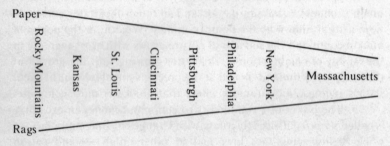

The price of raw materials tends to rise as we approach those places in which wealth most exists — those in which man is most enabled to associate with his fellow-man, for obtaining power to direct the forces of nature to his service. The prices of finished commodities move in a direction exactly opposite — tending always to decline as those of raw materials advance. Both tend thus to approximate — the highest prices of the one being always found in connection with the lowest of the other; and in the strength of the movement in that direction will be found the most conclusive evidence of advancing civilization and growing commerce.

That all the facts are in entire accordance with this view, will be obvious to those who remark that cotton is low in price at the plantation, and high in Manchester or Lowell; whereas, cloth is cheaper in Lowell than it is in Alabama or Louisiana. Corn, in Illinois, is frequently so cheap that a bushel is given in exchange for the silver required to pay for a yard of the coarsest cotton cloth;

whereas, at Manchester, it is so dear that it pays for a dozen yards. The English farmer profits doubly — obtaining much cloth for his corn, while increasing the quantity of corn by help of the manure that is furnished by his competitor of the West. The latter loses doubly — giving much corn for little cloth, and adding thereto the manure yielded by the consumption of his corn, to the loss of which is due the unceasing diminution of the powers of his land.

Looking backward in time, we obtain results precisely similar to those obtained in passing from countries in which associated men are found, and in which, consequently, wealth abounds, to those in which they are widely scattered, and in which they are, therefore, weak and poor. At the close of the fifteenth century, eight ecclesiastics, attending the funeral of Anne of Brittany, were royally entertained at a cost of 3.13 francs, of money of our time; while the silk used on that occasion is charged at 25 francs. The same quantity of silk could now be purchased for less than a franc and a half — a sum that would be entirely insufficient to pay for a single dinner. The owner of four quires of paper could then obtain for it more money than was required for the purchase of a hog, and less than two reams were needed for that of a bull. In England, hogs, sheep, and corn were cheap, and were exported, while cloth was dear, and was therefore imported. Coming down to a more recent period, the early portion of the last century, we find that corn and wool were cheap, while cloth and iron were dear; whereas, at the close of the century, the former were becoming dearer from day to day, while the latter were as regularly becoming cheaper.

6. Raw material tends, with the progress of men in wealth and civilization, to rise in price. What, however, *is* raw material? In answer to this question, we may say, that all the products of the earth are, in their turn, finished commodity and raw material. Coal and ore are the finished commodity of the miner, and yet they are only the raw material of which pig-iron is made. The latter is the finished commodity of the smelter, and yet it is but the raw material of the puddler, and of him who rolls the bar. The bar, again, is the raw material of sheet-iron — that, in turn, becoming the raw material of the nail and the spike. These, in time, become the raw material of the house, in the diminished cost of which are found concentrated all the changes that have been observed in the various

stages of passage from the rude ore — lying useless in the earth — to the nail and the spike, the hammer and the saw, required for the completion of a modern dwelling.

In the early and barbarous ages of society, land and labor are very low in price, and the richest deposits of coal and ore are worthless. Houses being then obtained with exceeding difficulty, men are forced to depend for shelter against wind and rain upon holes and caves they find existing in the earth. In time, they are enabled to combine their efforts; and with every step in the course of progress, land and labor acquire power to command money in exchange, while the house loses it. As the services of fuel are more readily commanded, pig-iron is more easily obtained. Both, in turn, facilitate the making of bars and sheets, nails and spikes, and all of these facilitate the creation of boats, ships, and houses; but each and every of these improvements tends to increase the prices of the original raw materials — land and labor. At no period in the history of the world has the general price of these latter been so high as in the present one; at none would the same quantity of money have purchased so staunch a boat, so fleet a ship, or so comfortable a house.

The more finished a commodity, the greater is the tendency to a fall of price — all the economies of the earlier processes being accumulated together in the later ones. Houses, thus, profit by all improvements in the making of bricks, in the quarrying of stone, in the conversion of lumber, and in the working of the metals. So, too, is it with articles of clothing — every improvement in the various processes of spinning, weaving, and dyeing, and in the conversion of clothing into garments being found gathered together in the coat — the more numerous those improvements, the lower being its price, and the higher that of the land and labor to which the wool is due.

With every stage of progress in that direction, there is an increasing tendency toward an equality in the prices of the more and the less finished commodities — and toward an approximation in the character of the books, clothing, furniture, and dwellings of the various portions of society; with constant increase in power to maintain commerce between those countries which do, and those which do not, yield the metals which constitute the raw material of money.

For proof of this, we may look to any of the advancing communities of the world. In the days when the French peasant would have been required to give an ox for a ream and a half of paper, wine was much higher than it is at present — peaches were entirely unattainable — the finer vegetables now in use were utterly unknown — a piece of refined sugar, or a cup of tea or coffee, were luxuries fit for kings alone — and an ell of Dutch linen exchanged for the equivalent of 60 frances — $11.25. Now — the price of meat having wonderfully increased — the farm laborer is better paid; and the consequences are seen in the fact that with the price of an ox the farmer can purchase better wine than then was drunk by kings — that he can obtain not only paper, but books and newspapers — that he can eat apricots and peaches — that sugar, tea, and coffee have become necessaries of life — and that he can have a supply of linen which would, in earlier times, have almost sufficed for the entire household of a nobleman. Such are the results of an increase in the facility of association and combination among men; and if we now desire to find the instrument to which they are most indebted for the power to combine their efforts, we must look for it in that to which we have given the name of money. Such being the case, it becomes important that we ascertain what are the circumstances under which the power to command the use of that instrument increases, and what are those under which it declines.

7. To acquire dominion over the various natural forces provided for his use, is both the pleasure and the duty of man; and the greater the amount acquired, the higher becomes his labor, and the greater is the tendency to increase of power. With each addition that each successive discovery proves to be but the precursor of newer and greater ones. Franklin's lightning rod was but the preparation for the telegraph-wires that connect our cities; and they, in turn, are but the precursors of those destined soon to enable us to read, at the breakfast-table, an account of the occurrences of the previous day in Europe, Asia, and Australia. Each successive year thus augments the power of man, and with every new discovery utility is given to forces that now are being wasted. The more they

are utilized — the more nature is made to labor in man's service — the less is the quantity of human effort required for the *reproduction* of the commodities needed for his comfort, convenience, or enjoyment — the less is the value of all previous accumulations — and the greater is the tendency toward giving to the labor of the present power over the capital created by the labors of the past.

Utility is the measure of man's power over nature. The greater it is, the larger is the demand for the commodity or thing utilized, and the greater the attractive force exerted upon it, wherever found. Look where we may, we see that every raw material yielded by the earth tends toward those places at which it has the highest utility, and that there the value of the finished article is least.† Wheat tends toward the grist-mill, and there it is that flour is cheapest. Cotton and wool tend toward the mills at which they are to be spun and woven, and there it is that the smallest quantity of money will purchase a yard of cloth. On the other hand, it is where cotton has the least utility—on the plantation—that cloth has the highest value. Therefore it is, that we see communities so universally prospering when the spindle and the loom are brought to the neighborhood of the plough and the harrow, to utilize their products.

Precisely similar to this are the facts observed in regard to the precious metals, everywhere on the earth's surface seen to be tending toward those places at which they have the highest utility — those at which men most combine their efforts for utilizing the raw products of the earth — those in which land most rapidly acquires a money value, or price — those, therefore, in which the value of those metals, as compared with land, most rapidly diminishes — and those in which the charge for the use of money is lowest. They tend to leave those places in which their utility is small, and in which combination of action least exists — those, therefore, in which the price of land is low, and the rate of interest high. In the first, there is a daily tendency toward increase in the freedom of man; whereas, in the last, the tendency is in the opposite direction — toward the subjugation of man to the control of those who live by the expenditure of taxes, rent, and interest. Desiring evidence of this, we

---

† Value is the measure of the obstacle interposed by nature to the gratification of the wishes of man.

have but to look around us at the present moment, and see how oppressively rent and interest operate upon the poorer portions of society — how numerous are the applications for the smallest office — and, above all, how great has been the increase of pauperism in the past three years, in which our exports of specie have been so large.

Looking to Mexico or Peru, to California or Siberia, we see but little of that combination of action required for giving utility to their metallic products — little value in land — and interest higher than in any other organized communities in the world. Following those products, we see them passing gradually through the West, towards the cities of the Atlantic, or through Russia to St. Petersburg — every step of their progress being toward those States or countries in which they have the greatest utility — those in which combination of action most exists, and in which, therefore, man is daily acquiring power over the various forces of nature, and compelling her more and more to aid him in his efforts for the attainment of further power.

8. For more than a century, Great Britain constituted the reservoir into which was discharged the major part of the gold and silver produced throughout the world. There it was, that the artisan and the farmer were most nearly brought together — the power of association most existed — the ultimate raw materials of commodities, land and labor, were most utilized, and the consumption in the arts, of gold and silver, was the greatest.† Now the state of things is widely different. From year to year, the land of the United Kingdom has become more consolidated — the little proprietor having been superseded by the great middleman farmer, and the mere day-laborer; and the result is seen in the fact that Great Britain has passed from being a place at which commodities are produced, to be given in exchange for the produce of other lands — to being a mere place of exchange for the people of those lands. With each successive year, there is a decline in the proportion borne to the whole population by the producing classes, and an increase in that borne by the non-producing ones, with corresponding dimin-

---

† Thirty years since, the annual consumption of the precious metals in Great Britain was estimated at £2,500,000, or $12,000,000.

ution in the power to retain the products of the mines of Peru and Mexico.

The gold of California does not, as we know, to any material extent, remain among ourselves. Touching our Atlantic coast, only to be transferred to steamers that bear it off to Great Britain, it there meets the product of the Australian mines — the two combined amounting to more than a hundred millions of dollars a year. Both come there, however, merely in transit — being destined, ultimately, to the payment of the people of Continental Europe, who have supplied raw products that have been converted and exported, or finished ones that have been consumed. Much of it goes necessarily to France, whose exports have grown, in the short period of twenty years, from 500,000,000 francs, to 1,400,000,000, and have steadily maintained their commercial character. Manufactures are there the *handmaids* of agriculture; whereas in the United Kingdom, they are, with each successive year, becoming more and more the *substitutes* for it. To a small quantity of cotton, silk, and other raw products of distant lands, France adds a large amount of the produce of her farms — thus entitling herself not only to receive, but to retain for her own uses and purposes, nearly all the commodities that come to her from abroad. Her position is that of the rich and enlightened farmer, who sells his products in their highest form — thus qualifying himself for applying to the support of his family, the education of his children, and the improvement of his land, *the whole of the commodities received in exchange.* That of Britain is the position of the trader, who passes through his hands a large amount of property, of which he is entitled to retain the *amount of his commission, and nothing more.* The one has immense, and wonderfully growing commerce, while the other performs a vast amount of trade.

9. The precious metals are steadily flowing to the north and east of Europe, and among the largest of their recipients we find Northern Germany, now so rapidly advancing in wealth, power, and civilization. Denmark and Sweden, Austria and Belgium, following in the lead of France, in the maintenance of the policy of Colbert, are moving in the same direction; and the consequences are seen in a growing habit of association, attended with daily augmentation in

the amount of production, and in the facility of accumulation, as exhibited in the building of mills, the opening of mines, the construction of roads, and the constantly augmenting power to command the services of the precious metals.

The causes of these phenomena are readily explained. Raw materials of every kind tend towards those places at which employments are most diversified, because there it is that the products of the farm command the largest quantity of money. Gold and silver follow in the train of raw materials; and for the reason, that where the farmer and the artisan are most enabled to combine, finished commodities are always cheapest. When Germany exported corn and wool, they were cheap, and she was required to export gold to aid in paying for the cloth and paper she imported; because they were very dear. Now she imports both wool and rags; her farmers obtain high prices for their products, and are enriched; and the gold comes to her, because cloth and paper are so cheap that she sends them to the most distant quarters of the world. So is it with France, Belgium, Sweden, and Denmark— all of which are large importers of raw materials, and of gold. In all those countries, raw materials rise in price; *and the greater the tendency to rise, the more rapidly must the current of the precious metals set in that direction.* The country that desires to increase its supplies of gold, and thus lower the price of money, is, therefore, required to pursue that course of policy tending most to raise the prices of raw material, and lower those of manufacturers. This, however, is directly the opposite of the policy advocated by the British school, which seeks, in the cheapening of all the raw material of manufactures, the means of advancing civilization.

10. The reverse of what is above described is found in Ireland, Turkey, and Portugal, so long the close allies of England — and so uniformly following in the course of policy now advocated by her economists. From each and all of them, there has been an unceasing drain of money — the disappearance of the previous metals having been followed by decline in the productiveness of agriculture — in the prices of commodities, in the value of land, and in the power of man.

France in the decade prior to the Eden treaty in 1786, was ad-

vancing in both manufactures and commerce with great rapidity, as
is shown conclusively in M. de Tocqueville's recent work.† Raw materials and the precious metals flowing in, and manufactured goods
flowing out, the result was seen in a daily increasing tendency toward the division of land, the improvement of agriculture, and the
increase of human freedom. From the date of that treaty, however,
all was changed. Manufactures flowed in, and gold flowed out, with
daily decline in the power of association, in the wages of labor, and
in the value of land. Universal distress producing a demand for
change of policy, its effect was seen in the calling together of the
States-General, whose appearance on the stage for the first time in a
hundred and eighty years, was so soon to be followed by a
revolution, that sent to the guillotine the most of those by whom that
treaty had been made.

Looking to Spain, we see her poverty to have steadily increased
from the hour, when, by expelling her manufacturing population,
she rendered herself dependent upon the workshops of other countries. Mistress of Mexico and Peru, she acted merely as the conduit
through which their wealth passed to the advancing countries of the
world, as is now the case with Great Britain and the United States.

Turning next to Mexico, we see her to have been declining

---

† "Simultaneous with these changes in the minds of the governed and
governors, public prosperity began to develop with unexampled strides.
This is shown by all sorts of evidence. Population increased rapidly; wealth
more rapidly still. The American war did not check the movement — it
completed the embarassment of the State, but did not impede private enterprise; individuals grew more industrious, more inventive, richer than ever.

"An official of the times states that in 1774 'industrial progress had
been so rapid that the amount of taxable articles had largely increased.' On
comparing the various contracts made between the State and the companies
to which the taxes were farmed out, at different periods during the reign of
Louis XVI, one perceives that the yield was increasing with astonishing
rapidity. The lease of 1786 yielded fourteen millions more than that of 1780.
Necker, in his report of 1781, estimated that 'the produce of taxes on articles of consumption increased at the rate of two millions a year.'

"Arthur Young states that in 1788 the commerce of Bordeaux was
greater than that of Liverpool, and adds that 'of late years maritime trade
has made more progress in France than in England; the whole trade of
France has doubled in the last twenty years'." — De Tocqueville, *The Old
Regime and the Revolution*, p. 210.

steadily in power from the day on which she obtained her independence; and for the reason that from that date her manufactures began to disappear. From year to year she becomes more and more dependant upon the trader, and more and more compelled to export her commodities in their rudest state; as a necessary consequence of which, her power to retain the produce of her mines is constantly diminishing.

11. The facts thus far presented, may now be embodied in the following propositions:—

Raw materials tend *towards* those countries in which employments are most diversified — in which the power of association most exists — and in which land and labor tend most to rise in price.

The precious metals tend towards the same countries; and for the reason, that there it is that finished commodities are least in price.

The greater the attractive force exerted upon those raw materials and this gold, the more does agriculture tend to become a science — the larger are the returns to agricultural labor — the more steady and regular becomes the motion of society — the more rapid is the development of the powers of the land, and of the men by whom it is occupied — the larger is the commerce — and the greater the progress towards happiness, wealth, and power.

Raw materials tend *from* those countries in which employments are least diversified—those in which the power of combination least exists—and those consequently, in which land and labor are least in price.

The precious metals, too, tend to leave those countries, because there it is that finished commodities are dearest.

The greater the expulsive force that is thus exhibited, the slower is the circulation of society, and the smaller is the amount of commerce — the more rapid is the exhaustion of the soil — the lower is the condition of agriculture — the less is the return to the labors of the field — the lower are the prices of the products of the farm — the less is the regularity of the motion of society — the greater is the power of the trader — and the stronger is the tendency towards pauperism and crime among the people, and towards weakness in the government.

The portions of the world *from* which the previous metals flow, in which agriculture declines, and men become less free, are those which follow in the lead of England — preferring the supremacy of trade to the extension of commerce — Ireland, Turkey, Portugal, India, Carolina, and other exclusively agricultural countries.

The portions *toward* which they flow are those which follow in the lead of France — preferring the extension of commerce to the enlargement of the trader's power. Germany and Denmark, Sweden and New England, are in this position. In all of these agriculture becomes more and more a science, as employments become diversified — the returns to agricultural labor increasing as the prices of raw materials tend to rise.

In all the countries *to* which they flow, the prices of raw materials and those of finished commodities tend to approximate — the farmer giving a steadily diminishing quantity of wool and corn in return for a constant quantity of cloth and iron.

In those *from* which they flow, those prices become from year to year more widely separated — the farmer and the planter giving a steadily increasing quantity of wool and corn for a diminishing quantity of iron, or of cloth.

Such are the facts presented by the history of the outer world, of both the present and the past. How far they are in accordance with our own experience we may now inquire.

12. The mining communities of the world having raw products to sell, and needing to purchase finished commodities, the gold and silver they produce flow naturally to those countries that have such commodities to sell; and not toward those which have only raw materials to offer in exchange. India has cotton to sell; Ireland and Turkey have grain; Brazil has sugar and coffee; while Alabama has only cotton; for which reason it is that money is always scarce in those countries, and the rate of interest high. Looking homeward, we find that whenever our policy has tended toward the production of combination of action between the farmer and the artisan, we have been importers of the precious metals, and that then land and labor have risen in price. The contrary effect has invariably been produced, whenever our policy has tended to the diminution of association, and the production of a necessity for looking abroad for making all our exchanges of food and wool for cloth and iron — limited, however, for the period immediately following the change,

by the existence of a credit that has enabled us to run in debt to Europe, and thus for a time to arrest the export of the precious metals. What was the precise course of the trade in those metals during the thirty years preceding the discovery of the California gold deposits, is shown by the following figures:

	Excess exports	Excess imports
1821-1825	$12,500,000	—
1826-1829	—	$4,000,000
1830-1834	—	20,000,000
1835-1838	—	34,000,000
1839-1842	9,000,000	—
1843-1847	—	39,000,000
1848-1850	14,000,000	—

In the closing years of the free trade system of 1817, the average excess of specie export was about $2,500,000 a year. To this adding a similar amount, only, for the annual consumption, we obtain an absolute diminution of five-and-twenty millions, while the population had increased about ten per cent. Under such circumstances, it is no matter of surprise that those years are conspicuous among the most calamitous ones in our history. At Pittsburgh, flour then sold at $1.25 per barrel; wheat, throughout Ohio, would command but 20 cents a bushel; while a ton of bar iron required little short of eighty barrels of flour to pay for it. Such was the state of affairs that produced the tariff of 1824 — a very imperfect measure of protection, but one that, imperfect as it was, changed the course of the current, and caused a *net* import, in the four years that followed, of $4,000,000 of the precious metals. In 1828, there was enacted the first tariff tending directly to the promotion of association throughout the country; and its effects exhibit themselves in an excess import of the precious metals — averaging $4,000,000 a year — notwithstanding the discharge, in that period, of the whole of the national debt that had been held in Europe, amounting to many millions. Putting together the discharge of debt and the import of coin, the balance of trade in that period must have been in our favor to the extent of nearly $50,000,000; or an average of about $10,000,000 a year. As a consequence, prosperity existed to

an extent never before known — the power to purchase foreign commodities growing with such rapidity as to render it necessary greatly
to enlarge the free list; and then it was that coffee, tea, and many
other raw commodities, were emancipated from the payment of any
impost. Thus did efficient protection lead to a freedom of commerce, abroad and at home, such as had never before existed.

The first few years of the compromise tariff of 1833 profited
largely by the prosperity caused by the act of 1828, and the reduc-
tions under it were then so small that its operation was but slightly
felt. In those years, too, there was contracted a considerable foreign
debt — stopping the export of specie, and producing an excess
import averaging more than $8,000,000 a year. Prosperity *seemed* to
exist, but it was of the same description that has marked the last few
years, during which the value of all property has depended entirely
upon the power to contract debts abroad — thus placing the nation
more completely under the control of its distant creditors. . . .

13. "In every kingdom into which money begins to flow in
greater abundance than formerly, everything," says Mr. Hume, in
his well-known Essay on Money, "takes a new face: labor and
industry gain life; the merchant becomes more enterprising, the
manufacturer more diligent and skillful; and even the farmer
follows his plough with more alacrity and attention.". . .

14. We are told, however, by the same writer — Mr. Hume —
and in that he is followed by the modern economists — that the
only effect of an increase in the supply of gold and silver is that of
"heightening the price of commodities, and obliging every one to
pay more of those little yellow or white pieces for everything he purchases." Were such really the case, it would be little short of a
miracle that we should see money always, century after century,
passing in the same direction — to the countries that are rich from
those that are poor; so poor, too, that they cannot afford to keep as
much of it as is absolutely necessary for their own exchanges. The
gold of Siberia leaves a land in which so little circulates that labor
and its products are at the lowest prices, to find its way to St. Petersburg, where it will purchase less labor and less of either wheat or
hemp than it would do at home; and that of Carolina and Virginia
goes steadily and regularly, year after year, to the countries to which
the people of those States send their cotton and their wheat, because

of the higher prices at which they sell. The silver of Mexico, and its cochineal, travel together to the same market; and the gold of Australia passes to Britain by the ship which carries the wool yielded by its flocks.

Every addition to the stock of money, as we are assured by the ingenious men of modern days engaged in compiling treasury tables and finance reports, renders a country a good place to sell in, but a bad one in which to purchase. To what countries, however, is it that men have most resorted when they desired to purchase? Have they not, until recently, gone, almost exclusively, to Britain? It has been so, assuredly; and for the reason, that there it has been that finished commodities were cheaply furnished. Where have they gone to sell? Has it not been to Britain? It certainly has been so; and for the reason, that there it was that gold, cotton, wheat, and all other of the rude products of the earth, were dear. Where do they now most tend to go when they desire to purchase cloths or silks? Is it not to France and Germany? So it certainly is; and for the reason, that there it is that raw materials are highest, and finished ones are cheapest. Gold follows in the train of raw materials generally — these last being found, invariably, traveling to those places at which the rude products of the earth command the highest price, while cloth, iron, and manufactures of iron and other metals, may be purchased at the lowest; and the greater the flow in that direction, the greater is the tendency to further enhancing the prices of the former, and reducing those of the latter. From this it would seem that increase in the supply and circulation of money, so far from having the effect of causing men to give two pieces for an article that could before have been had for one, has, on the contrary, that of enabling them to *obtain for one piece the commodity that before had cost them two;* and that such is the fact, can readily be shown.

It is within the knowledge of all, that manufactures have greatly fallen in price — the quantity of cotton cloth that can now be obtained for a single dollar being as great as would formerly have cost five — *and that the reduction has taken place in the very countries into which the gold of the world has steadily flowed, and into which it is now flowing* — whence it would appear quite certain that finished commodities tend to fall as money flows in, while land and labor — the ultimate raw materials of all — tend to rise in price.

The gold of California and Australia now goes to Germany, France, Belgium, and Great Britain, where money abounds and interest is low, because there manufactured commodities are cheap and money is valuable, *when measured by them*. It does not go to Spain, Italy, Portugal, or Turkey, because there manufactured goods are dear, and land and labor are cheap. It does not stop in Mississippi, Arkansas, or Texas, because there, too, manufactures are dear, and land and labor are cheap; but there it will stop at some future period, when it shall have ascertained that the plough and the harrow should always have for their near neighbors the spindle and the loom.

The higher products of a skillful agriculture — fruits, garden vegetables, and flowers — tend steadily to decline in price in all those countries into which money is flowing; and for the reason, that agricultural improvement always accompanies manufactures, and manufactures always attract the precious metals. Every one familiar with the operations of the West, knows that while corn and pork are there always cheap, cabbages, peas, beans, and all green crops, are invariably scarce and dear; and so continue, until, as around Cincinnati and Pittsburgh, population and wealth have given a stimulus to the work of cultivation. In England, the increase of green crops of all kinds has been immense, attended with the decline in price; and in France, a recent writer† informs us that, notwithstanding the increase in the quantity of money, the price of wine is scarcely more than a fourth of what it was three centuries since. By another we are told, that "every man in France, of forty years of age, must have remarked the sensible diminution of the price of garden produce, fruits of all kinds, flowers, etc.; and that most of the oleaginous grains and plants used in manufactures have fallen in like manner; while beets, carrots, beans, etc., have become so common that they are now fed to animals in the stable."‡

Food thus becomes more abundant in those countries into which gold is steadily flowing, and it becomes less so in those from which the gold flows, as is seen in Carolina, which has steadily exhausted her land — in Turkey — in Portugal — and in India. In all

---

† M. Moreau de Jonnes.
‡ De Fontenay, Du Revenue Foncier.

those countries, land and labor are low in price. Give them manufactures — thus enabling their people to combine their efforts —
and they will obtain and retain gold; and then they will make roads,
and the supplies of food will steadily increase as cloth and iron
become cheaper; and land and labor will then rise in price. . . .

16. The use of bank-notes tends, however, as we are assured, to
promote the expulsion of gold. Were it to do so, it would be in opposition to the great general law in virtue of which all commodities
tend to, and not *from,* the places at which they have the highest
utility. A bank is a machine for utilizing money, by enabling A, B,
and C to obtain the use of it at the time when D, E, and F, its
owners, do not need its services. The direct effect of the establishment of such institutions in the cities of Europe has always been to
cause money to flow *toward* those cities; and for the reason, that
there its utility stood at the highest point. Even then, however, there
were difficulties attendant upon the change of property in the money
deposited with the bank — the owner being required to go to the
banking-house, and write it off to other parties. To obviate this
difficulty, and thus increase the utility of money, its owners were at
length authorized to draw checks, by means of which they were
enabled to transfer their property without stirring from their houses.

The difficulty still, however, existed, that — private individuals
not being generally known — such checks could, in general, effect
but a single transfer, and thus the recipient of money found himself
obliged to go through the operation of taking possession of that
which had been transferred to him, after which he had, in his turn,
to draw a check when he himself desired to effect another change of
property. To obviate this, circulating notes were invented, and by
their help the ownership of money is now transferred with such
rapidity that a single hundred dollars passes from hand to hand fifty
times a day — effecting exchanges, perhaps, to the extent of many
thousand dollars, and without the parties being at any time required
to devote a single instant to the work of counting the coin. This was
a great invention, and by its aid, the utility of money was so much
increased that a single thousand pieces could be made to do more
work than without it could be done by hundreds of thousands.

This, of course, as we are told, supersedes gold and silver, and
causes them to be exported. So we are certainly assured by those

economists who regard man as an animal that must be fed and will procreate; and that can be made to work only under the pressure of a strong necessity. Were they, however, to look, for once, at the real *Man* — the being made in the image of his Creator, and capable of almost infinite elevation — they would perhaps, arrive at a conclusion widely different. The desires of *that* man are infinite, and the more they are gratified, the more rapidly do they increase in number. The miserable Hottentot dispenses with a road of any kind, but the enlightened and intelligent people of other countries are seen passing in succession from the ordinary village road to the turnpike, and thence to the railroad; *and the better the existing communications, the greater is the thirst for further improvement.* The better the schools and houses, the greater is the desire for superior teachers and further additions to the comforts of the dwelling. The more perfect the circulation of society, the larger is the reward of labor, and the greater is the power to purchase gold and silver, to be used for the various purposes for which they are so admirably fitted, and the greater is the tendency to have them flow to the places at which the circulation is established. Money promotes the circulation of society. The check and the bank-note stimulate that circulation — giving thereby value to labor and land; and wherever these checks and notes are most in use, there should the inward current of the precious metals be most fully and firmly established. . . .

That such *is* the case, is proved by the facts, that, for a century past, the precious metals have tended most to Britain, where such notes were most in use. Their use increases rapidly in France, with constant increase in the inward flow of gold. So, too, does it in Germany toward which the auriferous current now sets so steadily that notes which are the representatives of money are rapidly taking the place of those irredeemable pieces of paper by which the use of coin has so long been superseded.

Whence flows all this gold? From the countries in which employments are not diversified; from those in which there is little power of association and combination; from those in which, therefore, credit has no existence; from those, finally, which do not use that machinery which so much increases the utility of the precious metals, and which we are accustomed to designate by the term *bank note*. The precious metals go *from* California — *from* Mexico — *from* Peru — *from* Brazil — *from* Turkey — and *from* Portugal — the lands in which property in money is transferred only by means of actual delivery of the coin itself *to* those in which it is transferred by means of a check or note. It goes *from* the plains of Kansas, where notes are not in use, *to* New York and New England, where they are — *from* Siberia *to* St. Petersburg — *from* the banks of African rivers *to* London and Liverpool — and *from* the "diggings" of Australia *to* the towns and cities of Germany, where wool is dear and cloth is cheap. . . .

Financial Crises:
Their Causes and Effects

William Cullen Bryant was the United States' leading transcendentalist author. The editor of the New York Post, *Bryant was a staunch Jacksonian as well as a key "insider" in Martin Van Buren's Free Soil Party. Bryant was also considered the leader of the "Free Trade" wing of the Republican Party. In part, through this series of open letters to Bryant, Henry Carey was able to gain the recommitment of the Republican Party to the economic policies that characterized the American System at the party's convention that nominated Abraham Lincoln as its presidential candidate in 1860.*

Philadelphia, December 27, 1859

Dear Sir:

In your recent and highly interesting volume, which I have just now read, there is a passage to which, on account of its great importance as regards the progress of man towards an ultimate state of perfect freedom or absolute slavery, I feel disposed to invite your attention. It is as follows: "I am pained to hear such bad news from the United States — such accounts of embarrassments and failures, of sudden poverty falling on the opulent, and thousands left destitute of employment, and perhaps of bread. This is one of the epidemic visitations against which, I fear, no human prudence can provide, so far, at least, as to prevent their recurrence at longer or shorter intervals, any more than it can prevent the scarlet fever or the cholera. A money market always in perfect health and soundness would imply infallible wisdom in those who conduct its operations. I hope to hear news of a better state of things before I write again.''

Is this really so? Can it be, that the frequent recurrence of such calamities is beyond the reach of man's prevention? To admit that so it certainly was, would be, as it seems to me, to admit that Providence had so adjusted the laws under which we exist as to produce those ''epidemic visitations'' of which you speak, and of which the direct effect, as all must see, is that of placing those who need to sell their labor at the mercy of those who have food and clothing with which to purchase it — increasing steadily the wealth, strength, and power of these latter, while making the former poorer and more enslaved. Look around you, in New York, at the present moment, and study the effects, in this respect, of the still-enduring crisis of 1857. Turn back to those of 1822 and 1842, and see how strong has been their tendency to compel the transfer of property from the hands of persons of moderate means to those of men who were already rich — reducing the former, with their wives and children, to the condition of mere laborers, while largely augmenting the number and fortunes of ''merchant princes'' who have no need to live by labor. Look around you and study the growth in the number of your millionaires, side by side with a pauperism now exceeding that of Britain, or even that of Ireland. Look next to the condition of the men who labor throughout the country, deprived as they have been, and yet are, of anything approaching to steadiness of demand for their services, in default of which they have been, for two years past, unable to suitably provide for their wives, their children or themselves. Study then the condition of the rich money-lenders throughout the country, enabled, as they have been, to demand one, two, three, and even four and five percent per month, from the miners, manufacturers, and little farmers of the Union, until these latter have been entirely eaten out of house and home. Having done all this, you can scarcely fail to arrive at the conclusion, that unsteadiness in the societary movement tends toward slavery — that steadiness therein, on the contrary, tends toward the emancipation of those who have labor to sell from the domination of those who require to buy it — and that, therefore, the question referred to in the passage I have quoted, is one of the highest interest to all of those who, like yourself, are placed in a position to guide their fellow-men in their search for prosperity, happiness and freedom.

The larger the diversity in the demand for human powers, the more perfect becomes the division of employments, the larger is the production, the greater the power of accumulation, the more rapid the increase of competition for the *purchase* of the laborer's services, and the greater the tendency towards the establishment of human freedom. The greater that tendency, the more rapid becomes the societary action — its regularity increasing with every stage of progress. In proof of this, look to that world in miniature, your own printing-office, studying its movements, as compared with those of little country offices, in which a single person not unfrequently combines in himself all the employments that with you are divided among a hundred, from editor-in-chief to newsboy. The less the division of employments, the slower and more unsteady becomes the motion, the less is the power of production and accumulation, the greater is the competition for the *sale* of labor, and the greater is the tendency towards the enslavement of the laborer, be he black or white.

The nearer the consumer to the producer, the more instant and the more regular become the exchanges of service, whether in the shape of labor for money, or food for cloth. The more distant the producer and consumer, the slower and more irregular do exchanges become, and the greater is the tendency to have the laborer suffer in the absence of the power to obtain wages, and the producer of wool perish of cold in the absence of the power to obtain cloth. That this is so, is proved by an examination of the movements of the various nations of the world, at the present moment. Being so, it is clear, that if we would avoid those crises of which you have spoken — if we would have regularity of the societary movement — and if we would promote the growth of freedom — we must adopt the measures needed for bringing together the producers and consumers of food and wool, and thus augmenting their power to have commerce among themselves.

The essential characteristic of barbarism is found in instability and irregularity of the societary action — evidence of growing civilization being, on the contrary, found in a constantly augmenting growth of that regularity which tends to produce equality, and to promote the growth of freedom. Turn, if you please, to the *Wealth of Nations*, and mark the extraordinary variations in the prices of wheat in the days of the Plantagenets, from *six* shillings, in money of the present time, in 1243, to *forty-eight* in 1246, *seventy-two* in 1257, *three hundred and thirty-six* in 1270, and *twenty-eight* in 1286. That done, see how trivial have been the changes of France and England, from the close of the war in 1815, to the present time. Next, turn to Russia, and mark the fact, given to us by a recent British traveler, that, in those parts of the country that have no manufactures, the farmer is everywhere "the victim of circumstances" over which he has no control whatsoever — the prices of his products being dependent entirely upon the greater or smaller size of the crops of other lands, and he being ruined at the very moment when the return to his labor has been the most abundant. Look then to the changes throughout our own great West in the present year — wheat having fallen from $1.30 in May to 50 cts. in July — and you will see how nearly the state of things with us approximates to that of Russia. Compare all this with the movements of England, France and Germany, and you will, most assuredly, be led to arrive at the conclusion, that the stability whose absence you deplore, is to be sought by means of measures looking to the close approximation of the producer and the consumer, and to the extension of domestic commerce.

Five years since, British journals nearly all united in predicting the advent of a great financial crisis, the seat of which would be found in France and Germany. More careful observation might have satisfied them that the tendency toward such crises was always in the direct ratio of the distance of consumers from producers, and that the real places in which to look for that which was then predicted, were those countries which most seemed bent on separating the producers and consumers of the world, Britain and America — the one seeking to drive all its people into the workshops, and the other laboring to compel them all to seek the fields, and both thus acting in direct defiance of the advice of Adam Smith. The crisis came, spending its force upon *those two countries* — France, Belgium, and Germany escaping almost entirely unharmed, and for the reason, that in all these latter the farm and the workshop were coming daily more near together, and commerce was becoming more rapid, free, and regular.

Russia and Sweden have, however, suffered much — the crisis having become, apparently, as permanent as it is among ourselves. Why should this be so? Why should they be paralyzed, while France and Germany escape uninjured? Because, while these latter have persisted in maintaining that protection which is needed for promoting the approximation of producers and consumers, the former have, within the last three years, departed essentially from the system under which they had been so rapidly advancing toward wealth and freedom — adopting the policy advocated by those writers who see in the cheapening of the labor and of the raw materials of other countries, the real British road to wealth and power.

Throughout Northern and Central Europe, there has been, in the last half century, a rapid increase in the steadiness of the societary movement, and in the freedom of man — that increase being the natural consequence of increased rapidity of motion resulting from a growing diversification in the demand for human services, and growing competition for the *purchase* of labor. In Ireland, India, Spanish America, and Turkey, the reverse of this is seen — producers and consumers becoming more widely separated, and exchanges becoming more fitful and irregular, with growing competition for the *sale* of labor. Why this difference? Because the policy of the former has been directed towards protecting the farmer in his efforts to draw the market nearer to him, and thus diminish the wasting tax of transportation, while the latter have been steadily becoming more and more subjected to the system which seeks to locate in this little island of Britain the single workshop of the world.

How it has been among ourselves, is shown in the following brief statement of the facts of the last half century. From the date of the passage of the act of 1816, by which the axe was laid to the root of our then rapidly growing manufactures, our foreign trade steadily declined, until, in 1821, the value of our imports was less than half of what it had been six years before. Thenceforward, there was little change until the highly protective act of 1828 came fairly into operation — the average amount of our importations, from 1822 to 1830,

having been but 80 millions — and the variations having been between 96 millions in one year and 70 in another. Under that tariff,
the domestic commerce grew with great rapidity — enabling our
people promptly to sell their labor, and to become better customers
to the people of other lands, as is shown by the following figures, representing the value of goods imported:

1830-31	$103,000,000
1831-32	101,000,000
1832-33	108,000,000
1833-34	126,000,000

Here, my dear sir, is a nearly regular growth — the last of these
years being by far the highest, and exceeding, by more than 50
percent, the average of the eight years from 1822 to 1830. In this
period, not only did we contract no foreign debt, but we paid off the
whole of that which previously had existed, the legacy of the war of
independence; and it is with nations as with individuals, that "out of
debt is out of danger."

The compromise tariff began now to exert its deleterious influence — stopping the building of mills and the opening of mines,
and thus lessening the power to maintain domestic commerce. How
it operated on that with foreign nations, is shown in the facts, that
the imports of 1837 went up to $189,000,000, and those of 1838
down to $113,000,000 — those of 1839 up to $162,000,000, and
those of 1840 down to $107,000,000; while those of 1842 were *less
than they had been ten years before.* In this period, we ran in debt to
foreigners to the extent of hundreds of millions, and closed with a
bankruptcy so universal, as to have embraced individuals, banks,
towns, cities, States, and the national treasury itself.

That instability is the essential characteristic of the system
called free-trade, will be obvious to you on the most cursory examination of the facts presented by the several periods of that system
through which we have thus far passed. From more than
$100,000,000, in 1817, our imports fell, in 1821, to $62,000,000. In
1825, they rose to $96,000,000, and then, two years later, they were
but $79,000,000. From 1829 to 1834, they grew almost regularly,
but no sooner had protection been abandoned, than instability, with
its attendant speculation, reappeared — the imports of 1836 having

been greater, by 45 percent, than those of 1834, and those of 1840 little more than half as great as those of 1836.

Once again, in 1842, protection was restored; and once again do we find a steady and regular growth in the power to maintain intercourse with the outer world, consequent upon the growth of domestic commerce, as is shown in the following figures:

1843-44 .... $108,000,000
1844-45 117,000,000
1845-46 121,000,000
1846-47 146,000,000

We have here a constant increase of *power* to go to foreign markets, accompanied by a constant decrease in the *necessity* for resorting to them — the domestic production of cotton and woollen goods having doubled in this brief period, while the domestic production of iron had more than trebled.

Twelve years having elapsed since the tariff of 1846 became fairly operative, we have now another opportunity for contrasting the operation of that policy under which Russia and Sweden are now suffering, with that of the one under which they had made such rapid progress — that one which is still maintained by Germany and by France. Doing this, we find the same instability which characterized the periods which preceded the passage of the protective tariff acts of 1824, 1828, and 1842, and on a larger scale — the imports having been $178,000,000 in 1850, $304,000,000 in 1854, $260,000,000 in 1855, $360,000,000 in 1857, $282,000,000 in 1858, and $338,000,000 in 1859 — and our foreign debt, with all its tendency toward producing those crises which you so much deplore, having been augmented probably *not less than three hundred millions of dollars.*

Ten years since, there was made the great discovery of the Californian gold deposits — a discovery whose effect, we were then assured, was to be that of greatly reducing the rate of interest paid by those who labored to those others who were already rich. Have such results been thus far realized? Are not, on the contrary, our workingmen — our miners and manufacturers, our laborers and our settlers of the West — now paying *thrice* the price for the use of money that was paid at the date of the passage of the tariff act of

1846? Are not these latter, at this moment, paying three, four, five, and even as high as six percent per month? Are they not paying more *per month*, than is paid *per year* by the farmers of the protected countries of the European world? That they are so, is beyond a doubt. Why it is so is, that although we have received from California five hundred millions of gold, we have been compelled to export, in payment for foreign food in the form of iron and lead, cloths and silks, more than four hundred millions — leaving behind little more than has been required for consumption in the arts. Had we made our own iron and our own cloth, thus making a domestic market for the products of our farms, would not much of this gold have remained at home? Had it so remained, would not our little farmers find it easier to obtain the aid of capital at the rate of six percent *per annum*, than they now do at three, four, and five per cent *per month?* Would not their power of self-government be far greater than it is now, under a system that, as we see, makes the poor poorer, while the very rich grow richer every day? Reflect, I pray you, upon these questions and these facts, and then answer to yourself if the crises of which you speak are not the necessary results of an erroneous policy of which, during so long a period, you have been the steady advocate.

The history of the Union for the past half century may now briefly thus be stated: We have had three periods of protection, closing in 1817, 1834, and 1847, each and all of them leaving the country in a state of the highest prosperity — competition for the *purchase* of labor then growing daily and rapidly, with constant tendency towards increase in the amount of commerce, in the steadiness of the societary action, and in the freedom of the men who needed to sell their labor.

We have had three periods of that system which looks to the destruction of domestic commerce, and is called *free trade* — that system which prevails in Ireland and India, Portugal and Turkey, and is advocated by British journalists — each and all of them having led to crises such as you have so well described, to wit, in 1822, 1842, and 1857. In each and every case, they have left the country in a state of paralysis, similar to that which now exists. In all of them, the exchanges have become more and more languid, the societary movement has become more and more irregular, and the men who have needed to sell their labor have become more and more mere instruments in the hands of those who had food and clothing with which to purchase it.

All experience, abroad and at home, tends, thus, to prove that men become more free as the domestic commerce becomes more regular, and less and less free as it becomes more and more fitful and disturbed. Such being the case, the questions as to the causes of crises, and as to how they may be avoided, assume a new importance — one greatly exceeding, as I imagine, that which you felt disposed to attach to them when writing the passage which has above been given. To my apprehension, they are questions of liberty and slavery, and therefore it is that I feel disposed to invite you, as a friend of human freedom, to their discussion through the columns of your own journal, the *Evening Post* — that discussion to be carried on in the spirit of men who seek for truth, and not for victory. If you can satisfy me that I am in error as to either facts or deductions, I will at once admit it; and you, I feel assured, will do the same. As an inducement to such discussion, I now offer to have all your articles reprinted in protectionist journals, to the extent of 300,000 copies — thereby giving you not less than *a million and a half of readers*, among the most intelligent people of the Union. In return, I ask of you only, that you will publish my replies in your single journal, with its circulation of, as I am told, fifteen or twenty thousand. That this is offering great odds, you must admit.

It may, however, be said, that the replies might be such as would occupy too large a portion of your paper; and to meet that difficulty, I now stipulate that they shall not exceed the length of the articles to which answers are to be given — thus leaving you entire master of the space to be given to the discussion. Hoping to hear that you assent to this proposition, I remain, very respectfully,

Your obedient servant,

Henry C. Carey

Philadelphia, January 3, 1860

Dear Sir:

Allow me now to ask you why it is, that great speculations, followed by crises and by almost total paralyses, such as you have so

well described, *always* occur in free trade times, and *never* in periods
when the policy of the country is being directed toward the creation
of domestic markets, and toward the relief of our farmers from the
terrific taxes of trade and transportation to which they are now
subjected? That such are the facts, you can readily satisfy yourself
by looking back to the great speculations of the four periods of 1817,
1836, 1839, and 1856, followed by the crises of 1822, 1837, 1842,
and 1857 — and then comparing them with the remarkable
steadiness of movement which characterized those of the protective
tariffs of 1828 and 1842. Study our financial history as you may, you
will find in its every page new evidence of the soundness of the views
of Washington, Jefferson, and Hamilton, Adams, Madison, and
Monroe, each and all of whom had full belief in the accuracy of the
ideas so well enunciated by General Jackson, when he declared that
we "had been too long subject to the policy of British merchants" —
that it was "time we should become a little more *Americanized*" —
and that, if we continued longer the policy of feeding "the paupers
and laborers of England" in preference to our own, we should "all
be rendered paupers ourselves."

   Why is all this? Why must it be so? Why must, and that
inevitably, speculation, to be followed by crises, paralyses, and
daily-growing pauperism, be the invariable attendant upon the
policy which looks to the separation of the producer of raw products
from the consumer of the finished commodities into which rude
materials are converted? To obtain an answer to all these questions,
let us look again, for a moment, to the proceedings connected with
the printing and publication of the *Evening Post*. Dealing directly
with your paper-maker, you pay him cash, or give him notes, in
exchange for which he readily obtains the money — no artificial
credit having been created. Place yourself now, if you please, at a
distance of several thousand miles from the manufacturer, and
count the many hands through which your paper would have to pass
— each and every change giving occasion to the creation of notes
and bills, and to the charge of commissions and storage; and you
will, as I think, be disposed to arrive with me at the conclusion, that
the tendency toward the creation of artificial credits, and toward
speculation, grows with the growth of the power of the middleman to
tax the producers and consumers of the world.

Seeking further evidence of this, let me ask you to look at the circumstances which attend the sale of your products. Now, your customers being close at hand, you are paid in cash — your whole year's business not giving, as I suppose, occasion for the creation of a single note. Change your position, putting yourself in that of the Manchester manufacturers, at a distance of thousands of miles from your customers, compelled to deal with traders and transporters, and study the quantity of notes and bills, with their attendant charges, that would be created — the augmentation of price and diminution of consumption that would be the consequence — the power that would be accumulated in the hands of those who had money to invest, and desired to produce such crises as those which you have so well depicted — and you will, most assuredly, arrive at the conclusion that there is but one road toward steadiness and freedom, and that that road is to be found in the direction of measures having for their object the more close approximation of the producers and consumers of the products of the earth.

Studying next the great facts of our financial history, with a view to ascertain how far they are in accordance with the theory you may thus have formed, you will see that, in those prosperous years of the tariff of 1828, from 1830 to 1833, the quantity of bank notes in circulation was but 80 millions. No sooner, however, had we entered upon the free trade policy, providing for the gradual diminution and ultimate abolition of protection, than we find a rapid growth of speculation, consequent upon the growing power for the creation of artificial credits — the average circulation of the years from 1834 to 1837 having been no less than 149 millions, or nearly twice what it before had been. Under the protective tariff of 1842, the average was but 76 millions; but no sooner had protection been abandoned, than we find an increase so rapid as to have carried up the average from 1846 to 1849, to 113, and that of 1850 and 1851, to 143 millions. In that period speculation had largely grown, but prosperity had as much declined. When the circulation was small, domestic commerce was great — mines having been opened, furnaces and factories having been built, and labor having found its full reward. When, on the contrary, the circulation had become so great, mines were being closed and miners were being ruined — furnaces and factories were being sold by the sheriff, and our people were unemployed. In the one case, men were becoming more free, while in the other they were gradually losing the power to determine for themselves to whom they would sell their labor, or what should be its reward. In the one, there was a growing competition for the *purchase* of the laborer's services. In the other, there was increasing competition for their *sale*. Such having invariably been the case, can you, my dear sir, hesitate to believe, that the question to whose discussion I have invited you, *is not* one of the prices of cotton or woollen cloths, but *is*, really, that of man's progress toward that perfect freedom of action which we should all desire for ourselves and those around us, on the one hand, or his decline toward slavery, and its attendant barbarism, on the other? That, as it seems to me, you can scarcely do.

At no period in the history of the Union has competition for the *purchase* of labor, accompanied by growing tendency toward improvement in the condition of the laborer, been so universal or so great as in 1815, 1834, and 1847, the closing years of the several periods in which the policy of the country was directed toward the approximation of the producers and consumers of the country, by means of measures of protection. At none, has the competition for its *sale*, with corresponding decline in the laborer's condition, been so great as in the closing years of the free trade periods, to wit, from 1822 to 1824, and from 1840 to 1842.

Great as was the prosperity with which we closed the period which had commenced in this latter year, three short years of the tariff of 1846 sufficed for reproducing that competition for the *sale* of labor, relief from which had been the object of the men who made the tariff of 1842. From the decline with which we were then menaced, we were relieved by the discovery of the Californian mines, and by that alone. Since then, we have thence received more than five hundred millions of gold, and yet at no period has there existed a greater tendency to increase of competition for the *sale* of labor than at present — the two cities of New York and Philadelphia, alone, presenting to our view *hundreds of thousands of persons who are totally unable to exchange their services for the money with which to purchase food and clothing.* Is it not clear, from all these facts, that —

First, the nearer the place of consumption to the place of

---

production, the smaller must be the power of transporters and other middlemen to tax consumers and producers, and the greater must be the power of the men who labor to profit by the things produced?

Second, that the more close the approximation of consumers and producers, the smaller must be the power of the middlemen to create fictitious credits, to be used in the furtherance of their speculations?

Third, that the greater the power of the men who labor, and the larger their reward, the greater must be the tendency toward that steadiness in the societary action, in the perfection of which you yourself would find the proof of "infallible wisdom in those who conduct its operations"?

Fourth, that all the experiences of continental Europe, and all our own, tend to prove that steadiness is most found in those countries, and at those periods, in which the policy pursued is that protective one advocated in France by the great Colbert, and among ourselves by Washington, Franklin, Hamilton, Adams, Jefferson, and their successors, down to Jackson; and least in all of those in which the policy pursued is that advocated by the British school, which sees in cheap labor and cheap raw materials the surest road to wealth and power for the British trader?

Renewing my proposition to cause your answers to these questions to be republished to the extent of not less than 300,000 copies, I remain, my dear sir, with great respect,

Your obedient servant,
Henry C. Carey

Philadelphia, January 17, 1860

Dear Sir:

In one of his *Mount Vernon Papers*, Mr. Everett informs his readers, that —

"The distress of the year 1857 was produced by an enemy more formidable than hostile armies; by a pestilence more deadly than fever or plague; by a visitation more destructive than the frosts of Spring or the blights of Summer. I believe that it was caused by a mountain load of *Debt*. The whole country, individuals and communities, trading-houses, corporations, towns, cities, States were laboring under a weight of debt, beneath which the ordinary business relations of the country were at length arrested, and the great instrument usually employed for carrying them on, *Credit,* broken down."

This is all very true — a crisis consisting in the existence of heavy debts requiring to be paid by individuals, banks, and governments, at a time when *all* desire to be paid, and *few or none* are able to make the payments. That admitted, however, we are not, so far as I can see, much nearer than we were before to such explanation of the *causes* of crises, as is required for enabling us to determine upon the mode of preventing the recurrence of evils so frightful as are those you have so well described. Why is it, that our people are so much more burthened with debt than are their competitors in Europe? Why is it, that it so frequently occurs among ourselves that all need to be paid, and so few are able to pay? Why is it, that crises *always* occur in free-trade times? Why is it, that they *never* occur in protective times? Why is it, that it so frequently occurs that those who are rich are enabled to demand from the poor settlers of the West, as much *per month,* in the form of interest, as is paid *per year,* by the farmers of England, France, and Germany? These are great questions, to which Mr. Everett had furnished no reply. Let us have them answered, and we shall have made at least one step toward the removal of the evils under which our people so greatly suffer.

Let us try, my dear sir, if you and I cannot do that which Mr. Everett has failed to do — ascertaining the cause of the existence of so much debt, the constant preliminary to that absence of confidence which impels all to seek payment, while depriving so nearly all of their power to pay.

The commodity that you and I, and all of us, have to sell, is labor — human effort, physical or mental. It is the only one that perishes at the moment of production, and that, if not then put to use, is lost forever. The man who *does* put it to use, need not go in debt for the food and clothing required by his family; but he who *does not,* must either contract debt, or his family must suffer from want of nourishment. Such being the case, the necessity for the creation of debt should diminish with every increase in that competition for the *purchase* of labor, which tends to produce an *instant* demand for the forces, physical or mental, of each and every man in the community — such competition resulting from the existence of a power on the part of each and every other man to offer something valuable in exchange for it. On the contrary, it should increase with every increase in the competition for the *sale* of labor, resulting from the absence of demand for the human forces that are produced. In the one case, men are tending toward freedom, whereas, in the other, they are tending in the direction of slavery — the existence of almost universal debt being to be regarded as evidence of growing power, on the part of those who are already rich, to control the movements of those who need to live by the sale of labor.

Where, now, is debt most universal and most oppressive? For an answer to this question, let me beg that you will look to India, where, since the annihilation of her manufactures, the little proprietor has almost disappeared, to be replaced by the wretched tenant, who borrows at fifty, sixty, or a hundred percent, *per annum*, the little seed he can afford to use, and finds himself at last driven to rebellion by the continued exactions of the money-lenders and the government. Turn, next, to those parts of Russia where there are no manufactures, and find in the free-trade book of M. Tegoborski his statement of the fact, that where there is no diversification of pursuits the condition of the slave is preferable to that of the free laborer. Pass thence to Turkey — finding there an universality of debt that is nowhere else exceeded. Look, next to Mexico, and find the poor laborer, overwhelmed with debt, passing into servitude. Pass on to Ireland, and study the circumstances which preceded the expulsion, or starvation, in ten short years, of a million and a half of free white people — that expulsion having been followed by the passage of an Act of Parliament for expelling, in their turn, the owners of the land from which those laborers had gone. Look where you may, you will see that it is in those communities of the world which are most limited to the labors of the field, that debt is most universal, and that the condition of the people is most akin to slavery — and for the reason that there it is, that there is least competition for the *purchase* of labor. There, consequently, there is the greatest waste of the great commodity which all of us must sell, if we would have the means of purchase.

Turn, now, if you please, to Central and Northern Europe, and there you will find a wholly different picture — competition for the purchase of labor being there steadily on the increase, with constant augmentation of the rapidity of commerce — constant increase in the power to economize the great commodity of which I have spoken — and, as a necessary consequence, constant diminution in the necessity for the contraction of debt. Why should such remarkable differences exist? Because, in all of these latter countries, the whole policy of the country tends toward emancipation from the British free-trade system, whereas India, Ireland, Turkey, and Mexico, are becoming from day to day more subject to it.

Looking homeward, we may now, my dear sir, inquire when it has been, that the complaint of debt has been most severe. Has it not been in those awful years which followed the free-trade speculations of 1816-17? Has it not been in that terrific period which followed the free-trade speculations of 1837 to 1840 — that period in which a bankrupt law was forced from Congress, as the only means of enabling tens of thousands of industrious men to enter anew upon the business of life? Has it not been in the years of the present free-trade crisis, which present to view private failures of almost five hundred millions in amount? When, on the other hand, has there been least complaint? Has it not been in those tranquil years which followed the passage of the protective tariffs of 1828 and 1842? That it has been so, is certain. Why should it so have been? Because in protective times every man has found a purchaser for his labor and has been thereby relieved from all necessity for contracting debt; whereas, in free-trade times, a large portion of the labor power produced has remained unemployed, and its owners, *unable to sell their one commodity*, have been forced to choose between the contraction of debt on the one hand, or famine and death on the other.

Look next, my dear sir, to our public debt, and mark its extinction under the tariff of 1828 — its revival under the compromise tariff — its reduction under that of 1842 — and then study the present situation of a national treasury that, in time of perfect peace, is running in debt at the rate of little less than $20,000,000 a year!

Turn then, if you please, to our debt to foreigners, which was *annihilated* under the tariff of 1828 — swelled to hundreds of millions under the tariff of 1833 — and since so much enlarged, under the tarifffs of 1846 and 1857, that the enormous sum of $30,000,000 is now required for the payment of its annual interest.

France, with a population little larger than our own, and far less instructed, maintains an army of 600,000 men — carries on distant wars — builds magnificent roads — enlarges her marine and fortifies her ports — and does all these things with so much ease, that when the government has suddenly occasion for $100,000,000, the whole is supplied at home, and without an effort. Belgium and Germany follow in the same direction — not only making all their own roads, but contributing largely to the construction of those which are used for carrying out the rude products of our land, and bringing back the cloth, the paper, and the iron, that our own people, now unemployed, would gladly make at home. They are rapidly becoming the bankers of the world, for they live under systems even more protective than were those of our tariffs of 1828 and 1842. We, on the contrary, are rapidly becoming the great paupers of the world — creating seven, eight, and ten percent bonds, and then selling them at enormous discounts, to pay for iron so poor in quality that our rails depreciate at the rate of five, six, and even ten percent a year.

Looking at all these facts, is it not clear, my dear sir —

That the necessity for the contraction of debt exists, throughout the world, in the ratio of the adoption of the free-trade system of which you are the earnest advocate?

That the greater the necessity for the contraction of debt, the greater is the liability to the recurrence of commercial crises such as you have so well described?

That the more frequent the crises, the greater is the tendency toward the subjection of the laborer to the will of his employer, and toward the creation of slavery even where it has at present no existence? And, therefore —

That it is the bounden duty of every real lover of freedom to

labor for the re-establishment of the protective system among
ourselves?

At foot† is given, as you see, your notice of refusal to enter upon
the discussion to which you have been invited. For a reply thereto,
permit me, my dear sir, to refer you to the following exposition of
your own views in relation to free discussion, given by yourself, a few
days since, in the *Evening Post*:

> "Those Political Lectures. — As our readers know, a project has
> been under consideration to give a course of political lectures in this
> city during the present winter, and in which our prominent poli-
> ticians of all parties were to be invited to take a part. We now under-
> stand that the scheme has fallen through, mainly because no single
> Democrat could be found who was willing to ventilate his party
> opinions, and maintain them, in connection with a series of similar
> addresses by Republican, Radical, and American speakers. We are
> assured that of twenty Northern and Southern Democratic states-
> men, who have been invited, not one has accepted the invitation. It is
> proper to say that the signatures to the letter inviting speakers re-

---

† "Mr. Carey's Challenge. — Mr. Henry C. Carey, of Philadelphia, known
by various works on political economy, has challenged Mr. Bryant, one of
the editors of this paper, to a discussion, in the newspapers, of the question
of custom-house taxation. In behalf of Mr. Bryant, we would state that
challenges of this kind he neither gives nor accepts. It would almost seem
like affectation on his part to say that he has not read the letters — two in
number, he is told — in which this defiance is given on the part of Mr.
Carey, having, unfortunately, too little curiosity to see in what terms it is
expressed; but as such is the fact, it is well perhaps to mention it. His duties
as a journalist, and a commentator on the events of the day and the various
interesting questions which they suggest, leave him no time for a sparring-
match with Mr. Carey, to which the public, after a little while, would pay no
attention; and if he had ever so much time, and the public were ever so
much interested in what he had to say, he has no ambition to distinguish
himself as a public disputant. His business is to enforce what he considers
important political truths, and refute what seem to him errors, just as the
occasions arise, and to such extent as he imagines himself able to secure the
attention of those who read this journal, and he will not turn aside from this
course to tie himself down to a tedious dispute concerning the tariff question
at any man's invitation.

"The question of the tariff is not the principal controversy of the day. It
may seem so to Mr. Carey, who is suffering under a sort of monomania, but
the public mind is occupied just now with matters of graver import. To them

presented a number of our very foremost citizens, of all shades of politics. If a letter, so respectably signed as to guarantee every cour- tesy to all who took part in the course, failed to secure at least *one* speaker to uphold Democratic principles, we may safely suggest that the old *soubriquet* of the unterrified Democracy is a misnomer. We regret the failure of the proposed course of lectures, but are glad to know that many Republicans were willing to participate. Why cannot we have a few Republican speakers in an independent course?"

Obviously, these Democrats fear discussion. For years, they have been advocating doctrines that will not bear examination before the people. What, however, shall we say to the free-trade ad- vocates? Is there any one of *them* that would accept a proposition like to the one to which you have here referred? Would they even accept an offer that was so much better than this, that it would give them, of cool and reflecting readers, *five hundred times as many* as you could give to any Democrat, of mere auditors? Would Mr. Hal-

---

it is proper that a journalist should principally address himself, until they are disposed of. He may make occasional skirmishes in other fields of controversy, but here is the main battle. When the tariff question comes up again, it will be early enough to meet it; and even then, a journalist who understands his vocation would keep himself free to meet it in his own way.

"If Mr. Carey is anxious to call out some antagonist with whom to mea- sure weapons in a formal combat, and can find nobody who has an equal desire with himself to shine in controversy, we can recommend to him a person with whom he can tilt to his heart's content. One Henry C. Carey, of Philadelphia, published, some twenty years since, a work in three volumes, entitled 'Principles of Political Economy,' in which he showed, from the ex- perience of all the world, that the welfare of a country is dependent on its freedom of trade, and that, in proportion as its commerce is emancipated from the shackles of protection, and approaches absolute freedom, its people are active, thriving, and prosperous. We will put forward Henry C. Carey as the champion to do battle with Henry C. Carey. This gentleman who is now so full of fight, will have ample work on his hands in demolishing the positions of his adversary, with which he has the great advantage of being already perfectly familiar. When that is done, which will take three or four years at the least, inasmuch as both the disputants are voluminous writers, we would suggest that he give immediate notice to his associates, the owners of the Pennsylvania iron-mills, who will doubtless lose no time in erecting a cast-iron statue in honor of the victor."

lock, of the *Journal of Commerce,* accept the magnificent offer I have made to you, which, thus far, you have not accepted? Would it be accepted by Mr. Greene, of the Boston *Morning Post?* Will you accept it? If you will not, can you object to the course of the Democratic leaders to whom you have here referred? Scarcely so, as I think.

Hoping to hear that you have reconsidered the question, and have decided to accede to a proposition which will enable you to address to *a million and a half of readers,* all the arguments that can be adduced in support of free-trade doctrines, I remain, my dear sir,

Very truly and respectfully yours,

Henry C. Carey

How To Outdo England

This series of open letters to the Honorable Schuyler Colfax from Henry Carey was written just prior to the assassination of President Abraham Lincoln. On the whole, they are an argument for dirigist economic policy. It is not known, so one can only surmise that these letters were written at the request of Lincoln, in as much as Carey points out time and again in these letters that the Chief Executive was constantly forced to affix his signature on bills that he considered not in the national interest.

The letters polemicize against the anarchy that characterized the manner in which financial legislation was considered and carried out, and Carey argues for a national body under the control of the executive to plan national economic policy.

Lincoln used this debate to set up a Revenue Commission and appointed as its head a person presumed to be a Careyite — David Wells. The establishment of this body has been barely mentioned in most history books in spite of the fact that it held the key to the success or failure of the nation's industrial as well as postwar reconstruction policy.

As Carey argues, the best way to outdo England was for the United States to continue its rapid industrialization, to completely sever its currency from that of Great Britain [i.e., from the gold standard which backed the pound sterling], and to continue the policy of protective tariffs until the United States became strong enough to export its own technology and so destroy the British System world-wide.

Philadelphia, January 9, 1865

Dear Sir:

The preparation seems to have now been made for boring another hole through the protective system that has recently been so well established. This time it takes the form of a protest, of course in favor of the public revenue, against duties on spool cotton, under which, as we are told, "foreign spinners are now suffering in their attempts to contend against these heavy odds whereby importation is now stopped." Large exhibits are made therein of the quantity of gold that is thus prevented from passing into the treasury, but not a word is said in reference to the important fact, that, under the system which has thus far made us dependent on Britain for that important commodity, we have never yet been able to carry up our consumption even to the amount of six cents per head of our population. Selling cotton at three or four pence per pound we have been required to pay in gold, to the extent of millions of dollars per annum, for pennyweights of it combined with Russian and Egyptian corn, while the farmer of Iowa, unable to find a market for his grain, has found it expedient to convert it into fuel, and thus prevent its total waste. Here, as everywhere, we have been favoring the policy of slavery and barbarism, limiting our people to the raising of raw produce for the supply of distant masters, by whom they have been required to give the whole skin for a sixpence, receiving their pay in tails at a shilling. The answer to all that is now said in regard to the opening of the new rat-hole which is now proposed, is found in the words of the excellent article from the *Herald*, a part of which was appended to a former letter: "*If the price is very large and the demand is great, manufactories will spring abundantly into existence and prices will find their natural level.*" If the British manufacturers are really suffering in the manner above described, let them transfer themselves and their machinery here; let them bring their people with them to eat the food of Illinois and Iowa in place of that of Egypt; let them do this and the price of their commodity will soon be so far lessened that our consumption will rise to 20 cents per head; the Government will then receive, in the form of internal revenue, an amount far greater than these foreign agitators ever yet have paid at the custom-house; and we shall then have made a further step toward enabling ourselves to retain at home the gold that we ourselves shall so much need when the time shall have arrived for using the precious metals in the place of paper.

Having thus disposed of this new subject of agitation, the further examination of the great Iron Question comes now next in order.

To British free trade it is, as I have shown, that we stand indebted for the present civil war. Had our legislation been of the kind
which was needed for giving effect to the Declaration of Independence, that great hill region of the South, one of the richest, if not
absolutely the richest in the world, would long since have been filled
with furnaces and factories, the labourers in which would have been
free men, women, and children, white and black, and the several
portions of the Union would have been linked together by hooks of
steel that would have set at defiance every effort of the "wealthy
capitalists" of England for bringing about a separation. Such, however, and most unhappily, was not our course of operation.

Rebellion, therefore, came, bringing with it an almost entire
stoppage of the societary movement, with ruin to a large proportion
of those of the men engaged in producing coal and iron who had still
continued to exist notwithstanding the heavy losses inflicted upon
them in the sad five years which had just then elapsed. More than at
any previous period the Government stood then in need of iron in all
its shapes, from the needle with which the poor sewing woman
makes the shirt, to the great sheet required for plating the enormous
ship of war; and yet, such had been the extraordinary policy of the
country that, while fuel abounded rolling mills were idle and furnaces were out of blast, and the machinery for the needle and the
plate had not as yet been permitted to take its place at any single
point over our extensive surface. As a consequence, poor as was then
our Government, and unemployed as were then so large a portion of
our people, we were compelled to send abroad for millions upon
millions of dollars worth of the machinery of war, and there to encounter all the obstacles that could decently be thrown in our way by
men who prayed openly for the success of the rebellion, and who, almost at the instant of its first occurrence, had, by royal proclamation, placed the rebel Government on a level with that which
their predecessors had, in 1783, so unwillingly recognized. This
great adversity had, however, brought with it a remedy that, if now
properly applied, will cause our children and our children's children
to look back to the period of its occurrence as that in which there
had been an act of Providential interference in favor of a community
such as had had no precedent in the history of the world, prompting,
as it had done, men who for seventy years had wholly controlled the

action of the Government, to abdicate their seats and leave the direction of affairs to those who represented the poor and despised "mud-sills" of northern states. So great an act of insanity had never before been perpetrated by any body of intelligent men, and, most fortunately, its perpetration occurred at the moment when the public opinion of the North had been prepared to profit of it.

That preparation had come as a natural consequence of the terrific free trade crisis of 1857. Assembling in 1860, the politicians at Chicago accepted most unwillingly that new plank of the platform by which "protection to the farmer in his efforts for bringing the consumer to his side" was incorporated into the Republican creed; and great was their surprise when they found that public opinion, and especially the opinion of the great Mississippi Valley, had left them far behind. "We might have made it stronger," was the exclamation of one of its chief opponents after he had witnessed the enthusiastic applause with which it had been greeted. As yet, however, it could be nothing more than a declaration of good intentions to be carried into effect at some future time, the senatorial power appearing then likely long to remain in the hands of men who believed in human slavery as the corner-stone of all free government; in British free trade as the means by which slavery was to be perpetuated and extended throughout this continent; and in the "wealthy capitalists" of England, as the firm allies by whose aid their ambitious hopes were to be fully realized. To give practical effect to the new Declaration of Independence, it was necessary that those men should abdicate, and happily for the North, and for the world, abdication was not long delayed. Protection then at once became the law of the land, and under circumstances that should have tended to free forever the country from that agitation by means of which the British trader had so long controlled the societary movement, and had, with so much profit to himself, been enabled to fill the British treasury by means of taxes, direct and indirect, upon nearly all the foreign exchanges that our poverty had permitted us to make. Between skins at sixpence and tails at a shilling — cotton at cents per pound and cotton goods at shillings per ounce — corn at cents per bushel and wool and corn at dollars per pound — there was a large margin for the British trader and his superiors, and out of the taxes thus extorted have, to a large extent, the British nation and its government been supported by the people of the United States. Protection looked to the abolition of this taxation. That it has done much in that direction is proved by the great fact, that it has enabled us to contribute thousands of millions of dollars toward the suppression of the rebellion; that it has in so short a period given us a navy such as had been so long required for setting at naught the declaration that "not a flag but by permission spreads"; and that, notwithstanding all our vast expenditures, the productive power of the loyal States is greater at this moment than was that of the whole Union on the day on which, less than four years since, President Lincoln assumed the reins of government.

The need for iron soon became very great. Great, too, was the disposition of iron men to exert themselves for the supply of the wants the rebellion had now created. The Government had just then pledged itself to stand by them in their contest for the market of the world, at home and abroad, with the men who had so long controlled "that great instrument of warfare" by whose judicious use their predecessors had so generally been ruined. The pledge was accepted, and the results exhibit themselves in the facts:

I. That the production of pig-iron has already been carried up to more than 1,300,000 tons, and that it has been made certain that large as is the quantity, it can with ease, provided that the labor can be obtained, be trebeled in the next seven years;

II. That the rolling-mills of the country have now a capacity of nearly 700,000 tons, and that the only difficulty now standing in the way of the production of that quantity of sheet and bars is the one resulting from the scarcity of labor;

III. That the supply of railroad iron is now fully equal to the demand, and can be increased to any extent that may be required;

IV. That the conversion of iron into steel has been so much extended as to free us entirely from any further dependence on the "wealthy capitalists" of Britain;

V. That works required for the conversion of steel and iron into the various other machinery required for both public and private uses have been so extended as to enable their proprietors to meet the whole demand.

The industrial history of the world exhibits nothing at all comparable with what has here been done in regard to this great branch of manufacture. That it might be done every man who previously had been interested therein has been required to apply to the enlargement and improvement of his machinery not only every dollar that he could make, but in very many cases, all that he could borrow; and this they have done in the false confidence that consumers of iron had at last so far profited of past experience as to have become convinced that the way to have good and cheap iron was to be found in the direction of stimulating competition for its manufacture; and not in that of annihilating American competition for its *sale*, while promoting competition for its *purchase* from the very men who had always used their power in the direction of promoting agitation for the destruction of "foreign competition," and for enabling themselves to "gain and keep possession of foreign markets."

That it *was* a false confidence you will, my dear sir, see, after you shall have accompanied me in a brief review of the proceedings of iron consumers which it is proposed now to make. When you shall so have done, you will, as I think, agree with me that it would be difficult to find in the history of the world a case in which the proverb given in my last had been more thoroughly applicable than it now is in reference to the iron consumers of these United States. Often as they had been "brayed" in the British free trade "mortar," their "foolishness" had not departed from them.

By the tariff of 1861 the duty on railroad iron was fixed at $12 per ton of 2,240 pounds, being less than one-half of the charge upon it as established by the tariff of 1842 — that one under which iron generally was so cheaply furnished that the total consumption of the country was in four years carried up from 300,000 to 900,000 tons. It should have been placed at a higher rate than this, and so it would have been but for the exceedingly absurd and stupid jealousy which prompts so many persons to consider the iron manufacture the special property of Pennsylvania. Iron ore abounds in more than two-thirds of the States of the Union; fuel, too, almost as much abounding as the ore demanding to be smelted; and it is to the great credit of Pennsylvania that her ironmasters have never in a single instance allowed themselves to be influenced by the narrow idea, elsewhere openly expressed in regard to other branches of manufacture, that it was needed to "keep protection down, lest it might stimulate domestic competition." If there are any ironmasters in the country who can live without protection, they are those of that State. They are the men who have paid most dearly for their experience. To them the country is indebted for the fact that this great branch of manufacture, in nearly all its processes, is now ahead of Britain. They, however, know that Tennessee and Alabama, Missouri and Michigan, Virginia, Maryland, and Ohio, need protection; and they desire that they shall have it, quite assured that in the wise extension and general prosperity of the manufacture in which they are so well engaged will be found the key to that universal prosperity which enables men to extend their roads, to increase and improve their machinery, and to do all those things that make demand for iron and thus furnish proof conclusive of advancing civilization. Least in need of it, they stand foremost in the demand for efficient protection, asking it in the interest of the country at large, and not, as is in so many other cases done, exclusively in their own.

Accepting the rate of duty that had been fixed, they went promptly to work, and with the results that have been shown. The time came, however, when it became necessary to establish a system of Internal Revenue, and railroad iron was then subjected to a direct tax of $1.50 per ton, while upon coal and other commodities used in its production heavy duties were imposed. Incomes, too, were required to contribute, the general rate of contribution, by both the manufacture and the receiver of income, being fixed at *three* percent.

The war having thus produced a necessity for taxing both the materials of manufacture and its products, it was deemed proper to subject the foreign manufacturer to the payment of a like contribution, and duties generally were raised to the extent of *five* percent. To this, however, railroad iron was made an exception, the addition having been limited to the precise amount of the direct tax, $1.50 per ton, and no allowance whatever having been made for the taxes on coal, lime, machinery, or incomes. Such, my dear sir, was the paltry spirit in which were met the men who were at the moment, in their efforts to meet the wants of the Government, manifesting a larger liberality than any other body of men that could have been produced in the whole extent of the Union.

The necessity for further revenue becoming obvious, the last session of Congress gave us a new excise law by means of which pig metal was for the first time subjected to a tax, and that to the extent of two dollars per ton, the tax on coal being at the same time largely increased, and that on rails more than doubled, the general effect being that of giving a tax on the rail itself amounting to seven dollars per ton.

To this must now be added taxes on lime and other raw materials — taxes on machinery to a large amount — income taxes — taxes on licenses — taxes on sales — taxes on freight — taxes on leases — taxes on salaries — taxes on charters, notes of hand, and articles of agreement — the whole of which, when added to the $7 already obtained, will give at least $8.50 as the contribution in these several forms to be paid by each ton of railroad bars. — Adding now to this the large increase, consequent upon the existence of the war, of state, county, township, and borough taxes — the contributions for obtaining volunteers and for maintaining their families, it will be found that the amount, under this new law, furnished by each ton of bars, for the maintenance of the contest, cannot be estimated at less than $10.

Having thus shown what was the pressure brought by the Government to bear upon the men who were giving all their time, mind, and means to building up that great manufacture on which now rests the whole of our great societary machine, *and upon whose success or failure is dependent the whole future of this Union,* I propose in my next to show what were the measures at the same time adopted by the Government for enabling them successfully to compete with those "wealthy English capitalists" who were then giving all their time, mind, and means to the work of vilifying our people, destroying our credit, breaking our blockades, destroying our ships, and in every other way aiding a rebellion whose success, as they saw, could have no other result than that of reducing the country to a state of complete dependence.

It is with great regret, my dear sir, that I make so many demands upon your time and attention, but the question now to be settled is one of so great importance that you will, I am sure, excuse me. When the present war shall have been closed there will be another to be fought, and that one will be with England. By many it is desired that it may be a war of cannon balls; but it is not now with such machinery that she chiefly seeks to fight us. It is in the Halls of Congress she is to be met, and the machinery with which we have successfully to meet her is to be found in the adoption of those measures which shall enable us most speedily to profit of that inexhaustible store of fuel and of ores that nature has placed at our command. So believing, and hoping that all my countrymen may soon be led to the conclusion that there really is a way to *outdo England without fighting her*, I am, with great regard and respect,

Yours, very truly,
Henry C. Carey

Philadelphia, February 18, 1865
Dear Sir:
The measures now in preparation, as regards both the customs and internal revenues, tend, as it appears to me, in the direction of stoppage of the societary circulation, of rise in the rate of interest, of increase in the power of men engaged in the creation of financial water-spouts, and of permanent maintenance of a premium on the precious metals. If so, then, if we are ever again to witness here the regular redemption of promises to furnish gold and silver, it must occur as a consequence of the adoption of a course of policy directly the reverse of all that recently has been done, and all that, if we are to credit the public journals, is in the contemplation of those who are charged with the direction of our financial movements.

The existing derangement of the currency is wholly due to the action of those who manage *the windbag system* described in a former letter, and while their operations shall continue to be, as now they are, wholly unrestrained, financial crises must continue to reappear, and the price of gold must continue to be as uncertain as is their course of action. Such being the case, it is of high importance that proper checks be forthwith instituted, and now, for the first time in our history, is it in the power of Congress to let us have them. To that end, let us have a law declaring —

First, that no bank shall hereafter so extend its investments as to hold in any form other than those of gold, silver, U.S. notes, or notes of national banks, more than twice its capital:

Second, that in the case of already existing banks whose investments are outside of the limits above described, any extension thereof beyond the amount at which they stood on the first of the present month shall be followed by instant forfeiture of its charter.

Having thus established a check upon further extension, the next step should be in the direction of bringing the operations of existing banks within proper limits. To that end, let us have a provision imposing on all investments outside of the limits above described a tax which, when added to that already existing, shall amount for the present year to one percent. In the second year let it be made 1.25 percent on all over 90 percent in excess of the actual capital upon which dividends are paid. In the third, 1.5 percent over 80 percent; and in the fourth, 1.75 over 70 percent. Thenceforth let the tax grow at the rate of a quarter percent per annum until, by degrees, all banks shall have so enlarged their capitals, or so reduced their loans, as to free themselves from its further pament.

Holding interest-paying securities 70 percent in excess of its capital, a bank would be always in a condition of perfect safety, and could give to its stockholders dividends of at least 8 percent. Such stock would be preferable to almost any other securities in the market, and there would be no difficulty in so enlarging the foundation as to give to the whole structure the form of a true pyramid, instead of the inverted one which now presents itself to the eye of all observers.

Let us have a law embracing these provisions, and we shall then be fairly on the way toward the establishment of a financial system the most perfect the world has ever seen. Let us have it, and, as you will clearly see, the need for restrictions on the circulation will wholly have passed away. The day, indeed, will then be near at hand when banks will have ceased to be competitors with the Treasury for furnishing circulating notes of any kind, and when the nation may profit to the extent of 50, if not even 60 millions a year of the power to furnish the machinery of circulation.

Simultaneously with the passage of such a law, let the Government determine honestly to pay its debts. The soldier in the field, and the officer who is placing his life in daily hazard, have a right to demand of the Treasury that it shall give them such certificates of its indebtedness as will enable their wives and children to go to the neighborhood shop and purchase food and clothing.† The contractor and the shipbuilder have a right to claim that when certificates are issued they shall be in such a form as will enable them to avoid the further payment of the usurious interest to which they have so long been subjected. Paying promptly, the Government will buy cheaply; and should such payment have the effect of causing the supply of "greenbacks" to be in excess of the demand, the Treasury will thence derive a double benefit: first, in being thus enabled to borrow what it needs at reasonable rates; and second, in having its needs for borrowing diminished by reason of the increased stimulus thereby given to that societary circulation upon the rapidity of which it is dependent for both the maintenance and the growth of the Internal Revenue.

The whole South now requires reorganization, and one of the first steps in that direction should be found in furnishing machinery of circulation. As much in need of this stands the whole of that great West for the development of whose wonderful powers we are now exporting in that direction so many hundreds of thousands of our people. If the Government does not supply that machinery, who is there that can or will do so? Look carefully, I pray you, my dear sir, at the vast field that is to be occupied, and at the great work that is to be done, and then wonder with me that the Government should permit its soldiers to perish in the field, while it is debating the terms of a loan to be made to it by men all of whose interests are to be promoted by a diminution of the circulation and an increase of the rate of interest. Let our soldiers be paid, let the credit of the Government be once again reestablished, let the rate of interest be kept down, and let the Treasury reassert its independence, and all will yet go well.

Having thus, as paymaster, reestablished its credit, let it next place itself in a creditable position as regards those who had been led to see in the Morrill Tariff a pledge of protection against those "wealthy capitalists" whose fortunes count by millions, and who use those millions as "instruments of warfare" by means of which they are enabled to "overwhelm all foreign competition, and to gain and

---

† The amount now due to the army alone is stated by Senator Wilson at the enormous sum of one hundred and thirty-eight millions of dollars.

keep possession of foreign markets." Let it restore those great fundamental branches of industry which constitute the pillars of our national temple to the position in which they stood in 1861, increasing the duties on foreign products by just so much as the taxes since imposed on domestic ones, and the result will then exhibit itself in the fact that sugar, tea, coffee, soda ash, and other raw materials of food and manufacture, will twice over make amends for any loss that may be experienced by the revenue because of the substitution of domestic cloth or iron for that now made in foreign furnaces or on foreign looms.

Let these things be done, and we shall then cease to look abroad for purchasers of our bonds. Let this be done, and we shall soon find ourselves on the road toward becoming purchasers of those now held abroad, *every one of which should be redeemed before we ever again place ourselves in a position to be required to furnish gold and silver in payment of our notes.*

To many it might seem that this would be a postponement of resumption to a date so distant that none of them would live to see it. Let, however, all such persons study what was done in this respect in the brief period of the existence of the tariffs of 1828 and 1842; let them next look to what has been done in the past four years; and they will see that all that I have indicated as what is needed to be done, is only what, under a sound and permanent system, *may be done before the lapse of the next decade.*

As a rule, reformers desire to move too rapidly, and therefore fail to attain their objects. They omit to see that when Nature has important purposes to accomplish, she works slowly and with almost invisible machinery, as when she sends the daily morning dew. When she desires merely to destroy a ship or to root up a forest, she sends the tornado or the water-spout. Let us follow her example. We have a great work to accomplish, and we should now profit of the lesson read to the world in that period which followed the close of the great war of the French Revolution, and exhibited a scene of destruction that had never before, in time of peace, been witnessed. Believing it to be one that should be carefully studied, I now invite you, my dear sir, to accompany me in a brief review of the facts in the order of their occurrence.

For twenty years the Bank of England had been injecting gas

into the currency, but with the return of peace it became necessary that it should be steadily withdrawn. In the two years from 1815 to 1817, the bank directors had, by means of the very simple operation of calling in its claims on the one hand, and reducing its liabilities on the other, reduced the apparent quantity of money at the command of the community to the extent of £ 12,000,000, or little short of $60,000,000. So far as regarded the operations of society, this had been equivalent to a total annihilation of that large sum, and to that extent a contraction of the standard by which the community was required to measure the value of all other commodities and things. Had the yardstick been doubled in length, or the pound in weight, for the benefit of all persons who had contracted to purchase cloth or corn, the injury inflicted would have been trivial by comparison with the change that was thus effected. As compared with the property of the people of Great Britain, that sum was utterly insignificant, yet did its abstraction cause an arrest of the circulation almost as complete as would be that produced in the physical body by stoppage of the supply of food. Farmers and merchants were everywhere ruined. Of the country banks, no less than two hundred and forty — being one in four of their whole number — stopped payment; while one in ten and a half became actually bankrupt. "Thousands upon thousands," says Mr. McCulloch, "who had in 1812 considered themselves affluent, found they were destitute of all real property, and sunk; as if by enchantment, and without any fault of their own, into the abyss of poverty." Throughout the country, there was, to use the words of Mr. Francis Horner, "an universality of wretchedness and misery which had never been equalled, except perhaps by the breaking up of the Mississippi Scheme in France." *In the midst of all this ruin, however, the bank, which had supplied the gas, prospered more than ever, for the destruction of private credit rendered its vaults and its notes more necessary to the community.*

The groundwork having thus been laid by the bank. Parliament passed, in 1819, an act providing for the resumption of specie payments, and thus reestablished, as the law of the land, the standard that had existed in 1797 — among the most remarkable measures of confiscation to be found in the annals of legislation. For more than twenty years all the transactions of the United Kingdom had been based upon a currency less in value than that which had existed in 1796. In the course of that long period, land had been sold, mortgages given, settlements made, and other contracts of a permanent nature entered into, to the extent of thousands of millions of pounds, the terms of all of which were now to be changed for the benefit of the receivers of fixed incomes, and to the loss of those who had land, labor, or the produce of either, to sell. As a necessary consequence, land fell exceedingly in price, and mortgages everywhere entered into possession. Labor became superabundant, and the laborer suffered for want of food. Machinery of every kind was thrown out of use, and manufacturers were ruined. Manufacturers, being in excess of the demand, were forced upon foreign markets, to the ruin of the capitalists and workmen, miners and machinists, of the other countries of the world.

Peace had brought with it widespread ruin, but it everywhere enriched the money-lender — *his* commodity rising, while land became so cheap that he could purchase at less than half its previous price. The annuitant and office-holder profited — their dividends and salaries having become payable in coin, that would purchase double the quantity of food and clothing for which they had at first contracted. Farmers and laborers, mechanics and merchants, were impoverished — their taxes remaining unchanged, while their labor, and its products, commanded less than half the money for which they would before have sold.

Bad as is this, it will be *infinitely* worse with us if we shall attempt to follow the example here placed before us. Let us put our house in order; let us adopt the measures needed for making the Declaration of Independence something more than a mere word of small significance; let us do all this slowly and quietly, and we shall set to the world an example in peace even more remarkable than that which has been set in the course of the present extraordinary war — returning to the old standard, and without the occurrence of the slightest crisis.

That this may be done, it is needed only that those who direct our fiscal operations shall recollect that the National Treasury has now become a partner in, and entitled to the lion's share of, the profits of every mine, every furnace, every mill, every workshop, and every farm in the land, and that every increase in the prosperity of such works must be to it a source of double profit: first, that arising out of the direct contributions of the work itself; and second, that resulting from the increased consumption of sugar, tea, coffee, and other commodities consumed by those who mine the coal, roll the iron, and make the engines and the cloth. The day for a clear perception of the existence of this harmony of all real interests may or may not be near at hand. For the promotion of its arrival, we need to see extended throughout the Union the same principle of association that has proved to be so effective throughout the present war. We need to see *a great national league*, embracing men who grow wool, and others who convert it into cloth; men who make iron, and others who need railroad bars; men who raise food, and others who combine food and ore into iron; men who build ships, and others who consume the sugar and the tea that ships transport; and finally, men who pay taxes, and others who make the laws under which those taxes are collected. In the words of Jackson, we need to be *Americanized*. Whenever the day shall arrive when we shall have so become, then, and not till then, shall we have placed ourselves in a position successfully to contend for the control of the commerce of the world, and thus to

Outdo England Without Fighting Her.

That control will find its place among the hands and heads of the community that makes and uses the largest quantity of iron. A single decade of the system above described would suffice for placing us, in this respect, side by side with England. At the close of another, she would be left far behind, and we should then have vindicated our claim to that position in the world of which our people so often talk, and of the true means of obtaining which they so little think.

Hoping that the event may prove that the time for serious thought has now really arrived, and begging you to excuse my numerous trespasses on your attention, I remain, my dear sir, with great regard and respect,

Yours, faithfully,
Henry C. Carey

Open Letters to Hugh McCulloch

These open letters from Henry Carey to the Secretary of the Treasury Hugh McCulloch attacked his policy of contracting the Greenback currency and returning the country to the British gold standard. That policy, argued Carey, would inevitably lead to a new depression. The letters' effect was to push the U.S. Congress to put an end to the Secretary's power to reduce the currency supply, giving to U.S. iron manufacturers the time needed to complete their conversion to the new Bessemer steel-making process. A selection of these letters follows.

Philadelphia, January 28, 1866

Dear Sir:

Fully agreeing with you, as I do, in regard to many most important questions of public policy, it is with great regret that I find myself so wholly differing in reference to the existence of that "plethora of paper money" of which you speak, and to which you now attribute the "large importation of foreign fabrics"; the "splendid fortunes realized by skillful manipulations at the gold room or stock board"; the "rise in the prices of the necessaries of life"; the increase in the number of "nonproducers"; and the most important fact that "productive industry is being diminished."

That this, to a considerable extent, is an accurate exhibit of the actual state of affairs I am not at all disposed to doubt, but were I even to admit of its perfect accuracy the questions still remain: Why are such the facts? Why is it that men are now unemployed who but a twelve month since were so fully occupied? Why is it that our foreign debt so steadily increases? To these questions you furnish one general answer, that "paper money" is too abundant; and that if we should bring about a more healthy state of things its quantity must be diminished. I, on the contrary, hold that no such "plethora" exists, and that the real cause of all this error must be sought for in a direction precisely opposite, there to be found in measures of contraction with which the country has been threatened; and fully do I believe that if we would bring about a more healthy condition of affairs it is required that we move in a direction exactly the reverse of that which you so recently have indicated.

Differing thus widely, one of us must be much in error. It may be that I am wrong, but until I can look at the facts in a manner very different from that in which they now present themselves to my mind, I must continue to believe that I am right. The error may, possibly, my dear sir, be with yourself, and if it can be shown that such is the case, you will, I am sure, rejoice at being so convinced. So believing, I propose, with a view to the determination of the question whether such "plethora" does or does not exist, to furnish here a comparison of the actual circulation of the three chief commercial countries of the world, France, Great Britain, and the United States; of the needs for such circulation; and of their power profitably to use it. Should the result of such comparison be that of proving that not only is our medium of circulation not in excess in its relation to population and production, but that it is greatly short in the proportion which it bears to both, then, as I most respectfully submit, will it be necessary to look in a direction opposite to that of "plethora of paper money" for the cause of error, and there, on further examination, perhaps it may be found.

Seven years since the coin in use in France was estimated at 4,880,000,000 francs, or more than $900,000,000. Since then the quantity must have increased, the substitution of the convenient gold for the heavy and cumbrous silver coins that even then were still so generally in use having, as has been stated by a recent writer, had the effect of placing napoleons in pockets that before could carry only francs. Admitting, however, that the increase has been sufficient only to add to the coin in the hands of the public as much as before had been in the bank vaults, we have a hard money circulation of .... $900,000,000†

To which must now be added the "paper money" circulation, which may be taken at about   170,000,000‡

---

† From 1850 to 1865, the importations of the precious metals were in excess of the exportations to the extent of $334,000,000. The quantity held in 1852 was estimated by M. du Puynode at 3,500,000,000 (francs — ed.), or nearly $700,000,000.

‡ The amount in 1853 was only 395,000,000 francs. From that time it had grown with great steadiness until, in 1862, it had attained the figure of 869,000,000. In 1864, it was 804,000,000.

Giving a grand total of $1,070,000,000
Or nearly $30 per head.

The coin actually in use in Great Britain and Ireland was estimated a few years since at £60,000,000. Since then it must greatly
have increased, but, claiming no allowance on that account, I put it
here at the same figure, being the equivalent of only $300,000,000

The "paper money" circulation of the past few
years has varied between 37½ and 42½ millions.
Taking the means of these quantities we have the
equivalent of about   200,000,000

To this must now be added a paper circulation
of a character little known in this country, and
consisting of promises of individuals, in the form of
bills of exchange, to deliver money at a future day.
Of these, large quantities are in constant circulation, returning finally to their payers covered with
endorsements, sometimes 15, 20, and even more
in number, and having throughout the whole period of their existence performed all the service
that here is performed by bank notes. The whole
quantity of bills of exchange outstanding at any
given time was estimated, some years since, at
  200,000,000, and must now be greatly larger.
Allowing here but one-fifth of that sum to be used
for purposes of circulation, we have the equivalent
of   200,000,000

Giving a grand total of $700,000,000
Or but little less than $25 per head.

The actual circulation of the Union, as just now furnished by
the Comptroller, we know to be $460,000,000, being $12.50 per
head, or one-half that of Great Britain and Ireland.† Compared

---

† The amount of national bank notes in actual circulation on the 1st day of October was $171,321,903
The amount of State bank notes in circulation at the
same date, as appears by returns to the Commissioner of
Internal Revenue, was   78,867,575

Making the bank circulation of the 1st day of October
last   250,189,378

with that of France it stands in the ratio of but 5 to 12; and yet, for various reasons, we should be entitled to expect to find it bearing to population a larger proportion than in either one of those countries. Among the reasons are the following:

First. To pay any given number of mechanics or laborers required, before the war, more than twice the quantity of circulation

The amount of legal-tender notes and fractional currency issued and outstanding on the 1st of October was	704,584,658
National bank notes in the hands of banks not yet issued	19,525,152
National currency yet to be issued to banks	109,152,945
Making the aggregate amount of legal tender and bank notes in circulation as authorized to be issued to and by the banks	1,083,452,233
From which sum should be deducted, State bank circulation now outstanding that will be retired about as fast as national currency is issued to converted banks $78,867,575	
Also the amount of "compound interest notes" converted into 5-20 bonds since the 1st of October last 44,417,329	
	123,284,904
The amount then left as the available currency of the country is	960,167,326
In order to ascertain the amount of actual active circulation on the 1st day of October last, there should be deducted from the last mentioned sum —	
The amount of national currency delivered to banks, and not then in circulation $19,525,152	
National circulation not delivered to banks 109,152,945	
Amount of legal-tender notes held by banks, including $74,261,847 compound interest notes 193,094,365	
Compound interest notes, other than those held as investments by insurance and trust companies and savings banks, less say $10,000,000 in actual circulation 121,314,195	
Currency in the Treasury of the United States 56,236,440	
Total	499,323,097
Which will show the actual circulation to be	$460,844,229

This favorable exhibit of the amount of paper in actual circulation, is owing in a great degree to the accumulation of currency in the hands of the banks, in the absence of great demands of the government for currency since the close of the war. — *Report of the Comptroller of the Currency.*

that would have been needed in France; and one-half more than would have been required in Great Britain. The war having been accompanied by the establishment of a National Free Trade System there came a greatly increased demand for laborers with so large an increase of wages that the quantity of circulation now required for paying any given number of hands must be taken at twice that needed by the latter and thrice that required by the former.

Second. The proportion borne by circulation to numbers tends rapidly to increase as population becomes more widely scattered, and as rapidly to diminish as men are enabled to come more near together. That this is so, is shown in the fact that thousands of millions of exchanges are weekly performed in New York and other great commercial cities without the necessity for using a single note; whereas, among a scattered people like our own, every exchange, large or small, necessitates the delivery of a given quantity of coin or "paper money." Such being the case, the 36,000,000 of our people, dispersed over a territory eight times more extensive than that occupied by the 37,000,000 of France, and twelve times greater than that of the United Kingdom, might fairly be expected to demand a circulation, per head, thrice greater than that of either of those countries; and yet, as has been shown, it is but half as great as that in use in the one, and much less than half that employed by the other. Is it then, my dear sir, to be believed that there is among us, really, any of that "plethora" of which you have spoken? As it seems to me did we need to find one it would be beyond the ocean that we should seek it.

The grand error that, as it seems to me, we are accustomed to commit, is that which results from limiting ourselves to a comparison of the various periods of our own financial history, leaving wholly out of view the facts furnished by the history of other commercial nations. Thus, in the comparative view of our circulation given in your report it is shown that it grew from $60,000,000 in 1830 to $140,000,000 in 1836; and from $58,000,000 in 1843 to $207,000,000 in 1860; but those facts are not supplied by means of which your readers might be enabled to judge as to whether or not even the largest of these figures was in excess of the absolute wants of the community — whether it did, or did not, indicate the existence of any "plethora of paper money." That it did not do so has seemed to me, and must now, as I think, appear to you, to be very certain. On the contrary, when compared with other commercial countries it furnishes conclusive evidence that the supply of the medium of circulation had always been deficient, and thus enables us to understand more accurately the real cause of the extraordinary activity of the societary circulation which prevailed throughout the war, and to which our people have been indebted for power to give to the government the thousands of millions of dollars required for enabling it to dictate the terms of peace.

Of all the phenomena exhibited during the wonderful war in which we have been engaged, among the most extraordinary are those connected with the transportation of vast armies and all the vast supplies by them required, throughout a country of such vast extent, and over roads scarcely any portion of which south of the Delaware could boast of more than a single track, that, too, supplied with rails of the poorest kind. Never in the world, even under circumstances far more favorable, has such an amount of transportation been effected — never so large an amount of public work so well accomplished. Precisely so has it been, and now is, with the machinery by means of which circulation is effected from hand to hand, no country having ever yet performed so large an amount of exchanges by means of a medium of exchange the supply of which was so utterly disproportioned to the amount of production, to the quantity of exchanges needed to be made, or to the number of people empowered to make them. So far from "plethora" having either then or at any previous time existed, the financial history of the Union presents an uninterrupted series of figures the study of which is calculated to excite surprise that so much has always been done when the supply of machinery by means of which alone it could be done, has throughout our whole experience been so deficient. No other people, with such means, could so well have effected the transportation of the war; no other could, with such a supply of the medium of exchange, have so well effected the exchanges of both war and peace.

Proposing in another letter to examine into the influence of "paper money" on the action of the past five years, I remain, meanwhile, with great respect and regard,

Yours very truly,
Henry C. Carey

Philadelphia, February 3, 1866

Dear Sir:

Before proceeding to inquire into the changes of price so generally attributed to that "plethora of paper-money" of which you have spoken, it may be well to determine what, precisely, they recently have been. To that end, I give you here the actual prices of the New York market, as just now furnished by the *Merchants' Magazine,* for the closing week of the year which preceded the joint inauguration of Mr. Lincoln and of a national free trade policy, and for the corresponding week of the several years that since have passed, as follows:

	1800	1861	1862	1863	1864	1865
Ashes	$5.00	$6.25	$8.50	$8.50	$11.75	$9.00
Flour, State	5.35	5.50	6.05	7.00	10.00	8.75
Wheat, red	1.38	1.42	1.48	1.57	2.45	2.05
Corn	.72	.64	.82	1.30	1.90	.95
Hay	.90	.77	.85	1.45	1.55	.75
Hops	.25	.20	.23	.33	.40	.50
Hemlock leather	.30	.20	.27	.30	.42	.36
Lime	.75	.65	.85	1.30	1.15	1.10
Pork, old mess	16.00	12.00	14.50	19.50	43.00	28.50
Beef, city mess	6.00	5.50	12.00	14.00	20.50	20.00
Hams	.08	.06	.08	.11	.20	.16
Lard	.10	.08	.10	.13	123	.19
Butter	.18	.19	.22	.29	.55	.48
Cheese	.10	.07	.12	.15	.20	.18
Tallow	.10	.10	.10	.12	.18	.14
	$37.21	$33.62	$46.17	$56.05	$94.48	$73.11

From this list have been excluded cotton and naval stores, both of which, during the blockade, were so very high and have since so greatly fallen. For special reasons, however, many of these very articles might with equal propriety have been omitted. Of wheat, for instance, the crop of the last year was less by 12,000,000 bushels than that of 1864, that itself having been less by 16,000,000 than had been the one of 1863. This, of course, largely affects the present prices of both wheat and wheaten flour. Butter and cheese are higher than they would otherwise be, because of the very considerable diminution in the number of cows exhibited in the recent Report of the Commissioner of Agriculture. A corresponding diminution in the number of cattle generally, coupled with the existence of a cattle plague throughout a large portion of Europe, accounts for an increase in the prices of both beef and pork.† Allowing for all these circumstances, I would now, my dear sir, most respectfully beg you to reflect on the answers that might properly be given to the following questions, to wit:

First. Comparing present prices with those which ruled before the war, is there here exhibited any increase that might not have taken place had there been no change whatsoever in the circulation?

Second. Making the same comparison, and allowing for the fact that from the increased prices of 1865 is to be deducted the increased rate of freight, most of which has been rendered necessary by the heavy taxation of coal, iron, cars, engines, receipts, dividends, etc., etc. would the western farmer, except for the accidental circumstance of a deficient supply of wheat occurring simultaneously with the existence of a cattle plague abroad, receive today even as much in paper as he had before in gold?

Third. Leaving wholly out of view, with the single exception of a cattle plague occurring simultaneously with a diminution in our own supply of cattle, all of the circumstances above referred to, would there, in the prices current, now be found as great a change for the better as we should have been warranted in expecting from the creation of that great internal commerce which had resulted from the adoption, in 1861, of a policy having for its object the bringing together of the producer and the consumer, to the great advantage of both?

Fourth. Is there to be found in the above exhibit any evidence that the farmer now profits of the events of the past few years even to such extent as is absolutely required for enabling him to continue payment of the heavy taxes, local and national, now imposed?

Fifth. Must not any attempt at further forcing down prices, with a view to compelling export of our products in exchange for gold, be followed by inability to pay the taxes and by financial and political ruin?

---

†So much has the demand for beef exceed the supply, that, notwithstanding large imports from Canada, the number of cattle and oxen reported by the Commissioner of Agriculture is now nearly a million less than it was six years since.

Sixth. Do not all the facts above given show clearly, that what we really need is such a stimulation of the societary circulation as would cause that increased demand for all the products of the farm which would maintain their prices and diminish the necessity for employing our people in that which is the proper work of the barbarian and the slave, and of them alone, to wit, that of raising raw products for the supply of distant markets?

Throughout the period of Mr. Lincoln's administration that circulation was active to an extent never before known in any country of the world, and to that activity, as has been shown, have we been indebted for power successfully to prosecute the war. How we have been indebted to increase in the supply of the medium of circulation for promoting that activity, and thus enabling us to supply the thousands of millions rendered necessary by the war, has been also shown. What have been the precise facts connected with the change of prices above exhibited I propose, in my next, to show, and have now to ask for them your careful consideration. Meanwhile, my dear sir, permit me here to say a word or two in regard to my own position. Throughout the war I have been a heavy sufferer under the legal-tender system, having been, as I still am, compelled to accept paper in place of the gold that honestly was due me, and to pay double or treble price for almost everything I required to purchase. My *apparent* interests are, therefore, all on the side of an early return to specie as the standard, but well do I know that my *real* interests are so closely bound up with those of my neighbors that what must be bad for them cannot be good for

Yours truly and respectfully,

Henry C. Carey

Philadelphia, February 17, 1866

Dear Sir:

Influential Republican journals, by many supposed to represent the views of the Administration, are proving daily to the men of intelligence and enterprise — those "speculators" who have created the mills, furnaces, and mines to which we have stood indebted for power to make the war — that not only must they no longer rely upon the cooperation of the national authorities, but that they may count securely upon their opposition or oppression.

Appealing constantly to the ignorance, but never to the intelligence, of their readers, they denounce such men as belonging to a class whose ruin should afford just cause of triumph to all who in the past few years have sought to aid their country's cause.

Crippling those who had commenced the creation of new mills and furnaces, they have already closed many of those that had been throughout the war at work, and are now most effectually preventing the undertaking of any new enterprises tending towards development of our mineral wealth, or towards increase of our industrial forces.

Therefore is it:

That we are largely and rapidly diminishing the demand for human service, and lessening the power of the laborer, the mechanic, and the miner to claim reward for labor; this too being done at the very time when thousands and tens of thousands of ablebodied men have been, and are being discharged from the public service; the very time, too, when active and earnest men are engaged in an effort to draw from Europe the supplies of men required for enabling us to develop our vast resources:

That we are lessening the demand upon the farmer for the fruits of the earth, and compelling him to increased dependence on foreign markets:

That there is a decline in the power of our people to maintain with Britain that competition for the production and sale of cloth and iron to which alone can we look for such reduction of their prices as may compensate the farmer for the burthens of the war:

That, while reducing the prices of food and labor, we are largely and rapidly raising the general rate of interest, thereby enabling those who *do not* work to profit at the cost of those who *do*:

That we are making taxation more and more burthensome while lowering the rate of exchange to the great advantage of those who prefer to expend their incomes abroad rather than do the same at home:

That we are thus daily making it more impossible that our mills and furnaces should supply the domestic market; that those who "live at ease" should apply their means to the advantage of those who labor; that ships should be built to enter into competition with those of Europe; that we should in time of peace extend, or even maintain, that independence to which we have been indebted for recent success in war.

As consequences of all this, we are —

Supporting abroad, at an estimated annual cost of $100,000,000, a hundred thousand of our people engaged in consuming foreign food and paying for foreign labor:

Enabling foreigners to deluge our markets with cloth and iron in the production of which have been consumed hundreds of millions of bushels of foreign food:

Maintaining those foreigners in a monopoly of the carrying trade between this and Europe, and thus compelling our own people to the exclusive use of ships that represent both foreign labor and foreign food:

Increasing in every manner that can be devised the demand for the capital and the skill of Europe while destroying demand for the wonderful mechanical skill of people at home:

Raising the prices of all the things we need to buy, money included, while lowering those of all that we need to sell, stocks and bonds not excepted:

Buying now, annually, to the extent of hundreds of millions of dollars more than we have, or are like to have, to sell:

Exporting every ounce of gold yielded by California:

Increasing daily the necessity for going abroad to beg for loans, and thus adding to a foreign debt that now already exceeds a thousand millions of dollars:

Selling abroad at little more than half price bonds that must, at full prices, be redeemed in gold:

Paying thereon, on the security of the whole property of the Union, a rate of interest unknown to any really civilized people of the world; and more than thrice the rate at this instant paid by the British government with whom we should be now contending for control of the commerce of the world:

Compounding interest borrowing the money with which to pay it, and thereby doubling its amount in less than half a dozen years.

Such being our present course of operation, it may not be improper here to ask the questions: "Why it is that such things should now be done?" Why is it that we have so entirely abandoned the policy that carried us so triumphantly through the war? Seeking a reply thereto, we find it in the fact, that our eyes are closed to the existence of a very simple principle whose perfect truth has recently been so fully demonstrated as to make it absolutely marvellous that it should now be doubted — that principle being embraced in the following words: to wit, *The power of accumulation exists in the ratio of the rapidity of the society circulation*.

Throughout the war that circulation steadily increased in its rapidity, and for the reason that a really *national free trade policy* created demand for labor and its products, a really *national system of circulation* meantime giving to the internal commerce facilities of exchange such as it never before had known. Since the peace, however, we have been traveling backward, and undoing all that had so well been done — piling up taxes on one hand, while, on the other, not only refusing to our people the power to create for themselves machinery of circulation, but actually *frightening home* that which previously had been furnished; doing this, too, to such extent that *the quantity now in use bears to the exchanges needed to be performed a proportion that, with the exception of the closing years of our most calamitous British free trade periods, is less than has ever yet been known.*

The periods thus referred to are the following:

I. That one which followed the conclusion, in 1815, of *political peace* with Britain, to be followed by that *industrial war* which was proclaimed by Messers. Brougham, Hume, and other British *liberals*, when they announced in Parliament their determination to "strangle in the cradle" the then growing manufactures of America and of Europe; that one in which British hostility to American industry produced a general paralysis like to that which is now again so rapidly approaching, and thus enabled General Jackson, by aid of his admirable letter to Dr. Coleman, to reach the presidential chair:

II. That one in which bankruptcy of the Treasury and general ruin of our working men paved the way for expulsion of Mr. Van Buren from the chair of state:

III. That one in which public and private bankruptcy, civil war, and almost universal ruin, were exhibited to the world as the bequest of Mr. Buchanan, on his retirement from public life, to the people to whom he had stood so much indebted.

From all this we speedily recovered, doing so by aid of a *national* free trade tariff, and a *national* medium of circulation. *To* all of it we are now returning, having, by means of internal taxes, almost re-enacted the *British* free trade tariff, and being now engaged in frightening out of use even the existing circulation. Let us to continue, and we shall soon be called to witness a political revolution quite as thorough as were those which drove to private life the two of our public men who, of all others, had placed themselves most fully on record as opposed to progress in the direction of that substitution for coin of the circulating note by means of which the farmer, the laborer, and the mechanic are brought more nearly on a level with the great men who live at their expense — those who build palaces by aid of the performance of exchanges to the extent of thousands of millions without the use of a dollar of coin, and almost without being required to use a single note.

For all this the remedy, my dear sir, is clearly indicated by your present action in reference to the fractional currency, of which, as we are informed, nearly half a million per week has recently been sent to the Southern States. The people of those States needing such notes they are at once supplied. Why, however, should they be denied the use of notes of larger size, say of one, two, five, ten or twenty dollars? Why, even, deny them those of a hundred or a thousand dollars? Why compel them, when selling bales of cotton, to accept payment in notes of less than single dollar? Why not at once furnish them with facilities of exchange by means of which they may be enabled promptly to discharge each and every engagement they need to make? Why not do the same with the people of the West, thereby enabling the farmer to extend, instead of, as now, diminishing his cultivation? Why not place it in the power of our whole people to do as they did two years since, deal for cash with one another? The simple question that, so far as this question of credit is concerned, is now to be settled, is, whether throughout the whole country our people shall be buying and selling on credit, the poor man everywhere paying to the rich the ten, twenty, or even thirty percent demanded for the use of money; or, whether the Treasury shall make itself the general debtor to such extent as may enable all to deal for cash, thereby placing the poor man more nearly on a level with the rich one. Adopting this latter course the Treasury will give us once again those facilities of exchange to which we have stood indebted for that wonderful rapidity of circulation by means of which labor and capital were so much economized as to have enabled us to *donate* to the Treasury hundreds of millions, while *lending* it thousands of millions. Adopting the former, we shall rapidly return to the position in which, by reason of sluggishness of the circulation, labor and capital were *annually* wasted to an extent greater than the whole cost of four years of the most expensive war the world has ever seen. By means of the one, we shall so deepen the water as to enable the Treasury's ship to float securely, while advancing steadily in the direction of *resumption;* whereas, by adopting the other, the water must from day to day be made more shallow, until at last there will remain to us, as our only port, that of *repudiation.*

That we may hereafter move in the one here first indicated, all that is needed is that the Treasury shall make itself once again "master of the situation," controlling banks and brokers — excellent servants, but the worst of masters — instead of being controlled by them. To that end, let it give full consideration to the great fact, that, notwithstanding the density of population and consequent diminution of necessity for the use of any tangible machinery of exchange, *the coin alone* in actual use, in Great Britain, *is nearly equal in amount to the total quantity of that machinery here allowed for a population greatly larger, and scattered over almost a continent.* Let it remark the fact that, trivial as our allowance now is, the public mind is kept in a state of continual alarm by means of threats of measures of contraction. Let it reflect, that the more perfect the supply of that machinery by means of which alone exchanges are made *from hand to hand,* the more rapid must be the increase in the quantity of that required for making exchanges from place to place. Let it see that the injurious effect of deficiency in the supply thereof increases geometrically as distance from the great centers of commerce increases arithmetically, with constant tendency towards production, throughout the South and West, of that irritation which, if permitted once again to grow as it has in time past done, must result in final dissolution of our Union. Let it see, that in supplying that

In the depths of the 1837 depression, the panicked English and French demanded the payment of U.S. debts in specie. Free trade President Van Buren obliged, draining currency out of the U.S. and exacerbating the crisis of U.S. trade and credit. As Henry Carey argued, the best way to outdo England and defend the American System was to sever the U.S. economy from the British gold standard.

machinery it is therefore doing what is most required for producing harmony throughout the Union, while diminishing the taxation required for payment of interest on the public debt. Let it then grant to the men of the South, as regards exercise of the power to create banks, and to supply themselves with machinery of exchange, the same freedom that has been already granted to the loyal people of the North. Let it see that with the reincorporation of the South, and consequent extension of the field of commerce, there has arisen a necessity for exchanges greatly more numerous than were required to be performed when, two years since, there was found employment for a circulation greater by almost one-half, than that which now exists. Finally, let it see that the time has come for granting to our people facilities of exchange equal, at least, to those required during the war; and, that by so doing it will at once, and forever, bring to a close the practice of *shinning it* from day to day by aid of those "temporary loans" and "certificates of indebtedness" by means of which banks and brokers, at the cost of public creditors, are enabled to make enormous profits, the Treasury meanwhile paying for the privilege of thus postponing payment of its debts, to the extent of little less than a dozen millions per annum.

Let these things be done, and then will there at once reappear that *faith in our future* by means of which we had been enabled to make our way through the wonderful war that has just now closed. Let them be done, and activity and energy will at once replace the paralysis that now so much exists. Let them be done, and there will no longer be *a daily waste of capital and labor greater in amount than the total public revenue.* Let them be done, and at once our people will recommence the building of houses, mills, and furnaces, thereby making demand for the services of the laborer and the products of the farm. Let them be done, and the public revenue will so much increase as to enable you to dispense at once with all those taxes which now so much impede our internal commerce. Let them be done, and the world will soon cease to witness the extraordinary spectacle of a country flaunting the Monroe Doctrine in the eyes of foreign sovereigns, its people meantime besieging every little banking house in Europe, seeking thence to draw some small supply of the "sinews of war." Let them be done, and we shall at once re-enter upon competition with Britain for control of the commerce of the world. Let them be done, and great prosperity will enable our people to more and more retain the produce of California mines; and thus, with profit to all and injury to none, gradually to prepare for that resumption which both you and I so much desire to see achieved. Let them be done, and we shall not only cease, by the export of bonds, to increase our dependence on Europe, but shall gradually buy back those now held abroad, and thus increase our independence. Let them be done, and the great republican party will continue to control the movements of the great Ship of State. Let them be done, and the East and the West, the North and the South, will become from day to day more thoroughly knit together, the Union thenceforward marching steadily forward towards the occupation of that position which its wonderful natural resources, and the extraordinary intelligence of its people so well entitle it to claim, to wit, that of leader of the civilization, and controller of the commerce of the world.

Let them *not* be done and paralysis, to be followed by financial ruin, must pave the way for the destruction of that great party which has carried us through the war, but which, by reason of *deficiency of courage,* has thus far failed to give to the country that prosperity in peace for which it so well fought, and had so largely paid. Let them be *not* done, and there will be growing discord, ending in final dissolution of that glorious Union in whose behalf so many have fought, bled, and suffered. Let them be *not* done, and the public debt of the Union will, in the estimation of the world, and that at no very distant period, stand side by side with that of the Confederate States.

The question, my dear sir, now before you for determination is, in my belief, the most momentous one ever yet submitted to the decision of a single individual. We have just now closed a little internal difficulty, leaving yet for settlement the one great question as to whether the world is, in all the future, to be subjected to that *British* and *antinational* system which has for its especial object that of enabling bankers and brokers to enslave the farmers and laborers of the outside world; or, whether the Union shall now place itself in the lead of the now agricultural nations for resistance to that system, and for relief of the agriculturists of the world from the oppressions under which they so long have suffered. Contraction, by means of which the price of money is being so rapidly carried up, looks in the first of these directions and must result in giving the victory to England. Expansion, by means of which there shall be reestablished the alliance between the Treasury and the employers of money — farmers, laborers, artisans, and "speculators"— looks in the second, and will give the victory to us — health, wealth, strength, and the power of accumulation growing always with growth in the rapidity of societary circulation.

It may, however, be said that gold will rise in price. That for a brief period it must do so is very certain. So soon, however, as that rise shall have produced the effect of lessening the importations by which we now are being inundated, and so soon as we shall have established a small counter-current of bonds, it will fall again— that fall continuing until we shall have placed ourselves in a position to retain at home the produce of California, thereby enabling ourselves quietly and profitably to resume the use of precious metals.

Begging you now, my dear sir, to excuse my repeated trespasses on your attention, and earnestly hoping that you may be guided to a right decision, I remain, with sincere regard and respect,

Yours very truly,
Henry C. Carey

Open Letters to Henry Wilson

Henry Carey's open letters to the Honorable Henry Wilson exposed the fact that the delegations from New York and New England to the U.S. Congress were largely British agents-of-influence. Carey agitated for a "producing states" bloc of the West, Center, and South for "commercial prosperity and independence" from the "British and Eastern capitalists." A selection of these letters follows.

Philadelphia, August 26, 1867

Dear Sir:
...Slavery *did not* make the rebellion. British free trade gave us sectionalism, and promoted the growth of slavery, and thus led to rebellion. Had Mr. Clay been elected in 1844, all the horrors of the past few years would have been avoided. Why was he not? Because

free-trade stump orators of New York and Massachusetts, professing to be opposed to slavery, could not believe him radical enough to suit their purposes. They, therefore, gave us Messrs. Polk and Dallas, and by so doing precipitated the rebellion, for the horrors and the waste of which, North and South, they are largely responsible before both God and man. Judging, however, from recent letters and speeches, they are now willing to take the responsibility of the next secession movement, giving us at one moment the extremest antislavery doctrines, while at the next advocating that British free trade policy which had always commanded the approbation of southern slaveholders, and which has reduced, or is reducing, to a condition closely akin to slavery, the people of every community that has been, or is, subjected to it. Unable to see that any system based on the idea of cheapening the raw materials of manufactures, the rude products of agricultural and mining labor, tends necessarily to slavery, they make of themselves, the proslavery men, *par excellence*, of the world.

To what extent the policy of your State has, since that time, been in accordance with the teachings of such men, I propose in another letter to examine, meanwhile, remaining

Yours faithfully,
Henry C. Carey

Philadelphia, September, 1867

Dear Sir:

Forty years since, at the date of the agitation for the passage of that protective tariff of 1828, by means of which the country became first emancipated from the control of foreign money-lenders, the people of Massachusetts, as represented in Congress, were full believers in the advantages of the British free-trade system. Fourteen years having elapsed, during one-half of which they had, under protection, enjoyed the advantages derived from a peaceful and most profitable extension of domestic commerce; the other half having, on the contrary, furnished a series of free-trade and proslavery crises, ending in almost universal bankruptcy, and in an exhaustion of the national credit so complete that, after having, in 1835, finally extinguished the public debt, it had just then been found impossible to borrow abroad even a single dollar; Messrs. Choate and Sprague, representing Massachusetts in the Senate, are found gladly cooperating with Archer of Virginia, and other enlightened Southern Whigs, in the passage of the act of 1842, under which the consumption of iron and of cottons was, in the short space of less than half-a-dozen years, almost trebled; the country, meanwhile, resuming payment of its foreign debt, and reacquiring the credit which it had required but a similar period of British free-trade so entirely to annihilate.

The protection granted by the tariff of 1842, full and complete as it was, enabled Massachusetts — and for the first time — to compete in foreign markets for the sale of cottons. It enabled, too, the South to engage in their manufacture; and so rapid had, in 1848, been its progress, that Mr. Rhett, of the *Charleston Mercury*, was thereby led to predict, in a letter to Mr. Abbott Lawrence, that before the lapse of another decade, it would have ceased to export raw cotton. The prediction was one not likely to be so early realized, but even its half realization would have spared us all the cost in life, limb, and property, of the late rebellion, while it would so far have advanced the slave toward freedom as to have relieved the existing Congress from all the necessity for those measures of reconstruction of which you speak, and in which you have been, and are, so actively engaged.

The repeal of the act of 1846 was followed by a political revolution which placed General Taylor in the Presidential chair, and gave, or seemed to give, to the friends of American labor, and American interests generally, power for reestablishing protection. Forthwith a convention was held at Newport for the purpose of deciding what it was that needed to be asked for. The result of its deliberations was given to me a fortnight later by the then recognized head of the cotton interest of your State, in the few brief words: "We do not desire any protection that will stimulate domestic competition." To put this into other words, it was to say:

"We do not wish that the South or West should engage in manufactures, for that would make competition for the *purchase* of cotton, and raise the price of the raw material."

"We do not desire that the South or West should become

manufacturers, for that would produce competition for the *sale* of cloth, and reduce our profits."

"The tariff of 1846 having already closed the few mills of the Center and the South, we do not desire any tariff that could have the effect of reopening them, or of causing new ones to be erected."

"That tariff having broken down our competitors, has given us a monopoly, and we desire to keep it. Nevertheless, we desire to have the duties increased some five or ten percent, for that would benefit us, and would not suffice for producing domestic competition either for purchase of the raw material, or for the sale of finished goods."

It was a very narrow view of the question, wholly rejecting, as it did, the idea of any harmony between the interests of the producers and consumers of cotton. It was the right British idea, then first, as I think, naturalized in this country, and from that time forward, as I propose to show, made the rule of action of your representatives in both houses of Congress. It was the proslavery idea, common sense teaching that "raw materials" represent agricultural and mining labor, and, that whatever tends to increase competition for their sale, and thus to reduce their prices, tends directly to the subjugation of the laborer, black or white, to the will of those by whom his labor is directed. Wherever raw materials are low in price, man, be his color what it may, and whether found in Ireland or India, in Jamaica or Alabama, in Canada or Illinois, is little better than a slave, the only difference being in the form in which the master's whip presents itself for examination. The well-fed negroes of the South were, ten years since, less enslaved than were those Irish people so accurately described by Thackeray as "starving by millions." The Russian serf, paying *obrok* to his master, and comfortably supporting his wife and children on the proceeds of his labor, was far more master of his actions and himself than this day are the small remnant of those Pennsylvania miners that, in April, 1861, threw aside their tools and rushed to the nation's rescue, finding themselves, as they do, wholly without the employment by means of which they might be enabled to obtain better supplies of food and clothing. Competition for the purchase of labor *makes* men and women free. The ballot-box is useful as a means of *perpetuating* freedom. In your Address I find much in reference to this latter, but in regard to the former, and infinitely the most important, you are, as is much to be regretted, wholly silent.

The election of Mr. Cobb, in 1849, as Speaker of the House, threw the committees into the hands of the Democrats, and your manufacturers, as a consequence, wholly failed to obtain that small additional protection for which they so steadily had asked; just as much as, but no more than, would give security to themselves, while not in any manner "stimulating domestic competition" for purchase of cotton, or for the sale of cloth.

At the next step we find a coalition between British iron-masters and a self-constituted committee of three, having for its active head an ex-member of Congress from Massachusetts, since then presiding officer in one of the Republican conventions. This committee was, for a commission, to procure repeal of all duties on railroad iron, and return of much of those already paid. The movement failed; but for three years the sword of Damocles was held over the heads of all those engaged in the production of coal and iron, and at a cost to the mining interests of the country at large greater than would now suffice for buying and paying for all the cotton and woollen mills of your State, and all the towns in which those mills are placed.

Two years later the East proposed to the West, that, as compensation for granting it free wool, free raw material, and proslavery economic policy generally, it would itself generously consent to sacrifice the interests of its late colaborers of the mining center — of that section to which alone it had been indebted for the triumph of Whig principles in 1848. The proposition, in the form of an amendment to the appropriation bill, was strongly advocated by a distinguished Massachusetts member, shortly afterwards raised to the speakership, and it finally passed the House. It was defeated in the Senate, having there, on the last day of the session, been talked to death; this, too, in defiance of all the efforts of Massachusetts manufacturers, and of the readiness by them manifested to buy, and *pay for*, the silence of those engaged in the patriotic work.†

The first of those periods had been given to the closing of

---

† Should conclusive evidence on this subject be desired, it can at any hour be supplied.

existing rolling-mills, and preventing the building of others. In the second, it was claimed that because the mills were idle that, for that reason, the work of destruction should be further carried forward.

Simultaneously with these operations came the Canada reciprocity scheme, having for its object the cheapening of all the raw materials of manufacture that could be obtained from the country beyond the Bay of Fundy and the St. Lawrence, barley, wool, wheat, and coal, included. Wholly misunderstood, it passed the House, and was on the eve of becoming a law by means of senatorial action when I myself, for the first time, opened the eyes of Mr. Clay and other leading senators to the injurious, and even destructive, tendencies of the measure. From that hour the case became so hopeless that, as I think, the bill never afterwards came up for consideration. The election of Mr. Pierce, and consequent return of the proslavery party to power, brought about a change, however; it having then become to the South most clearly obvious that for preventing annexation of the British Possessions there was but a single remedy — that of granting to the Provinces all the advantages of being in the Union, while requiring of their people the performance of none of the duties, the bearing of none of the burdens, of American citizens. Such was the true intent and meaning of the treaty that then was negotiated, and that was carried through the Senate by aid of the combined proslavery and trading States, Massachusetts and New York steadily uniting with Carolina for preventing any change in the period for which it was to endure, and unanimously recording their votes against limiting it to one, two, three, and so on to nine years. To force through the House a bill providing for carrying it into effect was now the difficulty. That the work was done all know, but of the character of the means resorted to for having it done, few know who have not had the advantage I have had of hearing it fully described by one of the most honored and honorable members of the House. As in the case of the amendment to the appropriation bill above referred to, it seemed to be held that "the end" — the cheapening of raw materials at whatsoever cost to the farmers, miners, and laborers of the Union — "sanctified the means"; and "sanctified" them even in the eyes of men who long had found their chief employment in lecturing their fellow-citizens on the unchristian character of American slavery, and on the necessity for giving freedom to the Southern producers of those raw materials in the cheapening of which they found themselves so steadily engaged.

That this had been from first to last a Boston measure, is, of course, well known to you, as you must have seen the circulars asking subscriptions for moneys to be paid to the men who had succeeded in placing Canadians in a position far better than that occupied by our own citizens.

Close upon this followed the nomination of General Frémont, another British free-trade measure forced upon the States of the Center by extremists of the North and East. In the course of the campaign the agents of British makers of cloth and iron were, on one occasion, greatly gratified by a speech made in front of the New York Exchange by a gentleman of Massachusetts, who, in his character of Speaker of the House, had, but a few months previously, appointed committees entirely satisfactory to that portion of the body which had had full belief in *American* free-trade, and in the idea that every step in the direction of diversified industry tended toward emancipation for the laborer, black and white, foreign and domestic.

Coming now to 1857, we find the Ways and Means Committee, by its chairman, Mr. Campbell, of Ohio, reporting a bill for reduction of the revenue, somewhat satisfactory to the people of the Center and the West. Wholly changed by a senatorial proslavery committee, with Mr. Hunter, of Virginia, at its head, it was then advocated by yourself, my dear sir, in a speech in which occurs the following passage, to wit:

"The people of New England, Mr. President, and especially of Massachusetts, are very extensively engaged in the manufacture of articles in which wool, hemp, flax, lead, tin, brass, and iron are largely consumed. It is for their interest that the duties on these articles should be merely nominal, or that they should be duty free."

The opposition to this proslavery and cheap raw material substitute of the Virginia Senator was very vigorous, Mr. Seward taking therein a very decided part. So doubtful, at length, became its adoption, that its friends found it necessary to telegraph your colleague, Mr. Sumner, advising him that without his vote the friends of freedom for the American mining and agricultural

laborer, and of independence for the American Union, would
probably succeed in accomplishing its rejection. He came, then
presenting himself for the first time in the session, still suffering
under injuries caused by the attack of a Carolinian opponent of the
doctrine of diversified interests; and he then and there united with
Virginia, Carolina, and Mississippi in a vote, the true intent and
meaning of which was, that the farmers, miners, and laborers of
America, black and white, should, in all the future, be mere
"hewers of wood and drawers of water" for Southern slaveholders
and British and Eastern capitalists.

On more than one occasion I had said to your Colleague that
while he had spoken much of freedom, his senatorial votes on industrial questions had thus far always been given on the proslavery
side. Meeting him in Paris shortly after the one last above recorded,
I could not refrain from congratulating him on having so far
recovered from the effects of Carolinian brutality as to have been
enabled to unite with Carolinian senators in a vote for perpetuation
of slavery throughout the South. In the true Christian spirit he had
returned good for evil.

The passage of that act brought about a crisis, whose effect was
that of almost total stoppage of cotton and woollen mills throughout
the country north and south. For the moment Massachusetts suffered some little inconvenience, but she soon after resumed
operations, and with great advantage to herself, her rivals in the
Central, Southern, and Western States having been irretrievably
ruined. The danger of "domestic competition" had disappeared,
and the manufacturing monopoly had become assured.

The years that followed exhibited an almost total prostration of
the various industries of the country, yet it was determined by the
leaders of the Republican party, North and East, that the platform
to be adopted at Chicago should be a mere repetition of that of 1856,
all "new issues" to be entirely ignored. On the Committee of
Resolutions there was, however, one member who was determined
that the question of protection should be squarely met, and he
therefore notified his fellow-members that if they did not then and
there adopt a resolution to that effect they should be compelled to
fight it on the following day on the floor of the convention. In that
he, representing New Jersey, was sustained by the member from

Delaware, and the debate terminated by the adoption of a resolution in the following words, the reading of which, on the succeeding day, was followed by a storm of applause from the assembled thousands, the like of which has had no parallel on this Western Continent:

"That, while providing revenue for the support of the General Government by duties upon imports, *sound policy requires such an adjustment of these imposts as to encourage the development of the industrial interests of the whole country;* and we commend that policy of national exchanges which secures to the workingmen liberal wages, to agriculture remunerating prices, to mechanics and manufacturers an adequate reward for their skill, labor, and enterprise, and to the nation commercial prosperity and independence."

Such is the history of the decade. It is the history of a constant war by Massachusetts upon the greatest of all the national interest — a war for sixpences, carried on at annual cost to the mining and farming regions of the country five times greater than the receipts of California gold — a war more than half the cost of which was paid by Pennsylvania. To the Union at large its cost consists in this, that had Massachusetts fully, fairly, and honestly exerted her influence in the opposite direction, the iron manufacture of the Border States would probably have made such progress as to have prevented their secession, and thus prevented all the injury, as regards both property and life, they have been made to suffer.

Of what has since occurred I shall speak in another letter, meanwhile remaining,

Yours, very truly,
Henry C. Carey

Philadelphia, September, 1867

Dear Sir:

By the adoption, as part of its platform, of the resolution given in my last, the Republican party pledged itself to a policy the reverse of that advocated by yourself in 1857; one which looked to "stimulation of competition" for the purchase of raw materials, labor included; one which would "stimulate domestic competition" for the sale of finished commodities; one based on the idea, apparently unknown to our Massachusetts friends, that protection to the miner, by giving him means of purchase, is, in effect, protection to the maker of cloth; and that protection to consumers of his product is, in effect, protection to the farmer, there being a perfect harmony of interest among all the members of the social body.

Less than a year later, Congress redeemed the pledge then given, enacting into law the determination of the many thousands present at the Chicago Convention, a protective tariff having received the assent of Mr. Buchanan on the day before his quitting office. By it full protection was secured to the cotton manufacturer, and this was *then* most gladly accepted by the men of Massachusetts, the Cotton States having left the Union, and the danger of "stimulating domestic competition" having altogether ceased.

For means to carry on the war an internal revenue, however, came soon after to be required, and, as usual, the mining interest was made to suffer; taxes being piled upon iron at its every stage from the pig to the engine, while duties on the most important of all its products, railroad bars, were subsequently so diminished that the difference between contributions by the domestic and foreign article fell to little more than that which resulted from the fact that gold was required for the latter, while greenbacks sufficed for the former.

So long as the war endured, and the premium on gold continued large, this latter furnished all the protection which seemed to be required. With the peace, however, this so far dies away as to produce a necessity for such change in the tariff as would tend to counteract the nullification of protection caused by demand, for public use, for contributions on almost every article at every stage of manufacture. To this end the Secretary of the Treasury appointed a Commission, upon whose report was based a tariff bill which finally passed the House in the second week of July, 1866, and was on the following day received in the Senate. A Senator from Iowa forthwith moved that its consideration be postponed until the following December; and in the debate on this motion you yourself, as representative of the manufacturing interests of your State, spoke as follows:

"I shall vote, Mr. President, to commit this bill to the Committee on Finance, with instructions to report early in December. I shall so vote because I believe the permanent interests of the whole country demand that the adjustment of the tariff should be made after the most thorough examination, research, and care. Congress cannot take too much time, nor devote too much attention, to the proper adjustment of a measure that so deeply concerns the revenues of the Government and the varied productive interests of the country....

"What I objected to the other day, and what I object to now, is, that New England should be singled out and charged with the sin of the paternity of this measure. While the representatives of Massachusetts and of New England have voted on general principles for this bill, they have so voted with a great deal of hesitation, doubt, and reluctance. They saw what was clear to the comprehension of gentlemen of ordinary intelligence, that this measure imposed increased duties upon raw material, increased largely the cost of production, and subjected the manufacturing and mechanical interests of their section to the censure and hostility of those who spare no occasion to manifest their hostility to that section of our country."

Here, as ever, "cheap raw material" is, as you see, the one object to be accomplished. Pending the existence of the reciprocity treaty Nova Scotia coal had come in free of duty, and Boston capitalists had, as it is understood, become largely interested in the properties by which it had been supplied. The treaty having been abrogated, the special protection they had so long enjoyed was not to cease, and the fact that this new tariff bill did not provide for continued import of coal duty free, constituted the main objection to it. Here, as everywhere, the mining interests were made the object of attack; "cheap raw materials," whether "lead or tin, brass or iron," being, as you had told the Senate in 1857, essential to your constituents. Who, however, would, in this case of coal, have paid the duty? The manufacturers? Not one cent of it. The man who *must go* to market *must pay the cost of getting there*, as is so well known to the farmer of Iowa who sells for a few cents a bushel of corn that in Massachusetts would command almost a dollar. The price of coal is fixed by the domestic supply, and to that the importer must conform, whatever may be the cost of transportation, or charges of the revenue. The Boston owners of coal mines would have been required to pay the duty fixed by the bill before the Senate, yet was no effort spared for inducing the people of Massachusetts, and of New England generally, to believe that it was a tax to be paid by *them*.

In the division that ensued we find extremists of the North and

South combined for destruction of the common enemy, the miner and the laborer — Massachusetts and Kentucky voting together for postponing a measure having for its object the "stimulation of domestic competition" for purchase of the rude products of mining and agricultural labor; and New York and Massachusetts giving all the votes required for securing postponement of this important bill to another session.

At the next session a bill, nearly similar, passed the Senate; and now we find in the House a near approach to the senatorial action of the previous year. The majority of the latter was decidedly favorable to protection, and the state of the country demanded that it should be given. By no direct action could the bill be defeated; but here, as everywhere, there were indirect modes of accomplishing that which directly could not be done. Its management fell into the hands of a representative of Boston capitalists, and the result exhibits itself in the prostration of the industrial interests of the country; and in the fact, that not only do we export all the gold received from California, but that we are running in debt to Europe to an annual amount little less than $200,000,000. In this way it is that we are carrying into practical effect "the democratic idea of the Declaration of Independence," making our people from day to day more dependent on the capitalists of Massachusetts and of Europe.

It may be asked, however, if the Boston capitalist engaged in the cotton manufacture does not suffer equally with those elsewhere engaged in other industrial departments? He does not. Having secured an almost entire monopoly, all he desires is that nothing shall be done that will "stimulate domestic competition"; and to that end, as I understand, New England men have shown themselves inflexibly opposed to the granting of any more protection than that which they themselves required, or little more than that now allowed them. With them capital abounds, interest is low, and machinery exists in great perfection. Just now, they suffer in some small degree; but they find their compensation in the fact that, as before in 1848, and again in 1857, their competitors in the purchase of cotton and sale of cloth, are being ruined beyond redemption. In this State nearly all the mills have been already stopped, and the effect of this well exhibits itself in the fact that Eastern journalists now tell us, that "factory cloths are easy, with an upward tendency in prices, the stocks in first hand in all New England not exceeding 150,000 pieces." The more frequent the crises, the more dangerous the trade; and the more the free-trade cry can be raised, as is now being done throughout New England, the less is the danger of "domestic competition" for the purchase of cotton and for the sale of cotton cloth; and therefore is it that Eastern cotton manufacturers have been enabled to build up the immense fortunes that we find recorded. The system here pursued by them closely resembles that of the great British iron-masters, as below described; the latter being as much intent upon having a monopoly of the supply of iron to the world as are the capitalists of Boston upon monopolizing that of cottons for the Union.

> "The laboring classes generally, in the manufacturing districts of this country, and especially in the iron and coal districts, are very little aware of the extent to which they are often indebted for their being employed at all to the immense *losses* which their employers voluntarily incur in bad times, in order *to destroy foreign competition, and to gain and keep possession of foreign markets.* Authentic instances are well known of employers having in such times carried on their works at a loss amounting in the aggregate to three or four hundred thousand pounds in the course of three or four years. If the efforts of those who encourage the combinations to restrict the amount of labor and to produce strikes were to be successful for any length of time, the great accumulations of capital could no longer be made *which enable a few of the most wealthy capitalists to overwhelm all foreign competition in times of great depression,* and thus to clear the way for the *whole trade* to step in when prices revive, and to carry on a great business before *foreign* capital can again accumulate to such an extent as to be able to establish a competition in prices with any chance of success. *The large capitals of this country are the great instruments of warfare against the competing capitals of foreign countries,* and are *the most essential* instruments now remaining by which our manufacturing supremacy can be maintained; the other elements — cheap labor, abundance of raw materials, means of communication, and skilled labor — being rapidly in process of being equalized."

For "iron and coal" read cotton, and for "foreign competition" read "domestic competition," and you will have an almost perfect history of Massachusetts policy for the last twenty years.

Such, as I understand it, is the true history of your State in

relation to the question of *real* freedom of trade, *real* freedom for the
men who labor, *real* love for the whole Union, and *real* tendency
toward enabling freedmen of the South in any manner to profit by
the "bloody struggles" through which they and we have so lately
passed; and which you here describe as the "struggle on this continent between the democratic idea of the Declaration of Independence and human bondage." The one great object to be
accomplished has been that of having "cheap raw materials" at
whatsoever cost to the miner and laborer, black or white; and to that
end there has been coalition with Canada and Carolina against the
West; with Nova Scotia and the South against the Center; with any
and everybody, indeed, that could be made to contribute toward
placing the State you represent in the same position as regarded the
Union as is now occupied by Britain in reference to the world at
large. If it has, in any of its parts, been misrepresented, I shall be
most glad to give publicity to any correction that may seem to be
required. Postponing, for the present, all remarks thereon, I shall,
in another letter, present for your consideration a similar review of
the action of this State as representative of the mining interests, of
all others the most important in, and to, the Union; meantime
remaining,

                Yours faithfully,
                   Henry C. Carey

Protection and Revenue, Public and Private

The Honorable David Wells was the Special Commissioner on the Revenue. The 1869 report of that commission, which had been set up under President Abraham Lincoln, urged the United States to adopt the economic policy of the British System and chiefly targeted Henry Carey and his circle for their insistence on the American System.

Carey's open letters to Wells were printed in the millions, showing all how Wells had doctored the statistics — with the help of John Stuart Mill — to "prove" that economic growth occurred no matter what financial policy was adopted by the nation.

Philadelphia, January 23, 1869

Dear Sir:

Your report just now published contains a passage to which I desire here to invite your attention, as follows:

"As respects the relation of legislation by the national government to the results under consideration, if we except the adoption of a liberal policy in the disposition of the public lands, it is difficult, at least for the period which elapsed between 1840 and 1860, to affirm much that is positive, unless, in conformity with the maxim, that that government is best which governs least, absence of legislation is to be regarded in the light of a positive good. If important results followed the acquisition of California, such results were certainly neither foreseen nor anticipated; while as regards commercial legislation, a review of all the facts cannot fail to suggest a doubt whether the evils which have resulted from instability have not far more than counterbalanced any advantage that may have proceeded from the experience of a fluctuating policy.

"The Commissioner is well aware that this opinion will not be readily accepted by those who have been educated to believe that the industrial and commercial prosperity of the country was seriously affected by the legislation which took place during the years which elapsed from 1842 to 1846. But upon this point all investigation shows that the facts are entirely contrary to what may be regarded as the popular belief, which, indeed, in this particular, would appear to be based on little else than mere assertions, which, remaining for a long time unquestioned, have at last acquired historical truth. Thus, for example, it has been constantly asserted, both in Congress and out of Congress, that the production of pig iron was remarkably stimulated under the tariff of 1842 — rising from 220,000 tons in 1842 to 800,000 tons in 1848 — and that under the tariff of 1846 the same industry was remarkably depressed. Now, these assertions may be correct, but the most reliable statistics to which we have access, viz: those gathered by the American Iron Association, instruct us as follows:

"Production of pig iron in 1830, 165,000 tons; in 1840, 347,000 tons. Increase in 10 years, 110 percent.

"Production in 1845, 486,000 tons; increase in 5 years, 40 percent.

"Production in 1850, 564,000 tons; increase in 10 years, 62 percent.

"Production in 1855, 754,000 tons; increase in 5 years, 33 percent.

"Production in 1860, 913,000 tons; increase in 10 years, 61 percent.

"It thus appears that the great annual increase in the production of pig iron took place prior to the year 1840, and for 30 years was remarkably uniform at the rate of 10 to 11 percent per annum; and that since then, no matter what has been the character of the legislation, whether the tariff was low or high, whether the condition of the country was one of war or peace, the increase of the production has been at the average of about 8 percent per annum, or more than double the ratio of the increase of population.

"Again, as another curious illustration of an apparent misconception of the effects of past legislation upon the development of the country, take the following paragraph from the recent report of a congressional committee:

"No business man of mature age need be reminded of the revulsion which followed in consequence of the free-trade system of 1846 — the decline of production, of immigration, of wages, of public or private revenue, until the culmination of the system in the tariff of 1857, with the memorable crises of that period; the general ruin of manufacturers and merchants; the suspended payments of the banks; the reduction of the Treasury to the verge of bankruptcy, and the unparalleled distress among the unemployed poor."

Here follows a series of statements constructed in a manner similar to that above given in reference to iron, the object of their production being that of proving that the views of the committee thus presented had had no foundation in fact; that they had allowed themselves to be deceived by "mere assertions" on the part of others; and, that the time had now come for setting the stamp of falsehood on all they had been accustomed to believe in reference to the tariff of 1846, and for obtaining such accurate views of the last twenty years of our commercial history as might be entitled to claim to have "the force of accepted historical truths."

To whom, however, are to be attributed the oft-repeated mis-statements by which the committee had been deceived? No name is given, but you of course refer to me, the statements thus controverted having been first published over my own signature, so early as 1851, and since then many times republished; and the committee having been misled, if misled at all, by no other than myself. To me, therefore, it is that you have thus thrown down the glove, and I now take it up prepared on the one hand to prove the accuracy of the views you have thus called in question; or, on the other, to admit of having through a long series of years misled my fellow-citizens. Admit that such proof be furnished — that the "mere assertions" be now proved to be real "historical truths" fitted for even your own acceptance, where, I beg to ask, will you yourself then stand? Should it chance to be proved that it is not I that am required to impale myself on the horns of a dilemma which leaves but a choice between the admission of gross carelessness on the one hand, or grosser dishonesty on the other, does it not follow necessarily that you must be compelled to take the place you had prepared for me, and thus furnish yourself the proof required for establishing the fact that you are wholly disqualified for the office of public teacher? As it seems to me, such must be the case.

Leaving you, however, to reflect at leisure on the questions thus propounded, I propose now to analyze the "historical truths" of your report, first, however, giving a brief history of our tariff legislation for the last half-century, as follows:

The revenue tariff period which followed the close, in 1815, of the great European war, was one of great distress both private and public. Severe financial crises bankrupted banks, merchants, and manufacturers; greatly contracted the market for labor and all its products; so far diminished the money value of property as to place the debtor everywhere in the power of his creditor; caused the transfer of a very large portion of it under the sheriff's hammer; and so far impaired the power of the people to contribute to the revenue that, trivial as were the public expenditures of that period, loans were required for enabling the Treasury to meet the demands upon it. With 1824, however, there came a partial attempt at remedy of the evils under which our whole people were then so severely suffering, a tariff having been then established under which pig iron and potatoes were abundantly protected, pipes and penknives being admitted at moderate ad-valorem duties. The rude products of agriculture were, in effect, prohibited from being imported in their original forms, but when they presented themselves in those of cotton and woollen cloths little difficulty was found. Slight was the benefit resulting from such a measure, yet benefit did result, and hence it was that it came so soon to be followed by the admirable tariff of 1828, the first really protective one ever established by Congress. Under it all was changed, and with a rapidity so great that but five years of its action were required for giving to the country a prosperity such as had never before been known; for so increasing the public revenue as to render necessary the emancipation from import duties of tea, coffee, and many other articles the like of which was not produced at home; for taking thus the first step in the direction of *real* freedom of external commerce; for finally annihilating the public debt; and for causing our people to forget the state of almost ruin from which they had beeen redeemed by the combined action of the tariffs of 1824 and 1828.

Northern submission to Carolinian threats of nullification next gave us the Compromise of 1833, by means of which the country was, within the next decade, to be brought under a strictly revenue tariff of 20 percent. The South needed cheap food, and did not, therefore, desire that Western farmers should make a market at home which might tend to raise its price. Most generously, however, it permitted protection to remain almost untouched, until the first of January 1836, and how gradual were the changes then and for several years thereafter to be made, will be seen from the following figures representing the duties to be paid on an article that had stood originally at 50 percent:

1829-33	1834-35	1836-37	1838-39	1840-41	1842 to June 30	thereafter
50	47	44	41	38	29	20

For the first two years general prosperity continued to be maintained. Thereafter, however, we find the whole period of its existence presenting a series of contractions and expansions ending in a state of weakness so extreme that bankruptcy was almost universal; that labor was everywhere seeking for employment; that the public credit was so entirely destroyed that the closing year of that unfortunate period exhibited the disgraceful fact of Commissioners, appointed by the Treasury, wandering throughout Europe and knocking at the doors of its principal banking houses without obtaining the loan of even a single dollar. Public and private distress now, August 1842, compelling a return to the protective system we find almost at once a reproduction of the prosperous days of the period from 1829 to 1835, public and private credit having been restored, and the demand for labor and its products having become greater than at any former period.

Again, however, do we find our people forgetting that to the protective policy had been due the marvellous changes that were then being witnessed, and again, 1846, returning to that revenue tariff system to which they had been indebted for the scenes of ruin which had marked the periods from 1817 to 1828, and from 1835 to 1842. California gold now, however, came in aid of free trade theories, and for a brief period it was really believed that protection had become a dead issue and could never again be revived. With 1854, however, that delusion passed away, the years that followed, like those of the previous revenue tariff periods, having been marked by enormous expansions and contractions, financial crises, private ruin, and such destruction of the national credit that with the close of Mr. Buchanan's Administration we find the Treasury unable to obtain the trival amount which was then required, except on payment of most enormous rates of interest.

Once again, 1861, do we find the country drive to protection, and the public credit by its means so well established as to enable the Treasury with little difficulty to obtain the means of carrying on a war whose annual cost was more than had been the total public expenditures of half a century, including the war with Great Britain of 1812. Thrice thus, under the tariffs of 1828, 1842, and 1861, has protection redeemed the country from almost ruin. Thrice thus, under the revenue tariffs of 1817, 1833, and 1846, has it been sunk so low that none could be found "so poor to do it reverence." Such having been our experience throughout half a century it might have been supposed that the question would be regarded as settled, yet do we find an officer of the government whose special duty it has been made to inquire into all the causes affecting the public revenue, and who has had before him all the evidence required in proof of the above "assertions," now venturing to assure Congress and the people that —

> "There does not seem to be any reliable evidence which can be adduced to show that the change which took place in the legislative commercial policy of the country in 1846 had any permanent or marked effect whatever; while, on the other hand, the study of all the facts pertaining to national development from 1840 to 1860, and from 1865 to the present time, unmistakably teaches this lesson; that the progress of the country through what we may term the strength of its elements of vitality is independent of legislation and even of the impoverishment of a great war. Like one of our own mighty rivers, its movement is beyond control. Successive years, like successive affluents, only add to and increase its volume; while legislative enactments and conflicting commercial policies, like the construction of piers and the deposit of sunken wrecks, simply deflect the current or constitute temporary obstructions. In fact, if the nation has not yet been lifted to the full comprehension of its own work, it builds determinately, as it were, by instinct."

How much of truth there is in all this, and what has been your warrant for making such "assertions" it is proposed now to examine, commencing with the iron manufacture.

Yours respectfully,
Henry C. Carey

Philadelphia, January 28, 1869

Dear Sir:

The tariff of 1828 which was, as the country had been assured, almost to destroy the revenue, had, on the contrary, proved so very productive as to make it necessary wholly to emancipate from duty most, if not even all, of the commodities not competing with our domestic products, and had thus furnished conclusive evidence that the road toward financial independence and *real* freedom of trade was to be found in the pursuit of a policy leading to industrial independence. Further proof of this was now being furnished, the customs revenue, under what had been claimed as the true revenue system, having declined to half the amount at which it had stood in 1833, and Congress finding itself compelled, in 1841, to retrace its steps by remanding to the list of duty-paying articles a large proportion of those commodities which had been freed by the Act of 1832. Still, however, the necessary work remained undone, each successive day bringing with it new evidence of a need for total abandonment of a policy nearly the whole period of whose existence had been passed amid financial convulsions of the severest kind — convulsions whose effect had been that of almost annihilating confidence, and thereby bringing about a state of things destructive alike of public and private revenues.

With August 1842, therefore, we find the nation compelled to readoption of the protective and *real* revenue policy, followed at once by such restoration of confidence as enabled the Treasury to find all its wants promptly supplied at home. Thenceforth there was found no necessity for humbly knocking at the doors of foreign bankers, praying for relief. For the general restoration of confidence, however, much time was needed, ruin having been so widely spread as to make it indispensable that a bankrupt law should be enacted by means of which hosts of ruined merchants, miners, manufacturers, ship owners, land owners, might once again be enabled to get to work and seek the means by aid of which to repair their fallen fortunes. Mills and mines, too, needed to be repaired preparatory to setting laborers once again at work, and it was in such labors that the first year of the new policy was passed. Still another year was required for enabling the returning prosperity to make its way to the coal region, and it was not until the summer of 1844 that the men who had given their millions to its development became at length enabled to see reason for hope that they might at an early period be released from the burthen of debt imposed upon them in the revenue tariff period.† Thenceforth, however, all moved rapidly, new mines being opened, numerous furnaces being erected, and a rolling-mill for rails now for the first time making its appearance on the American soil. Throughout the long period of a dozen years British iron-masters had, by means of our own disastrous legislation, been secured in a monopoly of the control of supplies of rails, but the time had now come for obtaining that *real* freedom of trade which always results from the exercise of power to choose between buying at home or seeking supplies abroad.

The furnaces that in 1840, when pig had fallen to little more than half the price of 1837, had yielded but 347,000 tons, were now being driven to their utmost capacity, estimated at 450,000 tons, but, as there is good reason for believing, not less than   ... 430,000

To this we have here to add—

First, the produce of 8 new anthracite furnaces blown in
    from 1841 to 1844 inclusive, with a capacity of 40,000

Second, that of 52 new charcoal furnaces capable of
    yielding .... 52,000‡

Third, enlargements of old furnaces, estimated at 35,000

    Total capacity at the close of 1844 557,000

The actual produce of 1845 is given by you at 486,000 tons, but there exists no certain evidence in reference thereto, and I feel assured that it must have exceeded half a million. So great was then the demand for iron of all descriptions that, notwithstanding the large increase of domestic product, the import of 1844 and 1845 rose to 212,000 tons, exceeding by more than 25 percent that of the revenue tariff years 1842 and 1843.

---

† Coal and iron are always the last to feel the changes after a financial revulsion. In the present case, nearly two full years elapsed before there occurred any movement of property in the anthracite coal region. In proof of this it may be mentioned that in the early summer of 1844 it had been suggested to Boston capitalists that for the small sum of $3,000,000 they might be enabled to become owners of a full half of that region, together with improvements the cost of which had been probably five times that sum.

‡ The number of charcoal furnaces started in these years, in Pennsylvania alone, was 26. As many more are here estimated for all the remainder of the Union, but the real number was probably much greater than this.

To the quantity above obtained we have next to add as follows:
Eighteen anthracite furnaces blown in 1845 and 1846,
    with a capacity of .... tons 84,000
Eighty two charcoal furnaces capable of yielding 82,000
Enlargements estimated at 35,000
    Giving a total of 201,000

which added to the 557,000 already obtained makes a grand total of
758,000, or within seven thousand of the estimate then furnished by
the Secretary of the Treasury, thus confirming the accuracy of the
views that have heretofore been presented by myself.

    Nominally, the tariff of 1846 became operative at the close of
that year, but such was the general prosperity, greatly increased as it
was by a demand for food created by the Irish famine — a demand
that caused in that year an import from Europe of gold to the immense extent of $24,000,000 — that its operation was almost entire-
ly unfelt. In face of a large reduction of duty the price of pig-iron
rose more than 10 percent, and every existing furnace was tasked to
its utmost to meet the wonderful demand that then existed. Increase
of furnaces therefore went on, no less than 11 having been blown in,
in the anthracite region, in 1847 and 1848, with a capacity of
    .... tons 54,000
    Adding to this, for 18 charcoal furnaces in this State,
      and only as many estimated for all the other States,
      we obtain a further capacity of 36,000
                                        90,000

by adding which to the 758,000 of previous years we obtain a grand
total of 848,000 tons, admitting therein but 70,000 for enlargements
in each and every year of works previously in operation.

    By no correction of these figures that can even be attempted will
it be possible to reduce the quantity to 750,000. Admitting, however, that such reduction be made, there still remains an increase in
five years of more than 200 percent, population meantime having
grown less than 20 percent.

    Whence, you may ask, have the facts thus given been obtained?
In answer I have to say, that they have been drawn from a source to
which you yourself have had the readiest access, *the Statistics of the*

American Iron and Steel Association, the difference between the results obtained by you on one side, and by me on the other, consisting only in this, that whereas, I have now, as always heretofore, given all the facts; you have given only those which seemed best fitted for enabling you to prove that "no matter what had been the character of the the legislation, whether the condition of the country was one of war or peace, the increase of production had been at the average rate of about eight percent per annum, or more than double the ratio of the increase of population." How far there exists any warrant for this extraordinary assertion in reference to the years which followed the brilliant period above described, it is propposed now to show, commencing with those of 1849 and 1850.

With the summer of 1848 commenced a paralysis resulting from deluge of our markets by British iron, the fiscal year 1848-49 exhibiting an import exceeding by nearly a quarter of a million tons that of 1846, and largely exceeding 300,000 tons. Then, for the first time did the warehousing system exhibit its power for mischief, British iron masters filling the public stores with their various merchandise, and borrowing on the certificates money at the lowest rates of interest, their American competitors meanwhile piling up products upon which, while remaining on their premises, they could not borrow a dollar at any rate of interest whatsoever. For them there existed no public stores the like of those so carefully provided for their rivals, that the latter might be enabled at once to borrow nearly the whole value of their merchandise, and then apply the proceeds to the fabrication of other hundreds of thousands of tons by means of which they might, and with the smallest measure of inconvenience, be enabled to overwhelm those Americans by whom had been created the great market the control of which they were now determined to secure for themselves.

Worse even than 1848-49 was the state of things exhibited in the fiscal year 1849-50, the import having exceeded 350,000 tons, and prices having been forced down to the half of those of 1838, and but two-thirds of those at which they had stood even in the destructive year of 1841. To sell at $20 was ruinous to all but the favored few who enjoyed advantages greatly exceeding those possessed by the mass of those engaged in the manufacture. As a consequence, furnaces were closed one after another, and as early as 1849 the product was supposed to have fallen to 650,000. So steadily, however, did the work of destruction proceed that in 1850 it was fully believed that production had been reduced much below 500,000, and might not prove greatly to exceed 400,000. The actual product, as given in your report, was 564,000, furnishing proof conclusive that the production of previous years must have reached, and probably exceeded, 800,000. No one familiar with the facts of that calamitous period can for a moment hesitate to admit that the production of 1850 had been less than two-thirds of that of 1847-48; or, that to obtain the true figures of these latter years it would be required to add at the least one-half to those furnished by the former. Doing this we obtain 846,000, and that that presents more nearly than any other figure the quantity of iron actually produced in the closing years of that prosperous protective period is my firm belief.

How the great facts compare with those small ones so carefully selected by you is shown in the annexed diagram, the heavy line

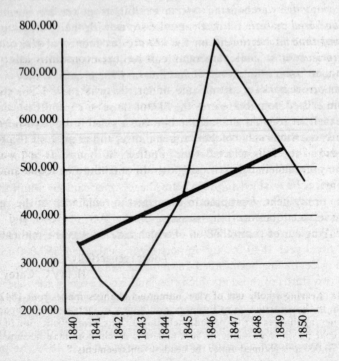

giving, as before, the picture presented by yourself in the following words:

"Increase in the production of pig iron: In 1840, 347,000 tons; in 1845, 486,000; in 1850, 564,775."

Having studied the above, and having seen how very carefully you had *suppressed* the calamitous revenue years 1841 and 1842; and then again *suppressed* the wonderfully prosperous period of protection from 1845 to 1848; I beg to ask that you then read again the following paragraph of your Report, and most particularly that portion of it here given in italics, as follows:

"The Commissioner is well aware that this opinion will not be readily accepted by those who have been educated to believe that the industrial and commercial prosperity of the country was seriously affected by the legislation which took place during the years which elapsed from 1842 to 1846. But upon this point *all investigation shows that the facts are entirely contrary to what may be regarded as the popular belief, which, indeed, in this particular, would appear to be based on little else than mere assertions, which, remaining for a long time unquestioned, have at last acquired the force of accepted historical truth.* Thus, for example, it has been constantly asserted, both in Congress and out of Congress, that the production of pig iron was remarkably stimulated under the tariff of 1842 — rising from 220,000 tons in 1842 to 800,000 tons in 1848 — and that under the tariff of 1846 the same industry was remarkably depressed. Now, these assertions may be correct, but," as you then proceed to prove by aid of carefully selected facts, there is really not, as you would have your readers believe, a single grain of truth to be found among them.

In my next, I propose to examine the remainder of the years that elapsed between the passage of the Act of 1846 and the breaking out of that rebellion of which latter it was the real cause.

Yours respectfully,
Henry C. Carey

Note: Leaving wholly out of view numerous changes made from 1842 to 1848, in the construction of furnaces with a view to increase their capacity, the new appliances of that period, including an extensive substitution of hot for cold blast, would alone, as it is believed, much more than account for the 70,000 tons claimed under the head of "enlargements."

Philadelphia, February 20, 1869

Dear Sir:

You have advised your constituents that —

"As respects the relations of legislation by the national government to the results under consideration, if we except the adoption of
a liberal policy in the disposition of the public lands, it is difficult, at
least for the period which elapsed between 1840 and 1860, to affirm
much that is positive, unless, in conformity with the maxim, that
that government is best which governs least, absence of legislation is
to be regarded in the light of a positive good. If important results
followed the acquisition of California, such results were certainly
neither foreseen nor anticipated, while as regards commercial
legislation, a review of all the facts cannot fail to suggest a doubt
whether the evils which have resulted from instability have not far
more than counterbalanced any advantage that may have proceeded
from the experience of a fluctuating policy."

That fluctuations of policy are to be avoided is very certain, but
what, I beg to ask, are those of which you have now been led to
speak? Are they to be found in the changes forced upon us in 1824,
1828, 1842, and 1861, by the almost universal ruin, public and
private, of the closing years of those British free trade periods which
commenced in 1817, in 1835, and in 1846? Are they not rather to be
found in those several *abandonments of American policy* which led
to the ruin of 1820, 1823, of 1841, 1842, of 1857, 1861? To one of
those systems of policy, the one American, the other British, you
here object, but to which of them you are thus opposed you do not
clearly state. Which is it? Are you in future to stand before the world
as advocate of the great British capitalists who would compel our
farmers to make all their exchanges in Liverpool; or of the farmer
himself who seeks to have the market brought so near to home as to
enable him to free his land and himself from that terrific "tax" of
transportation by means of which he, in the past, has been so nearly
ruined? We have here a very important question, and that you may
be enabled to answer it with satisfaction to yourself, I propose now
to furnish "a review of all the facts" that have thus far been developed, to wit:

British free trade almost crushed out the great iron manufacture in the period from 1817 to 1824; paralyzed it in that from 1835
to 1842; and did the same in that from 1848 to 1860.

American freedom of commerce, resulting from protection against the "warfare" of British "capitalists," more than trebled the iron production from 1824 to 1833; did the same from 1842 to 1848; and has doubled it since 1861.

British free trade never permanently added a single ton to the iron production in the whole thirty years of its existence.

American freedom of commerce has added 1,500,000 tons in the less than twenty years that the country has been ruled by the tariffs of 1828, 1842, and 1861.

British free trade closed the cotton mills that had been brought into existence during the war for freedom of navigation, and for sailors' rights, which commenced in 1807 and found its close in 1815. It wholly arrested progress in the period which closed in 1842; and almost wholly in that which ended in 1860; doing this in despite of that great discovery of California treasures by means of which the cotton manufacture should have trebled.

American freedom of commerce doubled the cotton consumption in the period ending in 1833. It almost trebled it in that ending in 1847-48. It has added fifty percent thereto in the last four years, and promises soon to exhibit an increase so great as to make a home demand for half the crop.

British free trade prevented the growth of either the iron or cotton manufacture in the South, and thus prevented the diversification of employments which would peacefully and profitably have given freedom to the slave, while increasing tenfold the value of land.

American freedom of commerce gave to the South a cotton manufacture that in 1847 was of the highest promise. It now proposes to give to it every variety of manufacture, thereby greatly aiding the cause of freedom, while largely increasing the fortunes of those who own the land.

British free trade bankrupted merchants and manufacturers, and filled our cities with paupers in 1820, 1842, and 1860.

American freedom of commerce gave prosperity to merchants and manufacturers, and profitable employment to the laborer, in the periods which closed with 1835 and 1848; and is now doing the same under the protective tariff of 1861.

British free trade prevented immigration in the period

preceding effective action of the tariff of 1828. It paralyzed it in that which closed in 1843-44. It had almost annihilated it in that which closed in 1861-62.

American freedom of commerce quadrupled immigration in the period controlled by the protective tariff of 1828. It quadrupled it again under that controlled by the tariff of 1842; and it has now been more than trebled under the tariff of 1861.

British free trade almost annihilated the railroad interest in the period which closed with 1842. It did the same in that which closed with 1861.

American freedom of commerce gave new life and vigor to the same interest in the period from 1842 to 1848. To a far greater extent it has done the same under the tariff of 1861.

British free trade, throughout its several periods of existence, has looked to crushing out the domestic commerce; to increasing the necessity for seeking distant markets; and to throwing on our farmers all the "tax" of transportation.

American freedom of commerce has sought to bring the market to the farmer's door, thereby freeing him from all such "tax," while throwing on the foreign manufacturer all the expenses standing between his market and himself.

British free trade, throughout its whole existence, subjected our farmers to taxes so heavy that to a frightful extent their properties, in 1818-23, 1840-42, and 1857-60, changed hands under the sheriff's hammer.

American freedom of commerce, in all its several periods, has given prosperity to the farmer; and has already so far relieved him from the "tax" of transportation that, and for the first time in our history, he is now almost everywhere free from the burthen of mortgage and other debts.

British free trade gave us the financial revulsions of 1818-23, 1837-42, 1857-60; ruining merchants and manufacturers; almost annihilating public and private revenues; making the rich everywhere richer and the poor everywhere poorer; and forcing the Treasury to the creation of burthensome debts.

American freedom of commerce filled the Treasury to repletion in the period ending in 1835, and saved it from bankruptcy in 1842.

It found the Treasury empty in 1861, and since then has supplied it with the means of making the most gigantic war recorded in the annals of the world.

British free trade, throughout, has looked to making Liverpool the hub of a great wheel of which American railroads were to be the spokes, as a necessary consequence of which there was no cohesion among the parts of which the Union had been composed. Of this discord, rebellion, civil war, were the unavoidable results.

American freedom of commerce looking, as it always *has* looked, to the creation of a great network of roads, tends toward bringing all the States into close communion each with every other, and thus establishing that complete *harmony of interests* to which alone can we look for the perpetuation of the Union.

2. Such is the "review" for which, in the extract from your Report above given, you have seemed to call. Having studied it, and having satisfied yourself that it contains nothing that may not be "accepted as historical truth," you may, perhaps be prepared to furnish answers to the following questions, to wit:

Why is it that, if protection be really adverse to freedom and to the general prosperity of our people, immigration always grows with such rapidity when protection is most complete?

Why is it that, if British free trade be really favorable to freedom, men who previously had come among us with intent to stay, have always in free trade times so largely re-emigrated to Europe?

Why has it been that in the last few years hundreds of thousands of Canadians have abandoned their free trade country, and have preferred to settle in these benighted and protected States?

Why is it that of the emigrants who arrive at Quebec and Montreal, and who have the choice between free trade on the one hand and protection on the other, nearly all prefer to take the latter, selecting homes in our Western States?

Why is it that Nova Scotia and New Brunswick are almost in a state of rebellion, because of their feeling of the absolute necessity for closer connection with these protected States?

Why is it that nearly the whole population of Ireland would desire to fly from British freedom of trade and seek for homes in this now partially protected country?

Why is it that British emigration to Australia diminishes, and that to us increases, almost precisely as our protective policy is made more and more complete?

Why is it that Australia, after a most severe political contest, has just now elected a protectionist parliament?

Why is it that furnaces are built and mines opened in protective times, and abandoned in British free trade times?

Why is it that when we build furnaces and open mines railroads are always profitable to their owners, and capital is easily obtained for the construction of new lines of road?

Why is it that when mines and furnaces are abandoned railroad property so far declines that it becomes most difficult to obtain the means for building further roads?

Why is it that financial crises, resulting in the ruin of trade, are the *never failing* accompaniments of the British free trade policy?

Why is it that such crises never occur in periods of protection?

Why is it that the deposits in our saving funds so much increase in times of protection, and so much diminish in those of British free trade?

Why is it that Sheriff's sales are so numerous in British free trade times, and so few in number in those of protection?

Why is it that British free trade periods always end in almost total failure of public revenue and almost total bankruptcy of the treasury?

Why is it that protective tariffs are so favorable to increase of public revenue, and to reduction of the public debt?

Why is it that a protective tariff now produces annually nearly as much revenue as was obtained by aid of an antiprotective one in the whole period of Mr. Buchanan's Administration?

Why is it that the Republican party — the party of liberty, of equal rights, of intelligence, and of sound morals — is so generally favorable to the protective policy?

Why is it that British free trade doctrines are so universally popular among men who believe in the divine origin of slavery — among sympathizers in the late rebellion — among foreign agents — among ignorant foreigners — and among the dangerous classes throughout the Union?

Why is it that, now that it diversifies its industry by raising its own food, the South obtains more for 2,000,000 bales of cotton than before it had received for 4,000,000?

Why is it that when the refining of our oil, thus fitting it for consumption, gives us now almost our only real free trade, the same results would not be obtained, and on a much larger scale, by finishing our cotton and fitting it also for consumption?

Why is it that France, in making her last treaty with England, established a tariff more intelligently protective than our own?

Why is it that the maker of that treaty, Mons. Chevalier, had been led to tell his countrymen that —

"Every nation owes to itself to seek the establishment of diversification in the pursuits of its people, as Germany and England have already done in regard to cottons and woollens, and as France herself has done in reference to so many and so widely different kinds of manufacturing industry. Within these limits," as he further says, "it is not an abuse of power on the part of the Government; on the contrary, *it is the accomplishment of a positive duty so to act at each epoch in the progress of a nation as to favor the taking possession of all the branches of industry whose acquisition is authorized by the nature of things.* Governments are, in effect, the personification of nations, and *it is required that they exercise their influence in the direction indicated by the general interest, properly studied, and fully appreciated.*"

Why is it that, small as are its natural advantages, France, the country *par excellence* of protection, has been enabled to establish a foreign commerce so vastly greater than our own?†

Why is it that Germany, the country that has most persistently carried into effect the policy of protection, now stands in the lead of Europe, although so recently a mere collection of loose fragments, ready to be moved about in whatsoever direction might be most agreeable to France or England at one moment, Russia or Austria at another?

Why is it that our Union, at the close of a long course of policy

---

† The average total of French foreign commerce for the last three years has been nearly $1,600,000,000, equivalent to more than $2,000,000,000 of our currency.

directly the reverse, has recently with such difficulty escaped being broken into fragments?

Why is it that British policy, that policy whose imitation is urged upon us by all the advocates of that antiprotective system which has invariably resulted in the destruction of revenue, has so entirely crushed out of existence that whole race of small British proprietors "whose touch," according to Arthur Young, "turned sand into gold?"

Why is it that the British agricultural laborer has, by means of that policy, been reduced to a condition so nearly akin to slavery as to have before him no future but the poor house?

Why is it that all the countries of the earth which find themselves compelled to submit to the, so-called, free trade policy now urged upon the world by British traders, are this day in little better than a state of ruin?

Leaving you to furnish answers to these important questions, I here close this protracted review of your labors with the request that you read once again the following passage of your Report, and that you then determine with yourself how far its broad "assertions" are to be regarded as making any approach toward "historical truth"; how far, too, the Report itself is such an one as we had a right to expect from a man who, holding a most important office, had been fully informed of the fact that money was being unsparingly used by British manufacturers in the effort now being made for perpetuating our industrial dependence as the most efficient mode of preventing the growth of political independence.

> "Study of all the facts pertaining to the national development from 1840 to 1860, and from 1865 to the present time, unmistakably teaches this lesson; that the progress of the country through what we may term the strength of its elements of vitality is independent of legislation and even of the impoverishment and waste of a great war. Like one of our own mighty rivers, its movement is beyond control. Successive years, like successive affluents, only add to and increase its volume; while legislative enactments and conflicting commercial policies, like the construction of piers and the deposit of sunken wrecks, simply deflect the current or constitute temporary obstructions. In fact, if the nation has not yet been lifted to the full comprehension of its own work, it builds determinately, as it were, by instinct."

Is there in all this a single word that you will now venture to reassert? I doubt it much.

Yours respectfully,
Henry C. Carey

Shall We Have Peace?

Henry Carey's open letter to General U.S. Grant restates the policy formulated by former President Abraham Lincoln of industrializing the South to ensure peace in the Union. Had that policy been followed through, the industrial classes of the South would by then have been determining the policy of that region and not the coalition of liberal Carpetbaggers and former Confederates.

Philadelphia, November 5, 1868

Dear Sir:

Let us have peace! In these brief words you express the unanimous wish of the loyal portion of the nation, North and South, and of whatsoever shade of color. It is the one great and preponderant desire of all that portion of our population which, at the close of a tedious and destructive war, has now succeeded in placing in the presidential chair the man to whom they had been most of all indebted for suppression of the armed rebellion. That there should be peace, and that it should be permanent, is to the true interest of all, whether loyalists or rebels, and it is in the interest of all that I now propound the great question, *Shall we have peace* — not a temporary one to be maintained by aid of military force, but such a peace as shall tend, day by day and year by year, so to bind together and consolidate the different portions of the Union as to render absolutely impossible a recurrence of scenes of war and waste like to those through which we so recently have passed? *Can* we have such a peace? For answer to this I have to say that such an one has recently, and on the largest scale, been established in Central Europe, and that all now needed among ourselves is that we study carefully what has there been done, and then imitate the great example which has there been set us.

Five and thirty years since, Germany presented to view a collection of loose fragments, most of which were mere tools in the hands of neighboring powers, France or England at one hour, Russia or Austria at another. A state of civil war had for centuries been the chronic condition of the country and, as a necessary consequence, poverty, and such poverty as in our loyal States is entirely unknown, had, with but few exceptions, been the condition of all classes of her people.

Brief as is the period which has since elapsed, an empire has been there created embracing a population little short of 40,000,000, among whom education is universal; with a system of communications that, with the exception of those provided for the very dense populations and limited territories of England and Belgium, is not excelled by that of any other country; with an internal commerce as perfectly organized as any in the world, and growing from day to day with extraordinary rapidity; with a market on the land for nearly all its products, and, as a necessary consequence, with an agricultural population that grows daily in both intelligence and power; with a mercantile marine that now numbers more than 10,000 vessels; with a public treasury so well provided that not only has it made the recent war without need for negotiating loans, but that it has at once made large additions to the provision for public education; and with private treasuries so well supplied as to enable its people not only with their own means to build their own furnaces and factories and construct their own roads, but also to furnish hundreds of millions to the improvident people of America, to be by them applied to the making of roads in a country the abundance of whose natural resources should long since have placed it in the position of money lender, rather than that now occupied of general money borrower.

To what now, has this all been due? To the quiet and simple operation of the protective features of the system of the Zoll-Verein, the most important measure of the century, and among the most important ever adopted in Europe. Under it labor has been everywhere economized. Under it, the producers and consumers of a whole nation have been brought into communication with each other, and thus has been created a great society which is destined ultimately, in all probability, to produce effects throughout the

Eastern continent fully equal to any that may, by even the most sanguine, be hoped for in this Western one.

2. Five and thirty years since, Germany and the American Union exhibited states of things directly antagonistic, the one to the other. The first was divided and disturbed, its internal commerce in every way embarrassed, its people and its various governments very poor, and with little hope in the future except that which resulted from the fact that negotiations were then on foot for the formation of a Customs Union, which, shortly after, was accomplished. In the other, on the contrary, everything was different, the internal commerce having been more active than had ever before been known, the public treasury filled to overflowing, the national debt on the eve of extinction, and capital so much abounding as to make demand, for the opening of mines, the building of houses and mills, and the construction of roads, for all the labor power of a people that then numbered thirteen millions.

The cause of these remarkable differences was to be found in the facts, that, up to that time, Germany had wholly failed to adopt such measures of coordination as were needed for establishing circulation among its 30,000,000 of population; whereas, our Union had, five years before, and for the first time, adopted measures having for their object development of all the powers, physical, mental, or moral, of its people, all the wealth of its soil, and all the wonderful mineral deposits by which that soil was known to be underlaid. The one had failed to bring together the producer and consumer of food and wool, and had remained dependent upon traders in distant markets. The other had just then willed that such dependence should, at no distant time, come to an end; that producers and consumers should be brought together; and there had thence already resulted an activity of circulation and an improvement in physical and moral condition, the like of which had never before been known to be accomplished in so brief a period.

But little later (1835), the two countries are once again found totally opposed, Germany having adopted the American system and thus provided for freedom of internal commerce, America simultaneously adopting that which to Germany had proved so utterly disastrous, and which had been there rejected. Thenceforth the former moved steadily forward in the direction of creating a great domestic commerce, doing this by means of a railroad system which should so bind together her whole people as to forbid the idea of future separation. The result already exhibits itself in the quiet creation of the most powerful empire of Europe. The latter meanwhile has constructed great roads by means of which it has exported its soil, in the forms of tobacco, corn, and cotton, to distant markets, and has thus diminished its power to maintain internal commerce — the result obtained exhibiting itself in a great rebellion that has cost the country, North and South, half a million lives, the crippling of hundreds of thousands of men, and an expenditure of more thousands of millions than, properly applied, would have doubled the incomes of its whole people, while making such demand for human force, mental, moral, and physical, as would, in a brief period, have secured the establishment of universal freedom, with benefit to all, white and black, landowner and laborer. Such have been the widely different results of two systems of public policy, the one of which looks to introducing into society that proper, orderly arrangement which is found in every well conducted private establishment, and by means of which each and every person employed is enabled to find the place for which nature had intended him; the other, meanwhile, in accordance with the doctrine of *laisser faire*, requiring that government should abdicate the performance of its proper duties, wholly overlooking the fact that all the communities by which such teachings are carried into practical effect now exhibit themselves before the world in a state of utter ruin.

3. Studying now our American railroad system, we find the great trunk lines to be, so far as regards the North and the South, purely sectional, all of them running east and west and the whole constituting a collection of spokes in a great wheel whose hub, wholly controlled by men like Laird and other workers in aid of the great rebellion, is found in Liverpool. As a consequence of this it had been that our dependence on such men had become more complete as those great lines had increased in number, and with every such increase our financial crises had become more frequent and more severe. Prior to the war a single turn of the British screw had sufficed for ruining thousands of those who had invested their means in

the opening of mines, the building of furnaces or factories, and for thus crushing out the most important portions of our domestic commerce. With each such crisis there came increased necessity for scattering our people over the land, and for limiting ourselves to that single species of employment which is the essential characteristic of semibarbarism—the raising of raw produce for the supply of distant markets. From year to year the tide of white emigration rose, following always the lines of road and canal of the extreme North, and carefully avoiding the Central States. Simultaneously, south of Mason and Dixon's Line, a black emigration depleted the Center, Virginia and Kentucky, Maryland and Delaware, furnishing the bone and the muscle required for consumption in the fields of Mississippi and of Texas. As a consequence of this, the extreme South and the extreme North grew steadily in the proportions borne by them to the whole system, until at length, as an unavoidable consequence, the body broke in two, with serious danger of seeing the parts forever separated.

Why was this? For the simple reason that the revenue tariff policy so long and so steadily pursued had effectively prevented development of the wonderful mineral resources of Maryland, Virginia, North Carolina, and the whole column of States extending west of these, embracing hundreds of millions of acres the like of which had elsewhere no existence. Had our policy been different — had we strengthened the center — there would have been such a growth of domestic commerce that roads would have been made running north and south, northeast and southwest, southeast and northwest, thereby so tying together the various parts of the Union as to render it wholly impossible that the idea of secession should continue to have existence. *Had that center been strengthened, as it should have been the slave would have been becoming gradually free, independence would have been fully established, we should have had no rebellion, and we should have been spared the mortification of feeling that the solution of the question as to whether or not the Union could be maintained rested almost wholly in the minds of men like Russell and Napoleon.*

Turning now to a railroad map of Germany, we find that each and every part of that now greatest of all European empires has been, and is daily being, more and more brought into communication with each and every other as direct and cheap as is now the case in our little New England States. Bavaria and Wurtemberg on the south, Mecklenburg and Westphalia on the north, are now so tied together that separation, under any circumstances, has become a thing to be no longer thought of. That this was so was clearly shown at the close of the recent war, the sovereigns of southern Germany having been compelled, notwithstanding the solicitations of France and Austria, not only to maintain but even to strengthen their relations with the *Zoll-Verein*. Peace and harmony within — strength for resistance to attack from without — material and mental wealth — political and industrial independence — all had grown together with the growth of that domestic commerce which with us has so studiously and carefully been destroyed.

Widely different would be now the state of Europe had Southern and Northern Germany been accustomed to do as we have done, making all their exchanges with each other through the medium of Paris and Lyons, Liverpool and Havre. Had they done so, the great German empire could never have had existence. Had we *not* done so — had we *not* continued Liverpool as the hub of our great political wheel — we should have escaped an expenditure of hundreds of thousands of lives, and of thousands of millions of dollars. For all that waste we stand this day indebted to the men who gave us the tariffs of 1846 and 1857 in lieu of that highly protective one of 1842 under which the nation was so rapidly achieving a real independence; and by means of which the reward of labor had so much increased that, and for the first time, immigration began to count by hundreds of thousands. — *Desiring now to prevent a recurrence of that waste, we must have a policy capable of giving us the great domestic commerce for which nature has so well provided as the basis of the greatest foreign commerce the world ever yet has known.*

4. The difference between the two systems consists in this, that while Germany has been unremitting in her efforts to make a piece of cloth, warp and woof, America has limited her efforts to the making of warp alone, the filling having been entirely omitted. The one has sought increase of domestic commerce, creating a great network of roads, and bringing consumer and producer more nearly together; the other, meantime, has looked exclusively abroad,

wholly overlooking the fact that each and every step tended to the further separation of producer and consumer, and to the further diminution of power to maintain commerce of any kind, either abroad or at home.

The road toward perfect peace, perfect union, perfect freedom of trade, and perfect political independence, lies through the establishment of perfect industrial independence. It is the one on which Germany for forty years has travelled; the one which we, and just at the moment when its vast advantages were being proved, so often have abandoned. It is the one on which we *must* travel if we would have peace.

President Lincoln's attention having been, at the opening of the war, called to the view that is here presented, he recommended to Congress the making of a road through Kentucky to and through East Tennessee, to connect with other roads leading to South Atlantic ports. Had that suggestion been adopted, Kentucky would this day be a loyal State, and Tennessee would be now engaged in works of development causing such an emigration from the North as would be giving to her loyal people a power of control such as would insure the maintenance of peace. Had it been adopted, another road would probably have been suggested, leading from the Northeast to the Southwest, the two tending to bring about between the North and the South the same intimate relations which now exist between the East and the West. Rejected by Congress, an opportunity was thus lost that with difficulty will again be found. Twenty millions spent in the manner that Mr. Lincoln would have advised would have given us an emigration southward that would have effectually controlled the men who are now assuming the direction of the movements of Georgia, Alabama, and Mississippi. Those few millions would before this time have produced results that would now be cheap at hundreds, if not even thousands of millions.

Long persistence in a policy directly the reverse of that which has in so short a period built up the great German empire, has given us a rebellion, and that rebellion has led to a state of things wholly adverse to the maintenance of a permanent peace. So must it continue to be unless the national government can now be brought to cooperate with loyal Southern men for production of a change. Unaided, the people of the Center, the South, and the Southwest cannot make the roads that are now most needed, and without which there can be no security for the maintenance of such a state of things as would warrant Northern men in opening Southern mines, in building furnaces or factories, by means of which the consumers and producers of the South might be brought together. Can they have such aid? Apparently they cannot, millions upon millions being lavished upon Eastern and Western roads which, useful as they may eventually prove to be, tend now to intensification rather than to obliteration of the sectional feelings under which we already so greatly suffered. Such roads need comparatively little help from government, Eastern capitalists being always ready for any measures tending to bring trade to the great cities, European or American, of the Atlantic coast. Northern and Southern roads — roads tending toward the development of the extraordinary mineral wealth of the Central States — roads tending to enable the cotton of the South to reach mills and factories in the West — *do* need it, and for the reason that those capitalists are not yet so far enlightened as at all to appreciate the idea that the larger the domestic commerce the greater must be the power to purchase those finer commodities for which the Center, the West, and the South are accustomed to look to Philadelphia and Baltimore, New York and Boston.

An expenditure for such purposes, involving an annual demand upon the Treasury for less than half a dozen millions, would add five times that amount to the annual public revenue, while giving to the domestic commerce a development that would add countless millions to the money value of labor and land, and by promoting immigration from abroad would do more for elevation of the downtrodden people of the eastern continent than has been done by all its sovereigns from the days of Charlemagne.

That we may have permanent peace, and that the desire of all loyal men may thus be realized, it is needed that our people be brought to understand that between the various portions of the Union there is a perfect harmony of real and permanent interests, all profiting by measures looking to establishment of perfect political and industrial independence, and all suffering from those which tend to prolong a dependence upon those foreign communities that hailed with so much joy the action of the men who initiated the great rebellion.

Throughout the world the tendency toward peace, freedom, and independence has grown as consumers and producers have been brought more nearly together, as the societary circulation has become more rapid, and as land and labor have become more productive. That peace may be here maintained — that all may really enjoy equality of rights — that the Union may be perpetuated — and, that the country may enjoy a real independence — we *must* have a system that shall tend toward enabling our whole people to make their exchanges with each other freed from the interference of foreign ships, or foreign merchants.

In another letter I propose to show the bearing of the measures above proposed upon the condition of the recently enfranchised people of the south, and through them on the Union at large, meanwhile remaining, with great regard and respect,

Yours truly,
Henry C. Carey

Abraham Lincoln

(1809-1865)

Discoveries and Inventions
Address at Pittsburgh, Pennsylvania
Annual Address to the U.S. Congress
The Military Order of Emancipation
To the Workingmen of Manchester, England
The Last Public Address

Discoveries and Inventions

Abraham Lincoln once described this speech as his favorite stump speech of the 1860 presidential campaign. It is Lincoln's clearest public enunciation of the humanist world outlook as his own world outlook. He uses the Bible to demonstrate that by the use of inventions and discoveries, man has made successive advancements in his culture. More importantly, he locates the fundamental distinction between man and beast in man's continuing ability to change his mode of labor through such discoveries and inventions.

All creation is a mine, and every man a miner.

The whole earth, and all *within* it, *upon* it, and *round about* it, including *himself*, in his physical, moral, and intellectual nature, and his susceptibilities, are the infinitely various "leads" from which, man, from the first, was to dig out his destiny.

In the beginning, the mine was unopened, and the miner stood *naked*, and *knowledgeless*, upon it.

Fishes, birds, beasts, and creeping things, are not miners, but *feeders* and *lodgers* merely. Beavers build houses; but they build them in nowise differently, or better now, than they did, five thousand years ago. Ants and honey bees provide food for winter; but just in the *same way* they did, when Solomon referred the sluggard to them as patterns of prudence.

Man is not the only animal who labors; but he is the only one who *improves* his workmanship. This improvement he effects by *Discoveries* and *Inventions*. His first important discovery was the fact that he was naked; and his first invention was the fig-leaf apron. This simple article, the apron, made of leaves, seems to have been the origin of *clothing* — the one thing for which nearly half of the toil and care of the human race has ever since been expended. The most important improvement he ever made in connection with clothing, was the invention of *spinning* and *weaving*. The spinning jenny, and power loom, invented in modern times, though great *improvements*, do not, *as inventions*, rank with the ancient arts of spinning and weaving. Spinning and weaving brought into the department of clothing such abundance and variety of material. Wool, the hair of several species of animals, hemp, flax, cotton, silk, and perhaps other articles, were all suited to it, affording garments not only adapted to wet and dry, heat and cold, but also susceptible of high degrees of ornamental finish. Exactly *when*, or *where*, spinning and weaving originated is not known. At the first interview of the Almighty with Adam and Eve, after the fall, He made "coats of skins, and clothed them" (Genesis iii: 21).

The Bible makes no other allusion to clothing, *before* the flood. Soon *after* the deluge Noah's two sons covered him with a *garment*; but of what *material* the garment was made is not mentioned (Genesis ix: 23).

Abraham mentions "*thread*" in such connection as to indicate that spinning and weaving were in use in his day (Genesis xiv: 23), and soon after, reference to the art is frequently made. "*Linen breeches*" are mentioned (Exodus xxviii: 42), and it is said "all the women that were wise-hearted did *spin* with their hands" (Exodus xxxv: 25), and, "all the women whose heart stirred them up in wisdom *spun* goats' hair" (Exodus xxxv: 26). The work of the "*weaver*" is mentioned (Exodus xxxv: 35). In the book of Job, a very old book, date not exactly known, the "*weaver's shuttle*" is mentioned.

The above mention of "*thread*" by Abraham is the oldest recorded allusion to spinning and weaving; and *it* was made about two thousand years after the creation of man, and now, near four thousand years ago. Profane authors think these arts originated in Egypt; and this is not contradicted, or made improbable, by anything in the Bible; for the allusion of Abraham, mentioned, was not made until after he had sojourned in Egypt.

The discovery of the properties of *iron*, and the making of *iron tools*, must have been among the earliest of important discoveries and inventions. We can scarcely conceive the possibility of making much of anything else, without the use of iron tools. Indeed, an iron *hammer* must have been very much needed to make the *first* iron hammer with. A *stone* probably served as a substitute. How could the "*gopher wood*" for the Ark have been gotten without an axe? It seems to me an axe, or a miracle, was indispensable. Corresponding with the prime necessity for iron, we find at least one very early notice of it. Tubal-Cain was "an instructor of every artificer in *brass*

and *iron"* (Genesis iv: 22). Tubal-Cain was the seventh in descent
from Adam; and his birth was about one thousand years before the
flood. *After* the flood, frequent mention is made of *iron,* and *instruments* made of iron. Thus "instrument of iron" at Numbers xxxv:
16; "bedstead of iron" at Deuteronomy iii: 11; "the iron furnace" at
Deuteronomy iv: 20, and "iron tool" at Deuteronomy xxvii: 5. At
Deuteronomy xix: 5, very distinct mention of "the ax to cut down
the tree" is made; and also at Deuteronomy viii: 9, the promised
land is described as "a land whose stones are iron, and out of whose
hills thou mayest dig brass." From the somewhat frequent mention
of brass in connection with iron, it is not improbable that brass —
perhaps what we now call copper — was used by the ancients for
some of the same purposes as iron.

Transportation — the removal of person and goods from place
to place — would be an early *object*, if not a *necessity*, with man. By
his natural powers of locomotion, and without much assistance from
discovery and invention, he could move himself about with considerable facility; and even, could carry small burthens with him.
But very soon he would wish to lessen the labor, while he might, at
the same time, extend, and expedite the business. For this object,
wheel-carriages, and water-crafts — wagons and boats — are the
most important inventions. The use of the wheel and axle has been
so long known, that it is difficult, without reflection, to estimate it at
its true value. The oldest recorded allusion to the wheel and axle is
the mention of a "chariot" (Genesis xli: 43). This was in Egypt,
upon the occasion of Joseph being made governor by Pharaoh. It
was about twenty-five hundred years after the creation of Adam.
That the chariot then mentioned was a wheel-carriage drawn by
animals is sufficiently evidenced by the mention of chariot *wheels*
(Exodus xiv: 25), and the mention of chariots in connection with
horses in the same chapter, verses 9 and 23. So much, at present, for
land transportation.

Now, as to transportation by *water*, I have concluded, without
sufficient authority perhaps, to use the term "boat" as a general
name for all water-craft. The boat is indispensable to navigation. It
is not probable that the philosophical principle upon which the use
of the boat primarily depends — towit, the *principle,* that anything
will float, which cannot sink without displacing more than its own

weight of water — was known, or even thought of, before the first boats were made. The sight of a crow standing on a piece of drift-wood floating down the swollen current of a creek or river, might well enough suggest the specific idea to a savage, that he could himself get upon a log, or on two logs tied together, and somehow work his way to the opposite shore of the same stream. Such a suggestion, so taken, would be the birth of navigation; and such, not improbable, it really *was*. The leading idea was thus caught; and whatever came afterwards, were but improvements upon, and auxiliaries to, it.

As man is a land animal, it might be expected he would learn to travel by land somewhat earlier than he would by water. Still the crossing of streams, somewhat too deep for wading, would be an early necessity with him. If we pass by the Ark, which may be regarded as belonging rather to the *miraculous* than to *human* invention, the first notice we have of water-craft is the mention of "ships" by Jacob (Genesis xlix: 13). It is not till we reach the book of Isaiah that we meet with the mention of "oars" and "sails."

As man's *food* — his first necessity was to be derived from the vegetation of the earth, it was natural that his first care should be directed to the assistance of that vegetation. And accordingly we find that, even before the fall, the man was put into the garden of Eden "to dress it, and to keep it." And when afterwards, in conse-quence of the first transgression, *labor* was imposed on the race, as a *penalty* — a *curse* — we find the first born man — the first heir of the curse — was "a tiller of the ground." This was the beginning of agriculture; and although, both in point of time, and of importance, it stands at the head of all branches of human industry, it has de-rived less direct advantage from Discovery and Invention, than al-most any other. The plow, of very early origin; and reaping, and threshing, machines, of modern invention are, at this day, the prin-cipal improvements in agriculture. And even the oldest of these, the plow, could not have been conceived of, until a precedent concep-tion had been caught, and put into practice — I mean the concep-tion, or idea, of substituting other forces in nature, for man's own muscular power. These other forces, as now used, are principally, the *strength* of animals, and the *power* of the wind, of running streams, and of steam.

Climbing upon the back of an animal, and making it carry us, might not occur very readily. I think the back of the camel would never have suggested it. It was, however, a matter of vast importance. The earliest instance of it mentioned, is when "Abraham rose up early in the morning, and saddled his ass" (Genesis xxii: 3), preparatory to sacrificing Isaac as a burnt-offering; but the allusion to the *saddle* indicates that riding had been in use some time; for it is quite probable they rode bare-backed awhile, at least, before they invented saddles.

The *idea*, being once conceived, of riding *one* species of animals, would soon be extended to others. Accordingly we find that when the servant of Abraham went in search of a wife for Isaac, he took ten *camels* with him; and, on his return trip, "Rebekah arose, and her damsels, and they rode upon the camels, and followed the man" (Genesis xxiv: 61).

The *horse*, too, as a riding animal, is mentioned early. The Red Sea being safely passed, Moses and the children of Israel sang to the Lord "the *horse* and his *rider* hath he thrown into the sea" (Exodus xv: I).

Seeing that animals could bear *man* upon their backs, it would soon occur that they could also bear other burthens. Accordingly we find that Joseph's brethren, on their first visit to Egypt, "laded their asses with the corn, and departed thence" (Genesis xlii: 26).

Also it would occur that animals could be made to *draw* burthens *after* them, as well as to bear them upon their backs; and hence plows and chariots came into use early enough to be often mentioned in the books of Moses (Deuteronomy xxii: 10; Genesis xli: 43; xlvi: 29; Exodus xiv: 25).

Of all the forces of nature, I should think the *wind* contains the largest amount of *motive power* — that is, power to move things. Take any given space of the earth's surface — for instance, Illinois; and all the power exerted by all the men, and beasts, and running-water, and steam, over and upon it, shall not equal the one hundredth part of what is exerted by the blowing of the wind over and upon the same space. And yet it has not, so far in the world's history, become proportionably *valuable* as a motive power. It is applied extensively, and advantageously, to sail-vessels in navigation. Add to this a few wind-mills, and pumps, and you have about all. That, as yet, no very successful mode of *controlling*, and *directing* the wind, has been discovered; and that, naturally, it moves by fits and starts — now so gently as to scarcely stir a leaf, and now so roughly as to level a forest — doubtless have been the insurmountable difficulties. As yet, the wind is an *untamed*, and *unharnessed* force; and quite possibly one of the greatest discoveries hereafter to be made, will be the taming, and harnessing of it. That the difficulties of controlling this power are very great is quite evident by the fact that they have already been perceived, and struggled with more than three thousand years; for that power was applied to sail-vessels, at least as early as the time of the prophet Isaiah.

In speaking of *running streams*, as a motive power, I mean its application to mills and other machinery by means of the "*water wheel*" — a thing now well known, and extensively used; but, of which, no mention is made in the Bible, though it is thought to have been in use among the Romans. (Am. Ency.-Mill), the language of the Saviour "Two women shall be grinding at the mill, etc." indicates that, even in the populous city of Jerusalem, at that day, mills were operated by hand — having, as yet had no other than human power applied to them.

The advantageous use of *Steam-power* is, unquestionably, a modern discovery. And yet, as much as two thousand years ago the power of steam was not only observed, but an ingenious toy was actually made and put in motion by it, at Alexandria in Egypt. What appears strange is, that neither the inventor of the toy, nor any one else, for so long a time afterwards, should perceive that steam would move *useful* machinery as well as a toy.

Address at Pittsburgh, Pennsylvania

Abraham Lincoln delivered this speech [excerpted here] on February 15, 1861, following his election to the presidency of the United States. He pledged to fulfill that section of the Republican Party platform which was written by Henry Carey and which called on the U.S. government to readopt the Whig policy of protection for the nation's industry and agriculture.

...The condition of the country is an extraordinary one, and fills the mind of every patriot with anxiety. It is my intention to give this subject all the consideration I possibly can, before specially deciding in regard to it, so that when I do speak, it may be as nearly right as possible. When I do speak, I hope I may say nothing in opposition to the spirit of the Constitution, contrary to the integrity of the Union, or which will prove inimical to the liberties of the people or to the peace of the whole country. And furthermore, when the time arrives for me to speak on this great subject, I hope I may say nothing to disappoint the people generally throughout the country, especially if the expectation has been based upon anything which I have heretofore said.

... If the great American people only keep their temper on both sides of the line, the troubles will come to an end, and the question which now distracts the country will be settled, just as surely as all other difficulties of a like character which have originated in this government have been adjusted. Let the people on both sides keep their self-possession, and just as other clouds have cleared away in due time, so will this great nation continue to prosper as heretofore.

... It is often said that the tariff is the specialty of Pennsylvania. Assuming that direct taxation is not to be adopted, the tariff question must be as durable as the government itself. It is a question of national housekeeping. It is to the government what replenishing the meal-tub is to the family. Ever-varying circumstances will require frequent modifications as to the amount needed and the sources of supply. So far there is little difference of opinion among the people. It is only whether, and how far, duties on imports shall be adjusted to favor home productions. In the home market that controversy begins. One party insists that too much protection oppresses one class for the advantage of another; while the other party argues that, with all its incidents, in the long run all classes are benefited. In the Chicago platform there is a plank upon this subject, which should be a general law to the incoming Administration. We should do neither more nor less than we gave the people reason to believe we would when they gave us their votes. That plank is as I now read:

> "That while providing revenue for the support of the general government by duties upon imports, sound policy requires such an adjustment of these imports as will encourage the development of the industrial interest of the whole country; and we commend that policy of national exchanges which secures to working-men liberal wages, to agriculture remunerating prices, to mechanics and manufacturers

adequate reward for their skill, labor, and enterprise, and to the nation commercial prosperity and independence."

... My political education strongly inclines me against a very free use of any of the means by the Executive to control the legislation of the country. As a rule, I think it better that Congress should originate as well as perfect its measures without external bias. I therefore would rather recommend to every gentleman who knows he is to be a member of the next Congress, to take an enlarged view, and post himself thoroughly, so as to contribute his part to such an adjustment of the tariff as shall provide a sufficient revenue, and in its other bearings, so far as possible, be just and equal to all sections of the country and classes of the people.

Annual Address
To the U.S. Congress

Addressing the second session of the thirty-seventh Congress on December 3, 1861, President Lincoln put to rest the many questions over how the nation's finances were to be carried out in the midst of the Civil War. He asserted a labor theory of value in opposition to British cost-accounting methods as the only appropriate method of accounting for wealth in an industrial-capitalist economy. The war effort, he announced, would be financed through government-funded debt — a Hamiltonian proposal — and not by hocking U.S. credit to the Rothschild and Baring banking houses. He urged all factions to support this policy.

December 3, 1861

Fellow Citizens of the Senate and House of Representatives:

In the midst of unprecedented political troubles, we have cause of great gratitude to God for unusual good health, and most abundant harvests.

You will not be surprised to learn that, in the peculiar exigencies of the times, our intercourse with foreign nations has been attended with profound solicitude, chiefly turning upon our own domestic affairs.

A disloyal portion of the American people have, during the whole year, been engaged in an attempt to divide and destroy the Union. A nation which endures factious domestic division, is exposed to disrespect abroad; and one party, if not both, is sure, sooner or later, to invoke foreign intervention.

Nations, thus tempted to interfere, are not always able to resist the counsels of seeming expediency, and ungenerous ambition, although measures adopted under such influences seldom fail to be unfortunate and injurious to those adopting them.

The disloyal citizens of the United States who have offered the ruin of our country, in return for the aid and comfort which they have invoked abroad, have received less patronage and encouragement than they probably expected. If it were just to suppose, as the insurgents have seemed to assume, that foreign nations, in this case, discarding all moral, social, and treaty obligations, would act solely, and selfishly, for the most speedy restoration of commerce, including, especially, the acquisition of cotton, those nations appear, as yet, not to have seen their way to their object more directly, or clearly, through the destruction, than through the preservation, of the Union. If we could dare to believe that foreign nations are actuated by no higher principle than this, I am quite sure a sound argument could be made to show them that they can reach their aim more readily, and easily, by aiding to crush this rebellion, than by giving encouragement to it.

The principal lever relied on by the insurgents for exciting foreign nations to hostility against us, as already intimated, is the embarrassment of commerce. Those nations, however, not improbably, saw from the first, that it was the Union which made as well our foreign, as our domestic, commerce. They can scarcely have failed to perceive that the effort for disunion produces the existing difficulty; and that one strong nation promises more durable peace, and a more extensive, valuable and reliable commerce, than can the same nation broken into hostile fragments.

It is not my purpose to review our discussions with foreign states, because whatever might be their wishes, or dispositions, the integrity of our country, and the stability of our government, mainly depend, not upon them, but on the loyalty, virtue, patriotism, and intelligence of the American people. The correspondence itself, with the usual reservations, is herewith submitted.†

---

† This correspondence may be found in Thirty-seventh Congress, Second Session, *Senate Executive Document No. 1,* I, 21-441 — A.S.

I venture to hope it will appear that we have practiced prudence, and liberality toward foreign powers, averting causes of irritation; and, with firmness, maintaining our own rights and honor.

Since, however, it is apparent that here, as in every other state, foreign dangers necessarily attend domestic difficulties, I recommend that adequate and ample measures be adopted for maintaining the public defences on every side. While, under this general recommendation, provision for defending our sea-coast line readily occurs to the mind, I also, in the same connection, ask the attention of Congress to our great lakes and rivers. It is believed that some fortifications and depots of arms and munitions, with harbor and navigation improvements, all at well selected points upon these, would be of great importance to the national defence and preservation. I ask attention to the views of the Secretary of War, expressed in his report, upon the same general subject.

I deem it of importance that the loyal regions of East Tennessee and western North Carolina should be connected with Kentucky, and other faithful parts of the Union, by railroad. I therefore recommend, as a military measure, that Congress provide for the construction of such road, as speedily as possible. Kentucky, no doubt, will cooperate, and, through her legislature, make the most judicious selection of a line. The northern terminus must connect with some existing railroad; and whether the route shall be from Lexington, or Nicholasville, to the Cumberland Gap; or from Lebanon to the Tennessee line, in the direction of Knoxville; or on some still different line, can easily be determined. Kentucky and the general government cooperating, the work can be completed in a very short time; and when done, it will be not only of vast present usefulness, but also a valuable permanent improvement, worth its cost in all the future.

Some treaties, designed chiefly for the interests of commerce, and having no grave political importance, have been negotiated, and will be submitted to the Senate for their consideration.

Although we have failed to induce some of the commercial powers to adopt a desirable melioration of the rigor of maritime war, we have removed all obstructions from the way of this humane reform, except such as are merely of temporary and accidental occurrence.

I invite your attention to the correspondence between her Britannic Majesty's minister accredited to this government, and the Secretary of State, relative to the detention of the British ship *Perthshire* in June last, by the United States steamer *Massachusetts,* for a supposed breach of the blockade. As this detention was occasioned by an obvious misapprehension of the facts, and as justice requires that we should commit no belligerent act not founded in strict right, as sanctioned by public law, I recommend that an appropriation be made to satisfy the reasonable demand of the owners of the vessel for her detention.

I repeat the recommendation of my predecessor, in his annual message to Congress in December last, in regard to the disposition of the surplus which will probably remain after satisfying the claims of American citizens against China, pursuant to the awards of the commissioners under the act of the 3rd of March, 1859. If, however, it should not be deemed advisable to carry that recommendation into effect, I would suggest that authority be given for investing the principal, over the proceeds of the surplus referred to, in good securities, with a view to the satisfaction of such other just claims of our citizens against China as are not unlikely to arise hereafter in the course of our extensive trade with that Empire.

By the act of the 5th of August last, Congress authorized the President to instruct the commanders of suitable vessels to defend themselves against, and to capture pirates. This authority has been exercised in a single instance only. For the more effectual protection of our extensive and valuable commerce, in the eastern seas especially, it seems to me that it would also be advisable to authorize the commanders of sailing vessels to recapture any prizes which pirates might make of United States vessels and their cargoes, and the consular courts, now established by law in eastern countries, to adjudicate the cases, in the event that this should not be objected to by the local authorities.

If any good reason exists why we should persevere longer in withholding our recognition of the independence and sovereignty of Hayti and Liberia, I am unable to discern it. Unwilling, however, to inaugurate a novel policy in regard to them without the approbation of Congress, I submit for your consideration the expediency of an appropriation for maintaining a chargé d'affaires near each of those new states. It does not admit of doubt that important commercial advantages might be secured by favorable commercial treaties with them.

The operations of the Treasury during the period which has elapsed since your adjournment have been conducted with signal success. The patriotism of the people has placed at the disposal of the government the large means demanded by the public exigencies. Much of the national loan has been taken by citizens of the industrial classes, whose confidence in their country's faith, and zeal for their country's deliverance from present peril, have induced them to contribute to the support of the government the whole of their limited acquisitions. This fact imposes peculiar obligations to economy in disbursement and energy in action.

The revenue from all sources, including loans, for the financial year ending on the 30th June, 1861, was $86,835,900.27, and the expenditures for the same period, including payments on account of the public debt, were $84,578,834.47; leaving a balance in the treasury, on the 1st July, of $2,257,065.80. For the first quarter of the financial year, ending on the 30th September, 1861, the receipts from all sources, including the balance of first of July, were $102,532,509.27, and the expenses $98,239,733.09; leaving a balance on the 1st of October, 1861, of $4,292,776.18.

Estimates for the remaining three quarters of the year, and for the financial year 1863, together with his views of ways and means for meeting the demands contemplated by them, will be submitted to Congress by the Secretary of the Treasury. It is gratifying to know that the expenditures made necessary by the rebellion are not beyond the resources of the loyal people, and to believe that the same patriotism which has thus far sustained the government will continue to sustain it till Peace and Union shall again bless the land.

I respectfully refer to the report of the Secretary of War for information respecting the numerical strength of the army, and for recommendations having in view an increase of its efficiency and the well being of the various branches of the service intrusted to his care. It is gratifying to know that the patriotism of the people has proved equal to the occasion, and that the number of troops tendered greatly exceeds the force which Congress authorized me to call into the field.

I refer with pleasure to those portions of his report which make allusion to the creditable degree of discipline already attained by our troops, and to the excellent sanitary condition of the entire army.

The recommendation of the Secretary for an organization of the militia upon a uniform basis, is a subject of vital importance to the future safety of the country, and is commended to the serious attention of Congress.

The large addition to the regular army, in connection with the defection that has so considerably diminished the number of its officers, gives peculiar importance to his recommendation for increasing the corps of cadets to the greatest capacity of the Military Academy.

By mere omission, I presume, Congress has failed to provide chaplains for hospitals occupied by volunteers. This subject was brought to my notice, and I was induced to draw up the form of a letter, one copy of which, properly addressed, has been delivered to each of the persons, and at the dates respectively named and stated, in a schedule, containing also the form of the letter, marked A, and herewith transmitted.

These gentlemen, I understand, entered upon the duties designated, at the times respectively stated in the schedule, and have labored faithfully therein ever since. I therefore recommend that they be compensated at the same rate as chaplains in the army. I further suggest that general provision be made for chaplains to serve at hospitals, as well as with regiments.

The report of the Secretary of the Navy presents in detail the operations of that branch of the service, the activity and energy which have characterized its administration, and the results of measures to increase its efficiency and power. Such have been the additions, by construction and purchase, that it may almost be said a navy has been created and brought into service since our difficulties commenced.

Besides blockading our extensive coast, squadrons larger than ever before assembled under our flag have been put afloat and performed deeds which have increased our naval renown.

I would invite special attention to the recommendation of the Secretary for a more perfect organization of the navy by introducing additional grades in the service.

The present organization is defective and unsatisfactory, and the suggestions submitted by the department will, it is believed, if adopted, obviate the difficulties alluded to, promote harmony, and increase the efficiency of the navy.

There are three vacancies on the bench of the Supreme Court — two by the decease of Justices Daniel and McLean, and one by the resignation of Justice Campbell. I have so far forborne making nominations to fill these vacancies for reasons which I will now state. Two of the outgoing judges resided within the States now overrun by revolt; so that if successors were appointed in the same localities, they could not now serve upon their circuits; and many of the most competent men there, probably would not take the personal hazard of accepting to serve, even here, upon the supreme bench. I have been unwilling to throw all the appointments northward, thus disabling myself from doing justice to the south on the return of peace; although I may remark that to transfer to the north one which has heretofore been in the south, would not, with reference to territory and population, be unjust.

During the long and brilliant judicial career of Judge McLean his circuit grew into an empire — altogether too large for any one judge to give the courts therein more than a nominal attendance — rising in population from one million four hundred and seventy-thousand and eighteen, in 1830, to six million one hundred and fifty-one thousand four hundred and five, in 1860.

Besides this, the country generally has outgrown our present judicial system. If uniformity was at all intended, the system requires that all the States shall be accomodated with circuit courts, attended by supreme judges, while, in fact, Wisconsin, Minnesota, Iowa, Kansas, Florida, Texas, California, and Oregon, have never had any such courts. Nor can this well be remedied without a change of the system; because the adding of judges to the Supreme Court, enough for the accommodation of all parts of the country, with circuit courts, would create a court altogether too numerous for a judicial body of any sort. And the evil, if it be one, will increase as new States come into the Union. Circuit courts are useful, or they are not useful. If useful, no State should be denied them; if not useful, no State should have them. Let them be provided for all, or abolished as to all.

Three modifications occur to me, either of which, I think, would be an improvement upon our present system. Let the Supreme Court be of convenient number in every event. Then, first, let the whole country be divided into circuits of convenient size, the supreme judges to serve in a number of them corresponding to their own number, and independent circuit judges be provided for all the rest. Or, secondly, let the supreme judges be relieved from circuit duties, and circuit judges provided for all the circuits. Or, thirdly, dispense with circuit courts altogether, leaving the judicial functions wholly to the district courts and an independent Supreme Court.

I respectfully recommend to the consideration of Congress the present condition of the statute laws, with the hope that Congress will be able to find an easy remedy for many of the inconveniences and evils which constantly embarrass those engaged in the practical administration of them. Since the organization of the government, Congress has enacted some five thousand acts and joint resolutions, which fill more than six thousand closely printed pages, and are scattered through many volumes. Many of these acts have been drawn in haste and without sufficient caution, so that their provisions are often obscure in themselves, or in conflict with each other, or at least so doubtful as to render it very difficult for even the best informed persons to ascertain precisely what the statute law really is.

It seems to me very important that the statute laws should be made as plain and intelligible as possible, and be reduced to as small a compass as may consist with the fullness and precision of the will of the legislature and the perspicuity of its language. This, well done, would, I think, greatly facilitate the labors of those whose duty it is to assist in the administration of the laws, and would be a lasting benefit to the people, by placing before them, in a more accessible and intelligible form, the laws which so deeply concern their interests and their duties.

I am informed by some whose opinions I respect, that all the acts of Congress now in force, and of a permanent and general nature, might be revised and rewritten, so as to be embraced in one volume (or at most, two volumes) of ordinary and convenient size. And I respectfully recommend to Congress to consider of the subject, and, if my suggestion be approved, to devise such plan as to their wisdom shall seem most proper for the attainment of the end proposed.

One of the unavoidable consequences of the present insurrection is the entire suppression, in many places, of all the ordinary means of administering civil justice by the officers and in the forms of existing law. This is the case, in whole or in part, in all the insurgent States; and as our armies advance upon and take possession of parts of those States, the practical evil becomes more apparent. There are no courts nor officers to whom the citizens of other States may apply for the enforcement of their lawful claims against citizens of the insurgent States; and there is a vast amount of debt constituting such claims. Some have estimated it as high as two hundred million dollars, due, in large part, from insurgents, in open rebellion, to loyal citizens who are, even now, making great sacrifices in the discharge of their patriotic duty to support the government.

Under these circumstances, I have been urgently solicited to establish, by military power, courts to administer summary justice in such cases. I have thus far declined to do it, not because I had any doubt that the end proposed — the collection of the debts — was just and right in itself, but because I have been unwilling to go beyond the pressure of necessity in the unusual exercise of power. But the powers of Congress I suppose are equal to the anomalous occasion, and therefore I refer the whole matter to Congress, with the hope that a plan may be devised for the administration of justice in all such parts of the insurgent States and Territories as may be under the control of this government, whether by a voluntary return to allegiance and order or by the power of our arms. This, however, not to be a permanent institution, but a temporary substitute, and to cease as soon as the ordinary courts can be reestablished in peace.

It is important that some more convenient means should be provided, if possible, for the adjustment of claims against the government, especially in view of their increased number by reason of the war. It is as much the duty of government to render prompt justice against itself, in favor of citizens, as it is to administer the same, between private individuals. The investigation and adjudication of claims, in their nature belong to the judicial department; besides it is apparent that the attention of Congress, will be more than usually engaged, for some time to come, with great national questions. It was intended, by the organization of the court of claims, mainly to remove this branch of business from the halls of

Congress; but while the court has proved to be an effective, and valuable means of investigation, it in great degree fails to effect the object of its creation, for want of power to make its judgments final.

Fully aware of the delicacy, not to say the danger, of the subject, I commend to your careful consideration whether this power of making judgments final, may not properly be given to the court, reserving the right of appeal on questions of law to the Supreme Court, with such other provisions as experience may have shown to be necessary.

I ask attention to the report of the Postmaster General, the following being a summary statement of the condition of the department:

The revenue from all sources during the fiscal year ending June 30, 1861, including the annual permanent appropriation of $700,000 for the transportation of "free mail matter," was $9,049,296.40, being about two percent less than the revenue for 1860.

The expenditures were $13,606,759.11, showing a decrease of more than eight percent as compared with those of the previous year, and leaving an excess of expenditure over the revenue for the last fiscal year of $4,557,462.71.

The gross revenue for the year ending June 30, 1863, is estimated at an increase of four percent on that of 1861, making $8,683,000, to which should be added the earnings of the department in carrying free matter, viz: $700,000, making $9,383,000.

The total expenditures for 1863 are estimated at $12,528,000, leaving an estimated deficiency of $3,145,000, to be supplied from the treasury, in addition to the permanent appropriation.

The present insurrection shows, I think, that the extension of this District across the Potomac river, at the time of establishing the capital here, was eminently wise, and consequently that the relinquishment of that portion of it which lies within the State of Virginia was unwise and dangerous. I submit for your consideration the expediency of regaining that part of the District, and the restoration of the original boundaries thereof, through negotiations with the State of Virginia.

The report of the Secretary of the Interior, with the ac-companying documents, exhibits the condition of the several branches of the public business pertaining to that department. The depressing influences of the insurrection have been especially felt in the operations of the Patent and General Land Offices. The cash receipts from the sales of public lands during the past year have exceeded the expenses of our land system only about $200,000. The sales have been entirely suspended in the southern States, while the interruptions to the business of the country, and the diversion of large numbers of men from labor to military service, have obstructed settlements in the new States and Territories of the northwest.

The receipts of the Patent Office have declined in nine months about $100,000, rendering a large reduction of the force employed necessary to make it self sustaining.

The demands upon the Pension Office will be largely increased by the insurrection. Numerous applications for pensions, based upon the casualties of the existing war, have already been made. There is reason to believe that many who are now upon the pension rolls and in receipt of the bounty of the government, are in the ranks of the insurgent army, or giving them aid and comfort. The Secretary of the Interior has directed a suspension of the payment of the pensions of such persons upon proof of their disloyalty. I recommend that Congress authorize that officer to cause the names of such persons to be stricken from the pension rolls.

The relations of the government with the Indian tribes have been greatly disturbed by the insurrection, especially in the southern superintendency and in that of New Mexico. The Indian country south of Kansas is in the possession of insurgents from Texas and Arkansas. The agents of the United States appointed since the 4th. of March for this superintendency have been unable to reach their posts, while the most of those who were in office before that time have espoused the insurrectionary cause, and assume to exercise the powers of agents by virtue of commissions from the insurrectionists. It has been stated in the public press that a portion of those Indians have been organized as a military force, and are attached to the army of the insurgents. Although the government has no official information upon this subject, letters have been written to the Commissioner of Indian Affairs by several prominent chiefs, giving assurance of their loyalty to the United States, and expressing a wish for the presence of federal troops to protect them. It is believed that upon the repossession of the country by the federal forces the Indians will readily cease all hostile demonstrations, and resume their former relations to the government.

Agriculture, confessedly the largest interest of the nation, has, not a department, nor a bureau, but a clerkship only, assigned to it in the government. While it is fortunate that this great interest is so independent in its nature as to not have demanded and extorted more from the government, I respectfully ask Congress to consider whether something more cannot be given voluntarily with general advantage.

Annual reports exhibiting the condition of our agriculture, commerce, and manufacturers would present a fund of information of great practical value to the country. While I make no suggestion as to details, I venture the opinion that an agricultural and statistical bureau might profitably be organized.

The execution of the laws for the suppression of the African slave trade, has been confided to the Department of the Interior. It is a subject of gratulation that the efforts which have been made for the suppression of this inhuman traffic, have been recently attended with unusual success. Five vessels being fitted out for the slave trade have been seized and condemned. Two mates of vessels engaged in the trade, and one person in equipping a vessel as a slaver, have been convicted and subjected to the penalty of fine and imprisonment, and one captain, taken with a cargo of Africans on board his vessel, has been convicted of the highest grade of offence under our laws, the punishment of which is death.

The Territories of Colorado, Dakotah and Nevada, created by the last Congress, have been organized, and civil administration has been inaugurated therein under auspices especially gratifying, when it is considered that the leaven of treason was found existing in some of these new countries when the federal officers arrived there.

The abundant natural resources of these Territories, with the security and protection afforded by organized government, will doubtless invite to them a large immigration when peace shall restore the business of the country to its accustomed channels. I submit the resolutions of the legislature of Colorado, which evidence the patriotic spirit of the people of the Territory. So far the authority of the United States has been upheld in all the Territories, as it is hoped it will be in the future. I commend their interests and defence to the enlightened and generous care of Congress.

I recommend to the favorable consideration of Congress the interests of the District of Columbia. The insurrection has been the cause of much suffering and sacrifice to its inhabitants, and as they have no representative in Congress, that body should not overlook their just claims upon the government.

At your late session a joint resolution was adopted authorizing the President to take measures for facilitating a proper representation of the industrial interests of the United States at the exhibition of the industry of all nations to be holden at London in the year 1862. I regret to say I have been unable to give personal attention to this subject,— a subject at once so interesting in itself, and so extensively and intimately connected with the material prosperity of the world. Through the Secretaries of State and of the Interior a plan, or system, has been devised, and partly matured, and which will be laid before you.

Under and by virtue of the act of Congress entitled "An act to confiscate property used for insurrectionary purposes," approved August 6, 1861, the legal claims of certain persons to the labor and service of certain other persons have become forfeited; and numbers of the latter, thus liberated, are already dependent on the United States, and must be provided for in some way. Besides this, it is not impossible that some of the States will pass similar enactments for their own benefit respectively, and by operation of which persons of the same class will be thrown upon them for disposal. In such case I recommend that Congress provide for accepting such persons from such States, according to some mode of valuation, in lieu, *pro tanto*, of direct taxes, or upon some other plan to be agreed on with such States respectively; that such persons, on such acceptance by the general government, be at once deemed free; and that, in any event, steps be taken for colonizing both classes, (or the one first mentioned, if the other shall not be brought into existence,) at some place, or places, in a climate congenial to them. It might be well to consider, too,— whether the free colored people already in the United States could not, so far as individuals may desire, be included in such colonization.

To carry out the plan of colonization may involve the acquiring of territory, and also the appropriation of money beyond that to be expended in the territorial acquisition. Having practiced the acquisition of territory for nearly sixty years, the question of constitutional power to do so is no longer an open one with us. The power was questioned at first by Mr. Jefferson, who, however, in the purchase of Louisiana, yielded his scruples on the plea of great expediency. If it be said that the only legitimate object of acquiring territory is to furnish homes for white men, this measure effects that object; for the emigration of colored men leaves additional room for white men remaining or coming here. Mr. Jefferson, however, placed the importance of procuring Louisiana more on political and commercial grounds than on providing room for population.

On this whole proposition, — including the appropriation of money with the acquisition of territory, does not the expediency amount to absolute necessity— that, without which the government itself cannot be perpetuated? The war continues. In considering the policy to be adopted for suppressing the insurrection, I have been anxious and careful that the inevitable conflict for this purpose shall not degenerate into a violent and remorseless revolutionary struggle. I have, therefore, in every case, thought it proper to keep the integrity of the Union prominent as the primary object of the contest on our part, leaving all questions which are not of vital military importance to the more deliberate action of the legislature.

In the exercise of my best discretion I have adhered to the blockade of the ports held by the insurgents, instead of putting in force, by proclamation, the law of Congress enacted at the late session, for closing those ports.

So, also, obeying the dictates of prudence, as well as the obligation of law, instead of transcending, I have adhered to the act of Congress to confiscate property used for insurrectionary purposes. If a new law upon the same subject shall be proposed, its propriety will be duly considered.

The Union must be preserved, and hence, all indispensable means must be employed. We should not be in haste to determine that radical and extreme measures, which may reach the loyal as well as the disloyal, are indispensable.

The inaugural address at the beginning of the Administration, and the message to Congress at the late special session, were both mainly devoted to the domestic controversy out of which the insurrection and consequent war have sprung. Nothing new occurs to add or subtract, to or from, the principles or general purposes stated and expressed in those documents.

The last ray of hope for preserving the Union peaceably, expired at the assault upon Fort Sumter; and a general review of what has occurred since may not be unprofitable. What was painfully uncertain then, is much better defined and more distinct now; and the progress of events is plainly in the right direction. The insurgents confidently claimed a strong support from north of Mason and Dixon's line; and the friends of the Union were not free from apprehension on the point. This, however, was soon settled definitely and on the right side. South of the line, noble little Delaware led off right from the first. Maryland was made to *seem* against the Union. Our soldiers were assaulted, bridges were burned, and railroads torn up, within her limits; and we were many days, at one time, without the ability to bring a single regiment over her soil to the capital. Now, her bridges and railroads are repaired and open to the government; she already gives seven regiments to the cause of the Union and none to the enemy; and her people, at a regular election, have sustained the Union, by a larger majority, and a larger aggregate vote than they ever before gave to any candidate, or any question. Kentucky, too, for some time in doubt, is now decidedly, and, I think, unchangeably, ranged on the side of the Union. Missouri is comparatively quiet; and I believe cannot again be overrun by the insurrectionists. These three States of Maryland, Kentucky, and Missouri, neither of which would promise a single soldier at first, have now an aggregate of not less than forty thousand in the field, for the Union; while, of their citizens, certainly not more than a third of that number, and they of doubtful whereabouts, and doubtful existence, are in arms against it. After a somewhat bloody struggle of months, winter closes on the Union people of western Virginia, leaving them masters of their own country.

An insurgent force of about fifteen hundred, for months dominating the narrow peninsular region, constituting the counties of Accomac and Northampton, and known as eastern shore of

Virginia, together with some contiguous parts of Maryland, have laid down their arms; and the people there have renewed their allegiance to, and accepted the protection of, the old flag. This leaves no armed insurrectionist north of the Potomac, or east of the Chesapeake.

Also we have obtained a footing at each of the isolated points, on the southern coast, of Hatteras, Port Royal, Tybee Island, near Savannah, and Ship Island; and we likewise have some general accounts of popular movements, in behalf of the Union, in North Carolina and Tennessee.

These things demonstrate that the cause of the Union is advancing steadily and certainly southward.

Since your last adjournment, Lieutenant General Scott has retired from the head of the army. During his long life, the nation has not been unmindful of his merit; yet, on calling to mind how faithfully, ably and brilliantly he has served the country, from a time far back in our history, when few of the now living had been born, and thenceforward continually, I cannot but think we are still his debtors. I submit, therefore, for your consideration, what further mark of recognition is due to him, and to ourselves, as a grateful people.

With the retirement of General Scott came the executive duty of appointing, in his stead, a general-in-chief of the army. It is a fortunate circumstance that neither in council nor country was there, so far as I know, any difference of opinion as to the proper person to be selected. The retiring chief repeatedly expressed his judgment in favor of General McClellan for the position; and in this the nation seemed to give a unanimous concurrence. The designation of General McClellan is therefore in considerable degree, the selection of the Country as well as of the Executive; and hence there is better reason to hope there will be given him, the confidence, and cordial support thus, by fair implication, promised, and without which, he cannot, with so full efficiency, serve the country.

It has been said that one bad general is better than two good ones; and the saying is true, if taken to mean no more than that an army is better directed by a single mind, though inferior, than by two superior ones, at variance, and cross-purposes with each other.

And the same is true, in all joint operations wherein those engaged, *can* have none but a common end in view, and *can* differ only as to the choice of means. In a storm at sea, no one on board *can* wish the ship to sink; and yet, not unfrequently, all go down together, because too many will direct, and no single mind can be allowed to control.

It continues to develop that the insurrection is largely, if not exclusively, a war upon the first principle of popular government—the rights of the people. Conclusive evidence of this is found in the most grave and maturely considered public documents, as well as in the general tone of the insurgents. In those documents we find the abridgement of the existing right of suffrage and the denial to the people of all right to participate in the selection of public officers, except the legislative boldly advocated, with labored arguments to prove that large control of the people in government, is the source of all political evil. Monarchy itself is sometimes hinted at as a possible refuge from the power of the people.

In my present position, I could scarcely be justified were I to omit raising a warning voice against this approach of returning despotism.

It is not needed, nor fitting here, that a general argument should be made in favor of popular institutions; but there is one point, with its connections, not so hackneyed as most others, to which I ask a brief attention. It is the effort to place *capital* on an equal footing with, if not above *labor*, in the structure of government. It is assumed that labor is available only in connection with capital; that nobody labors unless somebody else, owning capital, somehow by the use of it, induces him to labor. This assumed, it is next considered whether it is best that capital shall *hire* laborers, and thus induce them to work by their own consent, or *buy* them, and drive them to it without their consent. Having proceeded so far, it is naturally concluded that all laborers are either *hired* laborers, or what we call slaves. And further it is assumed that whoever is once a hired laborer, is fixed in that condition for life.

Now, there is no such relation between capital and labor as assumed; nor is there any such thing as a free man being fixed for life in the condition of hired laborer. Both these assumptions are false, and all inferences from them are groundless.

Labor is prior to, and independent of, capital. Capital is only the fruit of labor, and could never have existed if labor had not first existed. Labor is the superior of capital, and deserves much the higher consideration. Capital has its rights, which are as worthy of protection as any other rights. Nor is it denied that there is, and probably always will be, a relation between labor and capital, producing mutual benefits. The error is in assuming that the whole labor of community exists within that relation. A few men own capital, and that few avoid labor themselves, and, with their capital, hire or buy another few to labor for them. A large majority belong to neither class — neither work for others, nor have others working for them. In most of the southern States, a majority of the whole people of all colors are neither slaves nor masters; while in the northern a large majority are neither hirers nor hired. Men with their families — wives, sons, and daughters — work for themselves, on their farms, in their houses, and in their shops, taking the whole product to themselves, and asking no favors of capital on the one hand, nor of hired laborers or slaves on the other. It is not forgotten that a considerable number of persons mingle their own labor with capital — that is, they labor with their own hands, and also buy or hire others to labor for them; but this is only a mixed, and not a distinct class. No principle stated is disturbed by the existence of this mixed class.

Again: as has already been said, there is not, of necessity, any such thing as the free hired laborer being fixed to that condition for life. Many independent men everywhere in these States, a few years back in their lives, were hired laborers. The prudent, penniless beginner in the world, labors for wages awhile, saves a surplus with which to buy tools or land for himself; then labors on his own account another while, and at length hires another new beginner to help him. This is the just, and generous, and prosperous system, which opens the way to all — gives hope to all, and consequent energy, and progress, and improvement of condition to all. No men living are more worthy to be trusted than those who toil up from poverty — none less inclined to take, or touch, aught which they have not honestly earned. Let them beware of surrendering a political power which they already possess, and which, if surrendered, will surely be used to close the door of advancement against such as they, and to fix new disabilities and burdens upon them, till all of liberty shall be lost.

From the first taking of our national census to the last are seventy years; and we find our population at the end of the period eight times as great as it was at the beginning. The increase of those other things which men deem desirable has been even greater. We thus have at one view, what the popular principle applied to government, through the machinery of the States and the Union, has produced in a given time; and also what, if firmly maintained, it promises for the future. There are already among us those, who, if the Union be preserved, will live to see it contain two hundred and fifty millions. The struggle of today, is not altogether for today — it is for a vast future also. With a reliance on Providence, all the more firm and earnest, let us proceed in the great task which events have devolved upon us.

Abraham Lincoln

The Military Order
Of Emancipation

This military order, issued January 1, 1863, is perhaps one of President Lincoln's better-known declarations. What is not generally known, however, is that Lincoln was forced to issue this proclamation as a military order because emancipation legislation in Congress [like the Wade-Davis Bill] was tied to placing a debt lien on Southern cotton, and would have opened the South to looting of its resources rather than industrial reconstruction at the war's end.

By the President of the United States of America:

A Proclamation

Whereas, on the twenty-second day of September, in the year of our Lord one thousand eight hundred and sixty-two, a proclamation was issued by the President of the United States, containing, among other things, the following, to wit:

"That on the first day of January, in the year of our Lord one thousand eight hundred and sixty-three, all persons held as slaves within any State or designated part of a State, the people whereof shall then be in rebellion against the United States, shall be then, thenceforward, and forever free; and the Executive Government of the United States, including the military and naval authority thereof, will recognize and maintain the freedom of such persons, and will do no act or acts to repress such persons, or any of them, in any efforts they may make for their actual freedom.

"That the Executive will, on the first day of January aforesaid, by proclamation, designate the States and parts of States, if any, in which the people thereof, respectively shall then be in rebellion, against the United States; and the fact that any State, or the people thereof, shall on that day be, in good faith, represented in the Congress of the United States by members chosen thereto at elections wherein a majority of the qualified voters of such State shall have participated, be deemed conclusive evidence of such State, and the people thereof, are not then in rebellion against the United States."

Now, therefore I, Abraham Lincoln, President of the United States, by virtue of the power in me vested as Commander-in-Chief, of the Army and Navy of the United States in time of actual armed rebellion against the authority and government of the United States, and as a fit and necessary war measure for suppressing said rebellion, do, on this first day of January, in the year of our Lord one thousand eight hundred and sixty-three, and in accordance with my purpose so to do publicly proclaimed for the full period of one hundred days, from the day first above mentioned, order and designate as the States and parts of States wherein the people thereof respectively, are this day in rebellion against the United States, the following, to wit:

Arkansas, Texas, Lousiana (except the Parishes of St. Bernard, Plaquemines, Jefferson, St. Johns, St. Charles, St. James, Ascension, Assumption, Terrebonne, Larourche, St. Mary, St. Martin, and Orleans, including the City of New Orleans), Mississippi, Alabama, Florida, Georgia, South-Carolina, North-Carolina, and Virginia (except the forty-eight counties designated as West Virginia, and also the counties of Berkley, Accomac, Northampton, Elizabeth-City, York, Princess Ann, and Norfolk, including the cities of Norfolk and Portsmouth); and which excepted parts are, for the present, left precisely as if this proclamation were not issued.

And by virtue of the power, and for the purpose aforesaid, I do order and declare that all persons held as slaves within said designated States, and parts of States are, and henceforward shall be free; and that the Executive government of the United States, including the military and naval authorities thereof, will recognize and maintain the freedom of said persons.

And I hereby enjoin upon the people so declared to be free to abstain from all violence, unless in necessary self-defense; and I recommend to them that, in all cases when allowed, they labor faithfully for reasonable wages.

And I further declare and make known, that such persons of suitable condition, will be received into the armed services of the United States to garrison forts, positions, stations, and other places, and to man vessels of all sorts in said service.

And upon this act, sincerely believed to be an act of justice, warranted by the Constitution, upon military necessity, I invoke the considerate judgment of mankind, and the gracious favor of Almighty God.

In witness whereof, I have hereunto set my hand and caused the seal of the United States to be affixed.

Done at the City of Washington, this first day of January, in the year of our Lord one thousand eight hundred and sixty-three, and of the Independence of the United States of America the eighty-seventh

By the President: Abraham Lincoln

William H. Seward, Secretary of State.

To the Workingmen
Of Manchester, England

Abraham Lincoln drafted this letter in response to the support given the Union cause by Karl Marx and the International Workingman's Association. As Marx notes in his letters to Friedrich Engels, Lincoln made a clear distinction between the work of the IWMA and that of the British abolition societies which were working to subvert the United States. Lincoln praised the activities of the IWMA in support of the Union despite the hardships which the Manchester workers encountered during the war. Lincoln's reply to the bourgeois abolition societies, on the other hand, was curt and pro forma.

Executive Mansion, Washington
January 19, 1863

To the workingmen of Manchester:

I have the honor to acknowledge the receipt of the address and resolutions which you sent to me on the eve of the new year.

When I came, on the fourth day of March 1861, through a free and constitutional election, to preside in the government of the United States, this country was found at the verge of civil war. Whatever might have been the cause, or whosoever the fault, one duty paramount to all others was before me, namely, to maintain and preserve at once the Constitution and the integrity of the federal republic. A conscientious purpose to perform this duty is a key to all the measures of administration which have been, and to all which will hereafter be pursued. Under our form of government, and my official oath, I could not depart from this purpose if I would. It is not always in the power of governments to enlarge or restrict the scope of moral results which follow the policies that they may deem it necessary for the public safety, from time to time, to adopt.

I have understood well that the duty of self-preservation rests solely with the American people. But I have at the same time been aware that favor or disfavor of foreign nations might have a material influence on enlarging and prolonging the struggle with disloyal men in which the country is engaged. A fair examination of history has seemed to authorize a belief that the past action and influences

of the United States were generally regarded as having been beneficent towards mankind. I have therefore reckoned upon the for-
bearance of nations. Circumstances, to some of which you kindly
allude, induced me especially to expect that if justice and good faith
should be practiced by the United States, they would encounter no
hostile influence on the part of Great Britain. It is now a pleasant
duty to acknowledge the demonstration you have given of your
desire that a spirit of peace and amity towards this country may pre-
vail in the councils of your Queen, who is respected and esteemed in
your own country only more than she is by the kindred nation which
has its home on this side of the Atlantic.

I know and deeply deplore the sufferings which the workingmen at Manchester and in all Europe are called to endure in this
crisis. It has been often and studiously represented that the attempt
to overthrow this government, which was built upon the foundation
of human rights, and to substitute for it one which should rest exclusively on the basis of human slavery, was likely to obtain the
favor of Europe. Through the actions of our loyal citizens the
workingmen of Europe have been subjected to a severe trial, for the
purpose of forcing their sanction to that attempt. Under these circumstances, I cannot but regard your decisive utterance upon the
question as an instance of sublime Christian heroism which has not
been surpassed in any age or in any country. It is, indeed, an ener-
getic and reinspiring assurance of the inherent power of truth and of
the ultimate and universal triumph of justice, humanity, and freedom. I do not doubt that the sentiments you have expressed will be
sustained by your great nation, and, on the other hand, I have no
hesitation in assuring you that they will excite admiration, esteem,
and the most reciprocal feelings of friendship among the American
people. I hail this interchange of sentiment, therefore, as an augury
that, whatever else may happen, whatever misfortune may befall
your country or my own, the peace and friendship which now exist
between the two nations will be, as it shall be my desire to make
them, perpetual.

                                        Abraham Lincoln

The Last Public Address

Abraham Lincoln delivered his last public address in Baltimore, Maryland on April 11, 1865. Here he stressed again his commitment to place the newly freed men in apprenticeship training programs to develop the skills necessary for them to become useful citizens of an industrializing South.

We meet this evening, not in sorrow, but in gladness of heart. The evacuation of Petersburg and Richmond, and the surrender of the principal insurgent army, give hope of a righteous and speedy peace whose joyous expression can not be restrained. In the midst of this, however, He, from whom all blessings flow, must not be forgotten. A call for a national thanksgiving is being prepared, and will be duly promulgated, Nor must those whose harder part gives us the cause of rejoicing, be overlooked. Their honors must not be parcelled out with others. I myself, was near the front, and had the high pleasure of transmitting much of the good news to you; but no part of the honor, for plan or execution, is mine. To General Grant, his skilful officers, and brave men, all belongs. The gallant Navy stood ready, but was not in reach to take active part.

By these recent successes the re-inauguration of the national authority — reconstruction — which has had a large share of thought from the first, is pressed much more closely upon our attention. It is fraught with great difficulty. Unlike the case of a war between independent nations, there is no authorized organ for us to treat with. No one man has authority to give up the rebellion for any other man. We simply must begin with, and mould from, disorganized and discordant elements. Nor is it a small additional embarrassment that we, the loyal people, differ among ourselves as to the mode, manner, and means of reconstruction.

As a general rule, I abstain from reading the reports of attacks upon myself, wishing not to be provoked by that to which I can not properly offer an answer. In spite of this precaution, however, it comes to my knowledge that I am much censured for some supposed agency in setting up, and seeking to sustain, the new State Government of Louisiana. In this I have done just so much as, and no more than, the public knows. In the Annual Message of December 1863 and accompanying Proclamation, I presented *a* plan of re-construction (as the phrase goes) which, I promised, if adopted by any State, should be acceptable to, and sustained by, the Executive government of the nation. I distinctly stated that this was not the only plan which might possibly be acceptable; and I also distinctly protested that the Executive claimed no right to say when, or whether members should be admitted to seats in Congress from such States. This plan was, in advance, submitted to the then Cabinet, and distinctly approved by every member of it. One of them suggested that I should then, and in that connection, apply the Emancipation Proclamation to the theretofore excepted parts of Virginia and Louisiana; that I should drop the suggestion about apprenticeship for freed-people, and that I should omit the protest against my own power, in regard to the admission of members to Congress; but even he approved every part and parcel of the plan which has since been employed or touched by the action of Louisiana. The new constitution of Louisiana, declaring emancipation for the whole State, practically applies the Proclamation to the part previously excepted. It does not adopt apprenticeship for freed-people; and it is silent, as it could not well be otherwise, about the admission of members to Congress. So that, as it applies to Louisiana, every member of the Cabinet fully approved the plan. The Message went to Congress, and I received many commendations of the plan, written and verbal; and not a single objection to it, from any professed emancipationist, came to my knowledge, until after the news reached Washington that the people of Louisiana had begun to move in accordance with it. From about July 1862, I had corresponded with different persons, supposed to be interested, seeking a reconstruction of a State government for Louisiana. When the Message of 1863, with the plan before mentioned, reached New-Orleans, General Banks wrote me that he was confident the people, with his military co-operation, would reconstruct, substantially on that plan. I wrote him, and some of them to try it; they tried it, and the result is known. Such only has been my agency in getting up the Louisiana government. As to sustaining it, my promise is out, as before stated. But, as bad promises are better broken than kept, I shall treat this as a bad promise, and break it, whenever I shall be convinced that keeping it is adverse to the public interest. But I have not yet been so convinced.

I have been shown a letter on this subject, supposed to be an able one, in which the writer expresses regret that my mind has not seemed to be definitely fixed on the question whether the seceded States, so called, are in the Union or out of it. It would perhaps, add astonishment to his regret, were he to learn that since I have found professed Union men endeavoring to make that question, I have *purposely* forborne any public expression upon it. As appears to me that question has not been, nor yet is, a practically material one, and that any discussion of it, while it thus remains practically immaterial, could have no effect other than the mischievous one of dividing our friends. As yet, whatever it may hereafter become, that question is bad, as the basis of a controversy, and good for nothing at all — a merely pernicious abstraction.

We all agree that the seceded States, so called, are out of their proper practical relation with the Union; and that the sole object of the government, civil and military, in regard to those States is to again get them into that proper practical relation. I believe it is not only possible, but in fact, easier, to do this, without deciding, or even considering, whether these states have been out of the Union, than with it. Finding themselves safely at home, it would be utterly immaterial whether they had ever been abroad. Let us all join in doing the acts necessary to restoring the proper practical relations between these states and the Union; and each forever after, innocently indulge his own opinion whether, in doing the acts, he brought the States from without, into the Union, or only gave them proper assistance, they never having been out of it.

The amount of constituency, so to speak, on which the new Louisiana government rests, would be more satisfactory to all, if it contained fifty, thirty, or even twenty thousand, instead of only about twelve thousand, as it does. It is also unsatisfactory to some that the elective franchise is not given to the colored man. I would myself prefer that it were now conferred on the very intelligent, and on those who serve our cause as soldiers. Still the question is not whether the Louisiana government, as it stands, is quite all that is desirable. The question is "Will it be wiser to take it as it is, and to improve it; or to reject, and disperse it?" "Can **Louisiana** be brought into proper practical relation with the Union *sooner* by *sustaining*, or by *discarding* her new State Government?"

Some twelve thousand voters in the heretofore slave-state of Louisiana have sworn allegiance to the Union, assumed to be the rightful political power of the State, held elections, organized a State government, adopted a free-state constitution, giving the benefit of public schools equally to black and white, and empowering the Legislature to confer the elective franchise upon the colored man. Their Legislature has already voted to ratify the constitutional amendment recently passed by Congress, abolishing slavery throughout the nation. These twelve thousand persons are thus fully committed to the Union, and to perpetual freedom in the state — committed to the very things, and nearly all the things the nation wants — and they ask the nation's recognition, and it's assistance to make good their committal. Now, if we reject, and spurn them, we do our utmost to disorganize and disperse them. We in effect say to the white men "You are worthless, or worse — we will neither help you, nor by helped by you." To the blacks we say "This cup of liberty which these, your old masters, hold to your lips, we will dash from you, and leave you to the chances of gathering the spilled and scattered contents in some vague and undefined when, where, and how." If this course, discouraging and paralyzing both white and black, has any tendency to bring Louisiana into proper practical relations with the Union, I have, so far, been unable to perceive it. If, on the contrary, we recognize, and sustain the new government of Louisiana the converse of all this is made true. We encourage hearts, and nerve the arms of the twelve thousand to adhere to their work and argue for it, and proselyte for it, and fight for it, and feed it, and grow it, and ripen it to a complete success. The colored man too, in seeing all united for him, is inspired with vigilance, and energy, and daring, to the same end. Grant that he desires the elective franchise, will he not attain it sooner by saving the already advanced steps toward it, than by running backward over them? Concede that the new government of Louisiana is only to what it should be as the egg is to the fowl, we shall sooner have the fowl by hatching the egg than by smashing it? Again, if we reject Louisiana, we also reject one vote in favor of the proposed amendment to the national constitution. To meet this proposition, it has been argued that no more than three fourths of those States which have not attempted secession are necessary to validly ratify the amendment. I do not commit myself against this, further than to say that such a ratification would be questionable, and sure to be persistently questioned; while a ratification by three fourths of all the States would be un-questioned and unquestionable.

I repeat the question. "Can Louisiana be brought into proper practical relation with the Union *sooner* by *sustaining* or by *discarding* her new State Government?

What has been said of Louisiana will apply generally to other States. And yet so great peculiarities pertain to each state; and such important and sudden changes occur in the same state; and, withal, so new and unprecedented is the whole case, that no exclusive, and inflexible plan can safely be prescribed as to details and colatterals. Such exclusive, and inflexible plan, would surely become a new en-tanglement. Important principles may, and must, be inflexible.

In the present "*situation*" as the phrase goes, it may be my duty to make some new announcement to the people of the South. I am considering, and shall not fail to act, when satisfied that action will be proper.

William D. Kelley

(1814 - 1890)

Protection to American Labor

The South—Its Resources and Its Wants

*The Centennial Celebration and
International Exposition*

*The Causes and Authors of the Financial Depression
with Passing Hints at Remedial Measures*

Protection to American Labor

Pennsylvania Congressman William D. Kelley was one of Henry Carey's closest collaborators; he served in the House of Representatives for over twenty years. Kelley recruited to the "American System" faction William McKinley who, before he became President in 1897, took over from Kelley responsibility as the leading House spokesman for the American System when Kelley retired in the early 1880s.

Kelley delivered the speech which follows to the House of Representatives on January 31, 1866. He contrasts the British method of depressing the wages of their workforce to enable them to dump cheap British goods on foreign markets to the American policy of paying its workforce higher wages so that the entire nation will benefit from a population with a high skill level and standard of living.

. . . I have before me, sir, the yellowed pages of a pamphlet, printed in London in 1677, which contains a panacea for all our ills, the suggestions of which, illustrated by the experience of our own and other nations, will, if applied to our resources, bring permanent peace and prosperity to our country, elevate the freedman into the prosperous and intelligent citizen, bless the master spirits of the South with wealth beyond their past imaginings, and give them, as steady competitors in the race of life, "the mean whites," as they designate their poor neighbors; will reconstruct their broken railroads and canals, rebuild their ruined cities, towns, and villages, and make their barren and wasted fields bloom and blossom as those of the fairest portions of the North, of Belgium, Germany, France, or England.

This quaint old pamphlet was written by "Andrew Yarrinton, Gentleman," and is entitled, "England's Improvement by Sea and Land. How to outdo the Dutch without Fighting, to pay Debts without Moneys, to set at Work all the Poor of England with the Growth of our own Lands." It disposes very effectually of the gentleman's proposition that free trade "is the true theory of government."

When Andrew Yarrinton wrote, the Dutch were disputing the supremacy of the seas with England, and she was exporting raw materials and buying manufactured articles; and one object of his pamphlet was to relieve the English people from the taunt of the

Dutch that they "sold their whole skins for a sixpence, and bought back the tails for a shilling"— a commercial policy which the American people, with rare and brief exceptions, have steadily pursued. To Yarrinton and Sir George Downing, author of the Navigation Act, an American by birth, and a member of the first graduating class of Harvard College, England, in my judgment, owes more of her wealth and power than to any other two men, however illustrious their names may be in her history. Before they influenced her counsels Holland was mistress of the sea. But the Navigation Act and the employment of her people on the growth of her lands, transferred the scepter to England. The purpose of Downing's bill as declared in its preamble, was "to keep his Majesty's subjects in the plantations in a firmer dependence," to "increase English shipping," and to insure "the vent of English woollens and other manufactures and commodities." What Yarrinton and Downing taught their country we can practice for the benefit of ours. And as England outdid the Dutch without fighting, so can we outdo her by the arts of peace, and enforce the Monroe Doctrine against the world without firing a gun; and, vast as is our indebtedness, strangers will come and cast their lot with us and liquidate it if we so legislate as "to set at work all the poor of" the United States "with the growth of our own lands." They will bring with them arts and industries, and implements with which we are not familiar; will open new quarries, mines, and ore banks; will build new furnaces, forges, mills, and workshops; will revive wasted lands and open new fields, and by creating a home market will enable the farmer to practice skillful and remunerative husbandry, and will create American commerce by enabling our merchants to supply ships with assorted cargoes of American goods.

The One Want of Our Country

Sir, the pressing want of our country is men. We need not sigh for additional territory. We need go to no foreign nation for any product of agriculture. Abundant as are our ascertained stores of gold, silver, coal, iron, copper, zinc, lead, cinnabar, kaolin, petroleum, and the infinite number of substances man has utilized, the extent of our mineral wealth is unmeasured and unimagined. And our ocean-bound coasts, the immense inland seas that bound us on the north, the land-locked Gulf that laves our southern shores, and our grand rivers, impel us to commercial enterprise, and proclaim the one great want of our country to be men. Labor alone can make these unparalleled resources available; and when by securing to industry its just reward we shall develop and attract hither from other lands a supply of labor that will make the march of our conquest over the elements of our wealth steadily progressive, our debt, though expressed by the numerals required to tell it now, will shrink into comparative insignificance, and the Powers which by treachery and disregard of international law during the last four years would have destroyed us, will assume relatively Lilliputian proportions. . . .

But to make labor fully available it must be steadily employed and generously rewarded, and to secure these results the employments of a country must be largely diversified. A nation whose territory is broad and remote from dense populations cannot, by pursuing commerce and agriculture alone, prosper or endure. This is the decree of nature. Land, as well as man, requires rest and food; and a purely agricultural and commercial nation can afford neither of these. The social history of the world verifies this proposition. To make a nation prosperous remunerative employment must be accessible to all its people; and to that end industry must be so diversified that he who has not the strength for agricultural or other labor requiring muscle may make his feeble sinews available in some gentler employment. Agriculture and commerce afford few stimulants to inventive genius; diversified industry offers many. Childhood in a purely agricultural community is wasted in idleness, as are the winter months of robust men, and to realize the truth of the maxim that time is money, the varied industry of a country should offer employment to all for all seasons of the year, that each day may be made to earn its own subsistence. And herein is illustrated the harmony of interests, for where diversity of employment is successfully promoted, agriculture finds its readiest markets and earns its richest rewards: for within accessible distance from the city or town the farmer has a market for those perishable productions which will not bear extended transportation, but the cultivation of which, in alternation with white or hard crops, strengthens and enriches his land. But of this hereafter. . . .

Effect of Free Trade on the Poor Whites of the South

Mr. Chairman, having ascertained the result of the planters' free-trade policy upon their own interests and those of the people of the North, let us contemplate the condition of the masses of the people of the cotton States. I will not detain you by any reference to that of the slaves and free people of color. Other occasions will be more fitting for that. But on nearly one million of square miles of territory which the planters regarded as their exclusive domain, were some six or eight million people designated as "poor" or "mean whites," to whom were accorded all the rights of citizenship, and I will inquire whether their interests had been promoted by this policy? Let us, in contemplating their condition for a few moments, do it, not from our standpoint, but through the eyes of southern men.

Mr. Tarver, of Missouri, in the course of a paper on *Domestic Manufactures in the South and West*, published in 1847, says:

> "The free population of the South may be divided into two classes — the slaveholder and the non-slaveholder. I am not aware that the relative numbers of these two classes have ever been ascertained in any of the States, but I am satisfied that the non-slaveholders far outnumber the slaveholders — perhaps by three to one. In the more southern portion of this region, the non-slaveholders possess, generally, but very small means, and the land which they possess is almost universally poor, and so sterile that a scanty subsistence is all that can be derived from its cultivation; and the more fertile soil, being in the possession of the slaveholder, must ever remain out of the power of those who have none.

> "This state of things is a great drawback, and bears heavily upon and depresses the moral energies of the poorer classes. . . . The acquisition of a respectable position in the scale of wealth appears so difficult, that they decline in the hopeless pursuit, and many of them settle down into habits of idleness, and become the almost passive subjects of all its consequences. And I lament to say that I have observed of late years that an evident deterioration is taking place in this part of the population, the younger portion of it being less educated, less industrious, and in every point of view less respectable, than their ancestors."

Governor Hammond, addressing the South Carolina Institute

in 1850, spoke of this portion of the people of the South when he said:

> "They obtain a precarious subsistence by occasional jobs, by hunting, by fishing, by plundering fields or folds, and too often by what is in its effects far worse — trading with slaves, and seducing them to plunder for their benefit."

William Gregg, Esq., addressing the same Institute in 1851, said:

> "From the best estimate that I have been able to make, I put down the white people, who ought to work and who do not, or who are so employed as to be wholly unproductive to the State, at one hundred and twenty-five thousand. . . . By this it appears that but one-fifth of the present poor whites of our State would be necessary to operate one million spindles. . . . I have long been under the impression, and every day's experience has strengthened my convictions, that the evils exist in the wholly neglected condition of this class of persons. Any man who is an observer of things could hardly pass through our country without being struck with the fact that all the capital, enterprise, and intelligence is employed in directing slave labor; and the consequence is that a large portion of our poor white people are wholly neglected, and are suffered to while away their existence in a state but one step in advance of the Indian of the forest."

Hon J.H. Lumpkin, of Georgia, in a paper on the *Industrial Regeneration of the South*, published in 1852, in advocacy of the establishment of manufactures which had been attempted in Georgia, but which had been resisted on the ground that they would become hot-beds of crime and endanger the safety of slavery, said:

> "It is objected that these manufacturing establishments will become the hot-beds of crime. . . . But I am by no means ready to concede that our poor, degraded, half-fed, half-clothed, and ignorant population — without Sabbath schools or any other kind of instruction, mental or moral, or without any just appreciation of character — will be injured by giving them employment which will bring them under the oversight of employers who will inspire them with self-respect by taking an interest in their welfare."

Down to that time free trade had certainly done but little to bless the poor white people of the South. Nor does it seem from recent descriptions, and from our observation of them in military prisons and hospitals, to have materially benefited them down to the present day. J. R. Gilmore, Esq., "Edmund Kirke," in his discourse on the social and political characteristics of southern whites, before the Jersey City Literary Association, estimated the number known as the "mean whites" at over four millions, and described them as "herding together in sparse communities and gleaning a sorry subsistence from hunting, fishing, and poaching, in the mountain districts of Virginia, upper Georgia, Alabama, Mississippi, and in the sand hills of North Carolina and the barrens of Tennessee, and throughout the rest of the South; as hovering around the borders of large plantations, quartering themselves upon the 'chivalry,' stealing the deer from their forests and the hams from their smokehouses." He said they were tolerated by the planters for the two hundred thousand votes they gave for slavery and the mad theories of the planters, and added, "They are far below the slaves in morals and civilization; are indolent, shiftless, thieving, lying; given to whisky-drinking, snuff-dipping, clay-eating, incest, and all manner of social vices. Not one in a thousand of them can read; not one in ten thousand can write"; and that he "had met many who had never seen a book or newspaper, and some who had never heard of a Bible or a spelling-book."

Mr. B.C. Truman, an accredited correspondent of the *New York Times*, in a letter to that journal, dated Montgomery, Alabama, October 23, 1865, said:

"There is a class of beings in all the southern States known as poor whites. That little monosyllabic adjective does not give the faintest idea of these things with bodies and souls. How under the heavens they live is a question for the philanthropist, if indeed that paragon of benevolence has ever visited the region in which they exist — the 'homes' of the poor whites. In a visit to Spanish Fort a few days ago, in company with a naval officer, we stopped at the 'shebang' of one of this species. Most of these poor whites are natives. The individual whom we called upon, however, was a Scandinavian, but had lived in the place we found him for thirty years. For a long time he made his living by manufacturing turpentine; but the trees ran out years ago, and since then he has lived upon what he has raised, buying nothing but sugar and coffee, for which he traded chickens and eggs. His wife was of the regular mold, lean and long, with seven little children by her side, and a pipe in her mouth. I told her I was a newspaper correspondent, and she did not know what that was. I endeavored to explain, and found that she did not know what a newspaper was, *and yet she resides within twenty miles of Mobile.* The husband could not read or write his name, but could drink like a fish. Both husband and wife had on wooden shoes, while the children exhibited no feet covering except what nature had provided for them.

"Throughout the southern portion of Alabama, upon both sides of the river, is what is known as the 'piney woods country.' It is one of the most barren sections I have ever seen. Neither corn nor cotton will grow to any extent. Sweet potatoes are the chief product, and this vegetable and bacon, and a little corn bread, form the bill of fare morning, noon, and night all the year round. These people are scattered all through these piney woods, and live in log huts which in a way protect them from the tempestuous weather and violent storms of wind and rain which howl through this barren waste during certain periods of the year. Oh, how I pity these poor beings who have been the recipients of uncounted woes and unheard-of sufferings during the long, long years of African slavery!"

Dixon, the traveling correspondent of the *Boston Daily Advertiser,* whose admirable letters prove him to be a keen observer and faithful reporter, writing from Fort Valley, Georgia, November 15, said:

"Whether the North Carolina 'dirt-eater,' or the South Carolina 'sand-hiller,' or the Georgia 'cracker,' is lowest in the scale of human existence would be difficult to say. The ordinary plantation negro seemed to me, when I first saw him in any numbers, at the very bottom of not only probabilities, but also possibilities, so far as they affect human relations; but these specimens of the white race must be credited with having reached a yet lower depth of squalid and beastly wretchedness. However poor or ignorant or unclean or improvident he may be, I never yet found a negro who had not at least a vague desire for a better condition, an undefined longing for something called freedom, a shrewd instinct of self-preservation. These three ideas, or, let me say, shadows of ideas, do not make the creature a man, but they lift him out of the bounds of brutedom. The Georgia 'cracker,' as I have seen him since leaving Milledgeville, seems to me to lack not only all that the negro does, but also even the desire for a better condition, and the vague longing for an enlargement of his liberties and his rights. I walked out into the country back of Albany and Andersonville, when at those places, and into the country back of Fort Valley this morning; and on each occasion I fell in with three or four of these 'cracker' families. Such filthy poverty, such foul ignorance, such idiotic imbecility, such bestial in-

stincts, such groveling desires, such mean longings, you would
question my veracity as a man if I were to paint the pictures I have
seen! Moreover, no trick of words can make plain the scene in and
around one of these habitations; no fertility of language can embody
the simple facts for a northern mind, and the case is one in which
even seeing itself is scarcely believing. Time and effort will lead the
negro up to intelligent manhood; but I almost doubt if it will be
possible to ever lift this 'white trash' into respectability."

Sir, is not the gentleman from Indiana mistaken in asserting
that free trade "is the true theory of government," and can a policy
which produces such results as these writers have depicted be wise?
Can we rely on it to pay the interest on our debt, to meet the pensions we owe to those who have been disabled in our service, or to the
widows and children, or aged and dependent parents of those who
have laid down their lives in our cause? Such free trade as he advocates can produce but one result; and that is bankruptcy, personal,
corporate, State, and national. It is against the laws of nature and
the providence of God. It involves as a necessary consequence idleness for one half the year to all, and for all the year to many of our
people who would find adequate and remunerative employment
under a system of diversified industry.

How England Established Her Supremacy

The propositions I enunciate are not deduced from our experience alone. All history affirms them. Other nations have tried
free trade and ever with the same result. England, the workshop of
the world and mistress of the seas as she proclaims herself, tried it,
and from the time of Alfred to that of Edward the Confessor, sold
her skins for a sixpence, and bought back the tails for a shilling, by
exchanging her unwrought wool for Dutch and Flemish clothing;
and the question as to how population might be prevented from exceeding the ability of the land to feed the people perplexed her rulers
throughout the long period.†

Even so late as the thirty-sixth year of Elizabeth's reign a law

---

† Believing herself to be strong enough she has renewed the experiment,
and at the end of a quarter of a century of free trade, finds, herself agitated
as never before by the question, "How shall we feed our people?" Daniel
Grant says: "No man doubts the broad fact that we cannot feed ourselves. It

was enacted against "the erecting and maintaining of cottages,"
which, after reciting that "great inconveniences have been found by
experience to grow by erecting and building of great numbers and
multitudes of cottages which are daily more and more increased in
many parts of this realm," enacts that no such tenement shall be
erected unless four acres of land be attached to it. And Charles I, in
1630, issued a proclamation "against building houses on new
foundations in London or Westminster, or within three miles of the
city or king's palaces." This proclamation also forbade the receiving
of inmates in the houses which would multiply the inhabitants to
such an excessive number that they could neither be governed nor
fed. The population of England has quadrupled since then, and her
modern capitalists, regarding labor as raw material, maintain a

---

has been accepted by Parliamentary Committees, made the plea for large
Inclosure Acts, and it caused the repeal of the Corn Laws; equally as little
can it be doubted that this condition is ever on the increase, for it is shown
by the Registrar General's returns, and the ever-increasing competition for
work. Day by day the tell-tale of our population mounts higher, and its
results are to be found in the increasing requirements for foreign food. But
at great Manchester meetings men tabulate out this enormous increase, and
appeal to it as an evidence of the value of free trade; whilst the facts are that
our imports of food have only one meaning, viz: we import that food which
we cannot produce for ourselves. The relation that food thus bears to our
population makes itself felt in a variety of ways; it changes the character of
our pauperism, the conditions of our destitution, and the price of food
itself; it also enforces the importance of our export trade and the danger of
foreign competition. All these circumstances, so apparently remote, are
linked together by the one tie, that our land cannot feed our people.
    "With respect to the first point, the state of our pauperism, it is so
changed that it no longer represents its original elements. The first poor-law
was based on the idea that paupers were the idle and the worthless, and to
such a labor test was the natural limitation of help; but today men seek
work and cannot find it, enforced idleness saps energy, and thus it is they
sink slowly down to pauperism. The same may be said of destitution with
even greater force; that silent, hopeless, broken misery, which is too power-
less to create work, too feeble to force it, and too proud to beg — that
poverty which sinks, suffers, and dies; that destitution of all others the most
fearful, and the most real, also springs from over-population." — *Home
Politics*, by Daniel Grant, page 169, London, 1870. (This and the following
footnotes were added by Kelley in the compiling and editing of his *Speeches,
Addresses and Letters on Industrial and Financial Questions*, Philadelphia,
1872 — A.S.)

supply of laborers in sufficient excess of the demand to cheapen it to the lowest point, to which end the British islands raise for annual exportation, a quarter of a million of people, feeding them in their unproductive infancy and childhood.

The change has been wrought by the diversification of her industry, which has been accomplished by so legislating as to set at work all the poor of England with the growth of her own lands; and the spectacle which Ireland presents, of years of famine, and an industrious people whose attachment to their native land is intense, fleeing by millions from the homes of their childhood and the graves of their ancestors, is the result of that one-sided free trade which England, since the Union, has forced upon her, by which her woolen, worsted, silk, cotton, and linen factories have been destroyed. Protected by her legislation of 1783, these and other branches of diversified industry were prosperous and her people contented at the date of the Union. But English free trade having done its work nothing is now of so little value in Ireland as an able-bodied laborer with a good appetite. Let him who would understand the causes of the miseries of the Irish people and the depopulation of Ireland read the thirteenth chapter of Henry C. Carey's *Slave Trade, Domestic and Foreign.* It is a brief story, but pregnant with instruction upon the point under consideration.

I cannot tell, sir, when England first determined to abandon dependence on the production and exportation of raw materials, but find by reference to McCallagh's *Industrial History,* page 74, that in 1337 she passed an Act imposing

"A duty of forty shillings per sack on all wool exported by native merchants and sixty shillings on all exported by foreigners. The next year a Parliament was held at Westminster that went still further in the same direction, enacting that no wool of English growth should be transported beyond seas, and that all cloth-workers should be received, from whatever parts they should come, and fit places should be assigned them with divers liberties and privileges, and that they should have a certain allowance from the king until they might be in a way of living by their trade."

While England remained a purely agricultural country her capitalists encountered the difficulties which those of the South have to overcome, and Wade, in his *History of the Middle and Working Classes,* page 31, says:

"In the year 1376 we have evidence of a strong disposition to vagrancy among laborers, in a complaint of the House of Commons that masters are obliged to give their servants high wages to prevent their running away; that many of the runaways turned beggars and lived idle lives in cities and boroughs, although they have sufficient bodily strength to gain a livelihood if willing to work, and that the chief part turned out sturdy rogues, infesting the kingdom with frequent robberies."

There are those who utter such complaints in our days, and especially deplore the fact that they "are compelled to give their servants high wages to prevent their running away." At a meeting of the planters of Marlboro' district, South Carolina, the proceedings of which I find reported at length, and properly attested, in the *Charleston Daily News* of December 9, the following, with many like resolutions, were adopted:

"*Resolved,* That, if inconsistent with the views of the authorities to remove the military, we express the opinion that the plan of the military to compel the freedman to contract with his former owner, when desired by the latter, is wise, prudent, and absolutely necessary.

"*Resolved,* That we, the planters of the district, pledge ourselves not to contract with any freedman unless he can produce a certificate of regular discharge from his former owner.

"*Resolved,* That under no circumstances whatsoever will we rent land to any freedmen, nor will we permit them to live on our premises as employees.

"*Resolved,* That no system can be devised for the present which can *secure success* where the discipline and management of the freedman is entirely taken out of the hands of the planter, and we invoke the authorities to recognize this fact, which cannot but be apparent to them.

"*Resolved,* That we request the military to cease the habit of making negroes act as couriers, sheriffs, and constables, to serve writs and notices upon planters — a system so destructive to good order and discipline."

It is evident that neither the thunders of Gillmore's "swamp angel," nor the howl of her ponderous shells, had sufficed to awaken these somnolent gentlemen to consciousness of the fact that the fourteenth century had passed in the Palmetto State.

Englishmen in those early days exhibited the same elements of character as the negroes of our days, showing that however the complexion of races may differ, the impulses and yearnings of humanity are the same in all times and among the children of all climes. Each man embraces the elements of perfect manhood and the germ of every human faculty and emotion; and the Africo-American, in his new-found freedom, desires, as did the English laborer of the fourteenth century, to work for whom he pleases, at what he feels he can do best, and in the field which will give him the amplest reward.

Slight as the stimulants applied to British manufacturing industry by parliamentary protection had then been, they caused the land-holders to manifest as much anxiety for despotic control over the laboring people as do the pardoned rebels of the South; and Wade tells us that the complaints of the Commons in 1406 furnish evidence of the competition which had commenced between rural and manufacturing industry at that day, and that —

> "To avoid the statutes passed some years before for compelling those who had been brought up to the plow till they were twelve years of age to continue in husbandry all their lives, agricultural laborers had recourse to the expedient of sending their children into cities and boroughs, and binding them apprentices when they were under that age; and that further, in order to counteract this, it was enacted that no person, unless possessed of land of a rental of twenty shillings a year should bind children of any age apprentices to any trade or mystery within a city, but that the children should be brought up in the occupation of their parents, or other business suited to their conditions."

But even in those dark days the British Government seems to have been more enlightened than they who claim the right to legislate for the Southern States, or Brevet Brigadier General Fullerton, late Commissioner of the Freedmen's Bureau at New Orleans; for it provided that such children were nevertheless to be allowed to be sent to a school in any part of the kingdom; which their proposed legislation and his arbitrary orders for the government of the laboring people of Louisiana would effectually prohibit.

These stupid parliamentary restrictions on the freedom of

laborers were not to endure forever, and the progress of England in the development of her resources has been marked by a constantly growing system of protection, not always judicious, sometimes infringing the rights of the subject, but tending constantly to build up the power of the kingdom, increase the material comfort of the subject, and give her ascendancy over the nations of the world.

In 1727, Dean Swift, appealing to the Irish people in behalf of Ireland, said:

> "One cause of a country's thriving is the industry of the people in working up all their native commodities to the last; another, the conveniency of safe ports and havens to carry out their goods, as *much* manufactured, and bring those of others as *little* manufactured, as the nature of mutual commerce will allow; another, the disposition of the people of the country to wear their own manufactures and import as little clothing, furniture, food, or drink as they can conveniently live without."

These were not abstract notions with him, for by that time England had become thoroughly protective in her policy, and was increasing in population, wealth, and power; while Ireland, though not wholly disregarding the necessity of protecting her own workmen and developing her resource, exhibited a tendency to be governed by that plausible but shallowest of economical sophisms which teaches that it is wise, regardless of all other circumstances and conditions, to buy where we can buy for least money and sell where we can sell for most, and was sinking in the scale of national consideration. How protective England had become, is illustrated by the fact that from having for many centuries exchanged her raw wool for manufactured cloths, she had in 1660 prohibited the exportation of *unmanufactured* wool. This prohibition continued till 1825. And to protect her silk manufacturers, from 1765 to 1826, she prohibited the importation of silk goods manufactured in other countries, and confirmed the parliamentary prohibition by a reservation in the treaty of commerce concluded with France in 1786. She also prohibited the export of tools and machines used in the various branches of manufactures. In 1696 she prohibited by special act of Parliament the exportation of Lee's stocking-frame — a machine invented nearly a century before. She also prohibited by various acts the exportation of certain machinery used in woolen, silk, cotton, and linen manufactures. Such favor did protection to English labor find that her laws prohibiting exportation were made to embrace presses or dies for iron buttons, engines for covering whips, tools for punching glass; in fact, anything for which it was thought worth while on the part of any class of manufacturers or mechanics to seek protection at the hands of Parliament by securing Englishmen a monopoly of the implements required for the production of their goods.

And when, in 1824, a commission, created to inquire into the expediency of repealing these prohibitions, reported generally in favor of the repeal, it was unable to recommend their unconditional abrogation, but qualified the suggestion by recommending that the Privy Council should continue to exercise their discretion in permitting the exportation of such tools and machinery then prohibited as might appear to them not likely to be prejudicial to the trade or manufactures of the United Kingdom, "because it is possible that the circumstances may exist which may render a prohibition to export certain tools and machines used in some particular manufactures expedient." To justify even this conditional repeal the commission set forth the advantages England had derived from the protection of her infant or feeble industries in the following language:

> "Placed beyond all comparison at the head of civilization as regards manufacturing skill, *with capital far more ample than is possessed by any other people,* with cheap and inexhaustible supplies of iron and fuel, and with institutions every way favorable to the development of the industry and ingenuity of her citizens, she must always be able to at least maintain her superiority of position where circumstances are in other respects equal, and be ready to turn to the utmost advantage every improvement which may reach her in common with her less powerful rivals."

It was not, we perceive, until by adequate protection to her labor she had kept the balance of trade in her favor long enough to make capital so abundant as to secure a steady and ample supply of money at low rates of interest; and by setting all her people to work on the growth of her lands had trained artisans and accumulated an abundance of superior machinery, which had paid for itself by profits on its use, that England was willing to admit the labor of the world to compete with that employed in her varied industries.

Nor had she resorted to these devices alone in her progress to this assured position, for an English writer, Porter, in his history of the *Progress of the Nation,* says:

"Previous to 1825, the jealousy of our Legislature in regard to the progress of foreign manufactures was extended so far as to interfere even with the natural right of working artisans to transfer their industry to countries where it could be most profitably exerted. Any man who had acquired a practical knowledge of manufacturing processes was thereby rendered a prisoner in his own country, and not only might the arm of the law be interposed to prevent his quitting his native shores, but heavy penalties were imposed on all persons who should abet the expatriation of one of our artisans."

England Preaches But Does Not Practice Free Trade

These, however, were not the most effective means by which England has protected her capital and augmented her power. While prohibiting the exportation of tools and machines, and restraining her skilled workmen from emigrating, she was, from so early as 1337, as we have already seen, encouraging by special grants and privileges the artisans of other countries to bring the implements of their industry and employ them within her limits. Her policy is unchanged. The free trade she proclaims is theoretical and plausible, but to some extent false and delusive.†

The world hailed her admission of foreign grain free as a step toward really reciprocal free trade. Her statesmen, however, saw in it a master-stroke by which her manufacturing supremacy would be maintained. Sir Robert Peel knew that the manufactures of England were the source of her power; that cheap food for her laborers was an element of cheap production; and believed that so long as other nations would employ her to manufacture their raw materials it was immaterial whether she raised any grain, and that every acre of her

---

† England's enormous annual subsidies to Steamship Companies are part of an ingenious system of protection by which she hopes to maintain a monopoly of ship building and the carrying trade. She thus pays part of the freight on foreign raw materials used by her manufacturers, and the fabrics and wares they export. These subsidies amounted last year, as was stated by the Chancellor of the Exchequer in his speech of April 29, 1871, when presenting to Parliament his budget for this year, to £1,225,000 or over $6,000,000.

arable land not required to raise vegetables and fruits which do not
bear transportation, might be appropriated to sheep walks and pas-
turage, and, through her diversified industry she would draw from
the prairies of the United States, the banks of the Nile, and the
shores of the Baltic a supply of food far more generous than the in-
sular dimensions of England could possibly yield.

Her policy is to undersell all others. To do this she must depress
the wages of labor, and to accomplish this she must provide her
laboring people at the lowest possible prices with the simple and
coarse fare on which her low wages compel them to live. To have retained the duties on grain would have been, in so far, to tax raw
materials, as we do,† but she is too astute for that. She wants cheap
food for her slaves as the southern planters did for theirs, and seeks
to get it as they did by forcing British free trade on the American
people. She is the foe of the working-men of every country, and im-
pairs their wages by depressing those of the men upon whose toil her
own power depends.‡ She protects the capital of England as I wish
to protect the labor, ingenuity, and enterprise of the American
people. Her aim is to be the workshop of the world, and to bind the
people of all other lands to the rude employments of unskilled
agriculture.

Her agricultural interests resisted the repeal of the corn laws.

---

† The Act of July 14, 1870, reduced the duty on tea and coffee, and transferred to the free list many varieties of raw material which we cannot yet
produce; and I hope that Congress will, during the next session, make tea
and coffee free. The harmless stimulants taken morning and evening by the
farmer and laborer should not be taxed.

‡ Let us for a moment think what are the conditions of our poor today.
*Apart from the question of our agricultural population, whose almost help-
less lot is best told by the simple fact, that in many places the luxury of meat
is comparatively unknown;* apart from the questions of special emergency,
such as the cotton famine, or the East End Emigration Society, which has
been brought into existence for the purpose of relieving the great mass of
destitution and poverty in that neighborhood; apart from all such special
and exceptional cases, we have the general sense of depression and want
everywhere spread around us. It is not necessary to dwell on the scenes of
human misery, where wholesale suicides or cruel murders mark the profound despair of those who lay trembling on the confines of want. It is
equally unnecessary to recall those verdicts that appear time after time at
coroner's inquests under the simple but expressive phraseology — "Death

To admit grain duty free it was said would ruin the farmers and lessen the market and taxable value of the land of the kingdom. But experience demonstrated the laws of social science and proved the harmony of interests by increasing the agricultural products of England in a ratio equal to the increased amount of her import of raw material and food for her land and people. . . .

Free Trade Keeps Us in Subjection to England's Colonial Policy

Sir, this is a melancholy picture to contemplate — a country wasted in its youth, and its people impoverished in the midst of abounding natural riches. And, sir, what adds to its sombre character is the fact that it is not accidental — that it is not the result of Providence, save as Providence permits some men to trifle with their rights and interests, and others to take advantage of their wickedness, weakness, or folly. It is the work of man; it is the result of design; it has been brought about as the end sought to be obtained by the sagacious and far-seeing legislators who have guided the counsels of Great Britain and their allies, the free traders of the Democratic party of our country. The laws by which these melancholy results were produced are demonstrable, and have long been well understood. They are the golden rule as administered by selfish and perfidious England to young or feeble nations and her own colonies. They were understood by Locke when he prepared his essay on *Civil*

from Starvation." It is not necessary to recall these things, because the newspaper press of the country drives these truths home without stint and without compromise; but it may be important to remember that the individual cases, which thus come to the surface, are known only by accident, and that the great mass of misery that suffers and dies, — dies and tells no tale. Occasionally and by accident the curtain is drawn on one side, and we see into the midst of the life of poverty that surrounds us; and we then know by the glance thus afforded us, what the general life must be; wasted by poverty, decimated by fever, shattered by want; and it thus rises before us, in the full force of its appeal to that sense of human sympathy which is common to us all. But the general acceptance of the positions here stated will be aided by a few facts. Let us see what the barometer of pauperism has to tell us. Our pauper population in 1866, was 920,344; in 1867, 958,824; in 1868, 1,034,823; and the number is still increasing; yet these numbers show that our pauper population has increased 114,479 persons in two years, or at the rate of more than 1000 per week. —*Home Politics,* by Daniel Grant, p. 3, London, 1870.

Government. Dean Swift, as I have shown, expounded them when
he endeavored to inspire the people of Ireland with wisdom and save
to that unhappy country a future. They were understood by Andrew
Gee when he published his work on *Trade* in 1750, and among other
illustrations of his clear apprehension of them said:

> "Manufactures in our American colonies should be discouraged,
> prohibited. . . . We ought always to keep a watchful eye over our
> colonies, *to restrain them from setting up any of the manufactures
> which are carried on in Great Britain;* and any such attempts should
> be crushed at the beginning. . . . Our colonies are much in the same
> state as Ireland was in when they began the woolen manufactory,
> *and as their numbers increase, will fall upon manufactures for
> clothing themselves, if due care be not taken to find employment for
> them* in raising such productions as may enable them to furnish
> themselves with all the necessaries from us. . . . As they will have the
> providing rough materials to themselves, so shall we have the manu-
> facturing of them. If encouragement be given for raising hemp, flax,
> etc., doubtless they will soon begin to manufacture, *if not prevented.*
> Therefore, *to stop the progress of any such manufacture,* it is
> proposed that no weaver have liberty to set up any looms, without
> first registering at an office, kept for that purpose. . . . That all
> slitting-mills, and engines for drawing wire or weaving stockings, *be
> put down.* . . . *That all negroes be prohibited from weaving either
> linen or woolen, or spinning or combing wool, or working at any
> manufacture of iron,* further than making it into pig or bar iron.
> That they also be *prohibited* from manufacturing *hats, stockings, or
> leather of any kind.* This limitation will not abridge the planters of
> any liberty they now enjoy; on the contrary, it will then turn their in-
> dustry to promoting and raising those rough materials. . . . If we
> examine into the circumstances of the inhabitants of our plantations,
> and our own, it will appear that *not one-fourth of their product re-
> dounds to their own profit, for, out of all that comes here, they only
> carry back clothing and other accommodations for their families,* all
> of which is of the merchandise and manufacture of this kingdom.
> . . . All these advantages we receive by the plantations, *besides the
> mortgages on the planters' estates and the high interest they pay us,
> which is very considerable."*

I think, sir, that I have shown by the extracts I have made from
that remarkable book, *Cotton is King,* that the men of the South
understood the laws of trade (certain as that of gravitation) well
enough to comprehend the fact that free trade must ultimately
destroy the varied interests of the North. They may not, mad with

ambition as they were, have seen that the operation of the laws whose penalties they were inflicting upon others would involve them in common destruction; but that they understood the fatal operation of free trade upon the great interests of the country is apparent in every chapter of the essay from which I have quoted.

I know not, sir, whether the gentleman from Indiana has studied the laws of social science, but they have been thoroughly comprehended by the statesmen of England, and furnish the key alike to her diplomacy and legislation. Illustrative of this is the case of Portugal. In the latter part of the seventeenth century she had established manufactures of woolen goods, which were thriving, adding to the comfort and prosperity of her people, and to her own respectability and power. They, however, needed protection against the hostile capital and more fully developed industry of England, and in 1684 the Government, discovering the advantages it derived from these manufactures, resolved to protect them by prohibiting the importation of foreign fabrics of the kind. Thenceforward their increase was so rapid as to attract the attention of British capitalists, who determined upon their destruction. This was not to be accomplished at once; but, evading the technical language of the law, they manufactured articles under the names and of descriptions not precisely covered by the act of prohibition, which would supply their places, and threw them in great abundance into the Portugese markets.† The effect upon the industry of the country was soon felt, and the Government gave its attention to the matter, and prohibited

---

† This device has been practiced upon during the past two years to the great detriment of the public revenue and of the American wool grower and manufacturer, by invoicing woolen and worsted goods as manufactures of cow and calf hair. Mr. James Dobson, in a letter which appears in the *New York Daily Bulletin* of January 26, 1871, says: "In the first place, I would say that these so-called calf hair cloakings are not made from the materials the importers say they are, but in place of being made from cow or calf hair are only so in part — the balance being wool; and some goods that have been so classified contain nothing but wool. Out of two hundred and eighty-five invoices that had passed, between July 1 to November 7, 1870, under the assumption of being calf hair, there were seventy invoices of curled Astrachans which, if properly and honestly invoiced, would have paid duty as manufactures of worsted goods. Samples of these goods can be seen in the Appraiser's Office in New York, if they have not been destroyed since

the introduction of these "serges and druggets." But British capitalists were as determined that their fabrics should clothe the people
of Portugal as they have since been that we should consume their
cotton, woolen, steel, iron and other goods; and what they had been
unable to accomplish by the mere force of capital or by skillful eva-
sions of Portuguese laws, they at least achieved by diplomacy.
Portugal failing to perceive that England could not produce Portuguese wines, as she cannot produce American cotton, hemp, rice
tobacco, and grain, listened to the words of such diplomacy as induced us to enter into the Canadian reciprocity treaty, and subjected
the energy, ingenuity, and industry of her people to the control of
the Government and capitalists of England; the inducement to this
step, artfully put forward by Great Britain, was that the wines of
Portugal should be admitted into Great Britain at a duty one-third

November 7, 1870. If they have, then I can produce certified samples by the
Deputy-Appraiser who passed them. About twenty specimens of the poorer
quality of these so-called calf hair goods were submitted by the Treasury
Department for microscopic examination, for the purpose of detecting
whether any wool was contained in them, and in every instance wool was
discovered, some specimens contained seventy percent wool, while others
had variable proportions. You can find this report in the Treasury Department at Washington. You can also find it embodied in the Department
letters, of December 7 and 8, 1870, to the Collector of the Port of New York,
Again, your correspondent says that the assumption that one house in
Huddersfield had sent nine-tenths of these goods to the United States, is
groundless, like the rest of my statements. All I have to say to this is that I
here quoted a portion of the American Consul's letter written to the Collector of New York, calling his attention to the frauds that were daily perpetrated on the revenue of the country. The letter bears date September 17,
1870, a copy of which is on file both in New York and Philadelphia, also at
the Treasury Department at Washington, and is a public document. He
says:
" 'My attention having been drawn to the fact that certain manufacturers of this district have refused to give calf-hair certificates to the goods
sold this firm in question, because they knew them to be false and did not
wish to perjure themselves for the sake of gain, however the impression
gained ground that the sworn certificate was only a matter of form. I was led
to infer that this house in question must be the house who had so misled the
manufacturer, and the developments have reached such a form that I feel it
incumbent on me to call the attention of the revenue officers at New York to
all the invoices of this firm, which have passed through this agency.' "

less than that imposed on wines imported from other countries. The effect of this treaty on the industry of Portugal is narrated by an English writer, who says:

> "Before the treaty our woolen cloths, cloth serges, and cloth druggets were prohibited in Portugal. They had set up fabrics there for making cloth, and proceeded with very good success, and we might justly apprehend they would have gone on to erect other fabrics until at last they had served themselves with every species of woolen manufactures. The treaty takes off all prohibitions and obliges Portugal to admit forever all our woolen manufactures. Their own fabrics by this were perfectly ruined, and we exported £100,000 value in the single article of cloths the very year after the treaty.

> "The court [of Portugal] was pestered with remonstrances from their manufacturers when the prohibition was taken off pursuant to Mr. Methuen's treaty. But the thing was passed, the treaty was ratified, and their looms were all ruined." — *British Merchantmen,* vol. 3, p. 253.

In the spirit of the diplomacy of Methuen was the partliamentary eloquence of Henry, now Lord Brougham, in 1815. Having described the effect of the peace of 1814, which bound continental Europe to the use of British manufactures, and produced an excessive exportation of British goods in that direction, he said:

> "The peace of America has produced somewhat of the same effect, though I am very far from placing the vast exports which it occasioned upon the same footing with those to the European market the year before, both because ultimately the Americans will pay, which the exhausted state of the Continent renders very unlikely, and *because it was well worth while to incur a loss upon the first exportation in order by the glut to stifle in the cradle those rising manufactures in the United States which the war has forced into existence* contrary to the natural course of things."

Though I should not pause here, I cannot abstain from asking the gentleman from Indiana whether he is ready to permit "British capitalists" to glut our markets and stifle in the cradle the rising manufactures which the late war has called into existence? In further proof that they will do so, and if we do not protect them, throw the workmen engaged in our furnaces, forges, factories and workshops out of employment, let me add that the commission appointed under the provisions of the act of 5th and 6th Victoria, chapter ninety-nine, showed how well it understood that the supremacy of Great Britain depends on the maintenance, at whatever cost of her manufacturing supremacy. In its report to Parliament in 1854 it said:

> "I believe that the laboring classes generally, in the manufacturing districts of this country, and especially in the iron and coal districts, are very little aware of the extent to which they are often indebted for their being employed at all to *the immense losses which their employers voluntarily incur in bad times, in order to destroy foreign competition, and to gain and keep possession of foreign markets.* Authentic instances are well known of employers having in such times carried on their work at a loss amounting in the aggregate to three or four hundred thousands pounds in the course of three or four years. If the efforts of those who encourage the combinations to restrict the amount of labor, and to produce strikes, were to be successful for any length of time, *the great accumulations of capital could no longer be made which enable a few of the most wealthy capitalists to overwhelm all foreign competition in times of great depression,* and thus to clear the way for the whole trade to step in when prices revive, and to carry on a great business before foreign capital can again accumulate to such an extent as to be able to establish a competition in prices with any chance of success. *The large capitals of this country are the great instruments of warfare against the competing capitalists of foreign countries,* and are the most essential instruments now remaining by which our manufacturing supremacy can be maintained; the other elements — cheap labor, abundance of raw materials, means of communication, and skilled labor — being rapidly in the process of being realized." . . .

We Can Pay Our Debts "Without Moneys"

I have never been able to believe that a national debt is a national blessing. I have seen how good might be interwoven with or educed from evil, or how a great evil might, under certain conditions, be turned to good account; but beyond this, I have never been able to regard debt, individual or national, as a blessing. It may be that, as in the inscrutable providence of God it required nearly five years of war to extirpate the national crime of slavery, and anguish and grief found their way to nearly every hearth-side in the country before we would recognize the manhood of the race we had so long oppressed, it was also necessary that we should be involved in a debt of unparalleled magnitude, that we might be compelled to avail ourselves of the wealth that lies so freely around us, and by opening markets for well-rewarded industry, make our land, what in theory it has ever been, the refuge of the oppressed of all climes. England, if supreme selfishness be consistent with sagacity, has been eminently sagacious in preventing us from becoming a manufacturing people; for with our enterprise, our ingenuity, our freer institutions, the extent of our country, the cheapness of our land, the diversity of our resources, the grandeur of our seas, lakes, and rivers, we should long ago have been able to offer her best workmen such inducements as would have brought them by millions to help bear our burdens and fight our battles. We can thus raise the standard of British and continental wages, and protect American workmen against ill-paid competition. This we must do if we mean to maintain the national honor. The fields now under culture, the houses now existing, the mines now being worked, the men we now employ, cannot pay our debt. To meet its annual interest by taxing our present population and developed resources would be to continue an ever-enduring burden.

The principal of the debt must be paid; but as it was contracted for posterity its extinguishment should not impoverish those who sustained the burdens of the war. I am not anxious to reduce the total of our debt, and would, in this respect, follow the example of England, and as its amount has been fixed would not for the present trouble myself about its aggregate except to prevent its increase. My anxiety is that the taxes it involves shall be as little oppressive as possible, and be so adjusted that, while defending our industry against foreign assault, they may add nothing to the cost of those necessaries of life which we cannot produce, and for which we must therefore look to other lands. The raw materials entering into our manufactures, which we are yet unable to produce, but on which we unwisely impose duties, I would put into the free list with tea, coffee, and other such purely foreign essentials of life, and would impose duties on commodities that compete with American productions, so as to protect every feeble or infant branch of industry and quicken those that are robust. I would thus cheapen the elements of life, and enable those whose capital is embarked in any branch of production to offer such wages to the skilled workmen of all lands as would steadily and rapidly increase our numbers, and, as is always the case in the neighborhood of growing cities or towns of considerable extent, increase the return for farm labor; this policy would open new mines and quarries, build new furnaces, forges and factories, and rapidly increase the taxable property and taxable inhabitants of the country. Would the South accept this theory and enter heartily upon its execution, she would pay more than now seems her share of the debt and feel herself blessed in the ability to do it. Her climate is more genial than ours; her soil may be restored to its original fertility; her rivers are broad, and her harbors good; and above all, hers is the monopoly of the fields for rice, cane sugar, and cotton. Let us pursue for twenty years the sound national policy of protection, and we will double our population and more than quadruple our capital and reduce our indebtedness *per capita* and per acre to little more than a nominal sum. Thus each man can "without moneys" pay the bulk of his portion of the debt by blessing others with the ability to bear an honorable burden.

How protection, by animating, diversifying, and rewarding industry, will pay our debt is well shown by the experience of the last five years. And though we do not owe that experience to sagacious legislation, but, as I have said, to the exigencies of the war, it should guide our future steps. The disparity between gold and paper has added to the duties imposed on foreign products, and enabled our manufacturers to enter upon a career of prosperity such as they have never enjoyed, save for a brief period, under the tariffs of 1824 and 1828, and again for four years under that of 1842, a prosperity in which the farmers are sharing abundantly, as is shown by the fact that they are now out of debt, though most of their farms were mortgaged five years ago. When the war began we could not, as I have said, make the iron for a gun-barrel; we can now export better gun-barrels than we can import. We then made no steel, and had to rely on foreign countries for material for steel cannon and those steel-pointed shot by which alone we can pierce the five-and-a-half inch iron-clads with which we must contend in future warfare. Many of our regiments that came first to the capital came in rags, though every garment on their backs was new, and many of them of freshly imported cloth. But, sir, no army in the world was ever so substantially clothed and armed as that which for two days passed in review before the President of the United States and Lieutenant General after having conquered the rebellion, and which, when disbanded, was clad in the product of American spindles and looms, and armed with weapons of American materials and construction.

It is said that ten years ago "a piece of Lake Superior iron ore was a curiosity to most of our practical metallurgists." In 1855 the first ore was shipped from Marquette county. How rapid the enlargement of the trade has been is shown by the following statement:

In 1855 there were exported	1,445 tons
1856	11,594 tons
1857	26,184 tons
1858	31,135 tons
1859	65,679 tons
1860	116,948 tons
1861	45,430 tons
1862	115,720 tons
1863	185,275 tons
1864	235,123 tons

The production of charcoal pig iron in that region, we are told by Dr. Lamborn, commenced at the Pioneer works near the Jackson mine in 1858. Those works were the pioneers of a great army, and already the Collinsville, the Forrestville, the Morgan, and the Greenwood furnaces are in profitable operation. The production of charcoal iron in that county has been as follows:

In 1858 there were exported	1,627 tons
1859	7,258 tons
1860	5,660 tons
1861	7,970 tons
1862	8,590 tons
1863	8,908 tons
1864	13,832 tons

And though we produced no steel in 1860, a table constructed from information furnished by the report of the Commissioner of Internal Revenue for the year ending June 30, 1864, shows that the Government had in that year derived $391,141.39 of internal revenue from the steel made and manufactured in the United States during that year.

Time will not permit me to indicate the many new branches of industry which have sprung up, or the vast extension and improvement of those which, under our old free trade system, had found an insecure footing and were enduring a sickly existence. I may, however, venture on a few remarks upon this head. California is not a New England or an eastern State; she has perhaps been less affected by the war than any other State, unless it be Oregon; and I find that, though she raised in 1859 but 2,378,000 pounds of wool, she raised in 1863, 7,600,000, and in 1864, 8,000,000 pounds. She is, we are assured by her papers, realizing the advantage of bringing the producer and consumer together; and though during the last year she shipped to New York some 7,500,000 pounds of wool, she is showing that her people understand the importance of saving the double transportation they would otherwise pay on those of their own products they might consume — that for carrying the raw material to the factory, and that for bringing the fabrics back again. I find in one of her papers the following statement:

"California Woolen Mills — The Pioneer Mill, at Black Point, California, has thirty-one looms at work now, consumes annually 1,200,000 pounds of wool, employs 220 laborers, pays out $100,000 yearly in wages, uses a capital of $500,000, and runs fifty-two sewing machines. About one-fourth of the wool purchased is used in making blankets, the importation of which has now entirely ceased, the home production having taken entire possession of the market. Nearly half the production is flannel, which is gradually crowding the imported article out of the market. About one-third of the wool consumed at this mill is made into tweeds and cassimeres, which is mostly made up into clothing in San Francisco. Broadcloth is not made there in quantity, because of the scarcity of pure Merino wool. The Pioneer and Mission Mills together consume about 2,400,000 pounds of wool, employ about 450 laborers and $1,000,000 of capital, and pay out $200,000 in wages annually."

Well done, California. Your tweeds and cassimeres and blankets will crowd foreign articles not out of your own State alone, but out of the markets of the Pacific slope. You will soon need machinists to construct your sewing-machines and make the tools for those who do such work. Land around your cities will grow in value; and those who own it need not compete with farmers so distant from market as to limit them to production of grain alone. Hay, potatoes, turnips, and all other roots for the sustenance of man and beast, and fruits for the table, may engage their attention and give them ample reward for their labor.

Oregon has also felt the quickening influence of the times. She paid to the internal revenue department, during 1864, taxes on the manufacture of $128,620.67 of woolen cloth. . . .

Why An Export Duty Should Be Laid on Cotton

Mr. Chairman, permit me, in drawing to a conclusion, to repeat that we need not resort to the prohibitions which have been practiced by other countries. Our natural advantages and those which spring from our personal freedom, are sufficient to relieve us from all difficulty on this point. There is, however, one of our agricultural productions upon which, did the Constitution permit, I would lay an export duty; and that is cotton. And I hope the Constitution will be so amended as to permit it; for though for years — for the life of more than a generation — the country was ruled in the interest of slavery, to the destruction of the interests and rights of our free laborers, by the pretended apprehension that if American cotton were not cheapened rival fields would be developed, the delusion has been dispelled, and all men know that ours are the only available cotton fields of the world. For five years we maintained along the coast of the cotton States a blockade such as never was attempted before. The people of those States planted no cotton and burned much of what they had produced, and did all that madness or ingenuity could suggest to develop rival fields if any existed; and what is the result? Necessity constrained the temporary use of Indian cotton, and Calcutta became so rich that her *ryots* put silver tires around their cart wheels. But when the power of our armies had reopened the cotton fields of the South, when it became known that freedmen were working upon the Sea Islands, and that our Government was again to possess the cotton region of the South, there came a fearful revulsion in India, and all men acknowledged that God had given the United States a monopoly of the available cotton fields of the earth.† Upon that one production we should put an export duty,

---

† An export duty of 2 cents a pound on unmanufactured cotton, coupled with the free export of yarns and fabrics, would soon transfer the capital, skill, and machinery of Lancashire to our cotton growing States, in most of which exhaustless water-power runs to waste.

and the result would be that the men of the cotton States, no longer dependent on England for a market for their bulky raw material, would, with their cheaper fabrics, drive her cotton goods from the markets of the world. Though I would not, by legislation, prohibit the export of the elements of any branch of manufacture or machinery, I will endeavor to retain in the country many of the elements of manufactures that now go abroad, by making them more valuable in this country than in any other, and by impressing upon the American people the conviction, so long ago inculcated upon the people of Ireland by Dean Swift, that to enrich themselves they must

> "Carry out *their own goods as much manufactured* and bring in *those of others as little manufactured* as the nature of mutual commerce will allow."

To gratify our patriotic desires we need not resort to prohibitory duties. We can nationalize our policy by relieving from duty tea, coffee, and every raw material which we do not produce, but which enters into our manufactures or arts.† I would give the wool-growers protection, but would stimulate the manufacture of carpets and

---

† American production, furnishing all National power, is to the country, its commerce, and trade, on a large scale, what the water-wheel and the steam engine are to mills and machinery on a small one — the prime mover. In the absence of this great National prime mover, as it may be called, all motion, nay, even the life of the body politic itself must cease. As all of the people of the country must ultimately, directly or indirectly, live off of or from this production, so must all taxes, National, State, and local, be finally drawn from American producers, unless some portion of our taxation can be levied upon foreigners who seek our markets, and enjoy the advantages and profits thereof.

Such being the case, it follows that the American producer has a right to demand that his Government shall levy duties on foreign imports, and in so doing shall levy them, first and foremost upon those commodities the like of which *are produced* in this country, for the following reasons:

First. Because such commodities come in direct competition with the productions of American producers who are obliged to pay National, State, and local taxes; and to grant privileges to foreigners which are and must be withheld from ourselves would be manifest and gross injustice on the part of the Government to its own people.

Second. Inasmuch as these commodities are such as are produced in this country, foreigners may be made to pay the duties thereon, as, having American competitors with whom they must compete, these duties must

increase the demand for American wool by admitting free of duty those low grades which we do not produce; and would lay light duties on those articles in the manufacture of which machinery has been perfected and large capitals have been accumulated, especially where the original cost of the machinery has been returned in profits; and would make them heavier and heaviest upon those branches of industry which are most feeble but which give assurance of ultimate success. When we do this our country will cease to be a mere agglomeration of sections, and we will be a national people, homogeneous in our interests by reason of their immense diversity.

Such, sir, is my plan for enforcing the Monroe doctrine, acquiring Canada, paying the national debt, and by relieving the South of its embarrassment, recementing the shattered Union. The poor whites must be weaned from the rifle, net, and line, by the inducements of well-rewarded labor. Their idle wives and children may thus be brought to habits of order, method, and industry, and in a few years we shall cease to remember that in this nineteenth century, and under our republican Government, there were for several decades millions of people tending rapidly to barbarism. The same

---

first be paid by them before they can place themselves in a position for such competition. If not made to pay these particular duties, there are no other taxes which they can, by any possibility, be made to pay in selling in our markets; and the heavily taxed American has an absolute right to demand that, enjoying the advantages and profits of these markets, foreigners shall take with them some of the many drawbacks and disadvantages which he himself is obliged to bear.

Third. Because if these duties are in whole or in part levied upon productions the like of which we do not ourselves produce, and must or will have, they must ultimately and inevitably fall upon the shoulders of American producers, thus causing them to be again taxed, indeed almost encompassing them by a network of taxation, escape from which is impossible.

Hence we develop the grand and immutable principle: *That the moral right of the Government to levy duties on articles the like of which are not produced in this country, only commences when it has exhausted all the means of collecting duties on such articles as are produced in the country, or until it has reached a full measure of the burdens imposed upon American producers and still finds itself in need of revenue. Then, and then only, may it, consistently with the rights of American producers, resort to other sources of taxation, including duties on the importation of commodities the like of which are not produced in the country. — The Rights of American Producers.* By Henry Carey Baird, Philadelphia, 1870.

inducements will disclose, even to the eye of prejudice, the manhood of the freed man, and that kindly relation between employer and his employee which exists throughout the busy North and East will spring up in the South. Oppressed and degraded as he has been, the colored man will find that there are fields open to his enterprise, and a useful and honorable career possible to him, and will prove that, like other men, he loves property and has the energy to acquire it, the ability to retain it, and the thrift to make it advantageous to himself, his neighbors, and his country.

Let us then measure our resources by experiment and open them to the enterprise of the world; and the question whether we owe three hundred or three thousand millions will, then years hence, be one of trifling importance; and, as Andrew Yarrinton showed the people of England how to "outdo the Dutch without fighting," we will find that peace hath her victories for us also; Canada will come to us like ripe fruit falling into the hands of the farmer; and if Maximilian remain in Mexico, it will be as the citizen of a republic and an adherent of the Monroe doctrine.

The South —
Its Resources and Its Wants

Three speeches delivered by William Kelley during 1867 — one in New Orleans, one in Montgomery, Alabama, and one in Philadelphia — all addressed to crowds of up to 20,000 the necessity of developing the South's mines and of setting up new industries as the region diversified out of cotton. For Kelley and his collaborators, these considerations explain why the South as a region had more reason to support the American System than any other.

Kelley's New Orleans speech was reported in the New Orleans Republican; *his Montgomery, Alabama address was reported in the Montgomery* Sentinel. *His Philadelphia address, reported for the Philadelphia* Inquirer, *is not included in this selection. Editorial interjections by these newspapers have been retained.*

Address At New Orleans, May 11, 1867

Fellow-Citizens of Louisiana: In response to the invitation of your Governor and the Mayor of this beautiful city, I am here to counsel with you as to the best interests of our country. Let me, however, first congratulate you upon your enfranchisement, and thank the loyal men among you, without regard to race or color, who during the late struggle braved the dangers of battle in defense of the old flag, or quietly remained true to it amid the dangers which surrounded you, for the part you took in my enfranchisement. Having addressed a large and enthusiastic audience in Memphis on Tuesday night, and, standing in the midst of this brilliant scene in the city of New Orleans, I am at last able to proclaim that I am a free man in my native land, and may traverse its wide extent, carrying with me my conscience and convictions without fear of personal violence. This was impossible before the war. The institutions of the South were not cosmopolitan. Her *peculiar* system of labor not only controlled but contracted her civilization.

Disregarding the practice and precepts of the founders of our Government, and ignoring the admonitions of experience, the South turned a deaf ear to reason, refused to listen to remonstrance, and finally punished dissent from her judgment as a crime deserving outlawry and death. Attempting in a progressive age, and in a land of vast and varied resources, peopled by a generation more enterprising than any that had preceded it, to maintain a system which was "peculiar," and incapable of modification, save by absolute overthrow, she arrayed against her all the forces of civilization. No poet ever sang the charms of slavery. No limner ever embodied its beauties on canvas. No orator ever descanted upon its blessings; and though dumb dogs that could not bark proclaimed from many a pulpit the duty of servants to obey their masters as the sum and substance of the gospel, the voice of Christianity bade conscientious men do unto others as they would have others do unto them — be eyes to the blind and feet to the lame — and the cries of the wronged against those who withheld from the laborer his hire, ascended incessantly to the ears of the Lord of Sabaoth.

To this attempt on the part of the people of the South to isolate themselves, to exclude from their broad and fertile territory the advancing civilization of the age, may be ascribed the terrible war through which we have just passed. It made them intensely sectional, while the steady development of the North was demonstrating to its more rapidly increasing millions the beneficence of nationality. It created a separate and antagonistic system of civilization. The North welcomed all classes of emigrants from all lands. She made herself familiar with the inventions and discoveries of the day, and applied them to purposes of utility. She challenged the freest discussion of all topics and all systems. She provided liberally for the education of all her people, including the unhappy few to whom, in deference to Southern demands, she denied the full rights of citizenship. But the South, wrapt in its delusion, repulsed emigration — rejected all science and literature that controverted the divinity of slavery, and the justice and economy of unrequited toil. She denied to her laborers education, and consequently could not avail herself of, and was indifferent to the scientific and mechanical progress of the age. Thus, while the breach between the two sections was widening, the disparity in power between them was constantly increasing. Contrast, my friends, the development of the two sections; behold the great cities of the North. New York, with its environs, which are really, though not municipally, part of it, already exceeds Paris in wealth, splendor, trade, and population. London and Paris are the only transatlantic cities which exceed Philadelphia in these respects. Boston, Cincinnati, Chicago, and other cities, each exceed New Orleans in population. Yet New Orleans, past which the waters of sixty thousand miles of rivers flow, is the greatest city of the South.

Let me illustrate this point familiarly. The railroads connecting New York with Philadelphia, and Memphis with Grenada, Mississippi, differ in length less than ten miles. They are each a link in a great thoroughfare North and South. Over the former eight passenger trains pass daily each way; each train is made up of several cars. Over the latter one train of two cars passes daily. The fare from New York to Philadelphia is $3; but from Memphis to Grenada it is $8. The time required to make the journey from New York to Philadelphia is less than four hours, while it takes six and a half hours to pass between Memphis and Grenada. The land along the route, in New Jersey and Pennsylvania, for agricultural purposes, is worth from $250 to $400 per acre; that along the other can be bought from $3 to $20!

These contrasts are not accidental or arbitrary. They illustrate great principles — sleepless laws of social life.

When the sages of 1776 proclaimed that all men are born equal, and invested by nature with the right to life, liberty, and the pursuit of happiness, they uttered the law that was to fashion the institutions of America, and shape the civilization of her people. They were ever true to that law. They controlled the States at the time they framed the Constituion of the United States; and then every free man, without regard to color, was a voter in every State, except South Carolina; and while the Executive Government remained in their hands, and their personal influence controlled the legislation of the country, the free colored man was not denied the right of suffrage under any Territorial Government. Though South Carolina had steadily demanded his exclusion from 1778, in the convention for framing articles of Confederation, it was not until 1812 that she succeeded in inserting the word *white* in a law establishing a Territorial Government. That word appears for the first time in the law establishing the Territory of Missouri, which was enacted in that year.

The little monosyllable white, embodied in that law, was the germ of the war through which we have just passed. It involved an attempt to stay the course of American civilization — it was in conflict with its essential law — the great truth to which I have alluded, and involved strife between the spirit of liberty and the impulse of the masses on the one hand, and the grasping selfishness of an oligarchy and the wrongs of slavery on the other. From that time to this our country has not been free from agitation; and while the institutions of the North have been more and more republicanized by the spirit of democracy, the written law of the land, yielding to the reactionary spirit which won its first triumph in the Missouri contest, has been controlled by the spirit of slavery, and been marked by a total disregard of the vital principle of our Government. Our Government rests on two great sentiments — personal liberty and territorial unity; and any law which restrained personal liberty, or engendered or fostered sectional interest, was a necessary cause of discord and strife. When, therefore, yielding to Southern persuasion or dictation, the North consented to deprive the free colored man of suffrage in the Territories; and when, under the same influence, State after State, throughout the free North, made color a test of citizenship, until out of New England, citizens of African descent were everywhere disfranchised, they who made these concessions were not, as they believed, cementing the Union, but making war inevitable. Nations are not the creatures of chance. God's providence embraces the American continent. His judgment is its final law. And these abandonments of the principles upon which our Government was based — which had been reverently accepted by our forefathers as in harmony with His will — did not pass without His notice. Has He not repealed all these reactionary statutes, and by His breath wiped out these modern improvements of State constitutions? From the firing on Sumter to the surrender of the armies of Lee and Johnston, He was teaching us, by the terrible baptism of battle and blood, how infinite is His power and justice, and how easily He can make the folly and madness of man to praise Him. Had the South been national and truly democratic as the North, and had her legislation been progressive, slavery would have gradually disappeared, and the colored population of the country would have been absorbed into its citizenship without a crisis, and almost without special notice. But that was not to be. By an inscrutable law, all great blessings come to us through suffering. Blood has been the price of freedom to every nation. For it is the same with nations in this respect as with individuals. Who can tell the agony that is requited when the mother first beholds a smile play over the face of her sleeping infant? It is to the garden and the cross that we go, in sorrow and humility, for our highest hopes and most enduring promises, and amid the tumult and tortures of the battle-field, the horrors of the wreck upon the maddened ocean, or the wearying sufferings of the feverish bed, we pass from the cares of life to the beatitude of eternity. And, as Americans, we may look back on years of war, we may count the dead of the contending armies at nearly one million, and behold the fairest and most fertile regions of our smiling country, your own lovely South, scarred and desolated by war, and rejoice that the agony which was to purchase our country's great blessing is over. Henceforth it shall be the boast of every American that though his country embraces all climates, from the summer breezes that ever linger over your broad Gulf to the wintry winds that howl the requiem of gallant navies as they sweep over the mighty lakes of the North, its atmosphere is so pure that no slave can breathe it and remain in bondage. [Immense applause.]

Let me not be misunderstood: I charge this war not upon the South alone. It is, perhaps more largely due to the unprincipled men in the North, who should have met the issue at the threshold, and settled the question while it was susceptible of legislative control, than to the men of the South, who, prompted by the short-sighted demands of present interest, insisted upon concessions which sagacious men of principle would not have accorded. Let me illustrate: No statesmen had denied that slavery in the Territories was the subject of Congressional legislation until John C. Calhoun introduced into the Senate, on the 19th of February, 1847, three resolutions, embodying mere abstract propositions, the last of which was as follows:

> "That the enactment of any law which should, directly or by its effects, deprive the citizens of any State of this Union from emigrating with their property into any of the Territories of the United States, will make such discrimination, and would, therefore, be a violation of the Constitution and the rights of the States from which such citizens emigrate, and in derogation of that perfect equality which belongs to them as members of this Union, and would tend directly to subvert the Union itself."

The object of these resolutions was to extend slavery over the almost boundless territory then belonging to the United States. So repugnant was the proposition to the members of the Senate, largely Democratic, and with no Republican member in it, that Mr. Calhoun did not dare press his resolutions to a vote.

In May, 1848, the Democratic party met in convention at Baltimore, and Mr. Yancey, Calhoun's great disciple, submitted the following:

> "*Resolved,* That the doctrine of noninterference with the rights of property of any portion of this Confederation, be it in the States or Territories, by any other than the parties introduced in them, is the true Republican doctrine recognized by this body."

There were 282 members in that convention. The South was fully represented. But so novel and dangerous was this doctrine then considered that every delegate from the North and most of those from the South united in demanding a direct vote upon the question, that they might send to the people of the country an expression of their abhorrence of the new and dangerous dogma. But about one in eight delegates was then prepared to sustain it, the vote upon it being 36 for and 246 against. But behold the sequel: In less than twelve years the unprincipled men who governed the Democratic party brought on the fierce struggles in Kansas by accepting the doctrine they had thus promptly spurned, and persuading the Southern people that the North had abandoned the faith of the Fathers, and was in reckless disregard of the restraints of the Constitution robbing them of their rights. Impelled by ambition, and seeking wealth through the intrigues of a corrupt political era, they encouraged you to prepare for war. They assured you that if you would strike for your supposed rights they would stand by you on the battlefield, as they had done in caucuses, conventions, and on the floor of Congress.

I have seen a copy of a letter from one of them who had once filled the Presidential chair, saying to you, through one of your leaders, that if you seceded there would be no war; or that if there were it would be co-extensive with the country, and blood would flow in every village, town, and city of the North.

How little Franklin Pierce knew the real spirit of the people among whom he lived! How ignorant was he of the fact that the world is under moral government! Were his pledges kept? In what city of the North did blood flow? Between the citizens of which Northern States was there armed collision; and from which of the Northern States did men swarm to swell the ranks of the Confederate armies? As the echo of the guns fired upon the flag over Sumter reverberated through the glens and valleys of the North and swept over the broad prairies of the distant Northwest, these same false and unprincipled friends of the South, in obedience to the demands of popular sentiment, flung to the breeze, at their dwellings and places of business, the resplendent flag of the Union; and, with Fernando Wood at their head, made themselves prominent in the work of recruiting and organizing troops for your subjugation. How did they aid you? The whole North gave you two soldiers whose names are known — Gustavus W. Smith and Mansfield Lovell! Can any of you name a third? [Shouts of "no, no."] I'll tell you what they did give you, though. They gave you what the little girl, who was asked to contribute the value of the sugar she used to the missionary cause, gave. She replied, "No, grandpa, I don't think I can do that; but I'll tell you what I will do. I'll give the cause my prayers." [Laughter.] They gave your cause their prayers, and, as if fearing they might prove effective, hastened to meet their neighbors and swear they had done no such thing! [Immense cheering.] A hopeless minority in Congress throughout the war, unable to influence, much less to control a single act of legislation, they made speeches for distribution through the South, as if to encourage you in your hopeless struggle, so that when it ended you should be utterly exhausted. In so far, history will hold the North — especially the Democratic party of the North — responsible for the war.

Still, the million of graves, in which sleep the best and bravest of both sections, are chargeable to the South. It withdrew the questions involved from the forum of diplomacy and legislation, and submitted them to war's last dread arbitrament. To prepare the way for this, its controlling spirits had kept the mass of the people in profound and degrading ignorance. Each State having received large grants of land for educational purposes, none of them had provided schools for the people. The laws of each State prohibited, by penal statutes, the education of the slave population. This was inevitable. Intelligence and culture are incompatible with slavery; the penalty God attaches to the crime of holding a brother in bondage is that he who is so held shall be of little value to him who holds him; and sluggish indolence is, like ignorance, the inevitable law of slavery. The absence of schools, the want of diversified fields of employment, degraded the non-slaveholding whites of the South, and the most enterprising of them left the land of their birth to find happier homes. Thus the South, whose great need was population to develop her vast and varied resources, and build up cities, towns, and villages along her great lines of transit, and thus increase the value of her lands and diminish the cost of travel and transportation, was constantly expelling her own children. Nor did she welcome emigration. The German, the Irishman, the Englishman, and the Scotchman quit the scenes of their childhood and the graves of their fathers in pursuit of liberty and a higher degree of physical comfort than is accorded the laboring man in those lands. In their native homes they learn that in the North there is political equality for all, and that every fair day's work done by man, woman, or child, is assured by the law of the land a fair day's wages; and that westward, to the last frontier, there is no village, however small, in which the free school is not open to every child. Thus attracted, they have come to the North and West by millions. The immigration last year numbered more than 300,000, and added a sum greater than the total of our national debt to the wealth of the people whose numbers they swelled. I found this morning that I had with me by accident, a copy of an address made to my neighbors, October 3, 1856, from which, if it be only to show you that I teach no new doctrine, I beg leave to submit a brief extract:

"I have another set of illustrations to give you, and I now speak not of slaves, but of the free white men of the South. Men love their homes; the place of their birth; the institutions under which they pass happy childhood, prosperous youth, and enter into a successful career of manhood. There are thirteen millions of Northern men from whom emigrants might go, while there are but six millions of free people in the South, yet the census of 1850 found 609,371 persons who were born in the slave States living in the free States, while only 206,638 persons born in the free States were living in the slave States. Yes, my fellow-citizens, in 1850 there were 609,371 men and women of Southern birth living in the Northern States; they had fled from the blessings of labor owned by capital. But you may say, 'they had come to the cities to engage in commerce; had come to pursue the arts in Philadelphia, New York, Boston; had come to find employment in all the various pursuits of our great cities.' Let us see, therefore, how many people born in the planting States had emigrated into two States of the North — Indiana and Illinois — in which there are no great cities; in which you may say there are no universities; in which the arts have scarcely been developed; in which commerce has scarcely a footing; which are two of the young grazing and grain-growing States of the North.† In 1850 there were in those two States 47,026 who had emigrated from North Carolina, 8,231 from South Carolina, 2102 from Georgia, 45,037 from Tennessee, 1730 from Alabama, 777 from Mississippi, 701 from Louisiana, 107 from Texas, 44 from Florida; making the total of those who had left these nine planting States to go to those two agricultural and grazing States, 105,755."

Do you reproach me and others of the North that we did not in those days come and lay these arguments before you? Ah, my

---

† It must be remembered that these remarks were made in 1856, and are wholly inapplicable to those progressive States now. (This and the following footnotes were added by Kelley in the compilation and editing of his *Speeches, Addresses and Letters on Industrial and Financial Questions,* Philadelphia, 1872 — A.S.)

friends, you forget the terrible despotism you had established over yourselves. The fact that I entertained the opinions I am expressing made the climate south of the Potomac and Ohio so insalubrious for me that I did not dare breathe it for an hour. When you raised the cry of abolitionist against a Northern man, beings, with hearts as unrelenting as the bloodhound, pursued him to his death. Not only did you prohibit men who would have gladly sat with you at your hearthside and taken sweet counsel with you, from entering your beautiful region, but, through the arts of your politicians and the demagoguery of the Democratic leaders of the North, you hunted them to their very homes. While delivering the very address from which I have read to you, a shower of eggs was hurled at me by proslavery Democrats; and my only consolation was to thank God that the American Eagle laid fresh eggs at that season of the year. [Great laughter and applause.] Nor was this conduct ascribable to individuals only. The State of South Carolina seized from the deck of their vessels colored citizens of other States who chanced to enter the ports of that State, and incarcerating them as felons, made them chargeable with costs and jail fees, and in default of the payment of these, sold them and their posterity as slaves. And when, what Southern men called the Sovereign State of Massachusetts, sent one of her ablest and most venerable lawyers to raise the question of law arising out of this conduct, before a South Carolina court, the people of Charleston — not the roughs, but those who could do such an act with highest courtesy — the very pinks of the chivalry of that city, gave that distinguished man and the accomplished daughter that accompanied him the option of departure from the city in twenty-four hours or tar and feathers and jolly rides on rails. Again, it is known to all the North, though perhaps you may not be aware of the fact, that the State of Georgia, by solemn act of her Legislature approved by the Governor, and to be found among her printed law — offered a reward of five or twenty thousand dollars, I forget which, for the body, dead or alive, of a citizen of Massachusetts, who had never entered that State, or been so far South as the capital of his country; but who had had the temerity to publish, through the columns of his own paper, his disbelief in the divinity of slavery, and an assertion of the right of every woman to the possession of the body of every living child that had cost her the pangs of maternity.

You treated difference of opinion as the most heinous of crimes; and from each and all of the Southern States, native citizens, and some of them men of just distinction, were driven by threats of popular violence. Such was the case with the Grimkes, of South Carolina; Underwood, of Virginia; and Helper and Professor Hedrick, of North Carolina. Why did we not come and reason with you? Do you forget that you would not receive nor permit your neighbors to receive, through the post office, any papers or periodical that did not pander to your prejudices? The receipt through the post office of the *Liberator,* the *Anti-Slavery Standard,* the *Independent,* the New York *Tribune,* or any leading Republican paper, by one of your neighbors, branded him as an Abolitionist, and rendered his life insecure among you. The North would gladly have discussed the question. It opened its public halls to your orators, and its people swarmed to hear them. It received your papers, and its conscientious people were amazed at the infatuation which was driving the two sections headlong into war. But I come not to bandy crimination or recrimination with you. There is "ample room and verge enough" for that between you and the leaders of the Democracy of the North. But for myself and the Republican party, I say: shake not your gory locks at us, for you cannot say we did it. You spurned our counsels; and though we would gladly have embraced you as brothers, you refused to listen to our fraternal prayers.

Happily, these things belong to the past. Having endured the agony of four years of war, conducted with unequalled valor, and on a scale of unequalled magnitude, we rise as a new nation; to perfect the continental temple of freedom and equality, the foundations of which were so wisely laid by our forefathers. From those foundations we have removed the only two faulty stones — those on which were inscribed the fatal words, *Compromise* and *Slavery.* In all this broad land no man now owns his brother man. [Sensation.] You, men of color — you citizens of Louisiana, who wear the livery of Afric's burnished sun — give thanks unto God that he has turned and overturned, until the humblest of you stands erect in the majesty of free manhood, the equal of your fellow man before the laws of your country, as you are before the beneficent Father of all.

He guided the pen of Abraham Lincoln while writing the proclamation of emancipation. [Great enthusiasm and applause.] And they who enacted the civil rights bill and the military bill, to secure the enforcement of its provisions, went reverently to Him for counsel, and recognized His sovereign presence in their midst. The charter of your freedom is from Him. Freedom is His last, best blessing to you. Maintain it by sleepless vigilance, and by any requisite sacrifice; for in surrendering it you will be alike recreant to man and God. See to it, that a common school system, broad enough as is that of the North, to embrace every child born in the Commonwealth, or brought into it by emigration, is established by the constitution soon to be framed for your State. See to it, that the press is free; and be tolerant of opinion, for by the collision of opinion is the truth elicited. Welcome among you the people of every clime and nation; and remember that the prosperity of the State is but the aggregate prosperity of the individual citizens thereof. Will you not do this? [We will, yes, yes.] I know you will. And as this assurance thrills me, I behold a vision grander than that of Columbus; for I know that behind the islands lies a broad continent, sweeping from the rock-bound coast of the storm-lashed Atlantic to the golden shores of the sleeping Pacific. [Applause.] And that from the Rio Grande to the perpetual snows of Mount Hood, it is inhabited by one people, who, though differing in origin, are homogeneous in language, thought and sentiment; and who, though the citizens of many States, each having its own constitution, recognize as supreme one government, and that the freest yet devised by man. [Applause.] I cannot better illustrate the value of this unity than by pointing to the future of your own beautiful city. It is the entrepot for the commerce of the Gulf, the trade of which proceeds under our bright flag. The river that winds around you carries to the sea the waters of sixty thousand miles of river course. The valley it drains will sustain a population of five hundred millions of people. They will be free, intelligent, enterprising, and given to commerce; and your city will be the centre of their great commercial exchange. [Applause.] But as I look through the vista of a brief future, the glories of the great cities of antiquity fade away, and Florence, Venice and Genoa, recur to me as but so many distant villages. Not Paris or London will be your equal; for behind each of them lies a territory less in extent and resources than any one of a score of American States; while behind New Orleans lie the resources — agricultural, mineral and manufacturing — of a territory broader and richer than all Europe, and a people destined at no distant day to be more numerous than the people of Europe. And when those days shall come, loyal men of Louisiana, the name of Abraham Lincoln will be uttered with reverence by every lip, and all men will give thanks to God that He so ordered His providence as to establish political equality throughout the enduring Union of American States. [Tremendous applause followed this eloquent reference to the man whom all in the audience delight to hear spoken of.] My colored friends, permit me to thank you for the enthusiasm with which you greeted my advent among you. If at any time I have suffered for you, you have abundantly rewarded me by this exhibition of your generous appreciation. Permit me now to address a few remarks more especially to those who have not known as you, the woes of slavery or the consequences of disfranchisement under popular government. My white fellow-citizens, let me say to you that you are charged with a duty grander than is often confided to a generation of men. You are to unite with those whom through life you have been taught to despise as an inferior race, in organizing a party in Louisiana in harmony with the great Republican party of the North. That party is based on, vivified and cemented by two sentiments, love for the Union, and devotion to human freedom. Its whole creed may be summed up in the phrase, perfect and indestructible unity of the States, with the perpetual maintenance of the largest liberty of the individual citizen, consistent with the general welfare. If you fail to give full scope and power to either of these sentiments, you will in so far fall short of the due performance of your mission. Justice is blind, and knows no color; and justice is the law of the Republican party. In enfranchising our fellow citizens of African descent we must accept them as entitled to all the rights, privileges, and amenities of citizenship. We must not give a mere intellectual assent to the propositions on which we base our action; but accept them as animating and controlling sentiments. Rights not guaranteed by daily practice are not secured. Established habit is the only sure safeguard of personal liberty in our land. The Constitution of the United States has always guaranteed to every citizen the rights, privileges, and immunities of citizenship to the citizens of each State in the several States; but when, before this war, was I, or men who hold opinions in common with me, safe in attempting to exercise that constitutional right in any slave State? As I have shown you, dominant sentiment may override constitutional and legal provisions. Rest not, therefore, your experiment upon the embodiment in constitution or law of abstract principles; but see to it that they are embodied practically in the organization of primary caucus and convention, and ultimate organization of parish, city and State. If you rise to the prompt accomplishment of this great work the day of strife will have passed, and the American sword may be beaten into a ploughshare. A homogenous people, *bound together by the immense diversity of their varied interests,* by the most unrestrained personal intercourse and the freest interchange of thought through a free press, will find no issues that legislation or diplomacy may not settle. And a nation that, in its infancy, put into the field, and kept there for four years, during which the bloodiest and best-contested battles of history were fought, armies each numbering more than a million of men, need fear no foreign war. [Applause.] The prestige of this war is at the back of our European diplomacy, and if we listen to the voice of reason in our demands, American questions will be matters of easy and speedy solution by the courts of Europe. Let us, then, not grieve over the past, but bating no jot of heart or hope move onward in our great work, and the struggling millions of Europe will find encouragement in our labors, and innumerable posterity will rise to revere our country's flag, and call those who fell martyrs in its maintenance, and those who through the civil strife completed their work, blessed among men. [Long and continued applause.]

Address At Montgomery, Alabama, May 16, 1867

I have not come into your State, fellow-citizens of Alabama, for the purpose of fomenting discord between classes or races, or States or sections, but in the hope that possibly by some poor service I may heal the wounds of my bleeding country, and promote the welfare of all her citizens. We have gone through a war unparalleled in history by the breadth of its theatre, the number and valor of its armies, and the results of which in the long future of our country are destined to be more beneficent than those of any other war. While we rejoice that it is over, and deplore the fact that it could not have been averted, we have the satisfaction of knowing that the sufferings attendant upon it mark the birth of a new and grander nation than the world has yet seen. I know not why it is, nor can philosophers divine, that Providence has decreed that all our great blessings shall be purchased by suffering. As I remarked the other evening in New Orleans, a mother only can tell the pains and agonizing doubts that are requited by the first smiles which play over the face of her sleeping infant. It is through the storm of battle, the horrors of shipwreck upon the tempest-tossed ocean, or the weary pains of protracted sickness, that we pass from the woes of life to the bliss of immortality; and we go to the garden, the agony and the cross, for our highest and most enduring hopes. Let us, therefore, hope that in this war we have gone through the throes of the birth of a new and nobler nation.

I have traveled from my distant home as far South as New Orleans, and thence hither, and from the time that I passed the Ohio I have been constantly and painfully impressed with the difference between the country and the condition of the people South of that river and the Potomac, and those to the North of them. The results are apparent. But the causes of the contrast lie deeper than you think. You ascribe them to the war, but they existed before the war began. Nature has been more profusely lavish of her gifts to you throughout the whole broad South than to us. You have natural wealth in infinite abundance and variety; but much of our land is sterile, and throughout the North man has to toil for every dollar he gets. Our labor is more diversified and is gentler than that of your mere laborers in the field; and in spite of your greater natural wealth our people are richer than yours, are better educated, and enjoy more of the conveniences, comforts, and luxuries of life than have ever been accessible to the people of the South.

Alabama has more natural wealth than all the New England States together. Alabama abounds in iron, while New England is without any, save a little bed of ore on the borders of Connecticut and Massachusetts, so small that it would scarcely be noticed amid the broad veins of heaven-enriched Alabama. She has no coal, while coal and limestone in immense deposits lie in close proximity to your beds of iron ore. New England can grow but little wheat, corn or rye. So thin and sterile is the soil of Massachusetts in many places that her people sow rye, not for the grain but the straw, to manufacture into hats and other articles; and so wide apart do the stalks grow, that at the proper season children find employment in plucking them stalk by stalk, and laying them down perfectly straight, that those who are to work them into fabrics may have them at their greatest length. In my own dear Pennsylvania, it will be late August before the wheat is ripe, but yours in favored parts of the State is now ready for the sickle.

But ample and diversified as are the agricultural resources of Alabama, she has deemed it wise to devote herself to one single crop, (cotton,) and depend on other States for corn, hay, and other products of the soil. This was the great error of her people; for that State is richest, most prosperous, and independent that can supply all its wants within its own borders, and by the diversity of its productions provide remunerative employment for all its people. You should do this in Alabama. Every vegetable grown in the North can be successfully produced upon some of the beautiful hillsides of your extensive State. Do you doubt this, and say, as one of your citizens said to me, that you cannot raise root plants because of their tendency to run to woody fibre? I tell you that this is because your culture is artless, and because you continuously raise crops that exhaust the soil and make no return to it in manures containing the elements you abstract.

Invoke the aid of experience and science, and give to your land sufficient and appropriate food before you deny to a State so broad and varied in its topography and climate any measure of productive power. But to return to the contrast between your State and New England. She has no copper, lead, or gold, while nature has given them all to Alabama with lavish hand. I have been surprised in the last hour by discovering, through the kindness of your Governor, your capacity to supply the country with sulphur. Many of you probably do not know, indeed, I apprehhend that few of the best informed of you know, how primary an element of our life this is. A philosophic statesman has said that the best test of the advance of a people in civilization was to be found in the quantity of crude brimstone consumed *per capita* by its people. It enters into our chemicals, our cloths of all descriptions, and almost every department of science and the mechanic arts; and if you but develop your resources in that behalf, you will bring within your limits millions of dollars which we now send abroad every year for its purchase.

But who knows what the resources of Alabama are? They have not been tested by experience or explored by science. When interrogated as to them by strangers, you tell them that you have the everglades or piney woods, the broad, rich cotton belt, the wheat growing region to the north of us, and north of it again, but still within your limits, pasture and cattle lands in the hill country. Inadequate as this statement of your resources is, when you shall be able to proclaim it in connection with the fact that you have established a generous system of free schools, and secured by law fair wages for labor, millions of toiling men will come to dwell among you and alleviate the burdens that now oppress you.

But how do you use these advantages? You have failed to avail yourselves of them, or to permit others to do so. Believe me, citizens of Alabama, when I say that I have not come to triumph in your depression, and do not wish to wound your sensibilities; but have come as a brother to reason with his brethren upon subjects in which they have an equal interest. The whole country is ours. It is yours and mine, and will belong to our posterity. Go with me to my cold and distant home, and you will not only find the stars that render that flag above you so resplendent as the symbol of your country's power, but gazing above the flag, in the darkness of the night, you will discover that the stars with which you are familiar here will look down upon you there and tell you that you are still at home.

It is, therefore, in the interest of our country that I speak, when I ask you how you use the advantages with which nature has so bounteously provided you? and tell you that you have impoverished yourselves by treating them with contempt.

We turn our coal and iron to most profitable account. You permit yours to slumber in their native earth. Availing ourselves of their power, one man with us does the work of a hundred with you. One little girl, tending a machine in a factory, will spin or weave more cotton in a day than one of your women will in a year by the ancient method of the wheel and hand-loom still in use among you. You have not deemed your mineral wealth worthy of consideration. In your devotion to your peculiar system of labor you have forgotten that iron and coal are the most potent agents of modern civilization.

Mere muscular power has become a thing of secondary consideration. Iron is the muscles of modern civilization, and coal, ignited coal — fire — is the nervous force that animates it.

What is it that drags the long train of heavily freighted cars, hour after hour, and day after day, at a speed greater than that of the fleetest horse? Is it not iron fashioned into a locomotive? It was these rejected elements of your greatness that expanded my native city, a mere village in my childhood, into a city of 700,000 prosperous inhabitants. In some of our workshops from 1500 to 2000 hands find employment, none of whom do heavy, muscular labor. We throw that species of labor on iron and coal. A little girl or woman watches a machine simply to see that no loose thread mars the smoothness of the fabric, and so earns good wages. Thus we provide for the widows and orphan daughters of our soldiers. In the heavier workshops massive blooms are converted into finest plate or bar iron by the trip-hammer or rolling-mill, which steam operates, and men or boys do but guide. Few of you have ever seen a trip-hammer at work. In its full force it will flatten at a single blow a rounded mass of heated iron; but its power may be so controlled that it will crack and yet not break an egg.

We strive to develop and convert to immediate profit our coal and iron beds by connecting our city and great thoroughfare railroads with roads from every pit's mouth, and have thus tempted from England, Scotland, Wales, and the iron districts of Belgium and Germany, the most skillful of their miners and workmen in metals.

Will you notice how this has enriched others than the parties directly concerned? Lands within the corporate limits of Philadelphia, which twenty years ago were under the plow are now selling as town lots, at from seven thousand to twenty thousand dollars per acre, and others at from sixty thousand to a hundred thousand dollars per acre, and are covered by palatial residences or stores, crowded with stocks of goods gathered from every quarter of the globe.

While we thus add to our wealth we cheapen the conveniences and comforts of life. Let me illustrate this by some facts drawn from other States. The railroads from New York to Philadelphia, and from Memphis to Grenada, Mississippi, are both links in great lines running from North to South. They differ in length but a few miles, being one precisely, and the other nearly a hundred miles. Over that between Philadelphia and New York eight trains pass each way daily; over the other but one. From Memphis to Grenada the time is six hours and a half; between the other points it is less than four hours. From Philadelphia to New York, the fare is three dollars, and we complain of it as extortionate; but on the other road it is eight dollars. The traveler in either of the Northern cities, anxious to reach the other, need not wait over three hours at any time. At Memphis or Grenada he may be compelled to wait nearly twenty-four hours. In view of these facts may I not ask whether I do wrong in suggesting that there is something in our experience worthy of your study and adoption?†

In Philadelphia, almost every temperate and industrious laboring man is the owner of the house in which his family dwells. He may still owe part of the purchase money, and if so, he has an additional incentive to industry and economy. Young people who do not own, rent, each family a separate tenement, and he is regarded as a bad citizen who builds a working man's home and does not provide it with a bathroom, into which hot and cold water are introduced. This is deemed essential to cleanliness and health. In view of the assemblage by which I am surrounded, can I give offence by remarking that there is a vast difference between the comforts enjoyed by your laboring people and ours?

My native State — indeed, I may say, the whole North, from

---

† The Philadelphia citizen of 1870 travels five miles for 6.26 cents over the safest and smoothest roads of our surprising modern civilization. Of these magnificent city thoroughfares there are one hundred and seventy-five miles in Philadelphia alone, over which last year nearly sixty-five millions of passengers were transported.

The cost of these city railroads was six millions of dollars; their annual receipts are three millions eight hundred thousand; they run daily thirty thousand miles over our streets; *they employ four thousand horses, which consume eleven thousand tons of hay and twenty million pound of grain.* There are now three hundred and fifty miles of paved streets in Philadelphia. — *Address of Col. J. W. Forney,* July 4, 1871.

The working people are the chief patrons of these roads, and thus furnish our farmers with markets for horses, hay and oats, which they would not enjoy if under free trade our wares were made in foreign countries.

Maine to Kansas — is divided into districts, not congressional, not senatorial, not legislative, not judicial, but *school* districts; and every man throughout each State is taxed in proportion to his wealth, to build schools, furnish books, and pay teachers, so that every child, however poor, that is brought into the State, may receive a good elementary education; and we expect the bright apprentice boy of today to become the master of an establishment larger and more perfect than that in which he acquires his trade. We hold all places of honor or profit open to all our people, and thus stimulate every boy and man to give the State the best results of his industry, enterprise, or genius. Thus we draw from, or rather create upon even the sterile soil of New England, products that bring us in return the best results of the industry of all other people; and more cloth, more writing, printing, and wall paper, and greater varieties of well-prepared food, are consumed by our people *per capita*, than by those of any other section of our own or any other country in the world.

How are we to account for this difference? I behold around me a laboring population, not only poor but destitute; almost homeless, and untutored in all but the simplest arts of life. Tempting as are your boundless resources and genial climate, no emigrants come to settle in your midst. You have built no great city, New Orleans being the largest city of the South. Your cities would be only first class towns or villages in the North. You have no New York, Philadelphia, Brooklyn, Boston, Baltimore, Cincinnati, St. Louis or Chicago. Yet, north of the Potomac and Ohio are no such boundless and diversified stores of wealth as you possess. You have the choice cotton fields of the world; the rice, cane-sugar, hemp and tobacco fields of the United States are yours; and on some of your hillsides, or in your smiling valleys you may grow every plant or find every mineral that is native to the country east of the Rocky Mountains. How, my fellow-citizens, shall we account for the poverty and depression of the South, and the general and growing prosperity of the North? We can only do it by turning from nature to society. Our prosperity is the result of our development of *man*, by giving him a fair field for the exercise of all his energy and talents; and you lag behind because your system repressed man's energies, restrained his enterprise, and contracted the field of his usefulness. This must be the cause, for in all other respects our policy has been the same. The same flag represented our country's power and beneficence. In all other respects our institutions were the same. The same legislative, executive and judicial organization, the same division of the State into counties, townships, cities and boroughs. The one difference was that we knew at the North what you failed to perceive — that the boy who could read and write was worth more than one of equal strength and age who could not; and that the boy who saw before him the chance for wealth or distinction would strive to attain one or the other, and by study, industry, and economy, endeavor to gather capital with which to labor for himself rather than for another. Having provided for the education of all their children, the people of the Northern States made ample provision to secure a fair day's wages for every fair day's work that might be done by man or woman.

But you may say this would affect only the people in cities. This is your mistake, and has been to you a fatal delusion. The landholder whose estate has been absorbed by a growing town or city has often received more for a little building lot than his whole estate had cost him; and he who had invested the earnings of years in a poor home in the suburbs has been enriched by the city growing beyond him, and its increasing commerce or manufactures giving value to his lot. Thus, too, are our farmers enriched. I know not what land is worth in a circle of ten miles around your beautiful city. I doubt whether forty or fifty dollars would be too low an estimate, but you would not buy land in the North as near as large a city, with such wonderful capabilities, for less than hundreds of dollars. So it would be here, would you connect your city with the neighboring coal and iron districts, and build furnaces, forges, rolling mills, machine shops, and factories, and availing yourselves of the magnificent water power at Wetumka, spin and weave your own cotton, and create an Alabama Lowell or Manchester. You would then learn what your rich lands are capable of.

Nobody can estimate the agricultural value of the stimulants created by great towns and the refuse of factories. You have grown cotton until you have extracted the very life from the lighter soils of your States. As I passed through Mississippi I saw wide stretches of land so exhausted by cotton that they would not produce fibrous roots enough to prevent the soil from washing away. Soil was gone, and the wash had left little mounds, that, in the light of the setting sun, looked like red tongues of fire rising from the earth to avenge its wrongs.

Throughout the North crops are alternated, and in the neighborhood of cities, or even of new manufacturing towns, fields that had been exhausted by injudicious culture until they yielded but ten or twelve bushels of wheat to the acre, have been reinvigorated, and now yield thirty bushels, as they did in their primitive condition. Make Montgomery a great city, and you will add to the wealth of every man within a circuit of a hundred miles. Let it be your ambition to raise a fair amount of cotton, but let it also be your desire to supply the States bounding the gulf with corn, and to send it and your cotton hence behind locomotives and over rails of your own construction.

Do not tell me that you have not laborers intelligent enough to assist you in this great work. I saw yesterday in your freedmen's schools abundant evidence of the incorrectness of this statement. I am very familiar with the public schools of the North, but I was profoundly astonished by what I saw among the younger pupils of the freedmen's schools of this city, and say without reservation that I never saw in any school pupils of equal age whose attainments and general intelligence exceeded those of two, a boy and girl, one six and the other seven years old, who I examined yesterday. I doubted the fairness of the exhibition, and believed that they had been specially prepared for it, but taking the examination into my own hands, and testing them in spelling, reading, geography, and other branches, was not only convinced of the honesty of the public exhibition, but amazed at the proficiency of the children. Tell me not that the race from which they spring is wanting in intellect or adaptation, or that their little hands will not one day be competent to the most delicate or ingenious labor. Yes, gentlemen, you have competent laborers at hand for the wide diversification of your pursuits. To demonstrate this, you have but to give poor people, regardless of color, a fair field and generous inducements. I reiterate that I am endeavoring to wound none of your susceptibilities in speaking thus pointedly to you. I am simply laboring to induce you to enter into generous competition with us at the North. If you will, you may be blessed beyond us as much as we are beyond any other people.

I speak the more freely because I once shared your prejudices, but I long since came to know that we can only be happy as we accord to every other man, however humble he may be, every right that we demand from others for ourselves; and I seek in vain for any other cause for the disparity between the two sections than our respect for man's rights, and your contempt for man as *man*. Let me then implore you to enter earnestly upon the work of reconstructing your State upon the plan provided by Congress. Let not freedom and equality be forced upon you by others. Accept the inevitable and find in it a good providence.

Some of you may ask, as others have done, whether the military bill is a finality. *That, the controlling minds of the South must determine.* It was so meant by Congress, if it was fairly accepted by the South. No further congressional legislation touching the South will be had, unless by a spirit of resistance on the part of the Southern people its necessity is made manifest.†

I am gratified in being able to report that I have found generally throughout the South a generous spirit, a readiness to acknowledge the right of all to travel freely, and to discuss with frankness and candor all the issues of the day; and though in some quarters a different spirit prevails, I believe that in five years the South will be more liberal than the North has been.

Now a word to you, my colored fellow-citizens: you are free, and it is your duty, every one of you who can find employment, to labor, and to practice temperance and economy. If there be among you one able-bodied man who can find employment at wages, who wastes his time in idleness, he is committing a crime against himself and his race. Freedom means the assured right of a man to earn his livelihood, and to manage his affairs as he may deem best. I cannot better illustrate what liberty is than by a little incident that happened one day while I was walking with a friend, his arm resting in mine. He suddenly withdrew it, and I turned to discover why he had done so. There lay upon its back upon the ground a broad, green-backed insect, which the boys in our section call the gold bug, kicking upward for the ground. Working the end of his walking-

---

† Andrew Johnson's determination to nullify the reconstruction acts had not then been disclosed.

cane under it, he gave it a toss, and it lit on its feet. "Now go, poor devil,"said he; "hoe your own row; you have just as good a chance as any other bug of your kind."

Liberty is to each of you the assurance that the Government will secure to every one of you the right to hoe his own row with as good a chance as any other bug of his kind. Do you ask me what is your kind? It is *Mankind*. I hold that there is but one race of men, and if there be two, then one of two things is certain: that this Southern sun plays the deuce with the African's complexion, or there are large numbers of ex-slaves in the freedmen's schools that are not there by virtue of African descent.

Freedom establishes the fact that a good man is better than a bad one; that a wise man is better than a fool; that a learned man is better than one who is content to pass his life in ignorance; that an active man will win the race and take the prize from an indolent one. If you have a dollar, freedom will secure it to you; and if you acquire land, freedom will protect you in its enjoyment and possession. You have not always had the right to protect your wife, but freedom not only gives that right, but makes it your duty to do it, to deal tenderly with her in all things, and to put over her head the roof of your own home. Freedom requires you to see to it that your children occupy seats in the public schools, so that their chances in life may be better than yours, and by any amount of toil you can endure, to contribute in taxes your share of the common charge.

Some of you may desire to travel and to emigrate, but the great mass of you are to pass your lives here in Alabama, and freedom requires you to live in peace with your neighbors, for you now have common interests. By industry, sobriety, the improvement of your minds, and care and culture of your children, you will command the confidence and esteem of those among whom you dwell. God made you free. You did not win your freedom, nor did we give it to you. God guided the course of battles, and controlled events so that when the war closed every man of you was as free as his white brother. You are now involved in the duties of citizenship, and must look to it well that you so perform your duties as to maintain that freedom for yourselves and all other men within the broad limits of your country.

Many of you, I am told, are skillful mechanics, carpenters, bricklayers, house-wrights, shoemakers, tailors, or are skilled in other mechanical branches. See to it, those of you who are capable of engaging in business for yourselves, that you do not spend your lives in laboring for wages. You cannot all be employers and master workmen, but some of you can, and the number of such will increase if you are industrious and thrifty. Most of you have been bred to plantation or farm work. Let the aim of such be to acquire land, put up a dwelling and procure adequate stock to work your acres. The homestead law offers lots of eighty acres to each and every one of you, but I am told that the land offices are so few and distant, and the expense of travel and clearing the land is so great, that you cannot avail yourselves of its privileges; but Congress will remedy this at its next session, for it is its purpose to secure if possible a homestead for every family that desires to till the soil. Thus every one of you may aim at a manly and honorable independence in life, and a vigorous struggle in the pursuit of such aim will not fail to secure you the sympathy of all good men.

Addressing the white citizens, Mr. Kelley continued:

I do not come to the South as the agent of any faction or party, but, in conclusion, I must say something of the principles of the Republican party, because I believe that the welfare of our country is bound up with the success of that party for some years to come. The North, in which that party prevails, is intensely national. The South, in which it had no recognized existence or adherents, was on the other hand intensely sectional; its people, priding themselves on the sovereignty of the States, and looking to them rather than to the General Government for the maintenance of their rights. The Republican party is inspired by two grand sentiments: the first, national unity, and the second, individual liberty. It believes, as did Thomas Jefferson, that every man in endowed by nature with the right to life, liberty, and the pursuit of happiness. It holds with him that all men are born equal; not equal in stature, color, or intelligence, but with equal rights before the laws of State and country, as they are equal before the judgment-seat of Him who is the common father. It is not, as has often been alleged, the purpose of that party to overthrow the constitution or invade the rights of States, but to promote the welfare of all, and to cement the Union by watching over the general and external interests of every State.

Let me illustrate this. Under the State rights doctrine there could be no general levee system for the Mississippi river, and the result is that the rich low lands bordering that river and its tributaries, from Tennessee to the Gulf, are overflowed, and their owners and laborers driven from their occupancy. Under the State rights system, Tennessee, Mississippi, Louisiana and Arkansas each had separate levee regulations; and some of these States again remitted the duty of keeping the levees in order to the counties in which they lay. Thus it happened that negligence on the part of a country or State north of others which constructed proper levees, often causes the ruin of those whose levees would have protected them from danger. The Republicans regard the Mississippi river as a great national highway, that should be under the charge of the General Government, and desire that its banks shall be guarded by a general system of levees, of which the National Government shall have the care and responsibility.

In illustration of the Republican party's love of liberty, I point to the homestead law, by which it would convert the largest possible number of the people of the country into independent landholders. Thus it is pledged to maintain the equality of every man before the laws; to secure the largest liberty to individuals consistent with the public welfare, and to preserve an indivisible Union from the Gulf to the northern boundary, and from ocean to ocean.

Had the statesmen of the South, when slavery was overthrown and the armies of the Confederacy surrendered, accepted the situation cordially, and legislated for man as *man*, Congress would not probably have interfered with their local legislation. But when State after State enacted Vagrant Laws and Apprentice Laws, by which slavery was to be perpetuated under a new guise, and, failing to provide for the education of the people, they denounced as "school marms" and "nigger teachers" and persecuted the noble women who, sacrificing everything else but Christian duty, hastened here to prepare the ignorant freedmen for the proper enjoyment of the new condition upon which they were entering, Congress found a high duty devolved upon it, and did not shrink from its performance. Believing that a Democratic Republic can exist securely only so long as the equal rights of all are guarded and maintained, it exhibited its willingness to exercise its amplest powers in this behalf.

The people of the North want peace and amity to pervade the

whole land, but they feel that these blessings, with general prosperity, can only be assured when all shall acknowledge that the protection of the liberty of the citizens is the highest duty of the Government.

Citizens of Montgomery, I thank you for the courtesy and attention with which you have listened to me. You have heard the
remarks I intended to make to the citizens of Mobile; and though
some of you may deem them insulting and incendiary, you will
hardly say, as the people of that city did, that I ought to be shot for
attempting to utter them.

The Centennial Celebration
and International Exposition

*William Kelley addressed the House of Representatives on January
10, 1871 to argue for government backing and financing for the
nation's 1876 Centennial Fair. This was part of a national deployment
by Carey, Kelley, and others to guarantee the continued industrial
development of the United States despite the fact that at this time this
faction was losing its battle with Britain over U.S. financial policy.*

The House having under consideration the bill (H.R. No. 1478) to
provide for celebrating the one hundredth anniversary of American
independence by holding an international exhibition of arts, manufactures, and products of the soil and mine, in the city of Philadelphia and State of Pennsylvania, in the year 1876 —

Mr. Kelley said:

Mr. Speaker: This bill has been treated by its opponents as
though its object were a purely local one. It is not so. The city of
Philadelphia, the State of Pennsylvania, and the Franklin Institute
of Pennsylvania originated the movement for the centennial
celebration of the Declaration of Independence, and are willing to
take, under the auspices of the Government of the United States, the
responsibility for its preparation and management. And to that end
the bill does little more than ordain that such a celebration shall be
had at Philadelphia, and provide for the appointment by the
President of one commissioner from each State and Territory upon
the nomination of the Governor thereof.

The proposed exhibition is to celebrate events that are not merely of national but of world-wide interest. It is to commemorate not a day, but an epoch in universal history; not an event, but a series of events that occurred in rapid succession, gave birth to republican liberty, and organized a nation that stands today, when measured by the number of its population, the extent and geographical position of its territory, the intelligence and enterprise of its people, and the variety and volume of its resources and productions first and proudest, though but an infant among the nations of the world. London and Paris were venerable cities when the American continent was discovered, and this bill proposes to invite the people of London, Paris, and the world at large to behold the results of one century of republican liberty in a country whose people are the offspring of those of every land and clime, and to challenge them to present the best results of their genius, experience, and labor in comparison with those of this young and heterogeneous but free people.

The proposed celebration, sir, will prove to be of national importance by its relation to the business of the country. I hold in my hand one of the most instructive politico-economic works of the last year, *Home Politics; or, the Growth of Trade considered in its Relation to Labor, Pauperism, and Emigration,* by Daniel Grant, published in London. I request the attention of the House to a passage from this work with respect to the influence of the first and second expositions on the trade of England. It is as follows:

"In an early part of this chapter it was pointed out that the personal knowledge of buyer and seller forms an important link in the growth of trade, and in one sense the first exhibition aided this. Men who for years had known each other by name came to know each other as a matter of fact, and thus built up relations that produced a mutual good. The mere prestige of the 'world's bazaar' brought men from every quarter of the habitable world, and they carried away with them to their distant homes the memory of English productions, that bore fruit then and has borne fruit since. At the time, among the whole of our manufacturers, it was recognized as an unchallengable fact that the exhibition had stimulated trade, that orders were plentiful, and that its success was great.

"The statistics do more than bear this point out; the bound in our exports is both clear and decisive. It will be necessary to notice here that the direct results of the exhibition would not be manifest until the year after it closed, and would most probably extend twelve months beyond. The exhibition did not close until the end of the year; the orders given during the time would be delivered partly in the year 1851, and partly in 1852, and the return orders some months later, so that the effects would appear in the following years. The statistics here given show very markedly the growth of our exports at the particular epochs.

"Our exports in 1851, were £74,448,722, in 1852, £78,076,854, and in 1853, £98,933,780; showing an advance in two years of £24,485,050.

"The same results are apparent in the two years after our second exhibition.

"Our exports in 1862, were £123,992,264; in 1863, £146,602,342; and in 1864, £160,444,053; showing an advance in the two years of £35,456,789."

No one can consider these figures and the reflections of Mr. Grant without conceding that such an exhibition, held in one of our great cities, would largely expand the trade of the entire country, and would attract an enormous flow of immigration, especially of skilled mechanics, artists, and men of enterprise whose capital though too limited to produce a competence in Europe, might enable them to amass fortunes in this country of cheap land and undeveloped resources.

The question, therefore, is one of national importance, and should not be treated as a local one, because it is proposed that the commemorative exhibition shall be held in the city in which the events which it is to commemorate occurred. I regret exceedingly that the gentleman from New Jersey [Mr. Cleveland] is not in his seat. He proposed to hold such a celebration in New York, and, in support of his strange proposition, invited the attention of the House to the fact that for forty years New York has had an association for the promotion of the mechanic arts, known as the American Institute. Sir, forty-five years ago, I was a copy-reader in a printing office, and I remember well that among the copy which most puzzled me was that of Dr. Jones, who was then at the head of the Patent Office and editor of the journal of the Franklin Institute, an institution which had then been publishing its proceedings for several years. This was five years before the organization of the

American Institute. The Franklin Institute of Pennsylvania hailed
the organization of and has rejoiced in the prosperity of the
American Institute, and recognizes it as its most successful offspring
and as one of its most influential co-workers in developing our
manufacturing and mining resources and promoting the general
interests of our country.

The gentleman from New York [Mr. Brooks], in opposing the
bill, spoke of the inconsequential character of the preamble and
resolutions. Regarding the proposed exposition as a commemo-
ration only of the Declaration of Independence, he said that document had nothing to do with the progress of manufactures and the
arts. In this opinion he dissents from that of Thomas Jefferson, as he
will discover by turning to volume one of Jefferson's *Works*, page
129. He will there find that Mr. Jefferson assigns the attempt by
England to suppress manufactures and prevent their establishment
as a potent cause of the revolt of the Colonies. He says:

> "That to heighten still the idea of parliamentary justice, and to
> show with what moderation they are like to exercise power where
> themselves are to feel no part of its weight, we take leave to mention
> to his Majesty certain other acts of the British Parliament by which
> we were prohibited from manufacturing for our own use the articles
> we raise on our own lands with our own labor. By an act passed in the
> fifth year of the reign of his late Majesty, King George II, an Ameri-
> can subject is forbidden to make a hat for himself of the fur which he
> has taken perhaps on his own soil; an instance of despotism to which
> no parallel can be produced in the most arbitrary ages of British his-
> tory. By one other act, passed in the twenty-third year of the same
> reign, the iron which we make we are forbidden to manufacture; and
> heavy as that article is, and necessary in every branch of husbandry,
> besides commission and insurance, we are to pay freight for it to
> Great Britain, and freight for it back again, for the purpose of
> supporting, not men, but machines, in the island of Great Britain."

That gentlemen may perceive how well founded these complaints of the colonists were, let me quote a portion of the two laws
to which Mr. Jefferson refers. I might cite many kindred acts, but
parts of these will suffice. Let me read the fourth section of chapter
twenty-two of the fifth year (1732) of George II. It is as follows

> "Whereas the art and mystery of making hats in Great Britain
> hath arrived to great perfection, and considerable quantities of hats
> manufactured in this kingdom have heretofore been exported to his

Majesty's plantations or Colonies in America, who have been wholly supplied with hats from Great Britain; and whereas great quantities of hats have of late years been made, and the said manufacture is daily increasing in the British plantations in America, and is from thence exported to foreign markets, which were heretofore supplied from Great Britain, and the hat-makers in the said plantations take many apprentices for small terms, to the discouragement of the said trade, and debasing the said manufacture; wherefore, for preventing the said ill practices for the future, and for promoting and encouraging the trade of making hats in Great Britain,

"*Be it enacted by the king's most excellent majesty, by and with the advice and consent of the Lords spiritual and temporal and Commons in this present Parliament assembled, and by the authority of the same,* That from and after the 29th day of September, A.D. 1732, no hats or felts whatsoever, dyed or undyed, finished or unfinished, shall be shipped, laden, or put on board any ship, or vessel in any place or ports within any of the British plantations, upon any pretence whatsoever, by any person or persons whatsoever; and also, that no hats or felts, either dyed or undyed, finished or unfinished, shall be laden upon any horse, cart, or other carriage, to the intent or purpose to be exported, transported, shipped off, carried, or conveyed out of any of the said British plantations to any other of the British plantations, or to any other place whatsoever, by any person or persons whatsoever."

The ninth and tenth sections of the other act referred to, chapter twenty-eight of the twenty-third year (1750) of George II, are as follows

"IX. That from and after the 24th day of June, 1750, no mill or other engine for slitting or rolling of iron, or any plating forge to work with a tilt-hammer, or any furnace for making steel, shall be erected, or after such erection, continued in any of his Majesty's colonies in America; and if any person or persons shall erect, or cause to be erected, or after such erection continue, or cause to be continued, in any of the said Colonies, any such mill, engine, forge, or furnace, every person or persons so offending shall, for every such mill, engine, forge, or furnace, forfeit the sum of £200 of lawful money of Great Britain.

"X. *And it is hereby further enacted by the authority aforesaid,* that every such mill, engine, forge, or furnace so erected or continued, contrary to the directions of this act, shall be deemed a common nuisance; and that every Governor, Lieutenant-Governor, or Commander-in-Chief of his Majesty's colonies in America, where any such mill, engine, forge, or furnace shall be erected or continued, shall, upon information to him made and given, upon the oath of any two or more credible witnesses, that any such mill, engine, forge, or furnace shall be erected or continued, (which oath such Governor, Lieutenant-Governor, or Commander-in-Chief is hereby authorized and required to administer,) order and cause every such mill, engine, forge, or furnace to be abated within the space of thirty days next after such information given and made as aforesaid; and if any Governor, Lieutenant-Governor, or Commander-in-Chief shall neglect or refuse to do so within the time herein before limited for that purpose, every such Governor, Lieutenant-Governor, or Commander-in-Chief so offending shall, for every such offense, forfeit the sum of £500 of lawful money of Great Britain, and shall from thenceforth be disabled to hold or enjoy any office of trust or profit under his Majesty, his heirs or successors."

Thus, sir the history of the Colonies, the laws of England, and the express assertion of the author of the Declaration of Independence assure us that no character of celebration of the events we propose to commemorate could be more appropriate than one which would exhibit to the world the results of the mining, manufacturing, and artistic skill of a people who, one hundred years ago, were not permitted to manufacture a felt hat or a plow or nail from the productions of their own soil. Certainly no celebration could be more apposite or more fitting.

Then comes the question, "Where should it be held?" Why, sir, it should, in the judgment of the country, be held where the Continental Congress assembled, deliberated, and acted, and where Carpenters' Hall still stands, as it did when the first prayer for Congress was uttered. It should be in the vicinity of Independence Hall, where the Declaration of Independence was signed and proclaimed to the people, and where may be seen the old bell, whose peals summoned them, now shattered, but still perfect in form, and bearing the prophetic inscription, cast upon it about a century before the great event it announced. "Proclaim liberty throughout all the land unto all the inhabitants thereof." It should be near to the hall in which the Constitution was framed and adopted, and to that in which the first Congress of the United States assembled; and these are all in Philadelphia. Were the celebration of the centennial anniversary of this great epoch, embracing this series of grand historical events, to be held in any other city it would be out of place, and the people who might attend it would wander from its precincts to Philadelphia, in search of the scenes and halls amid which and in which the men whose deeds they would commemorate had consummated their great designs.

Can Philadelphia accomodate it? Sir, many of the members of this House, including members of the Committee on Foreign Affairs and the Committee on Manufacturing, have visited our city with reference to this question. They spent delightful hours in our park, unequaled in the world, either in extent or beauty, through which flow the beautiful Schuylkill and the romantic Wissahickon, and which contains more than twenty-six hundred acres of undulating land, embracing both banks of these beautiful streams. When Miss Frances Anne Kemble first visited us she was fresh from Italy and Switzerland, among whose mountains and lakes she had passed years; yet familiar as she was with the wondrous beauty of their scenary she found its equal within the limits of Philadelphia's park. Listen to what she said on the subject:

To the Wissahickon

My feet shall tread no more thy mossy side,
  When once they turn away, thou pleasant water
Nor ever more, reflected in thy tide,
  Will shine the eyes of the white island's daughter.
But often in my dreams, when I am gone
  Beyond the sea that parts thy home and mine,
  Upon thy banks the evening sun will shine,
And I shall hear thy low, still flowing on.
And when the burden of existence lies
  Upon my soul darkly and heavily,
I'll clasp my hands over my weary eyes,
  Though pleasant water, and thy clear waves see.
Bright be thy course, forever and forever —
  Child of pure mountain springs and mountain snow
And as thou wanderest on to meet the river,
  Oh, still in light and music may'st thou flow!
I never shall come back to thee again,
When once my sail is shadowed on the main;

Nor ever shall I hear thy laughing voice,
As on their rippling way thy waves rejoice;
Nor ever see the dark green cedar throw
Its gloomy shade o'er the clear depths below.
Never, from stony rifts of granite gray,
Sparkling like diamond rocks in the sun's ray,
Shall I look down on thee, thou pleasant stream,
Beneath whose crystal folds the gold sands gleam.
Wherefore, farewell! but whensoe'er again
  The wintry spell melts from the earth and air;
And the young spring comes dancing through thy glen,
  With fragrant, flowering breath, and sunny hair;
When through the snow the scarlet berries gleam,
Like jewels strewn upon thy banks, fair stream,
My spirit shall through many a summer's day
Return among thy peaceful woods to stray.

Here, sir, amidst these scenes of beauty, and in the midst of a collection of American trees and foliage such as is nowhere else to be found within the limits of a city, we ask that this exposition shall be held. Sir, we make this request not with reference to the beauty of the site alone, but to its utility and fitness also.

Through the Philadelphia park passes the junction railway, by which the goods shipped for exhibition from any part of the continent of America, which is connected with a through line of railway, may be delivered at the ground proposed to be set apart for the exhibition without transfer or breaking bulk.

Again, the great thing that the people of Europe would learn by visiting us, would be the effect of free institutions upon the masses of the people, and that which they would most admire, and which they could see nowhere else in such numbers and perfection, would be the homes of our working people. I repeat, sir, that by nothing that they would see in this country would the workingmen or the capitalists of Europe be more instructed than in looking at the homes of the workmen of Philadelphia. No tenement houses there. Each laborer who has a family dwells under a separate roof, which is most frequently his own; in a house lighted by gas, supplied with an abundance of pure hydrant water. In every house there is a bathroom, into which there run streams, warm and cold, of the pure water provided by the public. This is a startling contrast to the homes of the workingmen of England,† France, Belgium, Prussia, or any other land. To thus bring the people of Europe to a knowledge of how laborers live in our free Republic would give an upward impulse to the temporal condition of humanity everywhere.

Sir, the gentleman from New York [Mr. Brooks] said he was not hostile to Philadelphia, inasmuch as he regarded her as one of the principal suburbs of New York. I do not wonder at that, for in truth the two cities are each other's principal suburb. They are so near each other, their population is so nearly equal, and each is so thoroughly the complement of the other, that each may, without affectation, so regard the other. They are but little more than two hours apart, and the road that connects them is the one to which I have alluded that runs through the park.

London imports through Liverpool, Paris through Havre, and our merchants receive most of their importations through New York for precisely the same reasons that control those of London and Paris. They do it for greater convenience, and our imports thus swell the volume of New York's apparent greatness. In her we find one of our principal customers, and she is largely our factor and distributing agent.

We have no rivalry with New York. Her field of operations is with foreign countries; our is at home. We convert the raw material of our own and other lands into utilities and matters of taste and

---

† Toil as they may, our working-classes (and I do not limit the term to our manual-labor class), even under favorable circumstances, have a hard task in providing for their old age — for that night of life when no man can work. They have brought up families, and the family should do its duty so far as it can to the parent — the bread-winner, who supported its members in helpless infancy, and even, it may be, at no small cost to himself, started them in life. Yet in many cases, if not in all, the most a working man can do, is by contributing to sick-societies and others, to lay by so much as will keep himself during transient illness, or when temporarily out of employment. We regret to say it, but it really seems to us impossible for the working-classes as a body to lay by enough to keep them during the impotence of old age. — *The State, the Poor, and the Country* — *Patterson.*

House rent in our larger towns has risen, till anything like a wholesome dwelling is beyond the reach of the average workmen. — *Social Politics* — *Kirk.* (This and the following notes were added by Kelley in the compilation and editing of his *Speeches, Addresses, and Letters on Industrial and Financial Questions,* Philadelphia, 1872 — A.S.)

vertu. We are a producing people; they are a trading people. Our roots are fixed in the soil of our country; they move with the changes of commerce. And New York, but for the possibility of increasing her manufactures, which local taxation and excessive prices for real estate and high rents must retard, may one day follow the great cities that have, from time to time, been reared on the commercial routes of the past, and are now known only to history. A city depending exclusively upon trade may be regarded as possibly transitory, so long as the routes of commerce are liable to change.

Sir, in comparing the two cities (I have no idea of contrasting them, for, as an American, I rejoice in the growth and progress of each), let me tell you something of the people of Philadelphia and their products. The census just taken is incomplete. General Walker, the Superintendent of the Census Bureau, assured me today that the statement which I hold in my hand is from twenty to twenty-five percent too low in its aggregate of her manufacturing products. The total of imports into the country during the last fiscal year, not into New York, but into the country; not on the Atlantic coast, but on the Atlantic and Pacific coasts, amounted to a little more than four hundred and sixty-two million dollars. That was the value of our entire import of manufactured articles, and of raw material, whether for food or manufacture. The entire imports were, I say, but $462,377,587, while the products of industry, as far as ascertained, in Philadelphia alone were $251,663,921. Add to this, as I am authorized by the Superintendent of the Census to add, twenty percent, and it will be found that her productions alone were far greater than the manufactured imports of the country, and equal to more than two-thirds of the entire imports of raw materials and manufactured articles.

Philadelphia has, far as ascertained (and the numbers will be greatly increased by the revision now making), 6090 establishments, employing a capital of $205,564,238; employing in horsepower, of steam, 31,582, and of water, 2226; employing 88,631 males above sixteen years of age, 23,545 females above that age, 7356 children and youth; paying wages annually to the amount of $52,236,026; using materials to the value of $132,618,873; and yielding manufactured products, as I have already said, to the value of $251,663,921. And the Superintendent of the Census, from information already in

GENERAL ABSTRACT—SCHEDULE FOUR—RECAPITULATION
—CITY OF PHILADELPHIA, PENNSYLVANIA.

TITLES (not revised*)	No. of establishments	CAPITAL	HORSE-POWER Steam	Water	HANDS EMPLOYED Males above 16	Females above 16	Children and Youth	WAGES	MATERIALS	PRODUCTS
Boots and shoes	674	$2,274,636	42	—	4,620	1,380	215	$2,478,082	$3,279,548	$7,724,809
Boot and shoe fitters	17	57,150	—	—	88	114	6	67,743	61,411	150,657
Brick-makers	80	1,814,500	395	—	2,332	—	437	1,151,647	356,984	2,703,148
Breweries	53	3,221,450	445	—	485	4	7	327,440	1,706,106	4,182,050
Bakeries	391	768,075	119	—	1,091	27	86	298,981	1,714,462	3,004,189
Bread, cake, ice-cream, etc.	10	44,700	—	—	45	16	1	25,040	64,016	116,340
Blacksmiths	139	200,685	22	—	505	—	8	217,664	154,890	587,776
Brass founderies	23	383,750	96	—	275	—	12	134,438	170,548	532,067
Cigars	345	986,040	34	—	1,213	160	113	524,168	791,851	2,014,058
Carriages	118	1,707,497	181	—	1,502	3	15	865,880	660,264	2,103,884
" (children's)	4	59,100	20	—	45	—	14	32,452	28,070	83,922
Carpets	205	2,363,650	500	—	3,464	872	379	1,700,436	4,798,253	7,397,636
Confectionery	81	266,750	20	—	271	53	28	99,438	282,258	601,452
Cabinet-makers	138	1,767,955	402	—	1,682	18	53	1,006,190	1,097,080	3,004,873
Coopers	59	409,487	125	—	526	—	5	275,278	338,982	896,284
Clothing	310	4,369,114	—	—	4,038	4,464	73	2,032,639	6,546,731	10,707,008
Carpenters and builders	87	1,110,500	—	—	1,337	15	18	753,863	1,647,475	4,180,643
Carpenters	148	383,050	1	—	658	—	10	438,664	917,141	1,691,401
Cotton-mills	21	2,682,000	1,015	690	1,034	1,445	469	898,662	2,122,354	3,476,454
Drugs and chemicals	24	2,579,500	501	—	589	114	34	384,008	2,562,190	3,877,180
Founderies (Iron)	71	4,240,420	675	—	2,480	—	115	1,414,227	2,213,004	5,295,072

Grist-mills	21	597,500	1,017	131	157	—	1	107,060	3,827,085	4,835,593
Glass-works	9	1,226,016	170	—	727	28	560	552,610	482,792	1,560,643
Hosiery	50	1,627,700	469	—	797	1,664	557	834,870	1,921,546	3,265,807
Jewelers	84	811,800	39	—	630	74	42	389,980	744,643	1,515,476
Machinists	90	5,107,245	1,541	—	3,194	5	31	1,675,711	1,618,060	4,605,312
Machinery and tubing	1	5,000,000	800	—	1,300	—	—	750,000	2,528,000	5,000,000
Plumbers & gasfitters	97	293,400	35	—	478	—	21	211,426	421,188	876,434
Printers	123	4,974,200	762	—	2,119	239	190	1,820,285	2,559,485	6,301,397
Paper-mills	5	2,560,000	435	767	691	141	3	352,200	1,524,379	2,444,000
Painters	107	228,625	—	—	547	9	9	286,322	348,824	893,161
Pianos	8	493,000	121	—	278	2	3	173,250	111,200	431,800
Paints, lead and linseed oil	13	1,466,750	467	—	326	—	—	181,622	1,316,374	3,216,410
Patent medicines	27	1,405,774	43	—	158	105	8	126,045	2,681,502	5,591,832
Planning-mills	28	907,800	700	8	387	—	15	221,369	1,001,994	1,833,316
Sashes, doors, and blinds	41	829,735	820	—	537	1	17	395,592	709,886	1,451,804
Sewing-machines	5	700,000	59	—	312	2	3	195,440	182,380	671,000
Soap and candles	33	787,600	499	—	329	31	32	176,129	827,031	1,625,981
Sugar refiners	11	3,494,000	1,796	—	942	—	1	373,308	18,206,062	19,581,374
Tinsmiths	130	598,750	—	—	545	53	51	237,671	429,288	930,755
Woolen-mills	54	7,149,000	2,558	155	1,903	3,183	724	1,793,163	6,728,516	11,204,802
Yarns	44	2,255,000	1,237	225	779	581	375	536,084	3,226,851	4,952,904
All others	3,979	74,203,904	18,161	1,975	45,317	14,803	4,741	26,617,077	82,910,704	147,120,704
	2,111	131,360,334	13,421	250	43,314	8,742	2,615	25,618,949	49,708,169	104,543,217
Total	6,090	$205,564,238	31,582	2,226	88,631	23,545	7,356	$52,236,026	$132,618,873	$251,663,921

An abstract from the manufacturing returns of Philadelphia, as received from the assistant marshals—correspondence not completed—respectfully furnished for the information of Hon. William D. Kelley, U.S. House of Representatives. FRANCIS A. WALKER, *Superintendent Census.*

*I have not adopted a classification—F.A.W.

his possession, justifies me in swelling this amount to $300,000,000.† But for the further information of the House I will at this point incorporate in my remarks the table in detail imperfect as it is. (See previous page.)

Here, then, among these appliances for the conversion of raw materials into the comforts and luxuries of life; here among these busy mechanicians; here, in the home of Franklin, whose old printing press will furnish a striking contrast when put beside the "Hoe's last fast" or the latest patent press that will be operating in those days; here, where Jefferson and his compatriots consulted upon the problem of independence, where Washington presided over the Convention which framed the Constitution, where, under that Constitution, he dwelt as Chief Magistrate of the country, surrounded by the great men of that day from all the then States; here, where, in a park embracing more than twenty-six hundred acres of land, the dimensions of the exhibition may spread to a hundred or five hundred acres, from every point of which the eye shall be filled with natural beauty; here, at a spot accessible from every part of the country, blessed with a railroad, should this commemorative exhibition be held.

I am asked what it will cost. The amendment submitted by my colleague [Mr. Morrell] proposes to limit the amount that may be

---

† The following is an approximate summary of the Industrial Establishments of Philadelphia, their machinery and production for the census of 1870: as corrected (at Philadelphia) up to September 1, 1871.

No. of Establishments		8,119
Capital employed (not including value of land)		$172,079,754
No. of Factories driven by steam		1,668
Horse power of these		45,101
No. of Looms		15,692
No. of Spindles		189,757
No. of Machines drive by steam		51,152
No. of Men employed	86,939	
No of Females (over 16 years)	34,728	
No. of Boys and Girls (under 16 years)	9,202	
Total persons employed	130,869	
Aggregate wages paid		$58,997,010
Aggregate cost of raw material		174,139,094
Aggregate value of manufactures		325,371,943

expended by the Government to $50,000 a year until 1876, when the sum may be increased to $250,000, making a total expenditure of $500,000. Sir, I have no idea that under the provisions of this bill the first year's expenses of the commissioners will be anything like that amount. But, assuming that they will, we appropriated the same sum to send a few articles to the Paris Exposition.† Here we invite the people of every State and Territory to present in brilliant array among and in comparison with the best productions of other countries their best productions of field, mine, workshop, or studio. And the appropriation is asked for the benefit of the people of the more remote and poorer States, to whose borders many an immigrant would be attracted by a generous exhibition of the many and various elements of wealth, in which every part of the country abounds in such marvelous profusion.

The Causes and Authors of the Financial Depression With Passing Hints at Remedial Measures

Iron Age magazine published in 1876 this article by William Kelley which showed how the government's policy to refuse to back the Greenback currency and to sell the U.S. debt to Great Britain had caused the economic collapse and depression of 1873 to 1876.

When the war closed in June, 1865, the question of reconciliation and reconstruction became paramount. Whatever measure would promote social intercourse between the people of the North and those of the South, or tend to involve them in common interests, was one of the highest patriotism and entitled to the support of every department of the Government and of the citizens of every section of the country. The army and navy had done their work, and the pursuits of peace invoked the fostering care of statesmen and social economists.

To say that the South was prostrate, is to inadequately express

---

† These provisions were stricken from the bill. The U.S. Government is not to be responsible for any part of the cost of the exhibition.

the fact. Here people were dispirited and almost destitute. Their fenceless and untilled fields were without stock or implements of husbandry. Their homes were in ruins. Their industrial system was not only demoralized, but had been overthrown; and, after the protracted and terrible paroxysms of war, they were in the condition of a patient whose frame, worn well-nigh unto death by fever, had sunk into that typhoid state in which heroic treatment would be fatal, and the object of physician and nurse must be the strengthening of the system and the restoration of vitality and circulation by the use of such stimulants as the extremity of the case would permit. Little less grave and difficult of solution were the questions arising in the North. During the war the government had been the great customer, and, by its special necessities, had given direction to the forms of industrial development; but, with the return of peace, the demand for ships, arms, clothing and other munitions of war was to cease, and capital must discover new and profitable employment for the skilled men previously employed, and those who, having served in the army and navy, were to return by hundreds of thousands to the walks of civil life.

Where these discharged soliders would settle, and what part they would take in the restoration of prosperity, were questions demanding grave consideration. Many of them had learned by observation that the South was not a purely agricultural region — was not, as they had believed, one vast cotton, tobacco, rice and sugar field; but that, while it was wonderfully endowed with the capacity to produce these elements of national greatness and independence, and might rival India in the production of jute, ramee, and other fibrous plants, it was capable of producing all the grains, fruits, trees and plants they had known in the North, or the distant countries in which they had been born; that its minerals were more varied and richer than those of the North, and included gold, cinnabar, corundum, the peculiar ore for speigelizen, and others which are rare or unknown at the North; and that all these were attended by a climate and seasons which lessen the exactions of labor and increase the charms of life. Men from New England and the cold Northwest had been incredulous when told that in Georgia, Texas and elsewhere throughout the South, corn could be planted with the absolute certainty that the season would permit it to ripen and be gathered from fields from which a luxuriant crop of wheat had been taken in May, and that a volunteer crop of potatoes, equal almost in size and quantity to the cultivated crop, followed the latter in almost every field. But when their eyes beheld these things, their incredulity yielded, and they believed.

That, in view of such facts, there was a general impulse among the more intelligent and enterprising workingmen of the North to settle in the South, is not remarkable. Nothing could have been more natural or more beneficent than such a movement; and, but for the restrictive financial policy announced by Mr. McCulloch in the latter part of 1865, upon which he entered in 1866, and which, with the sanction of Congress, has been pursued by all his successors in the Treasury Department, such emigration, guided by intelligent enterprise, and sustained by abundant capital, would have penetrated every Southern State, and, under its benign influence, long ere this, the era of good feeling, which we hope is now dawning, would have been a consummate experience. How different would then have been the history of the last decade! Whose pen will attempt to depict the marvelous progress the South would have made under such an impulse of enterprise, skill and capital: to tell how many prosperous villages with school-houses and churches would have risen beside the abounding water-power that flows through her cotton fields, or in the midst of her rich deposits of coal, iron, copper, zinc, nickel, and other metals; or to indicate which of her chief towns would now be thriving cities, connected with each other by railroads, which, under the continuance of our present financial policy, will be premature a century hence? Mine will not essay the task.

How shall we set to work these millions of able-bodied people, including the freed people and poor whites of the South and the disbanded soldiers and sailors of the North — at such wages as will enable them, while largely consuming each other's productions, to make generous commercial exchanges with foreign countries? — should have been the all-absorbing question among those charged with the administration of the Government. There was special need for the labor of all of them: for there was not only no surplus of goods on the market, but never had there been a time when, measured by the necessities of millions of people, and their ability to produce the means of paying for them, an increased supply of general commodities was more urgently demanded. The fields of the South were to be fenced and stocked with cattle and implements; ancient homesteads were to be rebuilt, and new ones created and furnished; desolated and decaying cities and towns were to be restored, and the whole people were to be reclothed.

Dogmatists and doctrinaires are burdening the press with plans for the extension of our foreign trade as a means of relieving our people from want and despair begotten of enforced idleness; but none of them seem to conceive the magnitude of the home market that then opened upon us (and which, under a more statesmanlike management of our debt and currency, is still open to us), or condescend to discuss the social and political consequences that would have followed our entrance upon it. The offer of work at remunerative wages would have tempted the undisciplined poor of the South into habits of industry and thrift, and would have enabled freedmen and poor whites alike to imitate their more fortunate neighbors in the occupancy of homes with floors and the enjoyment of tables, chairs, plates, spoons, knives, forks, simple cottage furniture, and even such luxuries as carpets and wallpaper. The increased demand for these, and the infinitude of minor articles that are found in the homes of small farmers and skilled laborers in the North, would have taxed our producing capacity: — for the prosperity that would have attended such an extension of our market would have augmented the tide of immigration, which in 1872 reached 450,000 per annum, but which, under the policy of resumption by contraction, steadily shrinks to smaller numbers. The adoption of this stimulating policy of development must have obliterated antagonism between the sections, by establishing the fact that identity of interest results from diversity of productions. The demands of the South upon our workshops would have secured employment in legitimate channels to the labor and capital of the North; while the ability to furnish an increased supply of cotton, tobacco, rice, sugar, naval stores, and a growing quantity of ramee, American jute and other fibres, would have brought the comforts and conveniences of life to which I have alluded, within the easy reach of every thrifty family of the South.

Could the people of the South then have been furnished, in exchange for fields, mines, or water-power, with money to enable them

The Great Paper Deluge

The Artificial Sea In The Play Of "Money" In The National Theatre

Sherman [*sounding for bottom — gold basis*] — "I'm sure I almost touch bottom, and if you would only stop those porpoises from agitating this greenback sea, we should certainly get down to hard-pan."

Schurz — "I think I touched the solid rock, but these inflationists have rolled the water so much that it is hard to tell."

Norton [*to Kelley*] — "These fellows think they touched bottom, but if they had our fish-eyes they'd see that their poles are a long way from the hard-pan yet. The tide of greenbacks must go down a great deal before they can get a solid footing."

Kelley — "There is too much wind for the sea to go down; but I don't like that silver sunrise. It means that the clouds are breaking away, and that these men will soon see the gold."

This 1874 cartoon is aimed straight at Representative William D. Kelley and his American System allies who advocated an expanding national currency tied to an expanding national agricultural and industrial production. Searching for gold and a return to the British System are Senator John Sherman and his free trade ally, the German radical emigré Carl Schurz.

to engage in improving their condition by the application to the property they retained of the industrial methods and appliances of the North; could they have seen their countrymen come among them to help build up their waste places, and beheld immigrants from Europe landing by thousands at their wharves, they would have been diverted from politics. Industrial prosperity would have become their leading object, and politics have soon come to be regarded as an incident, and not the supreme object of life. The prosperity that would have attended this reorganization of labor, and the infusion of these new industrial elements, would also have demonstrated to the most obtuse the value of the services of the docile and faithful laboring people upon whom they had previously relied, and who are familiar with all their ancient industries. And more than all this, though but a secondary effect, long before this every prosperous person in the South would have been bound to the Union by the strong ties of direct personal interest. That where the treasure there will the heart be also, is true now as of old; and had not McCulloch departed from the policy of Chase, vast amounts of the public debt now held by foreigners would have passed into the possession of the Southern people, who being the recipients of a large share of the taxes collected by the Government, would not have tolerated the efforts now frequently made by the baser sort among them, to escape taxation even by means of conspiracy and fatal violence. Prosperity would have brought peace to the country.

These are not the unsubstantial fancies of a Utopian. They are results that lay in the pathway of our progress as inevitable consequences of causes then in active operation. To avert them required the diversion of the course of events by active and efficient measures. Had Mr. Secretary McCulloch been content to let well enough alone, and so far as the national debt and currency were concerned, to travel in the established paths of experience, the wonderful story of the rapid recuperation of France after her prostration by Germany, would have had a precedent in our history so far exceeding hers in the splendor of its results, as to have made what is now regarded as that page of her financial history which records the marvelous, seem natural and commonplace. Lincoln, Chase, Stevens, and the practical men with whom they consulted, had given us a financial system which, while providing for the expenses of the war, had furnished an adequate medium for such freedom of exchange between individuals as to have induced the creation of wealth as by magic. Let me not be understood as speaking of imaginary profits, or fortunes nominally increased by the inflation of prices, or any other unreal and unsubstantial thing. I allude to solid wealth — to the subjugation of prairie, hillside, and woodland to the purposes of civilization and settlement; to the creation of towns and the enlargement of cities; to the opening of mines, the construction of furnaces, forges, mills, and the utilization of water-power by the erection of factories and factory towns where land and water had both been waste; to the founding of schools, colleges, scientific institutions, and the erection of churches of all denominations, all of which had gone on between 1862, when the greenback was issued, and 1873, when, by its partial withdrawal, and the retirement of every other form of national credit which had been used as money, our financial system collapsed, and in place of social, intellectual and national progress, bankruptcy, poverty and despair began to overshadow the land.

By referring to Secretary Chase's last report, transmitted to Congress on the 10th of December, 1863, Mr. McCulloch would have found a chart marking all the financial shoals and quicksands that endangered the ship of state, and channels thoroughly sounded and amply buoyed, by sailing within which her voyage to the haven of unquestioned prosperity would have been calm and brief. He would there have learned how "the great evils brought upon us by the war might be transmuted by a wise alchemy into various forms of utility"; how, "from the bitter root of debt, great good might grow," and that $400,000,000 of national notes, with a reserve of $50,000,000 to meet convertible bonds, then known as temporary loan certificates, "if presented in excess of current deposits," had been found to be not in excess of the legitimate demands of the business of the country, or instrumental in inflating prices. On the last point Mr. Chase said:

"It is an error to suppose that the increase in prices is attributable wholly, or in very large measure to this circulation. Had it been possible to borrow coin enough, and fast enough, for the disbursements of the war, almost if not altogether the same effects on prices would have been wrought. Such disbursements made in coin would have enriched fortunate contractors, stimulated lavish expenditures, and so inflated prices in the same way and nearly to the same extent as when made in notes. Prices too would have risen from other causes. The withdrawal from mechanical and agricultural occupations of hundreds of thousands of our best, strongest and most active workers, in obedience to their country's summons to the field, would, under any system of currency, have increased the price of labor, and, of consequence, the prices of the products of labor; while the prices of many things would have risen in part from other causes, as, for example, the price of railroad bonds from vast increase of income through payments for military transportation, and the price of cotton from deficient supply."

Unfortunately for the country, the administration, of which Mr. McCulloch was a member, was not composed of practical statesmen like Mr. Chase, but of doctrinaires, who, influenced by the false teachings of purblind and shallow schoolmen, ignored the palpable truth that it is labor and not coin that supports the public credit and the framework of society. Regardless of the function of money, which is the life-blood of trade, they considered only the material of which, in their judgment, it should be made, and, in order to make it as costly and as difficult to be obtained as possible, resolved to withdraw paper, and, let the experiment bring what disasters it might upon industry and enterprise, to attempt to use gold as the sole legal tender of the American people. They applied heroic treatment to a typhoid patient. The system taught by their school required blood-letting; and though they knew the patient would probably die under the operation, bleed him they would, if but in honor of the professors at whose feet they had studied. In other phrase, they determined to reduce the amount of money in circulation, to increase the value of its unit, and give the holders of national, state, municipal, corporate and private debts, in payment of interest and principal, dollars which, measured by the average product of the labor of a day or yield of an acre, were two, four, or six times as valuable as those contemplated by both creditor and debtor when the obligation was contracted. They did not pause to consider whether the scheme was practicable. They would brook no discussion of their simple proposition that a gold dollar was intrinsically worth more than a paper dollar (which, when regarded simply as commodities, was a truism not to be disputed), and proceeded to make the experiment, let it cost the people what it might, and whether or not it could prove ultimately practicable.

The first of the inevitable results of this stupid or wicked policy was to make money scarce and increase the rate of interest on loans to individuals. Scarcity of money and high rates of interest produced industrial paralysis, and deprived labor of employment and laborers of the power to consume the products of each other's toil. Trade and commerce felt the shock. Each additional discharge of laborers or material reduction of wages, further contracted the market. Bankruptcies became frequent, and confidence was shaken. Capital was not needed to pay idle laborers; there ceased to be a market for money, and ceasing to circulate, money concentrated in the Treasury and the vaults of the banks as dead capital. Our shallow philosophers pointed to the fact that money had lost its use, and was lying idle, and claimed this untoward condition of things as proof that money was superabundant, that the currency was inflated, and pointed to the shrunken and depreciating stocks of goods in the warehouses of ruined merchants as evidence that an excess of money had caused a blameworthy over-production of commodities. And even now, when real estate does not earn rent, or money beget interest, and labor is denied the opportunity to earn wages, our rulers refuse to investigate the condition of the people, but, counseled by the oracles of the schools, whose faces should be on the backs of their heads, as their eyes are ever turned toward the past, attempt to pacify the starving masses by crying out "over-production," and demanding the discharge of other laborers, and the further reduction of wages and prices generally as essential preliminaries to the establishment of gold payments.

To this end the Government employs syndicates to induce foreigners to accept mortgages upon the land and annual earnings of the people, and, in order to accomplish this undesirable purpose, binds posterity by issuing bonds to run for a period so protracted that the bare suggestion of it would have made Mr. Chase recoil from him who submitted such a proposition as from one who would barter the interests of his country. As Secretary of the Treasury he deplored the fact that extreme exigencies compelled him in 1861, upon the breaking out of the war, to consent to the issue of a small amount of bonds which had so long as twenty years to run; and yet

Secretary Sherman demands plaudits from his countrymen for having induced foreigners to take our bonds with thirty years to run. On this point Mr. Chase was most explicit. On page 14 of his report, above referred to, he said:

> "The object of future controllability has also had a prominent place in the regards of the Secretary. Under the conditions which existed at the outbreak of the rebellion, he acquiesced in the necessity which seemed to dictate the negotiation of bonds payable after 20 years; *but he acquiesced with reluctance,* and, as soon as permitted by circumstances, recommended the enactment of laws authorizing the issue of bonds payable after shorter periods, as well as the creation of temporary debt in other forms. In harmony with these views, Congress provided for the issue of the bonds known as the 5-20's; and also for the issue of Treasury notes payable after three years from date, for certificates of indebtedness payable in one year, *and for temporary loans by deposits reimbursable after ten days' notice.* At the last session, Congress repealed some embarrassing restrictions of former acts, and authorized the issue of bonds payable after ten years, and of Treasury notes payable at pleasure or three years from date. *These Treasury notes were made legal tenders for their face value, or convertible for amount and interest into U.S. notes.* [Greenbacks.]

> "The Secretary availed himself of this legislation, by placing with the people as large an amount as possible of 5-20 bonds, and by using the other powers so as to put the whole debt, except the long loans first negotiated, in such a shape that prompt advantage can be taken of favorable circumstances to diminish the burdens it imposes on industry.

> "Whenever the constitutional supremacy of the nation shall be re-established over all its parts, *it will be within the power of Congress and the Secretary to fund the whole or any part of the temporary debt in bonds having a very moderate interest, and redeemable at the pleasure of the Government after very brief periods, or perhaps at any time after their issue.* Nothing further seems desirable on the score of controllability."

Mr Chase saw that the proper fund for the payment of taxes was the current profits of the people. He knew that so long as the taxes absorbed but a percentage of current profits, the people would pay them without regarding the government as an oppressor, as they do now when no form of productive industry yields a profit, and citizens are impoverished by paying their annual taxes out of their shrunken principal; and he therefore recognized the vital necessity of maintaining a medium adequate in amount to secure the most perfect freedom of exchange and the largest possible production of exchangeable commodities. The first object to be considered was, in his judgment, the prosperity of the people — the source of all public revenues. The next was the controllability of the debt, that it might under all the varying circumstances of the country and financial conditions of the world, be so managed as to impose the least possible burdens upon the people, and abstract the smallest possible percentage from their profits. To this end he sought to keep the debt at home, and make the American people the sole creditors of the American Government, and announced as a controlling proposition "that the burdens of debt, always heaviest when loans are held by a few, and especially by foreigners, diminish in proportion as the receivers of interest become identified with the payers of taxes."

The idea of transferring our debt to foreigners was repulsive to him from the first. On this point I have personal knowledge, having, at a very early day after Congress made provision for a loan, been selected, by the representative of a number of German capitalists, as a medium to offer the Secretary $40,000,000 on 20-year bonds. He heard the proposition, and remarked very quietly in reply that it would be time enough to seek foreign aid when the American people failed to provide the Treasury with means, and requested me to be at the hotel at which the agent was stopping in thirty minutes, that I might receive and deliver to him his answer in writing. At the appointed time the answer came, and was, as nearly as my memory serves me, and I think it is accurate, "The Secretary declines to seek funds in foreign markets for the present, and hopes to be able to rely on the resources of the American people for the means of carrying on the war." The following passages from the report from which preceding extracts were made, illustrate Mr. Chase's views on this point, and sustain the belief I have expressed, that the retention of the national debt in this country would have been a potent bond of union between the people of the different sections:

"The final object of the Secretary was to extract from the unavoidable evil of debt as much incidental benefit as possible.

"To this end he desired authority *to receive temporary loans in the form of deposits reimbursable after a few days' notice.* This measure was regarded by many with something less than favor at first; but the Congress, after full consideration, authorized the receipt of such deposits at an interest not exceeding five percent, to the amount of $25,000,000; then raised the limit to $50,000,000, and then to $100,000,000, *and provided a reserve of $50,000,000 of United States notes to meet demands for reimbursements beyond other convenient means of satisfaction.* It was not long before these deposits reached the highest limit, and before the flow could be well checked, somewhat exceeded it.

"The utility of the measure was very conspicuous on the recent occasion of great stringency in New York, when the Secretary was able to reimburse over fifty millions of these deposits during the last weeks of the year; by which action the pressure was sensibly alleviated, with the use of only a fifth of the reserve. In former reports the Secretary has stated his convictions, and the grounds of them, respecting the necessity and utility of *putting a large part of the debt in the form of United States notes, without interest, and adapted to circulation as money.* These convictions remain unchanged, and seem now to be shared by the people. *For the first time in our history has a real approach to a uniform currency been made,* and the benefits of it, though still far from the best attainable condition, are felt by all. The circulation has been distributed throughout the country, and is everywhere acceptable. So, too, real and great advantages are derived from the wide diffusion of the debt among the people, through business transactions, and through the exertions of the officers of the departments, and the agents for loans, already noticed. *It is impossible to estimate the advantages to national unity and national strength secured by this distribution.* Every holder of a note or bond, from a five cent fractional note to a five thousand dollar bond, has a direct interest in the security of national institutions and in the stability of national administration. *And it is another and no small advantage of the distribution that the burdens of debt, always heaviest when loans are held by few, and especially by foreigners, diminish, in proportion as the receivers of interest become identified with the payers of taxes.*

"In these several ways may even such great evils as are brought upon us by rebellion be transmuted, by a wise alchemy, into various forms of utility. The Secretary has endeavored to use this alchemy; with what success the country will judge when time and trial shall have applied to his work their unfailing tests."

Not only did Mr. Chase not regard $400,000,000 as too large a volume of national notes or greenbacks, but in the course of his report he recommended certain modifications of the law, among

which was a provision giving "a simple authority to the Secretary to
ascertain from time to time the amounts destroyed or lost, and to replace them by new issues." He did not believe in sudden contraction
of the currency, either deliberate or accidental, but knew the value
of a sufficient volume of the medium of exchange, and the importance to trade of its steady maintenance. Am I asked how the Secretary hoped to place the whole of the national debt "in bonds bearing
a very moderate interest, and redeemable at the pleasure of the
Government after very brief periods, *or perhaps at any time after
their issue"?* If so, I refer my interlocutor to the report from which
the foregoing quotations have been made. He will find by reference
to page 16 that it was by the adoption of the convertible bond
system, the support of which has brought upon me such derision
from the organs of foreign bondholders and their American allies.
He called them temporary loans, and a provision of the statute
which provided for their issue required ten days' notice of intention
to present them for redemption; but experience proved that this was
an unnecessary restriction, and the Assistant Treasurer at New York
gave notice that they would be paid on presentation without notice.
They were thus in all respects convertible bonds, such as are advocated by those who are known as the friends of the "rag baby," and
the unlimited issue of which, as was recommended by Secretary
Chase, would, by keeping our debt at home, have prevented the
mortgage of the land and productive power of the country to
foreigners. As to the safety of this system, its great value to the commerce of the country, and to those whose small earnings need a safe
place of deposit, he was most explicit, saying:

> "The limits of deposit for temporary loan are fixed at
> $100,000,000. The amount of this deposit on the first day of Decem-
> ber had been reduced to $45,506,120.01, and payments of
> $10,000,000 had been made from the reserve. The additional pay-
> ments will be confined within the narrowest possible limits, and can
> hardly exceed $25,000,000. The reflow of deposits has already
> begun, and will probably soon exceed reimbursements, and so arrest
> payments from the reserve. The whole reflow beyond the amount of
> these payments will be available as part of the additional loan re-
> quired, and may be stated without much risk of mistake at
> $25,000,000. *The Secretary perceives no solid reason for retaining
> the restriction on loans in this form to $100,000,000. It may, as he*

thinks, be usefully removed. As the advantages of these deposits become better and more generally understood, the loan in this form will, doubtless, in the absence of restriction, be largely increased, and the possibility of demands for reimbursements beyond means to meet them can be fully provided for by an increase of the existing proportion between deposits and reserve.

"Such an arrangement, the Secretary inclines to think, would operate beneficially by increasing the amount of currency when unusual stringency shall require increase, and reducing its amount when returning ease shall allow reduction."

Notwithstanding the length to which this communication has grown, justice to the subject requires me to extend it. To the weight of Mr. Chase's great name I wish to add that of another, whose death took from us one of the most sagacious counselors of the American people. I refer to Horace Greeley. How Mr. Chase's temporary loan system, which is, as I have shown, identical with the convertible bond system, would affect the commerce and general industries of the country, was set forth by Mr. Greeley with a clearness which I cannot hope to attain; and I therefore close this communication with an article from his pen, which appeared in the New York *Tribune* of November 9, 1871, and which the present managers of that paper will not, in response to any amount of persuasion, reproduce, but the existence of which they have frequently denied:

"How To Reduce The Interest On the National Debt"

"Mr. Boutwell's plan of funding the national debt has had a pretty fair trial. True, the times have been adverse, but we have generally found them so when we needed to borrow money.

"The sum and substance of the Secretary's success is the funding of $200,000,000 at five percent on the payment of a bonus of 1.5 percent to the syndicate of foreign bankers who have agreed to take the loan. We would not disparage this achievement, for we regard it as decidedly better than nothing. Add to the interest ($3,000,000) $1,000,000 more for the aggregate cost of printing the new bonds, advertising, explaining and commending the loan, and the entire cost of funding the $200,000,000 at 5 percent for ten years, is $4,000,000. It seems to us that this does not justify a hope that our $1,500,000,000 of instantly or presently redeemable sixes can be promptly funded even at 5 percent.

"Having given to the Secretary's efforts a hearty support throughout, we urge that a radically different plan may next have as fair a trial. Before we send another bond abroad to be hawked from banking house to banking house throughout Europe, we ask the Government to try — just earnestly to try — to fund the bulk of our debt at home. We could not have sold our bonds during the dark hours of our civil war to Europe at any price, no matter how ruinous, if we had not first shown our faith in them by taking hundreds of millions of them ourselves. So now, having seen how reluctantly they take our reissues at 5 percent, with discount, let us show them that we stand ready to take a larger amount at a lower rate of interest at par. Here is the gist of our proposition.

"Let Congress make our greenbacks fundable, at the pleasure of the holder, in bonds of $100, $1000 and $10,000, drawing interest at the rate of one cent per day on each $100 (or 3.65 per annum), and exchangeable into greenbacks at the pleasure of the holder. Now authorize the Treasury to purchase and extinguish our outstanding bonds so fast as it is supplied with the means of so doing by receipts for customs or otherwise, and to issue new greenbacks whenever larger amounts shall be required, every one being fundable in sums of $100, $1000 or $10,000, as aforesaid, at the pleasure of the holder, in bonds drawing an annual interest of 3.65 in coin per annum, and these bonds exchangeable into greenbacks whenever a holder shall desire it.

"The benefits of this system would be these:

"1. Our greenbacks, which are now virtual falsehoods, would be truths. The Government would pay them on demand in bonds as aforesaid, which is in substantial accordance with the plan on which the greenbacks were first authorized.

"2. Every person having greenbacks for which he had no present need would present them at some sub-treasury and exchange them at par for these bonds. Suppose he has $10,000, which he expects to use a month hence, he can make them earn him $30 meantime, without incurring the smallest danger of loss by bank failures or otherwise, and with a positive certainty that the money would be ready for him whenever he chose to take it.

"3. A merchant leaves New York with $1,000,000, which he proposes to invest in wheat at the West or in cotton at the South. He calls at our sub-treasury, exchanges his greenbacks for these bonds, and takes or sends these to Chicago, Saint Paul, New Orleans or Galveston, to be exchanged for use when needed. After looking about for a month, he buys greenbacks, receives $50 per day, or $1500 in all, as interest, and makes his payments. After traveling and looking about for another month, he invests the remainder of his capital, receives $3000 as interest thereon for the two months he has held the last half million of bonds, and lays his course homeward. His bonds may have lain nearly all the time he owned them in the vaults of some bank; but they were earning money, not for that bank but for him.

"4. Our greenbacks, no longer false, but convertible at pleasure into bonds bearing a moderate gold interest, and exchangeable as aforesaid, could not fail to appreciate steadily until they nearly reached the level of gold. Indeed, they would, unless issued too profusely, be really better than gold. Drawing a higher rate of interest than British consols, and convertible at pleasure, as these are not, they would in time obtain currency even in the Old World.

"5. The trouble so inveterately borrowed by thousands with respect to over-issues, redundant currency, etc., would (or at least should) be hereby dispelled. If there were at any time an excess of currency, it would tend to precipitate itself into the bonds aforesaid. If there should ever be a scarcity of currency, bonds would be exchanged at the Treasury for greenbacks till the want was fully supplied. Black Fridays and the locking up of greenbacks would soon be numbered with lost arts and hobgoblin terrors.

"6. Though the demand for these bonds might for months be moderate, their convenience and manifest utility would soon diffuse their populairty and stimulate an ever-widening demand for them. They would be a favorite investment with guardians and trustees who should expect to be required to pay over the funds held by them at any early day, whether fixed or uncertain. They would say, though I might invest or deposit these funds where they would command a higher interest, I choose to place them where I know they will be safe and at hand when called for.

"7. Ultimately, we believe they would become so popular that hundreds of millions of them would be absorbed at or very near the par of specie, and that with the proceeds an equal amount of our outstanding sixes might be redeemed and canceled, without advertising for loans or paying bankers to shin for us throughout Europe. The interest thus saved to our country would be an important item.

"Such are the rude outlines of a plan which we did not originate, but which we heartily endorse. Why not give it a trial? We should dearly like to inform Europe that, since she seems not to want any more of our bonds at 5 percent, we have concluded to take the balance ourselves at 3.66."

To the Editor of the Iron Age — Dear Sir: The number of letters of inquiry and suggestion I have received from your readers since you were kind enough to lay before them my paper on "The Authors and Causes of the Financial Depression," is my justification for appealing to you for the privilege of once again communicating with them. Surprise is expressed by one of your readers that the support of a measure which had been so earnestly approved by Secretary Chase and Horace Greeley should have caused papers like the New York *Tribune*, the paper Mr. Greeley founded, its namesake of Chicago, and the Cincinnati *Commercial* to brand me as a lunatic and to make me the object of almost universal derision and caricature, as they had done.

In common with your readers you will probably be surprised to learn that Secretary Sherman, then Senator from Ohio, was among the earliest and ablest advocates of the convertible bond theory, and as he thus held views more in accordance with the then prevalent financial opinions than those of the late William Pitt Fessenden, was made to displace that distinguished gentleman from the chairmanship of the Finance Committee of the Senate. Senator Sherman in supporting the measure appealed, as you will see by the following extract from his speech of February 27, 1868, to right and duty as well as to expediency:

"I desire now to make a few observations in regard to the sections of the bill relating to the United States notes, and these I consider as vitally important. We propose to restore to the United States note the right to be funded at the pleasure of the holder into the new bonds whenever he desires. There is more ground of discontent and more real discontent among the people of this country because of the discrimination made between the bondholder and the holder of the greenback than from any other cause. You compel every citizen of this country to take the greenback as money, willing or unwilling. It is the measure of the value of his labor, and yet it has no purchasable power except the hope that in some future time the United States will redeem it. It may be forced upon another man in payment of debt; it may be applied to pay taxes, but it cannot be converted into income except at a discount.

"A man cannot take United States notes payable on demand to any broker and receive in exchange any form of security issued by the United States. There is a wide discrimination made between the bondholder and the noteholder, which gives rise to popular clamor and is the cause of a great deal of just complaint. In 1863 we were compelled for wise purposes to take away the right of the holder of the greenback to fund it, because we wished then to force our loans upon the market, and while that right was outstanding we could not do it. Now that the war is over, that the whole process of funding is intended to be voluntary at the discretion of the noteholder, we ought promptly to restore this right to allow the note to be converted at any time into some kind of bond; and we propose, also, to allow the bond to be converted into notes, keeping within the limits of notes fixed by law. Then there is no discrimination; the bondholder and the note-holder are both public creditors; both depend upon the public faith. The noteholder may go to the Treasury of the United States and demand his bond; the bondholder may go also and demand his note. They are put on a basis of equality. This destroys all speculation in government securities. Both will then stand on the same footing, and both will be of equal value. The noteholder may, at his option, draw interest in gold by converting it into bonds; and the popular cry of demagogues, that we have provided gold for the bondholder and notes for the people, will be silent.

"And, sir, there is no reason why the note issued to the laboring man should be less valuable than any other form of government security. It makes one of those salient points before a popular audience just and correct, which is the cause of complaint, and will be until it is removed. An important effect of this provision will be to furnish money to redeem the bonds or any other securities that offer, and without resorting to a sale of bonds. I do not propose, nor do the committee contemplate, the issue of any new greenbacks. We propose that the process of funding these notes, they pouring into the treasury, will furnish ample means to redeem all the outstanding bonds and securities as they become redeemable. I have no doubt the same process will go on here that occurred in Europe — a very small amount of money will pay a large amount of bonds. The mass of the bonds will be exchanged without money. The transactions paid by money, compared with the transactions paid by checks and other forms of paper, are as one to a thousand. The daily balances in the exchanges in the New York clearing house amount to many millions, and yet the amount of currency to pay these balances is often less than one percent of their nominal amount. Other reasons may be given for the new feature of this bill, giving the holder of these bonds the right to convert them into notes. This is indispensably necessary to guard against sudden contraction and panic. There are times when the notes will float into bonds so rapidly as to contract the currency, and thus derange business and prevent the movement of crops. This privilege will give flexibility and movement to the currency of the country. Every exchange will be a benefit to the country. If the holder of a government security bearing interest surrenders it to the Treasury for a note without interest the United States saves the interest. If, on the contrary, the notes are funded for a bond, the notes may be used in the redemption of other bonds bearing a higher rate of interest. If the money market becomes stringent, if currency becomes scarce, the holder may be willing to surrender his bond, bearing five percent interest in gold, in order to get currency with which to pay his debts, and why not give him that privilege? It is a benefit to the United States, and it is the only mode by which, during the suspension of specie payments, we may make a flexible currency.

"And, sir, this loan will be the great saving fund of the people of the United States. Every man having money for a time idle will float it into these ten-forty bonds, and while we have the money we shall pay off bonds having a higher rate of interest. When he desires it again he can come back and get the bond, and so this operation may be carried on with perfect safety. Now the deposits in the savings banks amount to over $500,000,000. Why should not this money be deposited in the Treasury? Why should not these little streams of the savings of the laboring man help to float the public credit? The government of the United States ought not to feel too high to acknowledge the services of such a fund. They will be useful. They will enable the depositor to get the full value of his money. Now he deposits in savings banks where he gets four or five percent interest in paper money. Under this provision he may put his money in these bonds, and the money thus deposited will enable the government to pay off bonds bearing a higher rate of interest. In every view we could take of this proposition, after the most ample consideration, we (the Finance Committee) thought it was a wise provision, and would work well. The trouble and cost of printing these bonds and exchanging them one for another, being carried on at the Treasury Department or at the depositories or other proper places of exchange, will be done without cost, except that of printing. It is purely voluntary, and will be adapted to the wants of trade. It will tend to give increased value to the United States notes, and my firm conviction is that under the process both notes and bonds will gradually rise, step by step, until they reach the standard of gold, and then the whole process ceases, according to the provisions of the bill. I look upon this provision as the most rapid way to specie payments."

These were not casual or hasty utterances. They were made in the course of a two hours' speech in support of a bill the speaker had reported from the Committee on Finance; and, inasmuch as Mr. Sherman was interrupted with questions (not, however in this part of the speech), it was withheld for several days for revision, and appears in the appendix to the *Congressional Globe,* second session, Fortieth Congress, pages 187 and 188.

Are the American people ready to believe that Chase and

Greeley in the very prime of their intellectual vigor were lunatics, and that he who now administers with such terribly destructive power the finances of this government had, before the opening of 1868, been bereft of reason? Or, in deference to the memories of the great dead, and respect to the most potent citizen of the Republic, will they cease to brand the humble disciple of these men as one fit for a "straight jacket," and one who requires "bladders of ice about his fevered temples" when he travels? Should the organs of the contractionists, who have treated me with such want of candor, in this connection invite attention to the fact that Senator Sherman spoke of gold interest, those who have heard me speak on the subject or read my writings, will bear witness that I have always said if it were deemed preferable to make the interest payable in gold, so be it; but as my object was to diminish the difference between our paper and gold, I preferred to add a new use to the paper dollar, and withdraw one from the commodity which had long since ceased to circulate as money in our country. Hoping you will pardon this liberty, I remain,

Yours, very truly,

William D. Kelley

William Elder

(1800 - 1871)

The Debt and Resources of the United States
And the Effect of Secession Upon the
Trade and Industry of the United States

The Debt and Resources of the United States and the Effect Of Secession upon the Trade And Industry of the United States

William Elder was a member of Henry Carey's Vespers circle and an economist in Abraham Lincoln's Treasury Department. This pamphlet, which is excerpted here, was written in 1863 to explain the financial policy of the Lincoln Administration to pay off the debt generated during the Civil War through a program of rapid industrialization. The pamphlet also projects the rates of growth of various industries and those new resources, such as oil, which had barely been exploited. This pamphlet and others were shipped around the world as a "how to do it" guide to America's economic policy.

Our National Resources

We propose to treat this subject under the following heads:

First. The capital, or present value of the property of the people — estimates based upon the official returns of the Census Bureau.

Second. How the resources of the Union are affected by the secession of the rebel States.

Third. Our prospective resources.

First. Present Capital of the Loyal States

Having already given the official valuations, we give now only a brief recapitulation, with explanations:

	Year	Population	Real and Personal Property	Increased Valuation Percent	Products of the Year
United States	1840	17049453	$3,764,000,000	—	$1,063,135,000
United States	1850	23191876	6,174,349,828	64	1,985,831,000
Loyal States	1850	15924122	4,728,247,586	—	1,513,039,227
United States	1860	31429891	14,183,215,628	129.7	3,736,000,000
Loyal States	1860	22328133	10,716,109,961	126.6	2,818,336,919
Loyal States	1863	24000000	13,395,137,451	25	3,522,921,184

EXPLANATION OF THESE ESTIMATES

The authority for the population and valuation of the property of the country and the rate percent of increase for the years 1840, 1850 and 1860 is the official reports of those decades made by the Census office. The values of the products of the census years 1840 and 1850 are the estimates of Professor Tucker, based upon the census returns. The estimates of the products of 1860 are our own, following the same rule of computation. The population and valuation of 1863 are obtained by the same rule.

It will be observed that the products of the year 1850 are 32 percent and those of 1860 are 26.3 percent of the valuation of property.

These amounts are greatly below the truth. They do not yield a per capita production of annual values beyond the necessary consumption of the people, and, of course, can afford nothing to the constant accumulation of wealth. The obvious deficiency is owing to the following causes:

The census returns take no account of the agricultural products and domestic manufactures of our farmers consumed by their families and their employees; who in 1840 were quite three-fourths of the population, and were nearly in as large proportion in 1850, and approaching it in 1860.

Again, the vast total of mechanical products which individually fall below the value of $500 per annum, is omitted.

Nor is there any notice taken of the labor employed in clearing and improving lands, in building and repairing railroads, canals, houses, manufactories, steamships and other vessels; nor of the labor in transportation on the ocean, lakes, rivers, canals, railroads, highways, etc.; nor, of the labor in the mines and forests. The labor thus overlooked finds expression only in the reports of such products as go into market, by the addition it makes to their value. But very much the largest portion escapes all notice, except in the decennial valuation of the real and personal property of the people.

Another cause of disproportion between our estimated annual production and the enhanced value of property, is the great and rapid enhancement in the value of our real property, which is immense in the new States and Territories, and even more surprising in the older States.

In this brief and imperfect enumeration of the industrial products and services omitted by the Marshals, probably one-half of the annual yield of the country lies uncounted. Even in England, where the assessor and the exciseman watch the labor and business of the country with the vigilance and authority of inquisitors, it is believed that one-fourth of the industrial products escape them. How much more of this must happen among a people living in such abundance that the half of them take no note for themselves of what they acquire or consume.

Our official valuations, and the estimates of experts, are, for these reasons, very short of the mark; but they serve the purpose of comparative estimates very well. They probably correspond with sufficient exactness to give us, not the amount of our wealth, but the rate and proportions of its progress, and so enable us to measure the relative ability of the country at different periods to bear its burdens and provide for its expenditures—a subject already presented to the reader in sufficient fullness. Let us now endeavor to understand—

Second. How Our Resources Are Affected by Secession.

The Rebellion leaves our capital in real and personal property just where it was before secession.

The public domain lying within their limits, and the material wealth on its surface and under it, never did, and under the slave system, never would repay expenses of purchase and charges of the Federal Government; and with a thousand millions of acres of unseated lands, all lying north and west of the slave region, which the Government is ready to give free of charge to the occupants, it is not soil or minerals, forest or rivers, mountains or valleys that we need, (for any purpose) beyond that which is in our possession. (See Tabular Statement No. 4) These lands undisposed of, are practically unlimited in value to the nation, and indirectly to the Treasury. A national debt thrice the amount of England's could not outlast the period in which they will be coming into available value, or the production of taxable wealth to our people, as we shall presently see.

The abated resources of the nation in direct taxes, occasioned by the rebellion, may be stated in a word:

Congress by the act of 5th August, 1861, assessed a tax of twenty millions upon the whole United States, apportioning to each

TABULAR STATEMENT NO. 4

Statement showing the number of Square Miles, total number of Acres of Public Land, amount sold and otherwise disposed of, and amount remaining unsold in each of the following States and Territories of the United States, with the Population and value of the Real and Personal Private Property in 1850 and 1860, respectively.

State or Territory	Number of Square Miles	Total Number of Acres	Total No. Acres Disposed of	Total No. Acres Undisposed of	Population in 1850	Population in 1860	Value of Private Property 1850	Value of Private Property 1860	Inc'd Val. P. Ct.
California	158,687	101,659,680	7,645,978	94,013,702	92,597	379,994	$22,161,872	$207,874,613	838
Dakota Ter.	148,932	95,316,480	12,076,326	83,240,154		4,837			
Nevada Ter.	81,539	52,184,960	2,295,111	49,889,849		6,857			
Colorado Ter.	104,500	66,880,000		66,880,000		34,227			
New Mexico Ter.	121,201	77,568,640	8,857,955	68,710,685	61,547	93,516	5,174,471	20,813,768	302
Arizona Ter.	126,141	80,730,240		80,730,240					
Utah Ter.	106,382	68,084,480	6,427,567	61,656,913	11,380	40,273	986,083	5,596,118	467
Oregon	95,248	60,958,720	5,072,174	55,886,546	13,294	52,465	5,063,474	28,930,637	471
Idaho Ter.	326,373	208,878,720		208,878,720					
Washington Ter.	69,994	44,796,160	6,312,861	38,483,299		11,594		5,601,466	
Nebraska Ter.	75,995	48,636,800	5,511,704	43,125,096	Part of Kansas	28,841		9,131,056	
Illinois	55,410	35,462,400	35,461,467	933	851,470	1,711,951	156,265,006	871,860,282	458
Iowa	55,045	35,228,800	33,847,296	1,381,504	192,214	674,948	23,714,638	247,338,265	943
Missouri	65,350	41,824,000	31,417,663	10,406,337	682,044	1,182,012	137,247,707	501,214,398	265
Michigan	56,451	36,128,640	27,034,943	9,093,697	397,654	749,113	59,787,255	257,163,983	330
Minnesota	80,386	51,447,040	15,501,747	35,945,293	6,077	173,855	Not returned	52,294,413	
Wisconsin	53,924	34,511,360	22,437,353	12,074,007	305,391	775,881	42,056,595	273,671,668	551
Kansas	81,318	52,043,520	7,538,870	44,504,650		107,206		31,327,895	
TOTALS	1,862,876	1,192,340,640	227,439,015	964,901,625	2,613,668	6,027,620	$452,457,101	$2,512,818,562	455

Increase, 130 percent

State its constitutional share of the levy. Of this sum the portion charged upon the loyal States was $15,846,047; the portion of the Rebel States was $4,153,952, a trifle more than one-fifth of the whole amount. Even in this meagre amount 3,470,121 slaves are charged as 2,082,072 persons; an element of taxation which it is to be presumed would not long remain in the present aspect of this world's affairs, and which if deducted would leave the rebel states at one-seventh of the Union for this purpose, or liable for one dollar in seven of the direct taxes to be raised for the use of the nation.

Since 1816 the Slave States have contributed nothing to the Treasury in land or property tax. They have enjoyed the political power of a slave basis of representation in Congress and in the Electoral College, nearly half a century, in entire exemption from the cost of their side of the compromise.

So far then this is only a loss of that which we have not had, and, at best or worst, a very small one in any time of need. But the secession of the rebel States is a question of both

PROFIT AND LOSS.

Among other things, we are disburdened of near five millions per annum of mail expenses, which their accommodation cost the North. Along with this, innumerable items and grand aggregates of civil expenditure; annexation and filibustering enterprises — such as extinguishing Indian title to lands within their borders, or beyond them, for their use; and perpetual acquisitions of territory for their exhaustive slave culture, with the national wars and wickedness attending. Their contingent of one dollar in five or seven of direct taxes, weighs like a feather in the scale against these masses of expenditure made in their behalf at the cost of the free people of the nation.

One other item of the political account current —

THE INDIRECT TAXES,

paid by them into the Treasury as consumers of foreign imports, has been a source of strife ever since the customs, of which the five-sixths were paid by the North, seemed no longer necessary to save them from the payment of all other taxes. While the debt of the revolution and of the last war remained to be met, they were content to let the free states pay 86 percent of it in customs duties — the great nullifier of 1833 voting for the tariff of 1816. But so soon as the national debt was discharged, duties for protection became vastly more unconstitutional than nullification or rebellion.

As profit and loss this item stands thus: the South consumed of foreign imports something less than 50 percent of their proportion according to population, which runs their contribution down to 14 percent of the total import duties, or seven millions of the ordinary income from customs, per annum.

If they are sure that this was a loss to them, we know that it was not a corresponding profit to the North. Their incessant endeavor, and not unfrequent success, at reducing the productiveness of this branch of the revenue, really occasioned incalculable losses to the North. But such as it is, it must stand in finance reports as a loss, and we have given the full amount of it.

The effect of the severance of the Union upon the commercial and industrial interests of the North would, under the laws of trade be nothing. Commerce is not limited by political boundaries. But the rebellion, the war of the rebellion and the blockade, must have had some influence. Let us see:

FIRST. UPON OUR EXPORTS TO FOREIGN COUNTRIES—

which may be expressed in the reported money values, as the prices of commodities in foreign markets are unaffected by the rebellion and our domestic currency.

Our fiscal year ends on the 30th of June. During the year ending June 1862, trade with the seceded States was interdicted and suspended. For this year we have the official report of our foreign trade complete. In Tabular Statement No. 5 our domestic exports (exclusive of gold and silver) for the complete year 1861-62 are compared with those of all the States of the Union in the year 1859-60 the last complete fiscal year before the rebellion; showing also, the necessary decrease of Southern exports in 1861-62, and the increase and decrease of Northern exports in the latter fiscal year as compared with those of 1859-60.

The estimated share of the South in the exports of the year 1859-60 of animal and vegetable products, usually classed as agricultural, of tobacco, hemp, manufactures, etc. is carefully

TABULAR STATEMENT NO. 5

Domestic Exports in the years ending 30th June. 1860 and 1862. (exclusive of Gold and Silver,) with the Increase & Decrease.

	YEAR ENDING 30 JUNE, 1860	YEAR ENDING 30 JUNE, 1862	TOTAL EXPORTS OF 1862 COMPARED WITH THOSE OF 1860	SOUTHERN PROD'CTS. 1862. DECREASE OF EXPORTS	NORTHERN PROD'CTS. 1862 INCREASE	NORTHERN PROD'CTS. 1862 DECREASE
Products of the Sea	$4,156,480	$3,913,477	Decrease, $243,003	$67,528		$175,475
Products of the Forest	13,738,559	9,934,211	Decrease, 3,804,348	2,017,545		1,786,803
[Rosin and Turpentine	1,818,238	293,400	Decrease, 1,524,838]			
Products of Agriculture—Animal	20,215,226	38,580,964	Increase, 18,365,738	990,119	$19,355,857	
Products of Agriculture—Vegetable	27,590,298	84,925,206	Increase, 57,334,908	2,922,275	60,257,183	
[Rice	2,567,399	156,899	Decrease, 2,410,500]			
Cotton	191,806,555	1,180,113	Decrease, 190,626,442	190,626,442		
Tobacco	15,906,547	12,325,356	Decrease, 3,581,191	10,514,630	6,933,439	
Hemp	9,531	8,300	Decrease, 1,231	381		
Other Agricultural Products	736,839	1,046,644	Increase, 309,805	103,244	413,049	
Manufactures	37,146,953	23,053,027	Decrease, 14,093,926	519,261		13,574,665
[Tobacco and Cotton Manufactures	14,307,843	4,014,544	Decrease, 10,293,299]			
[Iron Manufactures	5,703,042	4,526,971	Decrease 1,176,071]			
Coal	740,783	837,117	Increase 96,334	5,203	101,537	
Ice	183,134	182,667	Decrease, 467			467
Quicksilver	258,682	1,237,643	Increase, 978,961		978,961	
Non-enumerated, manufactured	2,397,445	2,880,347	Increase, 492,902	29,445	522,347	
Non-enumerated, raw	1,355,391	1,770,916	Increase, 415,525	37,303	452,828	
Totals	$316,242,423	$181,878,988	Decrease..$134,366,435	$207,843,376	$89,015,201	
Coin and Bullion	56,946,851	31,044,651		Less Decrease,	15,538,260	$15,538,260
Total Domestic Exports	$373,188,274	$212,920,639		Northern Inc..,	$73,476,941	

made. The statement shows the increase of Northern exports, as follows: animal products, (agricultural) 19⅓ millions of dollars, vegetable 60½ millions, of tobacco near 7 millions, and of other articles of domestic production, the balance of 89 millions. The decrease in the products of the sea and forest together, is less than two millions; of manufactures, 13½ millions; 10¼ millions of this decrease being in cotton goods and manufactured tobacco, for lack of the staple of the former, and by closure of the Southern ports against the export of the latter. The total decrease amounting to 15½ millions; which leaves a resulting total increase of 73½ millions of exports of Northern products over their own total in 1859-60.

But the total exports, Northern and Southern, of 1859-60 exceeded the average of the preceding six years by 69 millions, and the highest of them, 1858-59, by 38 millions. To the average total exports of those six years the loyal States contributed 101 millions; in 1860, 108 millions; and in 1862, 181¾ millions; which makes the excess of 1862 full 80 millions above the average of the previous six years.

The amount of profit and loss in the export trade of the two years compared, therefore, stands thus: a gain in the proprietary profits of 73 millions worth of exports, against the commissions and transportation profits upon that portion, about one-twelfth perhaps, of 208 millions of Southern products which would otherwise have found their way out into the world through Northern hands.

None of the rules of arithmetic will prove that a loss is a gain, but the laws of productive industry have often converted losses into profits, "from seeming evil still educing good," as under their rule many an instance of great commercial gain has resulted in still greater loss.

This case of our foreign exports is an eminent instance of the truth of an apparent paradox; and in the effects of the rebellion upon the total productive industry of the loyal States, irrespective of their foreign trade, we have another grand instance of great benefit gathered from a rough trial, in which a people lose their largest customer, and gain thereby increased industrial productiveness and profit. This involves an inquiry into the mechanical and manufacturing industry of 1862-63 as compared with that of 1860.

COMPARATIVE STATE OF NORTHERN INDUSTRY
DURING THE SUSPENSION OF TRADE WITH THE SOUTH

This inquiry into the business affairs of the day, to be caught on the wing, before they have settled themselves into fixed and formally recorded results, throws us necessarily upon the estimates of experts. The results of the most reliable investigation are given in detail in our Tabular Statement No.6. Business men having the advantage of an inside view of their own specialties, will make their own corrections of the estimated productions of the current year, and we think it will be found that a cautious avoidance of excess and overstatement has kept down the figures considerably below the truth. The estimates were first made in December last for the use of the Bureau of Internal Revenue. In April Mr. Blodget felt assured that the advance in manufacturing during four months, required an increase in the quantities of about 15 percent; and we are now satisfied upon inquiry that another addition of 10 percent would not more than meet the increase indicated by the business of June. This would bring the manufacturing industry of the present year in the loyal States just up to the quantities produced in 1860. The middle column of the statement expresses the quantities or relative quantities in the prices of 1860; the third column is an estimate of the same quantities at the current wholesale or first cost prices of the present time, which in the average are 25 percent above those of 1860; some of them being fifty, a few seventy-five, but many of them below twenty percent higher than two years ago.

The total Northern manufactures of 1860, according to the census report, amounted to $1,754,650,000. About one hundred and fifty millions of these items are not compared with the like products of 1863, but assuming that these hold the same ratio as those estimated in the table, it would result that the temporary loss of customers, who formerly took six times more of our manufactured products than all the world besides, has affected this branch of our industry to the extent of barely 10¼ percent; or if our judgment be correct, has not lessened our production at all in quantity. We believe that business men generally will hold this higher estimate to be quite within the bounds of fact.

The knowledge of an immensely enhanced activity in all branches of industry is brought home to every body in the free States

TABULAR STATEMENT NO. 6

Estimate of Mechanical and Manufacturing products of the Loyal States, prepared by Lorin Blodget, Esq., Secretary of the Philadelphia Board of Trade, for the use of the Bureau of Internal Revenue in December, 1862, and revised by him for this publication in April, 1863.

The first column gives the value produced in 1860; the data taken from the consensus of that year and other sources. The second column estimates the relative *quantity* produced in the year ending October, 1863, in the prices current.

PRODUCTS OF 1860.		Quantity produced in 1862-63, expressed in the prices of 1860	Value of the products of 1862-63, at the current prices
Textile Fabrics	$181,949,685	$135,462,264	147,703,813
Iron and Steel	125,387,220	112,848,498	178,552,633
Steel Manufactures	11,196,514	11,096,105	15,534,650
Manufactures part Steel & Iron	21,293,000	16,628,576	19,358,604
Manufactures of Metals	31,860,070	20,964,121	29,181,751
Glass, Pottery & Earthen Ware	12,327,915	8,603,592	10,754,490
Paper and Manufactures of	19,129,800	15,714,385	21,999,270
Blank Books, Cards, Bills, Photograph Cases	6,968,380	5,395,097	7,013,627
Books, Bound Volumes	11,667,709	12,000,000	15,000,000
Leather and Manufactures of	156,000,000	127,507,000	170,957,000
Liquors, Spirit., Vinous & Malt	64,659,422	64,879,439	84,340,670
Tobacco Manuf'td and Segars	11,491,000	11,491,000	20,000,000
Petroleum	800,000	8,178,000	8,178,000
Soap, Candles, Oils	26,692,500	26,825,191	33,672,750
Refined Sugar, Confectionery, Maple Sugar	33,509,200	25,180,000	40,000,000
Chemicals, Paints & Fertilizers	13,260,000	11,812,800	14,766,000
Wood Manuf'rs, Furniture, &c.	41,000,000	34,889,000	41,900,000
Gas	10,000,000	10,000,000	12,000,000
Clothing, Hats, Millinery, Furs, Umbrellas, Inda Rubber Goods, Gloves, &c.	102,180,222	81,955,000	96,300,000
Miscellaneous taxed Manuf'rs.	290,500,000	250,442,000	300,000,000
Coal	18,702,274	21,507,614	27,959,899
Salt	1,800,000	1,800,000	2,340,000
Sawed and Planed Lumber	77,971,124	85,768,236	107,210,295
Flour and Meal	192,376,912	211,614,603	238,066,428
	$1,462,722,947	$1,312,562,521	$1,642,789,880
	1,312,562,521		1,312,562,521
	$150,160,426		$330,227,359
		Decrease of Quantity, 10.26 percent	Increase of Price, 25.15 per cent

by the almost perfect distribution of its benefits. One class, and one class only, of the people, and that a class which the general prosperity always injures, suffers something — the class of annuitants, salaried officers, and people living upon accumulated capital. Their incomes stand still at their former figure, and vast amounts of their investments in mortgages and funds secured upon property are paid off and sent seeking new investments. Debts of record are settled this year to three times the amount ever known before, and millions of property are liberated from encumbrances. But it is the fate of those who have thrown their support upon the industry of others to suffer alike by the general insolvency and general prosperity, with this difference, that in the one case they suffer irreparable loss, but in the other, must some way or other participate in the general advantage.

We speak not only upon common fame, but by the record on this subject. The Recorders of Deeds and Mortgages and Clerks of Courts of Record every where are our witnesses.

But the evidence is just as strong in every department of business. The house, shop, and factory building in Philadelphia, taken from the registry of permits, shows that in 1860, 636 buildings were in process of erection in the first four months of the year, whereas in the corresponding months of 1863, the number of permits rose to 911, and for the month of May the office reports a larger amount of Inspector's fees than ever was received in any month before. This report, better than the number of buildings, measures the value of the erections, for the fees are proportioned to the size of the structures.

The reports of the Savings Banks are to the same effect, and most remarkable among them is the state of those institutions in New England. In the five largest manufacturing towns, Lowell, Lawrence, Waltham, Fall River, and Taunton, where diminished incomes if not absolute destitution, among the people, who are the chief depositors, was expected from the suspension of the Cotton Mills, the account published in March last shows that in the year 1862 the number of depositors increased 2,687, and that the amount of deposits increased $1,162,264. The Bank Commissioners of Massachusetts in their report to the Legislature for 1862-63 exhibit an increase of 23,842 depositors and an increase of $5,618,235 in the deposits, for the year, in the Savings Banks of the State.

When New England, that was believed to live upon cotton, shows such an account at the end of two years of threatened ruin, the condition of the rest of the country may be considered safe and sound.

One other sign and a very significant one, deserves notice here. The price of paper, composition and other elements of the cost of book-making have advanced quite 25 percent, yet the best informed man in the trade, the publisher of the *Bookseller's Circular,* Mr. G.W. Childs, of Philadelphia, answers an inquiry put to him thus: "From present appearances I am satisfied that there will be more books sold this year in the loyal portion of the United States than were ever sold in any one year when we had the whole country to supply (both North and South.) Besides, business is done mostly for cash, which never could be done with the Southern trade. A leading house in Chicago writes me that they are selling more books than every before — the same report from Cincinnati."

Such is the present state of the manufacturing and mechanical industry of a people who have sent a million of their laborers and wealth-producers into the Army!

We make no estimate of the agricultural products of the present year. It is unnecessary. The region that in 1861-62, the first full fiscal year of the rebellion, could spare from the sustenance of its army in the field, eighty millions of bread stuffs and provisions for foreign trade above the amount of its greatest exports in any former year, needs no other proof of its capacity. The crops now ripening to harvest promise grandly. They will not fall below the best and largest. The soil will yield its usual abundance, and in the usual excess of the home demand; and it depends only upon the foreign demand to bring our exports of food up to the amount in 1862, or above it.

Such results as we have reached may well awaken some wonder. But such demonstration as we have been able to give them, though sufficient for the argument, may leave some doubt — rather, opinions surprised by such contradiction may require explanations before they admit the conclusions we have reached.

There is an inveterate opinion abroad that the profits of labor and the resulting wealth of a nation can be realized only through *foreign* trade; that a State grows rich only upon the profits of its traffic with some other State and the greater the distance between them the better.† The doctrine strengthens in proportion to the size of the community. A nation must bring its wealth across a sea, and *a fortiori,* we must infer that the only chance the globe has for growing rich all over, is by a trade with the moon or some other outlying province of the solar system. Consequently when a working community loses a large foreign customer it must go into bankruptcy. A very free-trader holds that a State can no more prosper by its own domestic commerce, than two boys can make five dollars *each* by exchanging their jackets. Yet he asserts that *foreign* trade yields reciprocal profits. Leaving this philosophy for the enjoyment of its inventors, let us see how

THE NORTH LOSES A LARGE CUSTOMER AND PROSPERS.

The half of our population of both sexes are over fifteen years of age. The same proportion held in 1850; but in that year only 27 percent of the total population were in the various classes of the "employed," which was but 54 percent, or a fraction more than half of those over 15 years of age, leaving 5⅓ millions unemployed.

The proportion in 1860 may be safely taken to be the same, taking care to remember, besides, how many of the "employed" were but half employed.

In 1863 the population of the loyal States by the usual rule of increase would be 24,400,000. Taking it at 24 millions, 27 percent of this number gives us 6½ millions as the number "employed" on the peace establishment, and leaves us 5½ millions of both sexes, as a reserve guard of industrial forces to draw upon. 2¾ millions of these are males above the age of 15 — An abundant source of supply to fill the places of one million of men in the military service.

But put these 2¾ millions of men, and the 5½ millions left after the military draft, upon full time at tempting wages, and all the wonder of the increased production of a period of war vanishes.

---

† If a nation's wealth grows only by its foreign trade, then the United States in the decade ending 1860 must have made 8,000 millions clear gain out of its 2,322 millions of domestic exports.

We could spare another million and carry on the nation's work to a higher figure than it ever has yet reached. Our calculations do not ask *more* than an increased productiveness of 25 percent above that of the year 1860. There is abundant provision for it. We have 12 millions of people above the age of 15. We send one million of them to the field, leaving us 11 millions. We put but 8¼ millions of them to work, against the 6½ millions employed in 1860, which gives us 27 percent increase in numbers merely, to say nothing of the greater productiveness of the mass, under the stimulus of war prices, choice of labor, and fullness of time, with all their earnings and savings. The fact that a large proportion of our soldiers were of the "unemployed" in 1860 makes still more margin for our estimates, and strengthens the explanation.

A close reader of these pages will notice that our calculations do not require an increase of 25 percent in the industrial products of the year. We have not put either the manufacturing or agricultural estimates above the products of 1860, but we have a lurking conviction that they are at least that much enhanced, and finding the causes ample, give a conjectural place to the effects, with abundant allowance for the inactivity or failure among the causes which we find potentially present.

The very best and healthiest of all the causes of this prosperity is that one which has given us our own work to do — the congressional legislation of 1861-62 upon import duties, aided by the high rate of foreign exchange.

For more than a year we have had the competing industry of Europe under a tolerable commercial blockade, and the policy which saves a nation's work for its own hands has had a demonstration of its wonder-working power among us, which will not be lost when gold falls to par and peace puts in practice the wisdom that war has taught.

Occupied with the horrors and evils, the waste and the terrors of this rebellion, some one may turn upon us with impatience and ask whether we mean to prove that war is a blessing? No, alas! No. War, Pestilence and Famine are a leash of evils, usually associated, but happily separated in our case, sparing us the most terrible, and so far modifying the fury of the leader of the train, and with this further mitigation, that for the time it has broken up a wretched system of commercial policy, greatly more destructive to the industrial interests of the nation than all the usual waste of war. It has muzzled the two blood-hounds that always hunt in couples, *slavery* and *free trade*, slavery ever crying for free *foreign trade*, and *free trade* meaning nothing but *slave men*. Even a national debt may be lighter than a paralyzed industry, and may indirectly give the strength to bear its burden, by protecting labor itself from foreign invasion, and keeping it free to build up a nation's wealth.

Prospective Resources of the United States

In the treatment of this subject, we limit ourselves to the simplest presentment of the principal data for the estimates and opinions to be formed of the available wealth of the nation in the immediate future which has our debt and expenditure to provide for. No reader, of common understanding in these affairs, can need our help in forming his conclusions.

THE PUBLIC LANDS

lying within the loyal territory of the Union, open to settlement, and undisposed of, are exhibited in Tabular Statement No. 4. This statement was prepared in the Land Office, in the month of May, 1863. We have added, from the official returns of the Census Bureau, the population of the several States and Territories, embraced in the statement, and the official valuation of the private property, real and personal, of the inhabitants in 1850 and 1860, with the rate of increase percent, to give some notion of the progress of which that region is capable. It appears that nearly a thousand millions of acres of these lands remain undisposed of, within an area of eleven hundred and thirty-two millions.

These lands, yet belonging to the Government, are not relied upon for revenue arising directly from their sale to the occupants. The liberal provisions of the law of May, 1862, granting homesteads to actual settlers, the bounty lands assigned to our soldiers, and the large donations made to the States and Territories for educational and other purposes, with the grants to rail road and telegraph companies, will, in the opinion of the Secretary of the Interior, prevent the receipt of any considerable revenue from that portion of these public lands fitted for agricultural and pastoral uses. A very moderate and very reasonable reservation of the products of the precious metals, it is believed would in good time pay off our whole public debt; but no such tax having yet been laid upon the miners of these treasures, they are not now considered as a source of national revenue.

It is only as contributing to the wealth of the cultivators, and thus to the taxable wealth of the nation, that they are now presented.

We see that in the region of these lands the private property of its inhabitants increased in value in the ten years from 1850 to 1860, from four hundred and fifty-two, to two thousand five hundred and twelve millions of dollars, or full 450 percent; and the population from 2,613,000 to 6,027,000 persons — a clear gain of 130 percent.

This is not the description of a wilderness, but rather realizes the idea of a "nation born in a day." A progress so stupendous at, and even before, the golden era of their destiny, scarcely allows any limit to the prospect which it opens.

No one, acquainted with the movement in this vast domain of 1,862,876 square miles, can have any doubt that the advance of the next ten years will immensely overpass the last. We are personally acquainted with hundreds of men who are as old as the States of Ohio, Indiana and Illinois, which now have an aggregate population of 5,400,000 souls, drawing their living from the *surface* of the soil. If this has happened within the limits of a human life-time, and within an area of 130,000 square miles, what is the promise of a space fifteen times their measure, as rich in agricultural forces, and underlaid with unlimited *mineral wealth?*

The Commissioner of the General Land Office, in his report of the 29th December, 1862, says:

"The great auriferous region of the United States, in the western portion of the Continent, stretches from the 49th degree of North latitude and Puget Sound, to the 30′ 30″ parallel, and from the 102nd degree of longitude west of Greenwich, to the Pacific Ocean, embracing portions of Dakota, Nebraska, Colorado, all of New Mexico, with Arizona, Utah, Nevada, California, Oregon and Washington Territories. It may be designated as comprising 17 degrees of latitude, or a breadth of eleven hundred miles, from

North to South, and of nearly equal longitudinal extension, making an area of more than a million of square miles.

"This vast region is traversed from North to South, first, on the Pacific side, by the Sierra Nevada and Cascade Mountains, then by the Blue and Humboldt; on the East, by the double ranges of the Rocky Mountains, embracing the Wasatch and Wind River Chain, and the Sierra Madre, stretching longitudinally and in lateral spurs, crossed and linked together by intervening ridges, connecting the whole system by five principal ranges, dividing the country into an equal number of basins, each being nearly surrounded by mountains, and watered by mountain streams and snows, thereby interspersing this immense territory with bodies of agricultural lands, equal to the support not only of miners, but of a dense population."

"These mountains," he continues, "are literally stocked with minerals; gold and silver being interspersed in profusion over this immense surface, and daily brought to light by new discoveries." "In addition to the deposits of gold and silver, various sections of the whole region are rich in precious stones, marble, gypsum, salt, tin, quicksilver, asphaltum, coal, iron, copper, lead, mineral and medicinal, thermal and cold springs and streams."

"The yield of the precious metals alone of this region will not fall below one hundred millions of dollars the present year, and it will augment with the increase of population, for centuries to come." "Within ten years the annual product of these mines will reach two hundred millions of dollars in the precious metals, and in coal, iron, tin, lead, quicksilver and copper, half that sum." He argues the propriety of subjecting these minerals to a Government tax of 8 percent, and counts upon a revenue from this source of 25 millions per annum, almost immediately, and upon a proportionate increase in the future. He adds that "an amount of labor relatively equal to that expended in California, applied to the gold fields already known to exist outside of that State, the production of this year, including that of California, would exceed four hundred millions." "In a word, the value of these mines is absolutely incalculable."

To open up these lands for immediate settlement, develop their wealth and connect them and the Atlantic States with the Pacific coast, Congress in July, 1862, incorporated a Company to construct a line of Rail Road and Telegraph: granting to the Company ten square miles of public land in ten alternate sections on both sides of the road and within ten miles of it, for every mile of road made, completed and equipped; engaged, also, to extinguish the interfering Indian titles along the route, and lending the bonds of the Government to the Company to the amount of sixteen thousand dollars for every mile of finished road, equipped and in running order, holding the road mortgaged for the payment of the interest and redemption of these bonds at maturity by the Company.

This, with all the independent inducements, promises an early achievement of the great enterprise of connecting the Pacific coast with the valley of the Mississippi; unlocking the treasures of the vast region traverse, and peopling the great belt of highway with a race destined to open the transcontinental trade of the civilized world, and ultimately occupy the vast basins of the Cordilleras from the 49th degree of North latitude to the heart of the semi-tropical Zone on their Southern border. These things are not merely in the possible of the far-future, they lie not only in speculation, with centuries for its range — we touch the things we contemplate: they are in our grasp, and answer to the exigencies of the present.

The people of the non-slave-holding States increased from 2,601,509 in the year 1800 to 13,330,650 in 1850 or nearly six times, before the Pacific coast had fairly opened to them, and while all the wealth of these 1,000 millions of acres lay unrealized and almost unknown. Upon that basis they swelled their numbers in the next ten years 41½, and their wealth 126 percent. This grand capital of men in the next 40 years will rise to 75 millions, and, their wealth beyond computation by the arithmetic of progress in the past. The loyal States today lack but one-fifth of the population of all the British Islands. They have in their hands a wealth in the useful minerals, independently of those usually called precious, capable of a hundred times the product of theirs; an agricultural sweep equal to feeding the world, and capable of bringing out of their domain all that man can compel nature to yield to his wants.

The new and the golden lies out large and grand along the track of our future, encumbered with a debt only one-third of the magnitude of that under which England has augmented her wealth in 45 years from eleven to thirty one thousand millions of dollars in value.

But this dazzling picture of our West and Northwest must not be allowed to overshadow the hope that is in the States now called the older of the Sisterhood. In the last ten years they have more than doubled the capital of their wealth and added 41½ percent to their free population. Old as they are called in the young family of the still younger, they are fresh in all their energies and resources as on their natal day; and stronger by all they have achieved for still greater achievement. The new States of the Northwest have contributed handsomely to the national growth, and greatly augmented their own, but while Ohio appreciated 136 percent, the old States, New Jersey increased 133, Connecticut 185, and New York and Pennsylvania, millionaries among the States, added respectively 70 and 96 percent to their great capitals of 1850.

Who, and what shall limit the probabilities in the immediate future, of such a people, the masters of such possessions? If the statesmen of England feel asured that their debt is not only lessening but relatively dwindling in the progress of their wealth, a debt which in 1816 was an incumbrance of $41.14 upon every hundred of the value of the three kingdoms but now only $12.34 on the hundred, though it stands in pounds sterling within a trifle of its highest figure, what will be the effect upon ours?

Under our greater rate of growth — three-fold greater in the last decade, we will not venture to say how much still greater in the next twenty years — what will be the burden of a debt of twelve or fifteen hundred millions, upon the wealth that shall spring from our mines, our fields, our work-shops and our commerce? Their acquisitions are the small profits extorted by ill-paid labor from sources limited in quantity and variety to a trifle in comparison; — ours are practically unlimited; measured, not by miles and acres but by degress of latitude and longitude, and varied by every shade of influence that the sun rains on civilized mankind; stored with every species of wealth that the world knows and wants; lying all along and covering the historic zone of civilization; measuring an area equal to all Europe, Russia excepted, and offering one-half of its tribute gratuitously, while with the other half it rewards industry at full four-fold the rate of profit known in the old world.

May we not now conclude that a people so situated, so circumstanced, may not only bear, but quickly discharge a debt relatively no heavier than that which they extinguished in less than a score of years, a whole generation since, with this important difference between them, that in the poverty of our national infancy the principal and profits of our loans went away from us into foreign hands, but now we are our own creditor; having all the advantage in the liquidation of our comparatively small debt that enables England to support her immense one. In the language of one of their best writers and thinkers, "The money collected and expended at home, equalizes itself and acts only as a force to increase activity of circulation."

This is sound doctrine. The business prosperity of the passing year is a demonstration; and we may assure ourselves that so long as this burden rests upon us, its profits to the lenders will return to the Treasury in abatement of that burden — a perpetual circulation, replenishing the Treasury as the rivers feed the sea, and reflowing upon the people as the sea refreshes the land.

Stephen Colwell

(1806 - 1885)

The Relations of Foreign Trade to Domestic Industry
And Internal Revenue

The Relations of Foreign Trade to Domestic Industry and Internal Revenue

Stephen Colwell, a collaborator of Henry Carey's and a member of David Wells's Revenue Commission, produced this report [excerpted here] in 1866, one of several reports that argue against the adoption of the British System in America. This report deals with the argument that trade with Great Britain would cheapen prices. Colwell demonstrates the contrary: The British habit of dumping finished manufactures onto foreign markets, despite the loss incurred, allowed the British to set their own trade terms once the competing manufacturers were wiped out.

Among the elements not to be overlooked in any estimate of our present financial position, are the facts that, for years, during the war the public expenditures amounted to two millions daily; that the industry of the country was largely turned from its usual channels to the purposes of military service; that the agents of Government were in the market, purchasing to the extent of nearly a million of dollars daily; that a million of laborers were withdrawn from the usual movements of productive industry; that this unusual condition of things opened the way for shrewd or adventurous men to make rapid and large fortunes, and to launch out in lavish expenditure; that in consequence, great excitement in business sprung up, business and prices became unsettled and irregular, and speculation ensued in almost every department of production and trade. There were heavy and continuous speculations in cotton, in coal, in iron, in provisions, in wool, and in almost every article largely consumed by the army or required by the Government. Some of these speculations were accompanied by combinations to raise and keep up prices. The people, in a few years, withdrew capital from the ordinary channels of investment to the amount of nearly three thousand millions of dollars, much of which would otherwise have been employed in aid of domestic production. Taxation followed; taxation so heavy as to act directly and adversely upon the cost of living and the profits of labor.

The influence of these, and many other similar events, acted strongly upon prices. The withdrawal of labor from all occupations requiring the effective labor of man, largely increased the price of coal, iron, lumber, and numberless other things; and as these things went up, those who had to pay advanced rates began to increase the price of their own products, and that general advance took place, which always attends the excitement, irregularity and extraordinary consumption of a protracted war.

During the progress of the war, it was not difficult for observing men to see, or rather, it was almost impossible not to see the causes which were constantly producing great fluctuations in prices; but, on the whole, increasing them. These influences were the subject of constant discussion, and no one could be blind to the fact that they were of many kinds: partial, general, local, temporary, and lasting. They referred to production and trade, to merchants and speculators, to the absorption of labor and the anomalies of war. These influences were so great, so much spoken of, and so much concerned the interests of everybody, that it is strange they can now be lost sight of, when high prices are the subject of complaint.

Many intelligent persons, however, unhesitatingly and without qualification, ascribe present high prices to expansion of the currency. If this opinion could be indulged, without evil consequences, it might go unchallenged, in preference to attempting to set it right by the difficult task of proving a negative. It is, however, too serious a mistake to go unnoticed. No man can show any specific effect of expansion upon prices; the disposition to account for an advance of prices by referring it to that cause, doubtless results, in part, from the ease with which this complicated matter can be disposed of by this method.

As a multitude of causes undeniably contributed to the result, it cannot be safe to attribute the advance to any one of these, for the purpose of avoiding all further analysis and investigation. No safe opinion as to the effect of the expansion upon prices, during and since the war, can be given, unless by some one competent to detect and estimate the chief influences operating upon prices in that period. Whoever has done this is in a condition to inquire into the effect of expansion. The facts first — the theory afterwards. Still, however, the inquirer should, for this purpose, not only keep in view the doctrine of currency, but study the history of expansions. Our case is not like such cases as the Mississippi scheme of Law, the assignats of France, the issues of paper currency in our Revolutionary war, or in our Provincial history preceding that war. The question of prices and currency meet us now in such a complication of facts and events, and in such magnitude of proportions, and with such momentous consequences depending, that no care can be too great and no discrimination can be too wise to do justice to the solution.

In the face of these considerations, which cannot be without weight, we should be cautious in attributing the advance to the simple influence of expansion.

This convenient mode of disposing of the question of a general advance of prices, is founded upon a theory which has prevailed, for a century, among a class of writers more addicted to abstractions than acquainted with the actual processes of trade and industry. Montesquieu, in his *Spirit of Laws*, gave this theory the support of his name and the benefit of the circulation of his popular work. He announced, in the 7th chapter and 22d book, that prices were always in exact proportion to the quantity of money in a country. He stated it as a mathematical adjustment. This simple and neat, but utterly absurd proposition, has been asserted as a truth not to be questioned by scores of writers since his day. A controversy arose in England, during the suspension of specie payments, in which the question of whether gold had risen or the currency had depreciated, was one of the questions agitated. The practical men, the bankers and merchants, and men of business, held that gold had risen in price; the gentlemen of study, the theorists and the champions of the nobility, held that the currency had depreciated. The position that gold had advanced in price was maintained with signal ability, backed by great commercial knowledge and financial experience.

A writer of the commercial class finally entered the field, with a determination of reviewing the whole question and of sifting all the facts accessible, to the bottom, and, if possible, of reaching a sound and final conclusion. When his work had reached four volumes, it was regarded as unanswerable. He traced the whole subject back for two centuries, and brought together a mass of facts, which proved, beyond cavil, that prices are not specially controlled by the quantity of currency, and that all commodities have, beside, many general influences which govern their prices, many belonging to each which affect and control their market rates, and that the quantity is only one of these and not the most potent. †

European experience and attentive observation of our own financial and commercial history, lead to the conclusion that Montesquieu, and all the writers who have followed him, are in error, and that the general prices of a country are not mainly, nor even considerably affected by the quantity of currency.

The fact that our currency was not regarded as depreciated in proportion to the advance in gold, is shown by this, that there has been no time, since the expansion of the currency, when hundreds of millions of dollars worth of our most productive real estate could not have been purchased with it, at prices not different from those of 1860. The voice of the nation was that gold had advanced; and that the currency had not depreciated according to the quoted premium upon gold; at the very time when the premium on gold was at its highest, and when some deemed the currency to have depreciated some 60 or more percent, it would have commanded real estate on the terms stated above. According to this theory, those who accepted currency for old debts received only about fifty percent of their debts. Yet, banks and bankers are supposed to know the value of currency, even if the holders of real estate did not, and were among those who received the sums due them in this depreciated currency, and this not merely in legal tender notes, though these were preferred, but in the notes of State banks of unquestioned solvency.

The idea that the currency of this country has thus depreciated, is a dangerous error; it confuses the minds of men in public life, as well as those connected with important commercial business; it may influence legislation and questions of national finance greatly to the public detriment. Before it can be safely decided that the currency has depreciated, it must be determined whether gold has not

---

† The author was Thomas Tooke, a London merchant, whose *History of Prices* has now reached six volumes, octavo.

This elaborate work of a practical man should be carefully consulted by those desirous of being well informed upon the subject of the influence of currency upon prices. He sustains himself at every step by incontestable facts.

advanced. In the language of trade and business, gold began to rise in price and continued to advance before anything occurred upon which to found an assertion that the currency had depreciated. Gold not only advanced in price, but it is well known that it carried up with it, not only the price of imported goods, but a large class of others. A current reason for increase of prices was the advance of gold. It was, in this way, one of the elements in the general advance of prices at the beginning of the war. But the other elements operating upon prices, soon became more influential than gold, or anything pertaining to it. The general prices continued to go up, whilst gold had a great fall, and remains down. It is incumbent on those who deny the local advance in the price of gold to explain the phenomena of its fall. If this is to be explained as an appreciation of the paper currency, then we should be informed what cause produced this great rise of the currency, which still preserved about the same relation to prices as before the decline of gold.

The doctrine that our currency is not only depreciated, but that its depreciation is to be measured by the high prices and the premium on gold, and that the whole disorder is due to the expansion of the currency, is of not less financial danger. If it be admitted that the currency is unduly expanded, the conclusion very naturally follows that contraction of the currency is the remedy. In the present case, several serious fallacies are involved in favoring this often fatal remedy.

One is, that the assertion of undue expansion is a mistake. No undue expansion has existed since 1860; none dangerous to the currency or to our national finances; none which, of itself, produced any considerable advance in prices. The rise of prices was plainly attributable to causes well understood and constantly remarked upon as the prices advanced. The actual effect of these various causes should be carefully ascertained and considered before any safe conclusion can be drawn as to the effect of an undue expansion, even if any existed. It is obvious that high prices had more influence in creating expansion than expansion had to do in advancing prices.

It would not be difficult to show that we are not now employing more currency, in proportion to the present business of the country, all things considered, than was used before the war, and that the actual increase was, in a large degree, a financial necessity. The general rise in prices, due to other causes than expansion of one hundred percent, demands double the amount of currency. The limited use of individual paper makes it necessary to employ more currency. The payment into the Public Treasury, on account of Internal Revenue, absorbs an average sum, weekly, of about five millions of dollars, which experiences a detention, on the average, of a month or more before it is returned to the channels of circulation. Besides this, the movement of all the taxes commodities and taxed persons demands a very large increase of currency.†

All things considered, the business of this country is now being carried on with as little undue expansion of the currency as it has been any time of activity these thirty years. There are special features of this business which require the attention of Government, but expansion is not one of our dangers. It is to be hoped that this apprehension will not withdraw attention from subjects of greater

---

† The following statement of the quantity of currency in circulation in France, Great Britain and Ireland, and in the United States, is taken from a letter of Henry C. Carey, to the Secretary of the Treasury, just from press:

"Seven years since the coin in use in France was estimated at 4,880,000,000 francs, or more than $900,000,000. Since then the quantity must have increased, the substitution of the convenient gold for the heavy and cumbrous silver coins that even then were still so generally in use having, as has been stated by a recent writer, had the effect of placing napoleons in pockets that before could carry only francs. Admitting, however, that the increase has been sufficient only to add to the coin in the hands of the public as much as before had been in the bank vaults,

We have a hard money circulation of $900,000,000*
To this must now be added 'paper money' circulation,
which may be taken at about 170,000,000**
Giving a grand total of $1,070,000,000
Or nearly $30 per head.

"The coin actually in use in Great Britain and Ireland was estimated a

---

* From 1850 to 1865 the importations of the precious metals were in excess of the exportations to the extent of $334,000. The quantity held in 1852 was estimated by M. du Puynode at 3,500,000,000, or nearly $700,000,000.

** The amount in 1853 was only 395,000,000 francs. From that time it had grown with great steadiness until, in 1862, it had attained the figure of 869,000,000. In 1864 it was 804,000,000.

moment. Our currency, kept within its present limits, is not of the kind which bursts like a bubble, or goes down with a collapse. The expansion of individual credit, followed by issues of individual paper, to an extent beyond the proper limits of business, such as proceeds from extensive speculation, is dangerous, though in such cases as in this case, the advance preceded the expansion. But, for more than four years there has been no such expansion of personal credit. There is probably, at this time, not one-fourth of the amount of individual notes and bills of exchange afloat that was extant in 1860. As public and private credit now stand, there is no danger of collapse, unless the currency shall be contracted.

The high prices are a sore inconvenience, but, like the public debt, they are a legacy of the war, which, by its urgent demands upon certain departments of industry, its disturbing influence upon the labor of the country, its vast absorption of laborers, and its

---

few years since at £60,000,000. Since then it must greatly have increased, but, claiming no allowances on that account, I put it here at the same figure, being the equivalent of only $300,000,000

"The 'paper money' circulation of the past few years has varied between 37.5 and 42.5 millions. Taking the mean of these quantities we have the equivalent of about 200,000,000

"To this must now be added a paper circulation of a character scarcely at all known in this country, to wit, the promises of individuals, in the form of bills of exchange, to deliver money at a future day. Of these large quantities are in constant circulation, returning finally to their payers covered with indorsements, sometimes 15, 20, and even more in number, and having throughout the whole period of their existence performed all the service that here is performed by bank notes. The whole quantity of bills of exchange outstanding at any given time was estimated, some years since, at £200,000,000, and must now be greatly larger. Allowing here but one-fifth of that sum to be used for purposes of circulation, we have the equivalent of 200,000,000

Giving a grand total of $700,000,000
Or but little less than $25 per head.

"The actual circulation of the Union, as just now furnished by the Comptroller, we know to be $460,000,000, being $12.50 per head, or one-half of that of Great Britain and Ireland."

constant interference with the regular processes of civil life, has produced them. But neither these prices nor the industrial, nor commercial condition of the country, bear any resemblance to the broken-down currency of the Confederates, nor to the state of things when our Continental currency collapsed. This was recognized by the people, in both cases, as they quoted and looked upon their currency as depreciated and depreciating. In popular estimation our currency has only been regarded as depreciated when compared with gold. It must be very hard to believe that our whole currency was, and is, changing in value, up and down, every day, and every hour of the day, for some two or three years.

Neither the popular voice, nor the popular feeling, at this time, regard the currency as seriously depreciated. Every business man, now, is ready to state many potent reasons for the advance of prices, without thought of depreciation.

Not the least important topic of this subject remains a question, without solution, of which it is vain to attempt reaching any safe conclusion. That is: To what extent has the price of gold advanced in the United States? There are many who hold that gold cannot advance in price, and that it is the other currency that is falling when gold seems to be rising.

But merchants who are in a position to learn anything of the movements of bullion, know that both gold and silver vary in price. Coinage only marks and weighs them; they remain still commodities of trade. Legal tender laws and regulations of Governments, intended to fix, permanently, the value or price of gold and silver, disturb the fluctuations of price, and raise questions which the astutest minds often fail to solve, and which have to be remitted to bankers and merchants, whose daily experience teaches them that the precious metals cannot be deprived, by mints or by public authority, of their character of commodities, nor of their tendency to fluctuate in price as such. Whoever will form a safe opinion of our national finances and of our public currency, must first know that gold and silver vary in price in circumstances which affect the demand for them, and then must determine to what extent the present price of gold is an actual advance, and to what extent it may indicate a depreciation of currency.

Without going into the inquiry here, further than thus to refer to it, I assume that gold has risen in price very nearly, if not altogether, to the extent exhibited by the quotations, and that the fluctuations, monthly, weekly, daily, and from hour to hour, are variations of the price of gold, and not indications of a varying value in the entire mass of currency. It surely requires more credulity to believe that the mass of our currency is changing value several times daily or hourly, than to believe that the comparatively small amount of gold in the market is thus changing.

To some it may seem unintelligible that a local advance in the price of gold could take place. But local differences in price, even in articles so easy of transportation as gold, are not uncommon. Nor is the local advance here to be marvelled at, if we remember that a million and a half in gold is required, weekly, for payment of Customs, and that no bank pays gold on demand, that there is none in general circulation, and that those who have duties to pay must purchase it from those who keep it to sell, and that the Government, which receives the gold for duties, must withhold from circulation, from six months to six months, sufficient to pay the interest on the gold-bearing bonds.

Whether the speculation, by which gold was advanced at one time to a premium of nearly 200 percent, could have been checked or prevented by proper financial measures, is a question which may be allowed to rest for the present. It was, and is, the most stupendous, mere speculation, that the history of commerce records; the values involved, the numbers and wealth of those by whom it was sustained, and the vaster number of people and interests which were drawn into its support as it progressed, leave it without a rival in magnitude or importance. But to treat this vast commercial and financial movement as the mere result of the expansion of the currency, is an error in public finance not less vast, and fraught with evil consequences far more momentous.

If the fact is, that gold has advanced in price, and has for two years been rapidly fluctuating to the financial damage of the public Treasury and to the complete derangement and disturbance of business, effective measures should be taken to bring down the premium upon gold. But this could not be done rapidly, without the greatest caution. Millions of contracts and interests are involved in this rate of gold, besides those which are concerned directly in upholding the speculation. The extent to which the present rate of gold is carried into all the ramifications of commerce and industry, is beyond any estimate. The evil, great as it may be, is immeasurably less than any mistakes or ill-considered efforts to reduce it. Every merchant who has paid gold duties, every holder or dealer in domestic commodities, every one who must sell stocks, personal or real estate, and finally among innumerable others, every holder of gold-bearing bonds of the United States; all these would be more or less damaged by any vigorous attempt to reduce the price of gold by contraction.

If the fact is, however, on the other alternative, that the high rate of gold only marks the depth of the depreciation of the mass of the currency, then the remedial measures will be directed toward increasing the value of the currency. But here also is a difficulty. If expansion is the cause of the evils to be removed, it must not be overlooked that it has been coming upon us for several years, and the whole frame and network of business is interwoven with it, and not by any fault of the people. The expansion has arisen from the events of the war, from the change in our banking system, and from the vastness of our public loans. It reaches and touches everybody, and every interest of domestic commerce and industry. Men could no more keep out of it, than they could out of the air they breathed. Any violent hand laid suddenly upon this structure, might inflict heavy pecuniary loss upon millions and utter ruin upon multitudes. When the fabric of credit is shaken, the mischief spreads like an epidemic in a poisoned atmosphere.

The usual remedy proposed for an expanded currency and high prices, is contraction. The meaning of this term can be understood only by those who have been in business in this country long enough to have experienced the working of a bank contraction, under our late banking system.

Contraction of currency, if too rapidly effected, means that those who have merely accomodated themselves to the state of things around them, must suffer severely in mind, body and estate, for such acquiescence; it means, that those who have purchased goods at current prices to sell again, must suffer a loss; that those, who in the regular course of business have undertaken to make payments, must fail to pay and be crushed; it means interest at from one to two or more percent monthly; it means a great check to productive industry; it means laborers out of employment; and mills and machinery standing still; it means, by the fall of prices, and the cessation of industry, a loss to individuals and the country, of more than would in the aggregate cover several years of the Internal Revenue. It is a mode of redress more to be dreaded than expansion itself. Its harvest is insolvency. The country either cannot pay the Internal Revenue under the process of contraction, or only pay by enormous sacrifices.

The evils of a contraction, it is true, depend upon the manner in which it is conducted, the skill exercised, and the time taken to accomplish it. For years after the suspension of specie payments in England, the outcry about the high prices, the depreciation of the currency, and the evils of expansion, became so strong as to compel special Parliamentary inquiry, which resulted in the celebrated Bullion Report of 1810. This Report asserted the depreciation of the currency, and recommended an early return to specie payments. Although a majority in Parliament held to the doctrine of that Report, and believed in the efficacy of contraction, it did not venture upon such a measure of contraction, as brought about specie payments in full before 1822. No doubt a resumption might have been reached sooner, but abundant caution prevailed over the strong party of Bullionists, who never ceased their efforts for resumption at any cost. As it was, the resumption did not take place without disaster, widespread not only in England, but which reached this country.

Even with the reduced amount of individual notes now being issued, it is very far within bounds to say, that payments amounting to fifty thousand millions are maturing every year in this country, of which ten thousand millions run off every three months, or upwards of a hundred millions daily. These engagements were made with reference to the currency, as it was at the time of incurring the debt, for if men delayed their business transactions, to wait the result of political movements or public financial measures, people would starve or go into rags. Manufacturers and merchants, wholesale and retail, accomodate themselves to the state of the currency. They must go with the current, whether the stream is high or low, muddy or clear. If a contraction were so enforced as to reduce prices ten percent in three months, it would inflict a loss upon the holders of goods of not less than a hundred millions on three months' supply; it would disable a vast number from procuring the currency to meet their payments, whilst those that failed would be the cause of failure to others depending on them. Interest would rise under such an operation to disastrous rates. But this picture need not be finished. Violent contraction equals the devastation of war.

The recovery from a contraction, with safety to those who are involved in it, is necessarily by the slow process of working through engagements to the amount of thousands of millions, by selling property to an equal amount in a falling market.

There is a feature in the contraction of currency now favored by some in theory, and by others whose interest it is to force prices down, that deserves a moment's thought, if those who believe that the price of gold denotes its advance and not a depreciation of the currency, are even partially right. If gold had not been acted upon by special combinations, and had not been subjected to special and increased demand, and had remained now at its normal price, with reference to other commodities, the object of contraction would be clearly to raise the currency to par with gold, and reduce the prices correspondingly of other commodities.

But if gold, on account of speculation and other special fluences, now stands at an actual advance of 40 percent above its normal rate, then it will purchase other commodities at that much advantage over what it will do at its normal rates. If the process of contracting the currency reduces the general prices of commodities, then gold will purchase other articles at still greater advantage, and the difference in price between gold and other commodities, will be increased and not lessened. That is an effect the opposite of what is proposed by contraction.

Those who are conversant with the ordinary progress of the internal trade of the country, know that the prices of domestic commodities are agreed upon by merchants, dealers, manufacturers, and farmers, in their negotiations with each other, according to cost and all the unlimited combination of circumstances which unite to form market values, and all the varied influences, hopes, fears, and wishes, which they can bring to bear on each other. These prices once fixed, the aggregate of transactions is expressed in the notes or bills given by purchasers. The prices must be made, of course, before notes are given. The individual paper thus given, expresses the value of commodities moving in the domestic trade, at the prices fixed by the parties to that trade. The prices are not fixed with any reference to the amount of currency in the banks, in their pockets, or in circulation, but mainly with reference to the state of markets and to business considerations connected with selling and reselling and the profits to be realized.

The paper thus given passes into the banks, is discounted and becomes currency, in the shape of bank notes or deposits. Just that much currency is needed to pay these notes, and the banks will take in payment of these notes the same currency they gave for them, that is, bank notes and bank deposits. There is in all this a constant increase of currency, but no expansion, because the demand for currency to pay these notes, absorbs the whole. The circulation thus issued, performs the office of aiding in all the retail operations pertaining to the distribution for consumption of the whole mass of commodities, the value of which was represented by this discounted paper.

This is a slight indication of the ordinary way in which prices are fixed and currency created. It is sometimes the case, according to this mode of proceeding, that owing to great activity in business, currency is doubled; at other times, owing to dullness of business, the currency falls greatly below the average. In all cases, however, the prices are fixed before the currency issues. The demand for currency is in proportion to the business which has been done.

The vast proportions of the war, the immense expenditure of the Government, and the issue of Treasury notes in large sums, greatly disturbed this ordinary mode of proceeding between the banks and men of business. The agents of Government appeared in the markets as purchasers of army supplies, of food, clothing, and equipments. These purchases, on a scale so vast, raised prices rapidly, and as these purchases continued for several years, they continued to advance, by a law of prices which never fails in its operation. A continued effective demand always increases prices. In this case, however, as in the other, the currency was not issued until after the prices were fixed. There was abundant cause for the advance, without attributing it nakedly to the issues of the Treasury.

Prices would have gone up largely, if the currency had been gold; war always increases the prices of the ordinary necessaries of life, as well as of mere military equipments. No doubt the issue of notes for circulation as a currency by the Treasury, was out of the usual course of proceeding, and unlike the ordinary practice of banks, and that it tended to disturbance in the channels of trade and industry. The Government in issuing notes acted as an individual; it went into the market to make large purchases, and it gave its own notes, which, because they were preferred to those of the banks, went immediately into circulation as currency. The regular course of business was thus greatly changed. The Treasury currency soon largely supplanted that of bank notes, which, being absorbed by payments to the banks, was not reissued. It is well remembered that the bank circulation disappeared before that of the Treasury. This shows that the tendency of the currency was not to indefinite increase. The banks employed the Treasury notes in place of their own. The amount at no time reached that state of expansion which denotes depreciation. It of course increased according to the advance of prices. And whilst in ordinary times, large stocks of commodities are stored in private warehouses, to meet the gradual progress of trade and consumption, in time of war vast quantities of commodities are purchased, paid for, and go into Government warehouses. This involved doubtless a considerable increase of currency. The tendency of this was towards undue expansion, but it was soon checked by internal taxation, which absorbed the issues of the Government, at the rate of over half a million of dollars daily, and by the funding of the indebtedness of the Government, which absorbed one or two millions daily. Now, though the currency absorbed in both cases was reissued, the operations of the Government in both cases required constantly a large sum of currency merely to carry them on. The separate business of the Treasury for civil, military, and naval service, and for the receipt and expenditures for account of Internal Revenue, involved a constant use of currency, of not less than two hundred millions.

Thus the tendency to expansion was effectually overcome. Many times during the war, when the issues of the Treasury were at a very high point, the want of currency for the usual transaction of business was such, that it was sought from one city to another among the banks, without obtaining the needful supplies.

There has been, then, no undue expansion since the war began; no injurious expansion exists now. When it is considered how much currency must have been actually required for the purposes of the Government, and how much for the people, no evidence of expansion can be found but the high prices, and when these are duly examined, it will be seen that other reasons for the advance are sufficient to account for the whole movement. Taking every chief commodity, it can be shown that its advance was owing to special causes, having little, if any, relation to the quantity of the currency.

In accounting for the rise of prices, one general cause should not be overlooked, which operates in all cases of protracted wars. Business is disturbed in its usual progress, a feverish uncertainty prevails, the prices of many things go up under the strong demands of Government, prices become generally unsettled, and the efforts of shrewd holders of goods are soon successful in raising their rates. The war and the general disturbance of business are the levers used to raise prices, but find abundant assistance, special and accidental.

It may illustrate the variety and potency of the causes which operate upon prices, to state that the scarcity of certain goods in New York, at the opening of the fall trade of 1865, was such that merchants of that city besieged the Eastern manufacturers, and begged to have their orders filled, at greatly advanced rates. Of course these manufacturers advanced the rates. The prices were, in fact, fixed by competition of purchasers. The makers of the goods regretted the sudden and large advance, as likely to recoil upon the demand and damage their business. This has occurred in some departments already, as they anticipated. Regular sales and steady prices are the great boon of domestic industry . . . .

Mathew Carey

(1760 - 1839)

Addresses of the Philadelphia Society for the Promotion of National Industry

Addresses of the Philadelphia Society for the Promotion of National Industry

This entire series of addresses by Mathew Carey, delivered during 1819, was devoted to attacking Adam Smith's Wealth of Nations and to defending the American System as enunciated by Alexander Hamilton. The "Addresses of the Philadelphia Society," which are excerpted here, were effective in keeping the United States committed to Hamilton's economic policy until Andrew Jackson's reelection in 1828.

I

Philadelphia, March 27, 1819

Friends and Fellow Citizens,

The Philadelphia Society for the Promotion of National Industry, respectfully solicit your attention to a few brief essays on topics of vital importance to your country, yourselves, and your posterity. They shall be addressed to your reason and understanding, without any attempt to bias your feelings by declamation.

Political economy shall be the subject of these essays. In its broad and liberal sense, it may be fairly styled the science of promoting human happiness; than which a more noble subject cannot occupy the attention of men endowed with enlarged minds, or inspired by public spirit.

It is to be regretted that this sublime science has not had adequate attention bestowed on it in this country. And unfortunately, so many contradictory systems are in existence, that statesmen and legislators, disposed to discharge their duty conscientiously, and for that purpose to study the subject, are liable to be confused and distracted by the unceasing discordance in the views of the writers.

It is happily, nevertheless, true, that its leading principles, which safely conduct to the important and beneficent results, that are its ultimate object, are plain and clear; and, to be distinctly comprehended, and faithfully carried into effect, require no higher endowments than good sound sense and rectitude of intention.

It is a melancholy feature in human affairs, that imprudence and error often produce as copious a harvest of wretchedness as absolute wickedness. Hence arises the imperious necessity, in a country where so many of our citizens may aspire to the character of legislators and statesmen, of a more general study of this science, a thorough knowledge of which is so essential a requisite, among the qualifications for those important stations.

To remove all doubt on this point, we shall adduce, in the course of these essays, instances in which single errors of negotiators and legislators have entailed full as much, and in many cases more misery on nations, than the wild and destructive ambition of conquerors. Unless in some extraordinary instances, a sound policy, on the restoration of peace, heals the wounds inflicted by war, and restores a nation to its pristine state of ease and comfort. But numerous cases are on record, wherein an article of a treaty, of ten or a dozen lines, or an impolitic or an unjust law, has germinated into the most ruinous consequences for a century.

It is our intention,

1. To review the policy of some of those nations which have enjoyed a high degree of prosperity, with or without any extraordinary advantages from nature; and likewise of those whose prosperity had been blasted by fatuitous counsels, notwithstanding great natural blessings;

2. To examine the actual situation of our country, in order to ascertain whether we enjoy the advantages to which our happy form of government and local situation entitle us; and, if we do not, to investigate the causes to which the failure is owing;

3. To develop the true principles of political economy, suited to our situation and circumstances, and calculated to produce the greatest sum of happiness throughout the wide expanse of our territory.

In this arduous undertaking, we request a patient and candid hearing from our fellow-citizens. We fondly hope for success; but if disappointed, we shall have the consolation of having endeavoured to discharge a duty every good citizen owes to the country which protects him; the duty of contributing his efforts to advance its interest and happiness.

As a preliminary step, we propose to establish the utter fallacy of some maxims, supported by the authority of the name of Adam Smith, author of *The Wealth of Nations,* but pregnant with certain ruin to any nation by which they may be carried into operation. This course is prescribed to us by the circumstance, that the influence of these maxims has been sensibly felt in our councils and has deeply affected our prosperity.

This writer stands so pre-eminent in the estimation of a large portion of Christendom, as the delphic Oracle of political economy, and there is such a magic in his name, that it requires great hardihood to encounter him, and a high degree of good fortune to obtain a fair and patient hearing for the discussion.

But at this enlightened period we trust our citizens will scorn to surrender their reason into the guidance of any authority whatever. When a position is presented to the mind, the question ought to be, not who delivered it, but what is its nature? and, how is it supported by reason and common sense, and especially by fact? A theory, how plausible soever, and however propped up by a bead-roll of great names, ought to be regarded with suspicion, if unsupported by fact — but if contrary to established fact, it ought to be unhesitatingly rejected. This course of procedure is strongly recommended by the decisive fact, that, in the long catalogue of wild, ridiculous and absurd theories on morals, religion, politics, or science, which have had their reign among mankind, there is hardly one that has not reckoned among its partisans, men of the highest celebrity.† And in the present instance, the most cogent and conclusive facts bear testimony against the political economist, great as is his reputation.

We hope, therefore, that our readers will bring to this discussion, minds wholly liberated from the fascination of the name

---

† Montesquieu, whose reputation was as great as that of Dr. Smith, and whose *Spirit of Laws* has had as extensive a currency as the *Wealth of Nations,* held the absurd idea, which remained uncontroverted for half a century, that the habits, manners and customs, and even the virtues and vices of nations, were in a great measure governed by climate, whence it would result that a tolerable idea might be formed of those important features of national character, by consulting maps, and ascertaining latitudes and longitudes. Bacon studied judicial astrology! All the great men of his days believed in magic and witchcraft! Johnson had full faith in the story of the Cocklane-Ghost! So much for great names.

of the writer whose opinions we undertake to combat, and a determination to weigh the evidence in the scales of reason, not those of prejudice.

In order to render Dr. Smith full justice, and to remove all ground for cavil, we state his propositions at length, and in his own language.

"To give the monopoly of the home market to the produce of domestic industry, in any particular art or manufacture, is in some measure to direct private people in what manner they ought to employ their capitals; and must, in almost all cases, be either a useless or a hurtful regulation. If the domestic produce can be brought there as cheap as that of foreign industry, the regulation is evidently useless. If it cannot, it must generally be hurtful.

"It is the maxim of every prudent master of a family, never to attempt to make at home what it will cost him more to make than to buy. The tailor does not attempt to make his own shoes, but buys them of the shoemaker. The shoemaker does not attempt to make his own clothes, but employs a taylor. The farmer neither attempts to make one nor the other, but employs those different artificers. All of them find it for their interest to employ their whole industry in a way in which they have some advantage over their neighbours; and to purchase, with a part of its produce, or, what is the same thing, with the price of a part of it, whatever else they have occasion for.

"That which is prudence in the conduct of every private family, can scarcely be folly in that of a great kingdom. If a foreign country can supply us with a commodity cheaper than we ourselves can make it, better buy it from them, with some part of the produce of our country, employed in a way in which we have some advantage.

"The general industry of the country being in proportion to the capital which employs it, will not thereby be diminished, any more than that of the above-mentioned artificers; but only left to find out the way in which it can be employed with the greatest advantage. It is not so employed, when directed to an object which it can buy cheaper than it can make. The value of its annual produce is certainly more or less diminished, when it is thus turned away from producing commodities evidently of more value than the commodity which it is directed to produce. According to the supposition, that commodity could be purchased from foreign countries cheaper than it can be made at home. It could, therefore have been purchased with part only of the commodities, or, what is the same thing, with a part only of the price of the commodities, which the industry employed by an equal capital would have produced at home, had it been left to pursue its natural course."†

There is in the subordinate parts of this passage much sophistry and unsound reasoning, which we may examine on a future occasion; and there is likewise, as in all the rest of the doctor's work, a large proportion of verbiage, which is admirably calculated to embarrass and confound common understandings, and prevent their forming a correct decision. But, stripped of this verbiage, and brought naked and unsophisticated to the eye of reason, the main proposition which we at present combat, and to which we here confine ourselves, is, that,

"If a foreign country can supply us with a commodity cheaper than we ourselves can make it, better buy of them, with some part of the produce of our own industry, employed in a way in which we have some advantage."

The only rational mode of testing the correctness of any maxim or principle is, to examine what have been its effects where it has been carried into operation, and what would be its effects in any given case where it might be applied. This is the plan we shall pursue in this investigation.

Great Britain affords a felicitous instance for our purpose. Let us examine what effect the adoption of this maxim would produce on her happiness and prosperity.

There are above a million of people, of both sexes and of all ages, employed in that country, in the woollen and cotton manufactures.‡ By their industry in these branches, they make for themselves and families a comfortable subsistence. They afford a large and steady market for the productions of the earth, giving support to, probably, at least a million of persons engaged in agriculture; and moreover, enrich the nation by bringing into it wealth from nearly all parts of the earth. The immense sums of money they thus intro-

† Wealth of Nations, Vol. I, p. 319.

‡ Dr. Seybert states, that in 1809, there were 800,000 persons in Great Britain engaged in the cotton manufacture alone. It has since increased considerably. It is, therefore, probable that the two branches employ at least 1,300,000 persons. — *Statistics*, p. 92.

duce into their native country afford means of employment, and ensure happiness to millions of other subjects — and thus, like the circles made on the surface of the stream by the central pebble thrown in, the range of happiness is extended so wide as to embrace the whole community.

From this cheering prospect, let us turn the startled eye to the masses of misery, which Dr. Smith's system would produce; and we shall then behold a hideous contrast, which, we trust, escaped the doctor's attention; for the acknowledged goodness and benevolence of his character, will not allow us to believe that he would have been the apostle of such a pernicious doctrine, had he attended to its results. We fondly hope, that, like many other visionary men, he was so deeply engaged in the fabrication of a refined theory, that he did not arrest his progress to weigh its awful consequences.

The East Indies could at all times, until the recent improvements in machinery, have furnished cotton goods at a lower rate than they could be manufactured in England, which had no other means of protecting her domestic industry, but by a total prohibition of the rival fabrics. Let us suppose that France, where labour and expenses are much lower than in England, has possessed herself of machinery, and is thus enabled to sell woollen goods at half, or three-fourths, or seven-eighths of the price of the English rival commodities. Suppose, further, that articles manufactured of leather are procurable in South America, and iron wares in Sweden, below the rates in England. Then, if the statesmen of the last nation were disciples of Adam Smith, as "foreign countries can supply them with those commodities cheaper than they themselves can make them," they must, according to the doctor, "buy from them with some part of the produce of their own country," and accordingly open their ports freely to those various articles, from these four particular nations. Who can contemplate the result without horror? What a wide spread scene of ruin and desolation would take place? The wealth of the country would be swept away, to enrich foreign, and probably hostile nations, which might, at no distant period, make use of the riches and strength thus fatuitously placed in their hands, to enslave the people who had destroyed themselves by following such baneful counsels. The labouring and industrious classes would be at once bereft of employment; reduced to a degrading state of dependence and mendicity; and, through the force of misery and distress driven to prey upon each other, and upon the rest of the community. The middle classes of society would partake of the distress of the lower, and the sources of the revenues of the higher orders be dried up.† And all this terrific scene of wo, and wretchedness, and depravity, is to be produced for the grand purpose of procuring broad-cloth, and muslins, and shoes, and iron ware, in remote parts of the earth, a few shillings per yard, or piece, or pound, cheaper than at home! The manufacturers of Bombay, and Calcutta, and Paris, and Lyons, and Stockholm, are to be fed, and clothed, and fostered by English wealth, while those of England, whom it ought to nourish and protect, are expelled from their workshops, and driven to seek support from the overseers of the poor. We trust this will not be thought a fancy sketch! Such a view of it would be an extravagant error. It is sober, serious reality; and puts down for ever this plausible, but ruinous theory. Ponder well on it, fellow citizens.

Let us suppose another strong case. The cotton produced in this country, amounts, probably to 40 millions of dollars annually.‡ We will suppose the minimum of the price, at which it can be sold, to pay for the labour and interest on the capital employed in its culture, to be 12 cents per pound. We will further suppose, that the southern provinces of Spanish America have established their independence, and are able to supply us with this valuable raw material at the rate of ten cents. Ought we, for the sake of saving a few cents per pound, to destroy the prospects, and ruin the estates of nearly 800,000 inhabitants of the southern states — to paralize a culture so immensely advantageous, and producing so large a fund of wealth, and strength and happiness? Should we, for such a paltry consideration, run the risk of consequences which cannot be regarded without awe, and which could not fail eventually to involve in ruin, even those who might appear in the first instance to profit by the adoption of the system?

It may be well worth while to proceed a step further, and take the case of a nation able to supply us fully and completely with

---

† No small portion of this picture is rapidly realizing in this country.

‡ Tench Coxe.

wheat and other grain at a lower rate than our farmers can furnish them. Thus then we should find ourselves pursuing Adam Smith's sublime system; buying cheap bargains of wheat or flour from one nation, cotton from another, hardware from a third; and, to pursue the system throughout, woollen, and cotton, and linen goods from others; while our country was rapidly impoverishing of its wealth, its industry paralized, the labouring part of our citizens reduced to beggary, and the farmers, planters, and manufacturers, involved in one common mass of ruin. The picture demands the most sober, serious attention of the farmers and planters of the United States.

It may be asserted, that the supposition of our country being fully supplied with cotton and grain, by foreign nations, is so improbable, as not to be admissible even by way of argument. This is a most egregious error; our supposition, so far as it respects cotton, is in "the full tide of successful experiment." That article, to a great amount, is even at present imported from Bengal, and sold at a price so far below our own, (difference of quality considered) that our manufacturers find the purchase eligible. Let it be considered, that in 1789, doubts were entertained whether cotton could be cultivated in the United States;† that in the year 1794, there were exported from this country, of foreign and domestic cotton, only seven thousand bags;‡ and yet, that in 1818, the amount exported was above ninety-two millions of pounds. No man can be so far misled as to suppose that Heaven has given us any exclusive monopoly of the soil and climate calculated for such extraordinary and almost incredible advances. The rapid strides we have made, may be also made by other nations. Cotton is said to be shipped at Bombay for three pence sterling per pound; and therefore, setting South America wholly out of the question, it can hardly be doubted, from the spirit with which the culture of that plant is prosecuted in the East Indies, and the certainty that the seeds of our best species have been carried there, that in a few years that country will be able, provided Adam Smith's theory continues to be acted upon here, to expel our planters from their own markets, after having driven them from those of Europe. It is not, therefore,

† Seybert's *Statistics.*

‡ Ibid., p. 94.

hazarding much to assert, that the time cannot be very remote, when southern cotton industry will be compelled to supplicate Congress for that legislative protection, for which the manufacturing industry of the rest of the union has so earnestly implored that body in vain; and which, had it been adequately afforded, would have saved from ruin numerous manufacturing establishments, and invaluable machinery, which cost millions of dollars — now a dead and irreparable loss to the enterprising proprietors. Had these establishments been preserved, and duly protected, they would have greatly lessened our ruinously unfavourable balance of trade, and of course prevented that pernicious drain of specie, which has over-spread the face of our country with distress, and clouded (we trust only temporarily) as fair prospects as ever dawned on any nation.†

We have given a slight sketch of the effects the adoption of this system would produce in England and the United States, if carried into complete operation; and also glanced at the consequences its partial operation has already produced here. We now proceed to

---

† This view may appear too gloomy. Would to heaven it were! A cursory glance at some of the great interests of the United States will settle the question. Cotton, the chief staple of the country, is falling, and not likely to rise: as the immense quantities from the East Indies have glutted the English market, which regulates the price in ours. Affairs in the western country, on which so many of our importers depend are to the last degree unpromising. The importers, of course, have the most dreary and sickening prospects before them. They are deeply in debt, their resources almost altogether suspended, and a large proportion ultimately precarious. Commerce and navigation languish every where, except to the East Indies, the most ruinous branch we carry on. Further, notwithstanding nearly eight millions of specie were imported by the Bank of the U. States at a heavy expense, in about one year; so great has been the drain, that the banks are generally so slenderly provided, as to excite serious uneasiness. We are heavily indebted to England, after having remitted immense quantities of government and bank stock, whereby we shall be laid under a heavy and perpetual annual tax for interest. Our manufactures are in general drooping, and some of them are one-half or two-thirds suspended. Our cities present the distressing view of immense numbers of useful artisans, mechanics, and manufacturers, willing to work, but unable to procure employment. We might proceed with the picture to a great extent; but presume enough has been stated to satisfy the most incredulous, that the positions in the text are by no means exaggerated.

take a cursory view (reserving detail for a future occasion) of its lamentable results in Spain and Portugal, where the statesmen are disciples of Adam Smith, and where the theory which now goes under the sanction of his name has been in operation for centuries. As "foreign countries can supply them with commodities cheaper than they themselves can make them," they therefore consider it "better to buy from them, with some part of the produce of their own country."

Fellow citizens, consider the forlorn and desperate state of those countries, notwithstanding the choicest blessings of nature have been bestowed on them with lavish hand; industry paralized, and the enormous floods of wealth, drawn from their colonies, answering no other purpose but to foster and encourage the industry, and promote the happiness of rival nations; and all obviously and undeniably the result of the system of "*buying goods where they are to be had cheapest,*" to the neglect and destruction of their domestic industry. With such awful beacons before your eyes, can you contemplate the desolating effects of the system in those two countries, without deep regret, that so many of our citizens, and some of them in high and elevated stations, advocate its universal adoption here, and are so far enamoured of Dr. Smith's theory that they regard as a species of heresy the idea of appealing to any other authority, on the all-important and vital point of the political economy of nations!

To avoid prolixity, we are obliged to postpone the consideration of other positions of Dr. Smith on this subject; and shall conclude with a statement of those maxims of political economy, the soundness of which is established by the experience of the wisest as well as the most fatuitous nations of the earth.

1. Industry is the only sure foundation of national virtue, happiness, and greatness; and, in all its useful shapes and forms, has an imperious claim on governmental protection.

2. No nation ever prospered to the extent of which it was susceptible, without due protection of domestic industry.

3. Throughout the world, in all ages, wherever industry has been duly encouraged, mankind have been uniformly industrious.

4. Nations, like individuals, are in a career of ruin when their expenditures exceed their income.

5. Whenever nations are in this situation, it is the imperious

duty of their rulers to apply such remedies, to correct the evil, as the nature of the case may require.

6. There are few, if any, political evils, to which a wise legislature, untrammeled in its deliberations and decisions, cannot apply an adequate remedy.

7. The cases of Spain, Portugal, and Italy, prove beyond controversy, that no natural advantages, how great or abundant soever, will counteract the baleful effects of unsound systems of policy; and those of Venice, Genoa, Switzerland, Holland, and Scotland, equally prove, that no natural disadvantages are insuperable by sound policy.

8. Free government is not happiness. It is only the means, but, wisely employed, is the certain means of insuring happiness.

9. The interests of agriculture, manufactures, and commerce, are so inseparably connected, that any serious injury suffered by one of them must materially affect the others.

10. The home market for the productions of the earth and manufactures, is of more importance than all the foreign ones, even in countries which carry on an immense foreign commerce.

11. It is impossible for a nation, possessed of immense natural advantages, in endless diversity of soil and climate — in productions of inestimable value — in the energy and enterprize of its inhabitants — and unshackled by an oppressive debt — to suffer any great or general distress, in its agriculture, commerce, or manufactures, (war, famines, pestilence and calamities of seasons excepted) unless there be vital and radical errors in its system of political economy. . . .

VII

Philadelphia, May 20, 1819

On almost every subject of discussion, fellow-citizens, there are certain hacknied phrases, which pass current as oracular, and though extremely fallacious, are received with scarcely any investigation. There is probably no science that has been more distorted in this respect than that of political economy, on which so much of human happiness depends.

We propose, in the present number, to consider a maxim of this description, fraught with destruction to any nation by which it is adopted; but which is implicitly believed in by a large portion of our citizens, and has had considerable influence on the legislature of the union.

This specious maxim is, that

"Trade Will Regulate Itself,"

which in all probability, led to that refusal of adequate protection to the national industry, which has overspread the nation with distress — lowered the price of some of our chief staples, by depriving them of a domestic market — bankrupted so many of our merchants and traders — deprived so many thousands of our citizens of employment — and, in a word, reduced us from the most towering prospects to a most calamitous reverse.

It will be perceived that this is a vital part of Adam Smith's doctrine — indeed, the basis on which he has raised his great superstructure; and that we have already animadverted on it incidentally. But its immense influence on the fate of nations, and its most destructive tendency, demand a more minute investigation, to which we now solicit your attention.

How far its advocates deem it proper to have it carried, we are not quite certain. In its strict acceptation, it means a total exclusion of all regulations of commerce, so that the intercourse between nations should be as free as between different provinces of the same empire. In fact, if it does not mean this, it is difficult to define what it can mean; for it a government enacts any regulation whatever, it cannot with truth or justice be said, that *"trade regulates itself."* We shall, therefore, consider it in its upmost latitude, as excluding all regulations. The result, however, would not be materially affected by any modification, or restriction of its provisions, short of effectual protection of national industry. These would, as the case might be, only accelerate or procrastinate the final catastrophe, to which it infallibly leads.

This maxim ought to have been consigned to oblivion centuries since, by the consideration that no trading or commercial nation has ever prospered without, *"regulation of trade";* that those nations which have devoted the most scrupulous attention to its regulation, have been the most prosperous; and that in proportion as it has been neglected, just in the same proportion have nations gone to decay.

The cases of England, France, Spain, and Portugal, offer powerful illustrations of these positions. But we shall not rest satisfied with this mode of defence. We shall trace the operation of the maxim in its full extent.

As it would be nugatory to suppose that the existing regulations of commerce could, by any convention, be annulled, and its entire freedom be universally established, we shall merely suppose it adopted only by a portion of the commercial world, and see what would be its effects on those nations wherein it was carried into operation?

To form an accurate idea on this or any other subject, the safest and best mode is to state the case on a small scale, which the mind can readily embrace without distraction, and then to argue to the widest range to which the subject extends.

We will, therefore, here confine our view to two nations, France and Spain, and suppose that in the latter country the maxim we combat is carried into full operation, and trade is allowed *"to regulate itself"* — but that in the former, it is "regulated" by the government, for the protection and encouragement of national industry, after the example of Great Britain, and indeed almost every other country in Christendom.

In order to do the maxim justice, we will assume, that both nations are on a perfect equality in every other respect than the *"regulation of trade."* We will further assume that at the commencement of the rivalry between them, each nation possesses a circulating medium of 20,000,000 of dollars, and has 200,000 people employed in the cotton, and as many in the woollen manufacture, who produce annually four millions of yards of each kind of goods, which are exactly adquate to their consumption. To simplify the discussion, we confine ourselves to those two branches. But the reasoning will equally apply to every other species of manufactures.

4,000,000 yards of cotton goods, say at 50 cents $2,000,000
4,000,000 yards of woollen, at 6 dollars 24,000,000
                                                                                                                         —————————
                                                                                                                          26,000,000

On which they realize a profit of twelve and a
half percent $3,250,000

To the French manufacturers, according to our hypothesis, the home market is secured. All foreign competition is effectually cut off. They have, therefore, every encouragement to extend and improve their fabrics; and in the first year of rivalship, having a surplus on hand, they export, we will suppose, 400,000 yards of each kind to Spain, and increase the exportation annually an equal amount. This operation produces the treble effect of lowering the price of the Spanish goods by the competition; circumscribing their sale; and depriving, during the first year, about 40,000 people of employment.

It being our determination to afford as little room for objection, as possible, we will suppose the reduction of price to be only seven and half percent which is far less than is usual in such cases.† Let us see the situation of the parties at the end of the

First Year:

The French manufacturers gain in their domestic market, as before ..	3,250,000	Wheras, the Spanish manufacturers, whose sales are reduced to 3,600,000 yards of each kind, amounting to 23,400,000, gain at 5 percent only
And on 400,000 yards of each kind, sold in Spain, amounting to 2,600,000, at 5 percent	130,000	
	$3,380,000	.........$1,170,000‡

This is the operation in the very first year, producing a difference at once of about 2,300,000 dollars of actual profit against the infatuated nation, which allows *"trade to regulate itself,"* and, according to Adam Smith, buys where *"goods can be had the cheapest."* The second year commences with increased energy on the part of the French, and dismay and discouragement on that of the Spanish manufacturers. The former double their exportations,

---

† Instances have recently occurred of domestic goods being reduced at once ten, fifteen, and twenty percent in our markets, in consequence of great quantities of similar articles suddenly introduced from Europe.

‡ This view of the effect of the rivalry has, we apprehend, almost wholly escaped the notice of our political economists. When the prices of our manufactures are reduced in the home market by foreign competition, the reduction is *on the whole we offer for sale.* Whereas the reduction to the rival nation is only on such part of her's as she exports to us. The contest is therefore carried on at immense inequality.

and send 800,000 yards into the rival markets, amounting to $5,200,000, of which we trace the operation.

Second Year.

French profit as before, in the home market ... 3,250,000
And on 800,000 yards of each kind sold in Spain, amounting to 5,200,000, at 5 percent 260,000
$3,510,000

Wheras the sales of the Spaniards are reduced to 3,200,000 yards of each kind, amounting to 20,800,000, on which they gain at 5 percent ... $1,040,000

Third Year.

French profit as before, on the home market .. 3,250,000
They increase their exportation to 1,200,000 yards of each kind, amounting to 7,800,000, at 5 percent 390,000
$3,640,000

The Spaniards find their sales diminished to 2,800,000 yards, amounting to 18,200,000 whereon they realize a profit of 5 percent ....
$910,000

Fourth Year

French profit at home, as before 3,250,000
They increase their exportation to 1,600,000 yards of each kind, amounting to 10,400,000, which, at 5 percent affords a gain of 520,000
$3,770,000

The Spanish manufacturers are reduced to 2,400,000 yards of each kind, amounting to 15,600,000, on which, at 5 percent, they gain $780,000

It is, we trust, needless, to pursue the calculation any further. You can readily, fellow citizens, perceive that the contest must soon terminate. The Spanish manufacturers, oppressed, impoverished, and dispirited, would be soon driven from the market, which would be monopolized by the more sagacious nation, which, we repeat, had the good sense to *"regulate trade."* Their immense gains would be at the expense, and to the destruction, of the nation, which was deluded by the specious maxim to *"let trade regulate itself."* The successful rivals would soon indemnify themselves for the temporary reduction of price, by a proportionate advance in the future.

Let us compare the result of the four years operations on the two nations:

France.		Spain.	
First year's profit	3,380,000	First Year's profit	1,170,000
Second Year	3,510,000	Second Year	1,040,000
Third Year	3,640,000	Third Year	910,000
Fourth Year	3,770,000	Fourth Year	780,000
	$14,300,000		$3,900,000

EFFECT ON THE WORKING PEOPLE

France.	Spain.
Six hundred thousand people industriously employed, supporting themselves in comfort and happiness, and adding to the wealth and strength of the nation.†	Four hundred thousand people gradually thrown idle;—dragging on a wretched existence in mendicity; or looking in vain for those *"collateral branches"* which sound so harmoniously in Adam Smith, but which are not elsewhere to be found; or emigrating to France, to strengthen that nation at the expense of their own.

We have hitherto confined our calculations of the effects of this plausible but destructive system, to the manufacturers alone. Its pernicious consequences, if they extended no farther than to this class of citizens, would be sufficient to induce liberal minded men — those worthy to legislate for this rising empire, to abandon the maxim. But those consequences, how deplorable soever, are but as *"mere dust in the balance"* compared with its general effects on the wealth, strength, resources, power, and happiness of any devoted nation which enlists itself under the banners of Adam Smith.

In the first year France sells to Spain to the

amount of	$2,600,000
In the Second	5,200,000
In the Third	7,800,000
In the Fourth	10,400,000
	26,000,000

---

† It is obvious that by the transfer of the manufactures from Spain to France, for every workman reduced to idleness in the former country, there would be one additional employed in the latter. We have, therefore, in the text assumed 600,000, as the average number in France.

This is a debt which, in the first place, drains all the metallic medium, as far as the merchants can collect it; and next all the evidences of public debt, or whatever valuable articles can be had. And still a heavy and oppressive debt is accruing from year to year afterwards!

The result is easily seen. A prosperous nation, with a specie capital of $20,000,000, is by this simple process in four years reduced to a most abject, impoverished, and dependent state. Its wealth is drained away to support a foreign nation. Every species of industry is paralized. Ships rot at the wharves. Trade languishes. Merchants and traders, as well as manufacturers, become bankrupts. Artisans, mechanics, and labouring people, who had largely contributed to the welfare of the state, are transformed into mendicants, or driven to desperate courses to prolong their existence; and desolation extends itself over the face of the land.

This, fellow citizens, is very nearly our present case. It is true, we have not absolutely let *"trade regulate itself,"* by a total absence of all duties. The necessities of the Treasury, which by many members of Congress were freely admitted to be the leading, and by some to be the only object of a tariff,† forbade the adoption of the maxim in its fullest extent: and therefore our imported merchandize pays duty. But it is obvious that where the tariff of one nation is so wholly inefficient, that she can be completely undersold in her own markets by another, as the people of the United States are at present, the ultimate effect is actually the same, as if *"trade were allowed to regulate itself."* The duties imposed by our tariff have merely delayed, not averted, the work of destruction. But that it is as sure in its operation, is placed beyond the reach of doubt by the desolation and ruin that pervade so many invaluable manufacturing establishments throughout the union, on which millions of dollars have been expended, and whose fall, as we have so often repeated,

---

† We have already stated that Colonel John Taylor, a popular writer in Virginia, has taken the broad ground, that every dollar imposed as duty on foreign merchandize, is a dollar robbed out of the pockets of the agriculturalists! This maxim, admirably calculated to excite the selfish passions of one class of citizens against another, has unfortunately had too many proselytes in and out of Congress.

and must re-echo in the ears of those who alone have the power of applying a remedy, involved the ruin of the citizens engaged in them.

The most cursory reader must perceive, and no one possessed of candour can deny, that we have given the advocates of the maxim, *"let trade regulate itself,"* far more advantage in the argument than was necessary, or proper. When we stated the reduction of price at seven and a half percent and a gradual increase of exportation from France to Spain, of only ten percent of the amount originally manufactured in each country, we did our cause manifest injustice. We might have assumed at once a reduction of price not of seven and a half percent — but of ten or more — and an exportation of double the amount, which, combined, would produce the immediate ruin of the Spanish manufactures, of whose fabrics a large proportion would remain on hand, and the residue be sold at or below costs.— This is and has ever been the uniform operation of the system of letting *"trade regulate itself."*

A physician who found his patient in a raging fever, and let the disorder take its course, or *"regulate itself,"* would be deservedly reprobated as unworthy of his profession. But his conduct would not be more irrational than that of a statesman, who saw the agriculture, manufactures, trade, and commerce of his country going to decay, and let them *"regulate themselves."* Government is instituted to guard the interests of the nation confided to its care: and by whatever name it may be called, is no longer estimable than as it fulfills this sacred duty. It was painful to us to state in a former address — it is equally painful to us to repeat — but we must repeat the appalling truth, that our manufacturers, a large and important class, embracing some of the most valuable members of the community, must, with mixed sensations of regret and envy, regard the situation of the manufacturers of England, Denmark, France, Russia, Austria, and most other countries in Europe, who enjoy that protection from their governments which the former sought in vain from their fellow citizens and representatives, who are now themselves involved in the general distress resulting from the want of that protection.

We refer you, fellow citizens, to the plain, but impressive lesson afforded by the fable of the belly and the members. The latter starved the former to death — and perished victims of their own folly. We need not pursue it in detail. It is on the mind of almost every individual in the country, young and old. We cannot refrain from expressing our fears, that posterity will pronounce our policy to be a full exemplification of the soundness of its moral, and of our destitution of those broad and liberal views, that regard with *"equal eye"* all descriptions of society.

It will probably be objected by those whose interests or prejudices enlist them in hostility to our views, that all we have here submitted to you, fellow citizens, is merely theory; that however plausible, it cannot be relied on in the regulation of the political economy of a great nation; that Adam Smith being the oracle of that science, no theory opposed to his should be received, at least without the support of strong, and well-established facts.

Well, we meet them, and are fairly at issue, on this ground — and are willing to stand or fall as we furnish this support to our theory. We offer an historical case which exemplifies the baleful consequences of a system exactly similar to ours in its features and operation — which blighted and blasted the happiness of a prosperous nation — and which pronounces a strong sentence of condemnation on the theory of Adam Smith.

"It was soon found that the staple of their wool was too short for bays; therefore their bay-makers were dismissed.

"But they proceeded in their manufacture of cloth; and soon brought it to such perfection, that in 1684, either in June or July, upon the Conde *d'Ereicera's* project to encrease their exportations, and lessen the consumption of foreign manufactures, as well as to encourage their own, the king of Portugal made a sumptuary law to restrain several excesses in the kingdom; and, among the rest, *the importation of all foreign woollen cloths was prohibited.*

"Upon this the foreign merchants in that country made several remonstrances; but could by no means obtain that the prohibition should be set aside: yet they gained a year's time to bring in those that were on the way, but were obliged to reship whatever should arrive after the time limited.

"The Portuguese soon became so expert in the manufacture of

woollen cloths, that they sent home our English clothiers in a dis-
tressed condition; and the renegadoes were forced for some time to
beg their bread."†

"The *Portuguese* went on successfully: their manufacture of
woollen cloths increased to that degree, that both *Portugal* and
Brazil were wholly supplied from their own fabrics: and the materials of this manufacture were their own and Spanish wool, and no
other.

"To make ourselves some amends, and to evade the ill consequences of this prohibition of our woollen cloths, we introduced into
Portugal in their stead cloth-serges and cloth druggets; *against
which their fabric of cloth which was then but in its infancy, would
have been as unable to contend, as against a free importation of our
woollen cloths. Therefore, that their own cloth might have no such
thing as a rival in their own country, they proceeded to prohibit
foreign cloth-serges and cloth druggets.* This happened about one
year after the first prohibition."‡

"Mr. Methuen's treaty, (1703,) by taking off the prohibition of
British cloths, and by providing, that neither these, nor any of the
British woollen manufactures in Portugal, should hereafter be pro-
hibited, was *the immediate ruin of all the fabrics in that country.*"§

"Our gain by the treaty, and so vast an enlargement of our exportations to Portugal, is, that we have saved vast sums of money,
which otherwise might have gone out of the nation to pay our armies
in Portugal and other countries; and *have greatly added to the treasure of the kingdom; that the balance annually due from Portugal
has subsisted great numbers of our people, employed in making
manufactures to the value of the balance.*

"*The product of the lands is a considerable part of every manufacture; the balance therefore due from Portugal has paid great
sums for the product of our lands; and our rents are nothing else but
the value paid for the product of the lands; and consequently all that
part of the Portugal balance which has been paid for the product of
the lands, is so much added to the rents of the kingdom. Yet this is*

---

† *British Merchant,* Vol. III, p. 70.

‡ Ibid., p. 71.

§ Ibid., Vol. II, p. 76.

not the whole profit the landed interest has received from this balance. The people that have been subsisted by that great over-balance of manufactures might otherwise have come very great numbers of them upon the parish; it is a gain to the landed interest to be saved from this charge. *Our gain then by our Portugal treaty, and our excess of exportations on that account, is a vast increase of the nation's treasure, the employment and subsistence of great numbers of manufacturing people, an augmentation of our rents, and the saving the landed interest from the charge of maintaining such numbers of poor, as have subsisted themselves by the excess of exportations.*"†

"The stipulation of the king of Portugal in this treaty, has helped us to so *prodigious a vent for our woollen manufactures in that country,* as has abundantly made up for the loss of that balance we heretofore received from Spain."‡

Previous to the Methuen treaty, Portugal coins were so rare in England, that they were almost regarded as medals. Whereas, after that treaty had taken effect, there was an annual balance in favour of England, *of one million sterling,* or about 4,444,000 dollars equal to 3 millions at present. Portugal was drained, as the United States are now, first of her silver, and then of her gold, so that she had, *"very little left for her necessary occasions."* This balance fully accounts for her impoverishment, and at that period was an immense sum, as will appear from the circumstance that the whole of the balance of trade in favour of England with all the world was then only £ 2,000,000 — and her whole exports hardly £ 7,000,000.§ In consequence, the coins of Portugal flowed into Great Britain so abundantly, that she was not only enabled to pay her armies abroad with them — but they formed a considerable portion of the circulating medium of the nation — and the chief part of the bullion melted and coined in her mint.

"During the twenty years prohibition, the Portuguese succeeded so well in their woollen manufactures, that we *brought thence no gold or silver; but after the taking off that prohibition we brought*

---

† Ibid., Vol. III, p. 254.

‡ Ibid., p. 38.

§ Ibid., Vol. II, p. 110.

*away so much of their silver, as to leave them very little for their
necessary occasions; and then we began to bring away their gold.*"†

"From that treaty's taking place, the balance of trade began to
take place: and the year 1703, was the first year *we began to bring
off the silver of that nation.*"‡

"The intent of the treaty was, to increase the consumption of
our woollen cloth in Portugal; and has it not been increased by
means of this treaty? *had we any balance before from Portugal, and
do we not now gain every year a million by that treaty?*"§

"We never before the treaty had any armies to pay in Portugal;
yet *we brought none of their coin to our mint; not such a thing as a
Portugal piece was seen in England; or if it was, it was almost as
great a curiosity as our medals.*"††

"Our exports to Portugal since that treaty have amounted to
£ 1,300,000. per annum, and perhaps to a much greater sum."‡‡

"*The payment of our armies, the coinage in the mint, the
quantities of Portugal coin still current in the country,* are so many
demonstrations that we have exported vast quantities of woollen
manufactures and other goods and merchandizes to that kingdom."§§

The analogy between the case of Portugal and that of the
United States is strong and striking. The important woollen manufacture was established and brought to such perfection in four years
in the former country, as not only to supply its own consumption but
that of its colonies. In the course of three to four years it was
completely destroyed.

"Thus did Portugal, by the spirited exertion of one able
minister, (the Conde *d'Ereicera.*) gain in a few years a perfect
knowledge in a principal branch of the woollen manufacture; which
they might have possessed, to the infinite emolument of the poor
subjects of his Faithful Majesty till this hour, *had not the nation, by*

---

† Ibid., Vol. III, p. 15.

‡ Ibid., Vol. II, p. 35.

§ Ibid., Vol. III, p. 33.

†† Ibid., Vol. III, p. 253.

‡‡ Ibid., p. 20.

§§ Anderson on *National Industry,* p. 267.

*the death of that patriotic nobleman, lost her best counsellor, and
been overreached by the more able British minister, Mr.
Methuen.''†*

*"Thus in four years did their woollen manufactures attain to
such perfection, as to enable them to dispense with foreign cloths
entirely."‡*

It may perhaps, be supposed that the total destruction of this
flourishing manufacture, could not have taken place so rapidly unless the English woollen fabrics were admitted duty free. This would
be an egregious error. The stipulation of the Methuen treaty was,
that they should not be prohibited, nor be subject to a higher duty
than before the prohibition had taken place. This was twenty-three
percent which, *like so many of the duties of the United States, was
found utterly inadequate to preserve the manufacture from destruction.*

"The duties of importation, before the prohibitions, had the
name of twenty-three percent. But *the goods were not undervalued;
those duties of twenty-three percent, were not above twelve percent
of their real value.* To such low duties has the king of Portugal
obliged himself with respect to the several sorts of woollen manufactures, which stood before prohibited in that country."§

We invite your attention, fellow citizens, to the striking similarity between the case of Portugal, as stated above, and that of the
United States. In this country, the woollen manufacture and that of
cotton rose to maturity during the three years of warfare: and had
the war continued two or three years more, or had they met with
adequate protection after the peace, they would probably have
attained to such maturity and taken such deep root, as to defy
foreign competition. But the four years of peace have crushed a
large portion of both descriptions. One of the most eminent merchants in Baltimore writes us — "I am sorry to say, that our cotton
manufactures are likely to fall through, unless more effectually protected — *English cotton goods have been selling at about half the
cost and charges.* Under such circumstances it is impossible for

† Ibid., p. 266.
‡ Ibid., p. 257.
§ *British Merchant,* Vol. III, p. 37.

home manufactures to stand the competition." A merchant in New York likewise writes — "The manufactures (of cotton particularly) will require all the aid they can get from Congress next session to sustain themselves. The enormous imports of foreign goods have so affected the price, that the cost cannot be obtained."

The preceding view of the enviable state of prosperity, and the rapid and lamentable downfall, of Portugal, demands the most pointed attention of every friend of the prosperity of this country. It is like the hand writing on the wall — the *"mene, tekel, upharsin"* — the warning to flee the road that is leading us to a similar state. Let these facts be carefully compared with the theory laid down in the commencement of this address, and they will afford the most irresistible proof of its soundness, as well as of the utter impolicy that has prevailed in the regulation of our tariff, which has done this country more injury in four years of peace than she suffered in both her wars. At the close of the last, she commenced her career under as favourable auspices as any nation in the world— A high character at home and abroad — her merchants wealthy and prosperous — her manufactures flourishing — her people all employed — her staples of immense value. What a deplorable contrast she exhibits at present! Who can reflect on it without agony! Her character impaired by the impracticability of her citizens paying their debts abroad — her merchants, one after another, daily swallowed up in bankruptcy — her manufactures prostrate — thousands and tens of thousands of her people unemployed — her staples sunk in value, probably more than 20,000,000 dollars per annum — and no prospect of relief at hand. If Adam Smith's work consisted of twenty volumes instead of two — and if the commentaries on it had extended to two hundred, were the whole thrown into one scale, and the single case of Portugal thrown into the other, the former would kick the beam.

We conjure you, fellow citizens, by your regard for our common country — by the duty you owe yourselves, your wives, and your children — by the memory of your Washington, Franklin, Hancock, and Adams — by the desire you must feel to arrest the progress of the depreciation of the grand staples of your agriculture, as well as the destruction of your manufactures, trade and commerce — all victims of a pernicious policy; by the claim posterity has on you to make a good use of the immense advantages you possess — by that liberty on which you justly pride yourselves, but which loses its value, if accompanied by beggary and ruin — in a word, by all you hold near or dear on earth — weigh well the subject of this address. Examine it in all its bearings and aspects. And should it satisfactorily establish, as we trust it will, the danger of the course you are pursuing, arouse from the lethargy in which you are enthralled — and, as Congress alone has the power of applying a remedy, memorialize your representatives to change their system — to follow the maxims of all the wise nations of ancient and modern times — to remove, as far as possible, the distresses of the nation — and to save from the vortex of bankruptcy those who have escaped the ravages of the storm which threatens to blast all our hopes of happiness, and to reduce us to the same state of prostration and decrepitude as Spain and Portugal, who, it is unfortunately true, have not made a worse use of the bounties of heaven than the United States!

The immense importance of the case of Portugal, induces us to place before the eyes of our fellow citizens two comparisons of her conduct with ours — in the one, the soundness of her policy places us in the back ground an entire century in point of political wisdom — in the other, her impolicy and her consequent sufferings and distress are the counterpart of the system we have pursued, and the calamities under which we writhe.

STRIKING CONTRAST

Portugal	*The United States*
"The Portuguese set up a fabric of their own, and proceeded in it with very good success, *after the prohibition of ours and all foreign coloured cloth.* We had then nothing left against their cloths, but to introduce our cloth serges and cloth druggets into that country. They quickly found that these gave some interruption to their manufactures, and therefore *they proceeded also to prohibit foreign serges and druggets.*"†	Prohibit nothing whatever — and afford utterly inadequate protection to the great and leading manufactures of cottons, woollens, and iron, lest *"the many should be taxed for the benefit of the few!!!"* and in order to *"buy where goods could be had cheapest!!!"*

---

† Ibid., p. 35.

STRIKING LIKENESS

Portugal

"Before the treaty our woollen cloths, cloth serges and cloth druggets were prohibited in Portugal. They had set up fabrics there for making cloth, and proceeded with very good success; and we might justly apprehend they would have gone on to erect other fabrics, till at last they had served themselves with every species of woollen manufactures. The treaty takes off all prohibitions, and obliges Portugal to admit forever all our woollen manufactures. *Their own fabrics by this were presently ruined.* And we exported £100,000 value in the single article of cloths, the very year after the treaty."†

"*The court was pestered with remonstrances from their manufacturers when the prohibition was taken off, pursuant to Mr. Methuen's treaty.* But the thing was past. *The treaty was ratified: and their looms were all ruined.* And yet there was no tendency to a revolt, although so many people were deprived of their employment in that country by taking off the prohibition."‡

"The balance was so very great, that notwithstanding we paid subsidies to the king of Portugal, and paid for troops, (there were also vast supplies of our armies in Valencia and Catalonia,) yet still the overbalance lay so much against them, that there

The United States

During the war, cotton, woollen, and other kinds of goods, were not, it is true, prohibited. There were, however, very few imported. The citizens of the United States set up fabrics for making cloth, both woollen and cotton; and, had the war continued, or had they received protection after it was concluded, they would have gone on to erect other fabrics, till they had serve themselves with every species of manufacture. The treaty of peace opened our ports to foreign merchandize, under duties utterly inadequate for protection, whereby *a large portion of our fabrics were wholly ruined —* and, probably within a year after the war $35,000,000 of cottons and woollens imported into this country.

Congress was most respectfully entreated for adequate protection, by the manufacturers, when the war was closed. It was refused: and the distress and ruin of the manufacturers and the impoverishment of the nation followed.

The balance of trade is so great, that notwithstanding we have shipped immense quantities of produce at high prices — and remitted probably from about $20,000,000 of government and bank stock, we are still heavily in debt, and unable to pay.

† Ibid., p. 253.
‡ Ibid., p. 75.

was then, twelve, and fifteen
percent difference between the
exchange and the intrinsic value
of the money."†

The following picture of the state of the western country, taken
from the *Frankfort Argus,* evinces the insanity of not making some
prompt and decisive effort to relieve the nation from its disastrous
situation.

"Never within the recollection of our oldest citizens has the aspect
of times, as it respects property and money, been so alarming.
Already has property been sacrificed in considerable quantities, in
this and the neighboring counties, for less than half its value. We
have but little money in circulation, and that little is daily diminishing by the universal calls of the banks. Neither lands, negroes, nor
any other article can be sold for half their value in cash; while
executions, to the amount of many hundred thousand dollars, are
hanging over the heads of our citizens. What can be done? In a few
months no debt can be paid, no money will be in circulation to
answer the ordinary purposes of human life. Warrants, writs, and
executions will be more abundant than bank notes: and the country
will present a scene of scuffling for the poor remnants of individual
fortunes, which the world has not witnessed."

VIII

Philadelphia, May 27, 1819

When we first ventured, fellow citizens, to call your attention to
the subject of political economy, we were influenced to adopt that
measure, by the calamitous situation of our affairs, public and
private. Agriculture had received a deep wound by the reduction of
the prices of its staple articles from twenty to forty percent — real
estate was reduced in the same proportion — navigation and commerce were languishing — manufactures were prostrated by an inordinate influx of foreign commodities, calculated to excite a spirit
of luxury and extravagance in our citizens — the narrow, illiberal,
and selfish maxims, *"to buy where goods could be had the cheapest,"* and *"not to tax the many for the benefit of the few,"* had produced a system whereby the wealth of our nation was converted into
a means of fostering and encouraging the industry of a distant hemi-

† Ibid., p. 91.

sphere, and supporting foreign governments, while our own citizens were turned adrift for want of employment, and many of them reduced to mendicity, and our country impoverished — we were involved in heavier debts than ever before, with diminished means of payment — and the character of our country, from the inability of her merchants to pay their debts, and their frequent bankruptcy, was greatly impaired in the eyes of the world. In a word, under whatever aspect our affairs were viewed, they presented the most serious cause of uneasiness and apprehension.

We looked around for the causes which, in the short space of four years, without war, famine, pestilence or failure of any of the bounties of heaven, have reduced to this state from the pinnacle of reputation and happiness — a people justly celebrated for their enterprise, their industry, their mechanical skill, their wealth, and enjoying in the highest degree, every gift of heaven, in soil, climate, and extent of territory.

Several causes, we found, had combined to produce this calamitous result. The prosperity of the country had engendered a spirit of extravagance — and the inordinate spirit of banking, carried in many cases to a most culpable excess, had done much mischief. But the great paramount evil, in comparison with which all the rest sink into insignificance, is the immoderate extent of our importations, whereby we are involved in debts, for which our produce, at the highest prices, would have been inadequate to pay; and their great recent reduction, of course, increases our disabilities. The evils arising from other sources would have gradually cured themselves — or involved in ruin only deluded parties. Whereas the loss of our industry, the drain of our specie, and the consequent impoverishment of our country, affect all classes of citizens, the economical and the extravagant — the labourer, the artisan, the cultivator of the soil, as well as the landholder, the manufacturer, the trader, and the merchant.

On the most mature consideration we have given the subject, we are persuaded that the only radical remedy for those evils is to limit the importation of such articles as we can manufacture ourselves, and thus foster our domestic industry. Other measures may be adopted to cooperate and aid in this great work. But without the grand restorative of *"buying less than we sell,"* which a proper tariff alone can effect, they will operate as mere palliatives of an evil whose immense extent and magnitude require prompt and decisive remedies. All our efforts have been directed to convince our fellow citizens of this truth, so important to their virtue, their happiness, their independence.

We are, like other men, liable to error. We may have viewed the subject through an incorrect medium. But we declare, as we can with truth, that should we be mistaken — should any man or body of men devise a better plan we shall rejoice in the discovery, abandon our present views, and support theirs with all our ardour. We contend not for victory, which is no object in the discussion of such a momentous question, involving the happiness or misery of millions. We contend for the happiness of our citizens — and for the honour and prosperity of our beloved country....

XII

Philadelphia, June 24, 1819

We have presented for your consideration, the essence of the able and luminous report of Alexander Hamilton, then Secretary of the Treasury, on manufactures. The principles contained in that admirable state paper, are the principles of political economy, that have been practised by those statesmen, whom the concurrent testimony of ages, have pronounced the most wise; and have constituted the policy of every nation, that has advanced in civilization; in which the principles of free government have been developed; or which has grown in wealth and power.

Did it comport with the design of these essays, it would be no difficult task to establish, by historical references the facts; that the amelioration of society; the evolution of those just rights, which are the inheritance of every individual; and the weight and influence of the people in their government, had their origin in the establishment of manufacturing industry. With its progression, have they progressed; and by the diffusion of wealth through every class of the community, which is its necessary concomitant, have been diffused civilization and knowledge. The principles by which these important results have been effected, we shall shortly elucidate. But other considerations first invite attention.

The arguments, by which Mr. Hamilton has sustained the

principles he advocated, are lucid and conclusive. We believe them to be irrefutable. At least, we have not as yet met with any opposing writers, who have shaken one of the positions he advanced. Those diversified combinations, which grow out of, and affect all human transactions, did not escape his penetration. They are too commonly overlooked by theorists, who intent on general principles, disregard the minuter circumstances, that arise out of their very action, and frequently render them impracticable in operation, however just they may appear in themselves.

In no science, are the general maxims of mere theorists more delusive, and more to be distrusted, than in political economy. This branch of knowledge is yet in its infancy. It is composed of relations so commingled and commixed together, that like a skein of tangled thread, they require to be traced out with great patience, per-severance, and close attention. Its principles are not yet established. Those which have been considered as the most fixed, have been overthrown; those which have been taught as self-evident, are questioned; and the whole the subject of ardent discussion. In this state of the science, general maxims can serve no other purpose, than to give flippancy on an abstruse subject, and to overleap difficulties, that cannot be removed.

While the elements of political economy are thus un-determined, we are called upon to set at naught the harmonising examples of the most prosperous states; the accumulated experience of centuries; and to confide the character, the resources, the power of this nation; the wealth and happiness of this people; the safety perhaps of the government itself, to the operation of abstract principles, which have not yet been confirmed by practice, nor even settled by authority.

In human affairs, abstract principles, though they may cap-tivate the fancy by their simplicity, are often defeated by those subordinate accidents, which they must necessarily exclude. The principles of "Political Justice," of the English, and the "per-fectibility of human nature" of the French Philosophers, as well as unlimited freedom of moral action, in the abstract, may be true. But overlooking the very constitution of human nature, the discordancy of its sentiments, the complexedness of its affinities, the variety of its affections, the perverseness of the human heart, and the obliquity of human intellect, they can only be regarded as the visions of benevolent enthusiasts.

The abstract principles of political economy, are of similar character. Resulting from general reasoning, which seldom descends to minute particulars, they bear all the evidences of correct deductions, until brought into practice. Their inefficiency is then disclosed, and their partial nature made manifest. The involutions and compound nature of human interest, we are convinced, set distinctive limitations at defiance. They often open suddenly into new channels that have not been traced, or flow through others, so obscure, that they have escaped our notice. Our generalities are defeated by unanticipated combinations, which give results never calculated; and re-actions are produced, that work effects never suspected.

In a science thus uncertain, and in things thus complicated and indistinct, it is the part of prudence to tread the paths of sober experience; to trust those guides, whose long practice has imparted substantial knowledge, and whose knowledge is verified by their success. To reject the long acquired wisdom of ages, and the well-earned experience of mankind, from confidence in superior wisdom, may justly subject us to the imputation of self-sufficiency, and hazard the dearest interests of our country.

It is against such visionary projects, that we have raised our hands; it is to warn you from the closet speculations of theorists, to invite you to common sense practice, founded on the nature of things, that we have intruded with the best intentions on your notice. We have presented to you in succession, the systems of the various powers in Europe, for the advancement of their welfare; and have shown some errors of policy, bearing a strong similarity to principles generally entertained in the United States, which proved fatal to those by whom they were adopted. We have, finally, presented you with a system, that has been proposed by one of our most enlightened statesmen, as best adapted to promote the wealth and power, by exciting and fostering the industry of this country, *in the circumstances of a general and continued peace in Europe.* This system was prepared with an experience of the operation of the peace policy of Europe on our affairs, subsequent to the peace of 1783, and after mature reflection on the commercial relations between this country and foreign powers. Its principles, founded on well substantiated facts, are drawn from the examples of the most prosperous and most powerful nations; and its materials derived from the abundant sources of European commercial legislation. These are circumstances which entitle it to great weight, and to be received with the most marked and serious attention.

Let it not be presumed, that we are influenced by any feelings of political partiality, in favour of Mr. Hamilton. Most of those, who thus tender the tribute of their applause to his merits as a statesman, and thus highly appreciate this particular fruit of his labours, were, and continue to be, the decided opponents of his political principles. It is bigotry alone, that denies or would obscure merit in those, beyond the pale of its own belief, in church or state. To this feeling, we wish to have no claim, and while we confess a contrariety of sentiment on some essential points, we would not withhold our acknowledgment of the brilliancy of the genius, the extent and solid nature of the acquirements, and the strength of intellect, that distinguished Alexander Hamilton.

In the present situation of the country, when it cannot be concealed, that its progress has received a sudden check, and society labours under the shock of a rapid recoil, the discussions of political parties sink into minor importance, in comparison with the great principles of the prosperity and happiness of the people and of the nation. These are the principles that should rise paramount in the view, occupy the thoughts, and animate the feelings of every citizen of the great American republic. Divesting yourselves, therefore, of party feeling, prejudices and partialities; casting aside, as derogatory to the character of American citizens, the petty jealousies of sectional interests, take into candid consideration that system of policy which, in the early establishment of our government, was deemed best to comport with our interests as an independent people. If its principles should appear to you just, and the reasoning by which it is sustained, consonant to truth; if you should be satisfied, it is the best adapted to our present and probable future circumstances, you will not hesitate to trust to it, for the advancement of individual and national prosperity.

An inquiry naturally arises into the causes, which led the government, after having matured this system, and contemplated its adoption, to lay it aside. They are developed in our commercial history, and will be found to strengthen the principles and views on which it was erected, and for which we contend.

The peace concluded in 1783, continued undisturbed; Europe offered but partial markets to our productions, while it closed its commerce to our marine. The annual value of our foreign exports, was less in amount than the annual value of our consumption of foreign commodities, and we possessed no collateral sources of wealth to compensate the deficiency. The government had assumed a large debt, which subjected it to a heavy annual interest; other expenses were accumulating, the increase of which might be confidently anticipated; and the prospects of revenue from foreign commerce, or an impoverished people, were but gloomy. In these circumstances, the attempts of our statesmen must have been directed to internal resources. Yet from this quarter could be derived little to inspire their hopes. Commerce brought no money into the country; circulation was limited and slow; the industry or labour power of the country was but partially exerted; and consequently much wealth lost, that might have been created. Without a circulating medium, and full employment for industry, a revenue must have been oppressive to the people, of difficult collection to the government, and uncertain in its proceeds.

The difficulties of the colonial governments, and the evils endured by the colonists, were then fresh in remembrance, and their causes were well understood. The commerce, to which they had been limited, was that which at this time is recommended to our adoption. Confined almost exclusively to the tillage of the soil, they exchanged their raw productions for the manufactured articles of the mother country. This kind of barter, or "mutual exchange," to which the colonies were *forced* by the colonial system of England, kept them poor to favour industry at home. This commerce, to which the jealous policy of Great Britain limited her colonial possessions in America, it was acknowledged both in and out of Parliament, in the colonies and in England, and cannot now be denied, was intended solely to render them subservient to her interests, to which theirs were unhesitatingly sacrificed. Their progression in wealth and power, was looked upon with a distrustful eye. In order to its retardation, to keep them poor and dependent, they were forbidden to manufacture, and compelled to supply their wants from England. Even the earl of Chatham, who is considered to have been the friend of America, as he was the advocate of her rights, was still so much an Englishman in this respect, he was unwilling that a single hob-nail should be manufactured in America.

The cultivation of the soil to its greatest extent, excited no apprehensions that it would enable the colonies to become independent. England well knew, that in the mutual exchange of raw products for manufactured goods, all the advantage was on her side, the loss on that of the colonies. She, therefore, restricted them to the cultivation of the soil, except permitting a few handicrafts of first necessity, and the fisheries to the New England colonies, which raised no production she required.

This system kept the colonies in a wretched condition. They were totally destitute of the precious metals, either to constitute or regulate a currency. Every hard dollar that found its way into them, was immediately exported to England in payment of debts. "Those that are acquainted with America, know as I do," said Captain Luttrel in a debate in Parliament, "that from Rhode Island, northwards, they have no money; that their trade is generally carried on by barter, from the most opulent merchant to the most necessitous husbandman. Sir, before your fleet and armies visited their coasts, you might almost as soon have raised the dead, as one hundred pounds in specie from any individual, in those provinces." †

In order to procure some kind of currency to make those mutual exchanges, which the wants of civilized life render indispensable, and which cannot with convenience be effected by barter, the colonists were forced into various expedients. They altered the standard of money; they issued paper money of different kinds; they constituted it a legal tender. But all was ineffectual. While they had to hire workmen in England to perform their labour, they could not retain their gold and silver, which was sent to pay wages abroad. Altering the standard did not affect the value of gold and silver, which could not be restrained by an arbitrary limitation:

---

† *Parliamentary Register.*

and their paper money having no guarantee for its safety, constantly depreciated.

Such, it was known to our government, were the results that had been produced by a commerce, engaged in the exchange of the productions of the soil, for manufactured goods. They could not, therefore, anticipate that a similar commerce would have other effects; and consequently, that by such a commerce, a metallic currency could be given to the people, or even a metallic basis acquired, for an adequate paper currency. There was then no other course left them to pursue, but to adopt the manufacturing policy of Europe. By supplying a portion of those wants with our own industry, for which the colonies had been compelled by the parent country to hire and pay for labour in England, we would diminish the amount of our imports, without diminishing the amount of our exports. Because England took from us no more of our productions, than she really wanted, and those she would take under any circumstances, while the other nations to which we traded, were never influenced by other views, than the mere supply of their wants. Thus the balance of our trade with the West Indies, which had always been paid in specie, but immediately remitted to England, would have been retained in circulation; while a portion of the balance with France and the Mediterranean, would also have found its way back to this country, instead of always being transferred to England. In this manner, and in this manner only, in a state of general peace in Europe, could a circulating medium have been procured, that could be kept pure, free from depreciation, and fluctuations.

But the rapid occurrence of events wholly unexpected, unfolded new prospects, and enabled the United States to acquire with ease and rapidity, the wealth and power necessary to give stability to their recently formed institutions. In the midst of the agitations of the French revolution, the crops failed in France and other parts of Europe. At once a market was opened to our agricultural production, stimulated to its greatest energy. The labour power of the country, was instantly employed to the full extent of its capacity. The war that soon ensued, and involved almost every power in Europe, constituted us at once the carriers of an immense commerce. Our sails swelled on every ocean, and our flag streamed on every shore. Every dollar of capital we possessed or could borrow, and every hand in the nation, before idle, found employment. A road was thus open to a rapid acquirement of wealth, and it was a natural policy to pursue it. The capital and industry of the country, before stagnant and depressed, rushed into the new formed channel. Manufactures under these circumstances were neglected and the project was dropped. All the benefits that were expected to arise from them, were to be obtained with certainty and expedition by prosecuting our newly disclosed and widely extended commerce. Wealth rolled in apace, and the metallic capital alone in the space of ten or twelve years, was increased to twenty or twenty five millions of dollars. But the whole of this prosperity, depended on contingencies. A general peace in Europe would bring it to a close. As it was, we could not enjoy it undisturbed. The celerity of our progress awakened the jealousy of a rival. It was sought to destroy, by new principles of national law, the advantages we derived from our neutral character. The difficulties that were thus generated, terminated finally in war, which arose, let it be remarked, not from a spirit of manufactures, but from a spirit of commerce. The expenses and sacrifices necessary to its prosecution, were in fact, a tax upon the country, in favour of commerce; yet it was cheerfully borne, by the agricultural and manufacturing interests.

Out of this contest, the nation came with an accession of character; whilst the rapidity of circulation, the full employment of capital, and its retention in the country, caused individuals to feel but little comparative distress, notwithstanding its burthens. The attack directed against the physical strength of the country, only served to develop its power and resources. The war now waging against its moral strength, has paralised its energies, and laid it prostrate in the dust. It is no exaggeration to assert, that the two last years of peace, have produced more commercial embarrassment and distress, a greater destruction of capital, and increase of individual misery, than was caused by the whole war.

This apparent anomaly deserves to be examined. We believe its solution will be attained in the following considerations. The general pacification of Europe, had preceded the treaty of Ghent, and most of the powers of the eastern hemisphere, had re-assumed their usual peace policy. The object of this policy is to foster their own marine,

agriculture and manufactures, to the exclusion of those of other
nations. We consequently had lost the commercial relations, that
had existed in a state of European warfare. In fact, we reverted back
to our old commercial position, prior to the French revolution, or
when colonies. Had this circumstance been understood, it would
have been foreseen, that the same effects would have grown out of
the same causes now as formerly. The principles, views, and
reasonings, adapted to the then situation of the country, it would
have been perceived, were again applicable. But the habits and
modes of thinking, which had been formed during twenty years of a
lucrative commerce; the complete mutations which had taken place
in the commercial world, during that time, leaving few individuals
possessed of a practical knowledge of the effects of a general peace,
on the interests of the country, occasioned the revolution our
commerce had undergone to be overlooked or disregarded.

Most of those engaged in commerce, who also, it will be
recollected, preside over the monied institutions which regulate our
currency, had little other experience of commerce, than such as
existed during the wars of the French revolution. They naturally
supposed, that it would continue to work the same effects, as during
that period, except in smaller amount. The failure of two successive
crops in Europe, in 1815 and 1816, which stayed for a time the
operation of the new state of affairs, served to continue this
delusion. The time, however, is not remote, when we shall be
awakened to the true situation of our commercial relations with
Europe, and its consequences. The evils, which now press on us,
many vainly flatter themselves, are mere temporary effects, similar
to those which have before arisen from slight derangements of
commerce. We are firmly persuaded, they are of a very different
character, and of a more formidable nature. We have no doubt, that
they are the same, as the evils under which this country suffered
when colonies, and during the peace subsequent to the revolution.
The sooner we satisfy ourselves that such is the case, the earlier we
shall extricate ourselves from the embarrassments, that must grow
out of this position, in which we are placed. We propose to enter into
the examination of this subject in a future number, and trust we
shall exhibit by a comparison of the commerce of the colonies, and
the effects it produced on them, extracted from authentic

documents, with the present commerce of this country, and the effects now begun to be felt, that they are of similar character. We fear, from this view of the subject, though little flattering to our pride, it will be apparent, that after having expended the best blood of the nation, and millions of treasure to shake off the yoke of colonization, we have voluntarily adopted the colonial policy of England, and placed ourselves with respect to her, and in truth to most of the world, in the situation of colonies. From this state of humiliating and injurious dependency, the United States are bound to vindicate the sovereignty of a free people. For in vain will they make pretensions to a perfect independence, while they incur through the medium of their wants, all the consequences of subjection.

XIII

Philadelphia, July 5, 1819

Various causes concur to produce the present unhappy state of affairs. It is our belief, however, that the main root, whence branch all the evils we suffer, is the neglect of furnishing full employment, to the productive labour of the country.

National wealth does not consist in land, people, or the precious metals, but in the possession of products or values, created by labor.

A country with an extended territory, and a scattered population, must be poor and feeble. Such is Spain at this moment, and such was this country when in the state of colonies.

There is a paper in the *Spectator*, No. 200, that contains some excellent reflections on this subject, which, as they cannot be better expressed, we shall extract in full.

"If the same omnipotent Power, which made the world, should at this time raise out of the ocean and join to Great Britain, an equal extent of land, with equal buildings, corn, cattle, and other conveniences and necessaries of life, but no men, women nor children, I should hardly believe this would add either to the riches of the people, or revenue of the prince."

And again —

"That paradox, therefore, in old Hesiod, πλέον ἥμισυ παντός, or half is more than the whole, is very applicable to the present case; since nothing is more true in political arithmetic, than that the same people with half a country, is more valuable than with the whole. I began to think there was nothing absurd in Sir W. Petty, when he fancied if all the Highlands of Scotland and the whole kingdom of Ireland, were sunk into the ocean, so that the people were all saved and brought into the lowlands of Great Britain; nay, though they were to be reimbursed the value of their estates by the body of the people, yet both the sovereign and the subjects in general, would be enriched by the very loss."

The same sentiment is contained, and placed in a striking point of view in relation to this country, in a petition to Parliament, in the year 1767. General Phineas Lyman, it appears, contemplated the establishment of a settlement on the Ohio, in the present state of Illinois; and for this purpose applied to Parliament for a tract of land. He enforced the propriety of the measure, by the argument, that there could be little danger of the colonies becoming independent, if confined to agricultural pursuits, and the inhabitants were diffused over the country. The position is perfectly correct, and is a very suitable and forcible reply to those who are incessantly advising the same policy to these free and independent states, instead of promoting manufacturing industry on the seaboard, and the already thickly settled parts of the country. This is purely an English doctrine, and one which the English government unquestionably warmly approves.

"A period," the petition we allude to observes, "will doubtless come, when North America will no longer acknowledge a dependence on any part of Europe. But that period seems so remote, as not to be at present an object of rational policy or human prevention [and] it will be made still more remote, by opening new scenes of agriculture, and widening the space, which the colonies must first completely occupy." †

While it is thus demonstrated, that territory thinly peopled confers neither riches nor power, we have examples in Egypt, modern Greece, and other provinces of the Turkish empire, and in Persia, that people deficient in industry, contribute as little to national wealth or strength; while Spain and Portugal are familiar instances, that they are not necessarily concomitant with the possession of the precious metals.

When we reflect on the distribution of labour in society, which

---

† Macpherson's *Annals of Commerce,* 1767.

is necessary to give value to production, we shall be more sensible of the truth and operation of the principles laid down.

It has been judged from experience, and admitted by the best authorities, that the labour of twenty-five persons, will procure all the common necessaries of life, as food, drink, apparel, housing, furniture, etc. for one hundred persons. This supposition takes the above articles as coarse, though plentiful and good. One half, it is supposed, from being too old, or too young, sick or infirm, will produce nothing. There will then remain about twenty-five individuals of every hundred, capable of working, who are necessarily idle or non-productive. Now, on the quantity and quality of the employment, with which these twenty-five individuals are occupied, depend the wealth, power, intelligence, and degree of civilization of a nation.

The objects which can alone occupy this class, which, for the sake of distinction, we shall call non-necessary producers, as there is sufficient of sustenance and rainment, etc., for necessary wants, produced without them, must be, in part, to give to those products greater refinement, and consequent value: that is, to give to food a higher relish and more diversity; and to apparel, furniture, etc., more of ornament and beauty. These operations are the chief constituents of manufacturing industry, and absorb a considerable part of the labour, which would otherwise be idle. The cultivation of letters, of the fine arts, of the physical and abstract sciences, the offices of state, and its protection in the army or navy, in civilized society, give occupation to the remainder.

When that portion, which is employed in creating material products or values, finds full occupation, and is predominant, then national wealth is on the increase; circulation is kept full, brisk and steady; contentment and ease, comfort and happiness, are in the power of each individual to obtain; the government is invigorated, and its finances in a flourishing state. This is the situation of a prosperous people, and to attain and preserve it, should be the constant aim of an enlightened government.

The reverse of this state of productive industry, brings on a lamentable change in the affairs of a nation. In proportion as the employment of this class diminishes, national production or wealth declines; circulation becomes dull, languid and stagnant; embarrassments and difficulties surround traders; poverty and misery assail labourers; being idle, they become vicious; and, oppressed by pauperism, they become criminal. The materials for riots, and civil commotions; the ready instruments of designing demagogues, are formed and accumulated, to the hazard of all good citizens, and the safety of civil government.

It is not improbable, that it was this state of things, which was one of the principal causes of the violences of the French revolution. The derangement of the finances; the immense and unequal exactions of the government, which fell chiefly on the industrious poor; the vacillation of its measures, which overthrew all confidence; and the operation of the impolitic treaty of commerce with England of 1786, all tended to ruin the productive industry of France. Large fragments of its population were thus disjointed from their usual situation, and floated loose and unemployed, endangering the existence of organized society, with the first agitations that should arise.

The commencement of the revolution seems a demonstration of the fact. A starving multitude surrounded the Hotel de Ville, vociferating for bread; and, whenever the king appeared in public, his ears were stunned with the same incessant clamour from the crowd, that thronged around his coach.

The same principle, explains satisfactorily the cause of the extraordinary military energy of France, at that period. Her commerce ruined; her manufactures languid; her trades sinking from diminished consumption; her agriculture oppressed and declining; and the total destruction of her finances, threw an immense mass of physical and labour power out of employment. The army offered the only mode of occupation, by which it could be absorbed. Hence, more than a moiety of the non-necessary producers, whose labour had been appropriated on a thousand different objects, was suddenly devoted to arms. In the armies of the republic were found every rank and grade of society, and every variety of trade and profession.

Europe, which had confederated against that devoted country, and anticipated an easy conquest, was surprized, alarmed, and confounded, at the spectacle presented by this nation, which had seemed prostrated with calamity, sending forth at one time "eleven distinct armies" † to the field, and her extended frontier bristling with bayonets.

This principle was so well understood in England, before the establishment of manufacturing industry secured permanent employment, that it became a maxim with her kings to engage in wars, whenever this portion of her population accumulating, became idle, restless, and discontented.

"It was the dying injunction of the late king, (Henry IV.) to his son, not to allow the English to remain long in peace, which was apt to breed intestine commotions; but to employ them in foreign expeditions, by which the prince might acquire honour; the nobility, by sharing his dangers, might attach themselves to his person; and all the restless spirits find occupation for their inquietude."‡

By this means employment was found for her superabundant labour, which had become oppressive and troublesome to the government, because it could not find any other occupation.

On the disposition which is made by the government, of this class of non-necessary producers, depends the character of a nation. If the greater portion be occupied in agricultural and manufacturing industry, the nation will be wealthy and prosperous, but not enlightened. This is the case with China and Hindostan.

If engaged in arts, letters, and sciences, it will be distinguished for its writers, poets, philosophers, historians, orators, statesmen, sculptors, and painters. Greece in its maturity, Rome in the Augustan age, and Italy at the time of the revival of letters, illustrate our doctrine.

If arms be made their trade, the people become warlike, make extensive conquests, and are renowned for heroes, commanders, and warriors. This was the character of Greece in its early history, of Macedon, and of Rome. It is also the condition of the most semibarbarous states; like the Scythian tribes, which destroyed the western empire; and the Arabs, who carried the crescent over more than half the world, and have thundered at the gates of most of the capitals of Europe. In the vigour of its feudal institutions, Europe presented the same aspect. Arms and a rude agriculture constituted

---

† Stevens's *Wars of the French Revolution,* Vol. i, p. 266.

‡ Hume's *History of England,* Vol. 2, Chap. XIX, p. 59.

the chief employment of its inhabitants, who, poor and oppressed, were the dependant vassals of their lords.

Unoccupied by trades or manufactures, they were ever ready to follow their chieftains to the field, reckless of the cause which summoned them to the work of destruction. Under the banners of the cross, were arrayed such multitudes, that Europe, remarks Anna Comnena, loosened from its foundations, and impelled by its moving principle, seemed in one united body to precipitate itself on Asia. † The plains of Palestine and the borders of the Nile, for near two centuries, were deluged with the blood of millions of human beings, vainly shed in the fruitless battles of the crusades. . . .

---

† Alexias, lib. 10.

Bibliography

Baird, Henry Carey. *The British Credit System, Inflated Bank Credit as a Substitute for "Current Money of the Realm."* Philadelphia: H.C. Baird, 1875.

Carey, Henry C. *Miscellaneous Works of Henry C. Carey.* Philadelphia: H.C. Baird, 1872.

Carey, Henry C. Papers. Pennsylvania Historical Society, Philadelphia.

Carey, Mathew. *Autobiographical Sketches in a Series of Letters Addressed to a Friend Containing a View of the Rise in Progress of the American System, The Efforts Made to Secure its Establishment, The Causes Which Prevented Its Complete Success.* Philadelphia: John Clark, 1829.

Carey, Mathew. Papers. Pennsylvania Historical Society, Philadelphia.

Colwell, Stephen. Papers. Pennsylvania Historical Society, Philadelphia.

Colwell, Stephen. *Report on the Influence of the Duplication of Taxes upon American Industry.* U.S. Department of Treasury Report No. 9. Library of Congress, Washington, D.C.

Colwell, Stephen. *Report Upon the Relations of Foreign Trade to Domestic Industry and Internal Revenue.* U.S. Department of Treasury Report No. 10. Library of Congress, Washington, D.C.

Colwell, Stephen. *Report on Iron and Steel.* U.S. Department of Treasury Report No. 12. Library of Congress, Washington, D.C.

Colwell, Stephen. *Report on Wool and Manufactures of Wool.* U.S. Department of Treasury Report No. 13. Library of Congress, Washington, D.C.

Elder, William. *Questions of the Day — Economic and Social.* Philadelphia, 1871.

Kelley, William D. *Speeches, Addresses, and Letters on Industrial and Financial Questions.* Philadelphia, 1872.

Lincoln, Abraham. *The Collected Works of Abraham Lincoln.* Edited by Roy P. Basler. 8 Vols. New Brunswick, N.J.: Rutgers University Press, 1953.

McCulloch, Hugh. "Our National Debt and Financial Future: Address at Fort Wayne, Indiana, October 11, 1865." Hugh McCulloch Papers. Library of Congress, Washington, D.C.

McCulloch, Hugh. Papers, Library of Congress, Washington, D.C.

Marx, Karl. *Grundrisse.* Translated and edited by David McLellan. New York: Harper and Row, 1971.

Marx, Karl and Friedrich Engels. *The Civil War in the United States.* New York: International Publishers, 1937.

Marx, Karl and Friedrich Engels. *Selected Correspondence.* Moscow: Foreign Languages Publishing House, 1956.

Wells, David A. Papers. Library of Congress, Washington, D.C.

In addition the following newspapers and periodicals published between 1850 and 1876 were consulted: *Chicago Daily Tribune, Iron Age, The Nation, New York Daily Tribune, New York World, North American Review,* and the *Philadelphia Press.*

Secondary

Adams, Henry. *The Education of Henry Adams.* New York: Houghton Mifflin Co., 1918.

Beale, Howard K. *The Critical Year: A Study of Andrew Johnson and Reconstruction.* New York: Harcourt Brace and Co., 1930.

Beard, Charles A. and Mary R. *The Rise of American Civilization.* New York: The McMillan Co., 1944.

Bradsher, Earl. *Mathew Carey, Editor, Author, and Publisher.* New York: Columbia University Press, 1912.

Del Mar, Alexander. "Henry C. Carey's Round Table." *Gunton's Magazine,* XIII, August 1897.

Dorfman, Joseph. *The Economic Mind in American Civilization.* New York: The Viking Press, 1946-1959.

Elder, William. *A Memoir of Henry C. Carey.* Philadelphia: The American Iron and Steel Association, 1880.

Executive Committee for the Federal Republic of the European Labor Party, "The German Constitutional State and Terrorism." *The Campaigner.* Vol. 11, No. 1.

Ferleger, Herbert Ronald. *David A. Wells and the American Revenue System, 1865-1870.* New York: Columbia University, 1942.

Green, Arnold W. *Henry Charles Carey, Nineteenth Century Sociologist.* Philadelphia: University of Pennsylvania Press, 1951.

Hammond, Bray. *Banks and Politics in America from the Revolution to the Civil War.* Princeton: Princeton University Press, 1957.

Kaplan, Abraham D. *Henry Charles Carey: A Study in American Economic Thought.* Baltimore: Johns Hopkins Press, 1831.

Katz, Irving. *August Belmont, A Political Biography.* New York: Columbia University Press, 1968.

LaRouche, Lyndon H., Jr. *The Case of Walter Lippmann.* New York: Campaigner Publications, Inc., 1977.

Marcus, Lyn (aka, Lyndon H. LaRouche, Jr.) *Dialectical Economics.* Lexington, Mass.: D.C. Heath and Co., 1975.

Mitchell, Wesley Clair. *A History of the Greenbacks, with Special References to the Economic Consequences of their Issues, 1862-1865.* Chicago: University of Chicago Press, 1903.

Oberholtzer, Ellis Paxon. *Jay Cook, Financier of the Civil War.* Philadelphia: George W. Jacob and Co., 1907.

Sharkey, Robert P. *Money, Class, and Party: An Economic Study of the Civil War and Reconstruction.* Baltimore: Johns Hopkins Press, 1959.

Smith, George Winston. *Henry C. Carey and the American Sectional Conflict.* Albuquerque: University of New Mexico Press, 1951.

Spannaus, Nancy B. and Christopher White. *The Political Economy of the American Revolution.* New York: Campaigner Publications, Inc., 1977.

Spaulding, Elbridge Gerry. *History of the Legal Tender Paper Money Issued During the Great Rebellion.* Buffalo: Express Printing Co., 1969.

Sylvis, James C. *The Life, Speeches, Labor, and Essays of William H. Sylvis, Late President of the Iron Moulders International Union and also of the National Labor Union.* Philadelphia, 1872.

Tarbell, Ida M. *The Tariff in Our Times.* New York: The McMillan Co., 1911.

Unger, Irwin. *The Greenback Era.* Princeton: Princeton University Press, 1964.

Woodward, C. Vann. *Reunion and Reaction: The Compromise of 1877 and the End of Reconstruction.* Boston: Little Brown and Co., 1951.

Index

Abolitionist movement, 16, 17, 22, 24, 29, 38, 41, 78, 245, 293-294
Adams, Charles Francis, 41
Adams, John, 30, 130, 133, 408
Adams, John Quincy, 2, 9
Alfred, King of England, 262
American Institute, 312, 313
American Iron Association, 187
American Revolution, 1, 6, 8-11, 17, 24, 38, 112n, 126, 369
American System of political economy, 1, 3, 6, 6n, 9, 13-14, 16, 18, 20, 23, 25-29, 32, 33, 35, 38-40, 48-52, 59, 62, 71, 72, 75, 91, 121, 186, 207, 327
American Workers' League, 28
Anne of Brittany, 105
Anti-Slavery Standard, 294
Arbatov, Georgii, 19
Archer, Mr., 174
Articles of Confederation, 287
Associated Banks of New York and New England, 7, 16, 33, 37, 46-47
Association for the Promotion of National Industry, 9, 12-13, 14
Atkinson, Edward, 17, 41, 43, 52, 55, 56, 59, 61, 64

Bacon, Francis, 387n
Baird, Henry Carey: *The Rights of American Producers*, 283
Bank of England, 51-52, 151
Banks, Nathaniel Prentiss, 248
Baring Bros.: financial house of, 7, 16, 19, 33, 41, 51-52, 55, 57, 59, 65, 68, 70, 95, 96, 224
Baring, Thomas, 17, 55, 56
Belmont, August, 16, 26, 38, 43, 46, 51, 60, 65
Bentham, Jeremy, 10, 11, 41

Bessemer process, 57, 155
Bible, 217; books of, 217, 218, 219, 220, 221
Biddle, Nicholas, 4, 60
Black Friday, 67-68
Blaine, James G., 69
Blodget, Lorin, 353, 354
Boston Daily Advertiser, 261
Boutwell, George, 63, 67, 68, 336
British Merchantmen, 275
British System of political economy, 1-3, 6, 6n, 13, 18, 20-23, 25, 39, 50-53, 55, 57, 63, 65, 67, 68, 72, 78, 91, 111, 140, 171-186, 327
Brookings Institution, 7
Brooks, Rep., 313, 318
Brougham, Lord, 169, 275
Brown, John, 29
Bryant, William Cullen, 26, 29, 30, 31, 38, 41, 42, 43, 65, 67, 71, 121, 138n
Buchanan, James, 2, 26, 167, 181, 190, 202
Burr, Aaron, 9

Calhoun, John C., 9, 289
Cameron, Simon, 229
Campbell, John A,. 230
Campbell, Rep., 178
Canada, 30-31
Canada reciprocity treaty, 177, 182, 274
Carnot, Lazare, 8n
Carey, Henry, 2, 3, 4, 5, 5n, 7, 14, 34, 41, 43n, 46, 51, 52, 54, 57, 58, 60, 61, 63, 64, 65, 66, 68, 69, 75, 78, 121, 138n, 139n, 140, 155, 172, 186, 205, 222, 255, 264, 310, 345, 367, 372n; and Karl Marx, 18-20, 23-25; and Russia, 39; defense of a

433

Political economy, continued
20, 66, 385-387, 394-395, 403, 411, 413-416
Polk, James, 173
Porter: *Progress of the Nation,* 269
Priestley, Joseph, 10
Progress: idea of, 18, 37; technological and scientific, 4-6, 20, 21, 23, 27, 71
Protection: policy of, 6, 21, 23, 26-27, 29, 32, 34, 38, 39, 48, 52, 55, 56, 58, 62-68, 72, 76, 91, 92, 116, 127, 128, 130-140, 143-146, 150, 173, 174, 176, 179, 181, 189, 190, 192, 206, 222, 223-224, 266-276, 278-280, 358-359, 393-395, 412-413
Puynode, M. du, 372n

Raymond, Daniel, 10, 12, 13, 14
Reagan, Ronald, 71
Refunding legislation: debate over, 59-62, 67, 68
Republican Party, 2, 4, 25, 26, 28, 30, 34, 38, 41, 59, 60, 61, 65, 95, 121, 138-139, 171, 202, 222, 294, 296, 308, 309; 1860 convention of, 29, 31-32, 143, 179, 180, 181, 223
Rhett, Robert, 174
Ricardo, David, 7, 11, 18, 19, 21, 41, 49; theory of rent, 20, 21, 23
Rothschild family: banking houses of, 7, 16, 19, 22, 26, 33, 38, 41, 43, 51-52, 57, 59, 65, 68, 70, 72, 95, 96, 224
Rothschild, Nathan Meyer, 22
Royal Society, 7
Russia, 8, 38-39, 75n
Russian Revolution of 1917, 18
Russell, John, 209

Sandburg, Carl, 26
Say, Jean-Baptiste, 19
Schlesinger, Arthur M.,Jr., 18, 19
Schurz, Carl, 43n, 327
Scott, Lieutenant General, 239
Secessionists, 16, 30-31, 32
Seligman, Joseph, 43, 51, 65, 67, 68, 69
7:30 bonds, 33, 37, 51

Seward, William, 17, 26, 29, 29n, 35, 38, 50, 178, 244
Seybert, Dr., 389n
Seymore, Horatio, 60, 65
Sharkey, Robert P., 3-4, 7; *Money, Class, and Party,* 3-4
Sherman, John, 57, 60, 64, 72, 327, 332, 339, 341, 342
Skinner, William, 75
Slavery, 16, 17, 22, 23, 25, 27, 29, 30-31, 41, 42, 43, 48, 78-95, 122, 135, 137, 172, 173, 235, 242-244
Slidell, John, 33
Smith, Adam, 7, 13, 14, 41, 49, 80, 124, 385, 387, 387n, 392, 394, 396, 398, 400, 403, 408; *The Wealth of Nations,* 11, 12, 20, 20n, 124, 385, 387, 387n
Smith, Caleb. B., 233
Smith, E. Pershine, 29n
Smith, Gustavus, W., 290
Social Science Associations, 65
Society for the Promotion of Useful Manufactures, 12, 385
South, 2, 7, 16, 26, 27, 30, 32, 33, 34, 38, 40-43, 49, 61, 62, 68, 142, 150, 170, 171, 205, 208, 209, 211, 224-225, 247-251, 258-262
Southey, Robert: *Espriella's Letters,* 82
Special Commission on the Revenue, 49, 51, 52-53, 55, 62, 367; 1869 report of, 62, 63, 64, 65, 140, 186
Specie, 33, 37, 46, 48, 49, 51, 55, 58-60, 152, 163, 341
Spectator No. 200, 422
Sprague, Mr., 174
Springfield Republican, 64
Stanton, Edwin McMasters, 42, 50
States rights, 17, 32, 42, 308-309
Statistics of the American Iron and Steel Association, 195
Stevens, Thaddeus, 46, 53, 61, 62, 328
Stewart, Andrew, 13
Stewart, A.T., 65, 67
Stowe, Harriet Beecher, 16, 29, 41, 61, 78; *Uncle Tom's Cabin,* 22, 78

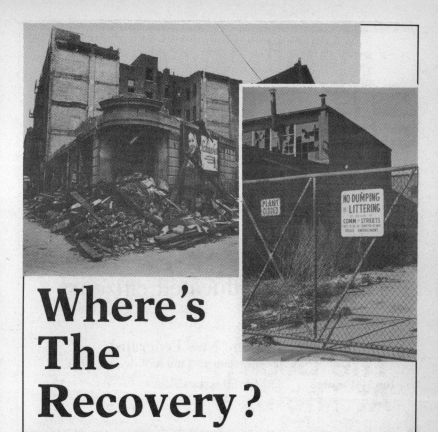